P9-DFC-535

# Bullying

## Implications
## for the
## Classroom

This is a volume in the Academic Press
**EDUCATIONAL PSYCHOLOGY SERIES**

*Critical comprehensive reviews of research knowledge, theories, principles, and practices*

Under the editorship of Gary D. Phye

# Bullying

## Implications for the Classroom

EDITED BY

## Cheryl E. Sanders
## Gary D. Phye

ELSEVIER
ACADEMIC
PRESS

*Amsterdam • Boston • Heidelberg • London • New York • Oxford*
*Paris • San Diego • San Francisco • Singapore • Sydney • Tokyo*

Elsevier Academic Press
525 B Street, Suite 1900, San Diego, California 92101-4495, USA
84 Theobald's Road, London WC1X 8RR, UK

This book is printed on acid-free paper. ∞

**Library of Congress Cataloging-in-Publication Data**
Application submitted.

**British Library Cataloguing in Publication Data**
A catalogue record for this book is available from the British Library

ISBN: 0-12-617955-7

For all information on all Academic Press publications
visit our Web site at www.academicpress.com

Printed in the United States of America
04 05 06 07 08 09  9 8 7 6 5 4 3 2 1

# Contents

## 3.  A THEORETICAL REVIEW OF BULLYING: CAN IT BE ELIMINATED?

*Adrienne Nishina*

## 4. IN THE LOOKING GLASS: A RECIPROCAL EFFECT MODEL ELUCIDATING THE COMPLEX NATURE OF BULLYING, PSYCHOLOGICAL DETERMINANTS, AND THE CENTRAL ROLE OF SELF-CONCEPT

*Herbert W. Marsh, Roberto H. Parada, Rhonda G. Craven, & Linda Finger*

## 5. THE BULLY IN THE FAMILY: FAMILY INFLUENCES ON BULLYING

James R. Holmes & Heather A. Holmes-Lonergan

## 6. PEER INFLUENCES

Helen Cowie

## 7. SCHOOLS AND BULLYING: SCHOOL FACTORS RELATED TO BULLYING AND SCHOOL-BASED BULLYING INTERVENTIONS

*Allison Ann Payne & Denise C. Gottfredson*

## 8. BULLYING DURING MIDDLE SCHOOL YEARS

*A. D. Pellegrini*

## 9. EVALUATING CURRICULUM-BASED INTERVENTION PROGRAMS: AN EXAMINATION OF PRESCHOOL, PRIMARY, AND ELEMENTARY SCHOOL INTERVENTION PROGRAMS

*Faith L. Samples*

## 10. RESEARCH BASED INTERVENTIONS ON BULLYING

*Jaana Juvonen & Sandra Graham*

# Contributors

*Numbers in parentheses indicate the pages on which the authors' contributions begin.*

**Helen Cowie** (137), European Institute of Health and Medical Sciences, University of Surrey, Surrey GU2 7TE, United Kingdom

**Rhonda G. Craven** (63), SELF Research Centre, University of Western Sydney, Penrith South, 1719, Australia

**Linda Finger** (63), SELF Research Centre, University of Western Sydney, Penrith South, 1719, Australia

**Denise C. Gottfredson** (159), Department of Criminology and Criminal Justice, University of Maryland, College Park, Maryland 20742

**Sandra Graham** (229), Department of Psychology, University of California, Los Angeles, Los Angeles, California 90095–1512

**James R. Holmes** (111), Center for Psychological Services, University of Western Florida, Pensacola, Florida 32514

**Heather Holmes-Lonergan** (111), Department of Psychology, Metropolitan State College of Denver, Denver, Colorado 80217–3362

**Jaana Juvonen** (229), Department of Psychology, University of California, Los Angeles, Los Angeles, California 90095–1512

**Herb Marsh** (63), SELF Research Centre, University of Western Sydney, Penrith South, 1719, Australia

**Xin Ma** (19), University of Kentucky, Lexington, Kentucky 40506–0017

**Adrienne Nishina** (35), Department of Education, University of California, Los Angeles, Los Angeles, California 90095–1521

**Roberto Parada** (63), SELF Research Centre, University of Western Sydney, Penrith South, 1719, Australia

**Allison Ann Payne** (159), Department of Criminology and Justice Studies, The College of New Jersey, Ewing, New Jersey 08628

**Anthony D. Pellegrini** (177), Department of Educational Psychology, University of Minnesota/Twin Cities Campus 55455–0208

**Faith L. Samples** (203), Center for Violence Research and Prevention, Columbia University, New York, New York 10032

**Cheryl Sanders** (1), Department of Psychology, Metropolitan State College of Denver, Denver, Colorado 80217–3362

# About the Authors

*Dr. Helen Cowie* (Chapter 6) is Professor of Mental Health and Youth and Director of the UK Observatory for the Promotion of Non-Violence (www. ukobservatory.com) at the University of Surrey in the European Institute of Health and Medical Sciences. She obtained her first degree in psychology at the University of Glasgow, her master's degree at the University of Birmingham, and her doctorate at the University of London. She has published widely in the field of child development, specializing in the fields of bullying, violence in schools, mental health and young people, and peer support as an intervention to promote non-violence. The textbook *Understanding Children's Development* (co-authored with Peter K Smith and Mark Blades and published by Blackwell) is now into its fourth edition and has become one of the major undergraduate developmental psychology texts in the UK. Her book *Peer Support in Action*, co-authored with Patti Wallace and published by Sage, has been influential in disseminating the theory and practice of such peer support methods as conflict resolution, peer-led listening services, and counseling-based approaches to the problem of bullying. Her most recent research project, Violence in Schools Training Action (VISTA), is funded by the European Union and is designed to disseminate the most effective anti-violence initiatives across Europe. Helen has three grown-up children, Julian, Anna, and Ben, and is the proud grandmother of Corrie, Isabel, and Haruki.

*Dr. Rhonda G. Craven* (Chapter 4) (diploma in Teaching, Alexander Mackie CAE; B.A. [Hons], University Medal; Ph.D. [Educational Psychology] University of Sydney) is Deputy Director of the SELF Research Centre and is Associate-Professor in the School of Education and Early Childhood Studies. As an educational psychologist, her research focuses on large-scale quantitative research studies in educational settings. She has attracted substantial prestigious external funding to conduct her research. Her research interests include the structure, measurement and enhancement of self-concept, the relationship of self-concept to desirable educational outcomes, the effective teaching of aboriginal studies and aboriginal students, and interventions that make a difference in educational settings.

Linda Finger (Chapter 4) was awarded First Class Honors in the School of Psychology at the University of Western Sydney in 2002. Her research interest focuses on examining the psychological determinants of bullying and the consequences of being a victim in educational settings. She plans to pursue her work in this area as a Ph.D. Candidate.

Dr. Denise C. Gottfredson (Chapter 7) is a Professor at the University of Maryland Department of Criminal Justice and Criminology. She received a doctorate in Social Relations from The Johns Hopkins University. Dr. Gottfredson's research interests include delinquency and delinquency prevention, and particularly the effects of school environments on youth behavior. She currently directs evaluations of Baltimore City's Drug Treatment Court and the Maryland After School Opportunity Grant Fund Program, both of which address important policy questions for the state of Maryland. She is co-principal investigator on an evaluation of the Strengthening Washington D.C. Families Program and directs a grant to work with the prevention community in the State of Maryland to increase the use of research-based prevention practices.

Dr. Sandra Graham (Chapter 10) (Ph.D., University of California, Los Angeles, 1982) is a professor in the Department of Education at the University of California, Los Angeles. Her major research interests include the study of academic motivation, peer aggression, and juvenile delinquency, particularly in African American children and adolescents. Dr. Graham has published widely in developmental, social, and educational psychology journals and is currently the principal investigator on grants from the National Science Foundation and the W.T. Grant Foundation. She also is the recipient of an Independent Scientist Award, funded by the National Institute of Mental Health, a recipient of the Early Contribution Award from Division 15 (Educational Psychology) of the American Psychological Association, and a former fellow at the Center for Advanced Study in the Behavioral Sciences in Stanford, California. Among her professional activities, Dr. Graham is an associate editor of Developmental Psychology, a member of the National Research Council Panel on Juvenile Crime, Prevention, and Control, and a member of the MacArthur Foundation Network on Adolescent Development and Juvenile Justice.

Dr. James R. Holmes (Chapter 5) is a licensed psychologist in Pensacola, Florida. He received his doctorate in clinical psychology from the University of Colorado. For 27 years, until his retirement, he was an Associate Professor and Director of the Counseling Center at the University of West Florida. He is a past president of the Society for Descriptive Psychology and is the editor of the Society's *Bulletin*. He enjoys applying applications of descriptive psychology to complex problems. He has written a book on depression that he hopes to publish this year.

Dr. *Heather Holmes-Lonergan* (Chapter 5) has a doctorate in developmental psychology from the University of Florida. She is currently an assistant professor of psychology at the Metropolitan State College of Denver, and has also been an assistant professor at Southeastern Louisiana University. She teaches courses in infant, child, and lifespan development, and conducts research on social and cognitive development in young children.

Dr. *Jaana Juvonen* (Chapter 10) (Ph.D., University of California, Los Angeles, 1989) is a Professor and Chair of Developmental Psychology at UCLA and Adjunct Behavioral Scientist at the RAND Corporation. Her areas of expertise are young adolescent school adjustment and bullying. Dr. Juvonen publishes in educational and developmental journals, and she serves on the editorial boards of *Developmental Psychology, Journal of Educational Psychology*, and *Child Development*. She has written a book with her RAND colleagues called *Focus on the Wonder Years: Challenges Facing the American Middle School*, to be published in 2004. She has also co-edited two books, *Social Motivation: Understanding Children's School Adjustment*, 1996, and *Peer Harassment in School: The Plight of the Vulnerable and Victimized*, 2001. Dr. Juvonen is currently a co-principal investigator on a longitudinal study of 2000 public middle schools students, funded by the National Science Foundation and the William T. Grant Foundation. Dr. Juvonen is a former recipient of a National Academy of Education Spencer Fellowship and Senior Fellowship of the Academy of Finland.

Dr. *Herb Marsh* (Chapter 4) (BA [Hons] Indiana, MA; Ph.D., UCLA; DSc, University of Western Sydney, Australia Academy of Social Science) is a Professor of Education and founding Director of the SELF Research Centre. He is the author of internationally recognized psychological tests that measure self-concept, motivation and university students' evaluations of teaching effectiveness. He has published more than 240 articles in top international journals, 22 chapters, 8 monographs, and 225 conference papers. He was recognized as the most productive educational psychologist in the world, as one of the top 10 international researchers in higher education and in social psychology, and the 11th most productive researcher in the world across all disciplines of psychology. His major research and scholarly interests include self-concept and motivational constructs, evaluations of teaching effectiveness, developmental psychology, quantitative analysis, sports psychology, the peer review, gender differences, peer support, and anti-bullying interventions.

Dr. *Xin Ma* (Chapter 2) is an associate professor of mathematics education in the Department of Curriculum and Instruction at the University of Kentucky. He got his doctorate from the University of British Columbia in Canada. He is a fellow of the United States National Academy of Education. His main research interests include mathematics education, school effectiveness, policy analysis, and quantitative methods. He has published referred articles on school bullying in the past couple of years in academic journals including *American Educational Research Journal, Research Papers in Education,* and *School Effectiveness and School Improvement.*

Dr. *Adrienne Nishina* (Chapter 3) completed her doctorate in clinical psychology and is currently a postdoctoral fellow in applied human development in the Department of Education at the University of California, Los Angeles. Her research interests include adolescent mental health, peer relations, contextual factors, school-based prevention, and methodological issues.

*Roberto Parada* (Chapter 4) has a BA (Hons), a masters in psychology, is psychology doctoral candidate at the University of New South Wales, and is a registered psychologist in New South Wales (NSW). Under the supervision of Professors Marsh and Craven, he is the Project Manager of one of New South Wales' largest projects investigating the psychological effects of bullying and the effectiveness of interventions to prevent it. He was awarded a highly prestigious Australian Postgraduate Award (Industry) to pursue this research that will form the basis of his Ph.D. With a background in education and psychology, Mr. Parada has worked in child and adolescent psychiatry and has overseen the evaluation of numerous projects at the Department of Child and Adolescent and Family Psychiatry, Westmead Hospital including the Positive Parenting Program (Triple P), a NSW strategy for the prevention of conduct disorders. He has clinical experience in working with victims of bullying and has worked with both parents and teachers in the implementation of anti-bullying interventions. He has written reports for the NSW Centre for Mental Health assessing stakeholder needs for young children and adolescents. Mr. Parada has published journal articles and book chapters in the area of bullying in schools, has presented at numerous conferences in the area of early intervention and has been featured in the Sydney Morning Herald and The Western Australian, and on SBS television and ABC Radio. He has also authored a number of instruments to assess peer relations including bullying.

Dr. *Allison Ann Payne* (Chapter 7) is an assistant professor at The College of New Jersey, Department of Criminology and Justice Studies. She received her Ph.D. from the University of Maryland, Department of Criminology and Criminal Justice in May, 2002. Her research interests include juvenile delinquency, school-based delinquency prevention, and program evaluation. She has previously worked on an evaluation of Positive Action Through Holistic Education (PATHE) in Charleston, South Carolina and an evaluation of the Strengthening Washington D.C. Families Program and has recently published in criminology.

*Anthony D. Pellegrini* (Chapter 8) is a Professor of Psychological Foundations of Education in the Department of Educational Psychology, University of Minnesota, Twin Cities Campus, His e-mail is pelle013@umn.edu. He completed his doctorate at Ohio State University in 1978 on the role of private speech in children's cognitive processing. His current research interests relate to methodological issues in the general area of human development, with specific interests in direct observations of aggression, dominance, and social bases of cognitive processes.

*Dr. Gary D. Phye* is the editor of the Academic Press *Educational Psychology Series*. Gary received his academic training in educational psychology at the University of Missouri under the tutelage of Allan J. Edwards. He is currently a member of the College of Education faculty at Iowa State University and is a professor in the Department of Psychology and in the Department of Curriculum and Instruction. Gary indicates that this has been a wonderful set of authors to work with and he has benefited intellectually from the new ideas being generated in this very important discussion.

*Dr. Faith L. Samples* (Chapter 9) currently holds the position of Project Director and Investigator at the Treatment Research Institute (TRI) at the University of Pennsylvania. She is also on faculty in the Department of Sociomedical Sciences at Columbia University. At TRI, Dr. Samples is involved in research on substance abuse research and prevention. Prior to joining TRI, Dr. Samples held a joint faculty and research appointment at Columbia University's Mailman School of Public Health, served as Chair of the Columbia Center for Youth Violence Prevention's Community Response Team, and was Research Director at the National Center for Children in Poverty. Dr. Samples' areas of interest include adolescent, school, and community violence, violence prevention, adolescent substance abuse, social contextual research, and program evaluation. Dr. Samples received her bachelor's degree from Howard University in child and adolescent development and psychology. She completed advanced graduate training at Cornell University, where she received both her masters and doctoral degrees in program evaluation and planning.

*Dr. Cheryl Sanders* (Chapter 1) is currently an assistant professor in the Psychology Department at the Metropolitan State College of Denver. She earned a master's degree in higher education and a doctoral degree in psychology at Iowa State University. She has conducted and published research on various aspects of moral development including moral development of college students and gifted children. In addition, she is currently investigating the effectiveness of various character education programs and effects of video game playing on development.

# Preface

In a time when concern regarding violence in schools is at an all-time high, this book attempts to accomplish an important goal. As authors of this book, we expect that our readers—students, teachers, educators, practitioners, researchers, and professionals in related fields—will come one step closer to understanding the phenomenon of bullying. A strong need exists to acquire a better understanding of why bullying occurs, how bullying occurs, and what effects it has on all individuals involved. Last, there exists a strong desire to "fix" the problem by using an effective intervention technique. This book attempts to provide some of the current theoretical views and current research findings related to these aspects of bullying.

Today, bullying is considered a worldwide issue. Evidence suggests that bullying occurs in schools of numerous countries and is receiving widespread interest not only by the educational community but also by the research community. Because the topic of bullying has received a tremendous amount of international research attention, all chapters within this book attempt to incorporate and capture an American as well as an international focus.

This book is divided into three sections. The first section is an introduction to the topic of bullying. Three chapters provide definitions and theoretical perspectives on bullying and victimization. Emphasized is the overwhelming consensus that a widely accepted definition for bullying and victimization is still needed. The second section of this book introduces prevalent issues concerning bullying. Discussions include possible correlates of bullying, such as personality traits, family environment peers, and school influences. Bullying is a complex phenomenon that is multifaceted.

The third and final section of the book offers insights about effective intervention techniques. Can bullying be eliminated with the right tools? These chapters focus on current research efforts for validating the effectiveness of intervention approaches that take either a systems/curriculum approach or an individual/clinical psychological approach.

*Cheryl E. Sanders*

# Acknowledgements

We greatly appreciate the contributions of the authors whose expertise in the field allowed us to formulate a book on bullying that is based on the most current theoretical and experimental views of the field. We also appreciate the commitment and helpfulness of Nikki Levy, Publisher for Social Sciences.

I would also like to thank my coeditor, mentor, and friend, Gary Phye, for allowing me the opportunity to coedit this book with him. His patience and countless hours of directing me through the process are greatly appreciated. I cannot thank you enough for all you have taught me.

Last, I would also like to thank my husband, Steve, and my children, Christa, Courtney, and Jake, for the tremendous support they always give me.

CHAPTER

1

# What Is Bullying?

CHERYL E. SANDERS
*Department of Psychology*
*Metropolitan State College of Denver*

In February of 2003, a 13-year-old girl attending middle school in a Denver suburb had to switch schools for fear of her life (Kirksey, 2003). This wasn't the first time she thought she was going to die. As a 9-year-old, she lost her right leg to synovial carcinoma. That was a big enough scare for a child her age. As a young amputee, she should have made friends easily and received empathy from her peers, but instead she experienced bullying. An "underground" group of eight to ten girls used verbal aggression to intimidate her. Sending profane and threatening messages such as "die, bitch, die" and "you better watch your back" via a website on the Internet as well as communicating with her at school were the primary venues for the bullying. After 5 months of living through this horror, she (with her mother's encouragement) chose to leave the neighborhood middle school and enroll at a different school. They hoped to find an inviting environment where she could flourish, learn, and feel safe. Unfortunately, statistics indicate that this young girl and others like her are likely to experience the same aggression at a new school (Beale & Scott, 2001).

According to Ross (2002), bullying has been a societal problem for hundreds of years. Bullying occurs in the workplace, homes, prisons, and nursing homes (Smith & Brain, 2000). Most predominantly, it occurs in schools. When referring to historical accounts of bullying in educational settings, one finds that many instances of bullying occurred in boarding schools

(Smith & Sharp, 1994) and were commonly described in literature (Hughes, 1857). However, it appears that bullying in the 1990s and the current decade is more volatile and occurs more often than it did in the past (Beale & Scott, 2001; Ma, 2001; Marsh, Parada, Yeung, & Healey, 2001; Olweus & Alsaker, 1991). Sad as it may seem, bullying will occur in most school environments (Smith & Brain, 2000). In addition, many students should expect to be bullied as researchers have estimated that 49 to 50% of all students will experience some form of bullying during their educational experience (Charach, Pepler, & Ziegler, 1995; Farrington, 1993).

## RESEARCH ATTENTION: NATIONAL AND INTERNATIONAL

Although bullying has been a problem for centuries, it did not receive significant research attention until the 1970s (Olweus, 1978). Olweus was the first scientist to focus on the topic and to contribute scientific data to the literature. He is considered a pioneer of the field (Camodeca, Goossens, Schuengel, & Terwogt, 2003) and has generated insurmountable research interest from scientists of various countries and continents.

As indicated by Olweus (1978), research on bullying began in Scandanavian and British countries. Research attention in Norway and Sweden in the 1980s led to the first national intervention campaign against bullying. The success of this research motivated other countries such as Finland, United Kingdom, Ireland, and Japan to study bullying (Ross, 2002; Smith & Brain, 2000). Since the late 1980s, the World Health Organization (WHO) has conducted cross-national studies every fourth year on health behavior in school-aged children. Samples of 11-, 13-, and 15-year-olds from numerous countries are assessed, and bullying is included as an important aspect of the research (Merrick, Kessel, & Morad, 2002). Thus, the issue of bullying is receiving increasing worldwide attention (Boulton, 1997; Camodeca M., Goossens, F. A., Schvengel, C., Terwogt, M. M. 2003; Carney & Merrell, 2001). Evidence suggests that bullying exists in many countries, including the United States, Canada, Japan, Australia, New Zealand, Germany, Belgium, Italy, Spain, Portugal, France, Switzerland, England, Ireland, and Finland (Ross, 2002; Smith, Morita, Junger-Tas, Olweus, Catalano, & Slee, 1999) and has taken a front seat in the research arena in many of these countries (Smith *et al.*, 1999).

Japan is a good example of a country that has made attempts to understand bullying and develop ways to prevent bullying. The Japanese word *ijime* translates as "bullying" in English. According to Kawabata (2001), *ijime* refers to bullying that results in trauma and, in some cases, school phobia. In addition, Tanaka (2001) describes *shunning* as a type of bullying typically found in Japan. *Shunning* is one type of bullying whereby a group of peers collectively ignore and exclude a victim. During the 1980s, research activity was high in Japan because bullying was believed to be largely a Japanese problem (Smith & Brain, 2000). After various results became available, many were led to believe that there was a decline in the problem; thus, research activity subsided. Between 1993 and 1995, however, Japan experienced a number of suicides due to bullying. As a result, research interest has increased dramatically (Morita, Soeda, Soeda, & Taki, 1999). Although rates of bullying in the United States and other countries are comparable or lower than the rate in Japan (Treml, 2001), the United States has placed bullying high on its research agenda.

In the United States, bullying is clearly a serious issue (Nansel, Overpeck, Pilla, Ruan, Simons-Morton, & Scheidt, 2001). According to Ross (2002), bullying is considered the most predominant form of aggression found in American schools and impacts the largest number of students when compared to other forms of violence. However, since many Americans view the phenomenon as a normal occurrence—"a part of growing up" (Siris, 2001) and a "character forming experience" (Smith & Brain, 2000)—it is not surprising to report that bullying has only become a part of the U.S. educational agenda fairly recently, mainly in the 1990s (Ross, 2002). Nonetheless, concern for individual rights and child protection from abuse have aided in giving bullying more serious attention in this country (Smith & Brain, 2000). Still, some feel that the United States could do a better job of addressing the issue of bullying and claim that this area of research is still largely neglected (Dupper & Meyers-Adams, 2002).

## DEFINITION OF BULLYING

Most experts in the field of bullying agree that there is considerable debate on a clear definition for the term *bullying* (Boulton, 1997; Crick & Dodge, 1999; Sutton, Smith, & Swettenham, 1999). An exhaustive literature search on the topic of bullying revealed that this problem of clarity in defining bullying is mentioned in the majority of publications. Ross (2002) indicated that researchers agree bullying is a common problem; however, very few agree on a widely accepted definition of bullying.

Many researchers use Olweus's (1993) definition of bullying, which states, ". . . a student is being bullied or victimized when he is exposed repeatedly and over time to negative actions on the part of one or more other students" (p. 9). The term *negative actions* encompasses a wide variety of behaviors ranging from nonverbal aggression, such as stares and teasing, to serious physical assaults. Olweus specified "repetition" in the definition to exclude occasional minor incidences. He indicated, however, that a single serious instance "under certain circumstances" should be considered bullying

(Olweus, 1993). Ross (2002) insisted that a more in-depth operational definition of "certain circumstances" is needed to conduct high quality research on bullying. In addition, this clarification would aid in developing effective intervention programs.

Smith and Sharp's (1994) definition of bullying is also popular in the field. They claim that bullying is "a systematic abuse of power" (p. 2). This definition incorporates the repetitive nature or bullying similar to Olweus's (1993) explanation. In addition, it implies an imbalance of power within the interaction. That is, the victim cannot defend him or herself easily for various reasons such as being outnumbered or being physically inferior. This definition also implies that others are obligated to intervene if the rights of the victim are taken into consideration (Smith & Brain, 2000). According to Crick and Dodge (1999), this definition is too vague and is vulnerable to encompassing too many interactions that should not necessarily fall into the bullying category.

Most definitions of bullying categorize it as a subset of aggressive behavior that involves an *intention* to hurt another person (Camodeca *et al.* 2003; Olweus, 1978; Rivers & Smith, 1994; Smith & Thompson, 1991). This negative intentional behavior can be manifested in a variety of ways. Not only can it be displayed physically, but it also can be subtle and elusive. As indicated by Rivers and Smith (1994), verbally aggressive notes can be passed in the classroom without teachers even being aware that bullying is taking place. Most recently, bullying has been labeled as a form of terrorism in that it involves an "unprovoked attack" with the intention to cause harm on the victim (Ross, 2002).

One narrow definition of bullying involves physical harassment (Ma, 2001). This is the most common view of bullying. McCudden (2001) notes that many children believe that if they have not physically touched another person, they have not bullied that person. Even some educators have indicated that various verbal harassment should not be considered bullying. Many adults (including educators) consider most verbal bullying as "normal" and "harmless" (Hazler, 1992). Boulton (1997) interviewed 138 teachers from Northwest England preschools, junior schools, and secondary schools and reported that one in every four teachers did not believe bullying involved name calling, spreading rumors, intimidating by staring, and taking other people's belongings. The top three behaviors that were considered as bullying were (1) hitting, pushing, kicking, (2) forcing people to do things they do not want to do, and (3) threatening people. In addition, Shields and Cicchetti (2001) found that professionals in education (teachers and counselors) felt that physical threats or abuse were significantly more severe than verbal and/ or social and emotional abuse. These results are disturbing in that educators did not consider elements of social exclusion serious offenses. Nonetheless, research indicates long-term effects from social exclusion are detrimental to healthy development (Sharp, Thompson, & Arora, 2000). Emotional harassment is much more difficult to identify and prove but should still be included under the definition of bullying.

Hazler and his colleagues attempted to clarify the definition of bullying by identifying specific characteristics of bullies and specific characteristics of victims (Hazler, Carney, Green, Powell, & Jolly, 1997). They interviewed 14 experts in the field to determine which of 70 characteristics were most typical of bullies and victims. They were able to quantify the expert agreement and compiled a list of 19 characteristics for bullies (see Appendix A) and 19 characteristics for victims (see Appendix B). Ross (2002) argued that results from this research "should be mandatory reading for those interested in the problem of bullying and victimization." Moreover, it may be beneficial to include these characteristics in a widely accepted operational definition of bullying.

## TYPES OF AGGRESSION INVOLVED IN BULLYING

Rivers and Smith (1994) identified three types of aggression involved in bullying: *direct physical aggression, direct verbal aggression*, and *indirect aggression*. Direct physical aggression involves tangible behaviors such as hitting, pushing, and kicking. Direct verbal aggression includes name-calling and threats. The least identified and most difficult to prove is indirect aggression. This involves behaviors such as spreading rumors and telling tales. Direct aggression is explicitly exhibited from the aggressor to the victim whereas indirect aggression involves a third party. Sharp (1995) studied over 700 13- to 16-year-olds and found that the majority of the youth reported indirect verbal bullying as being the most stressful and hurtful. In addition, Sharp and Smith (1991) reported that name-calling was the most common form of bullying when they interviewed more than 7,000 primary and secondary students in the United Kingdom. They also found that girls were more likely to experience direct and indirect verbal aggression while boys were more likely to be victims of direct physical aggression.

Dodge (1991) introduced the notion of two types of aggression: *proactive aggression* and *reactive aggression*. Reactive aggression involves angry and defensive reactions to frustration, while proactive aggression is characterized by goal-directed, dominant, and coercive behaviors. An individual displaying proactive aggression is cold-blooded and will utilize aggression to reach his or her goal. On the other hand, reactive aggressors often misinterpret social cues and attribute hostile intentions to their peers (Camodeca *et al.*, 2003). These two types of aggression have been attributed to deficits or mistakes in the processing of social information (Crick & Dodge, 1996). (Social information processing theory and how this theory relates to bullying are presented later in this chapter.)

Crick and Dodge (1999) have applied reactive and proactive aggression to the phenomenon of bullying and hypothesized that bullies would exhibit proactive aggression while their victims would display predominantly reactive aggression. Salmivalli and Nieminen (2002) studied over 1000 youth (10 to 12 years of age). They assessed the amount of proactive and reactive aggression displayed by each youth via peer and teacher reports. Their results revealed that bully-victims (individuals who at times were bullies and at other times were the victims) displayed the highest level of aggression (both proactive and reactive) than any of the other youth. Bullies displayed significantly higher levels of aggression than victims and controls. Youth who were labeled as victims displayed predominantly reactive aggression. These results partially supported Crick and Dodge's (1999) original hypothesis.

## CLASSIFICATION OF BULLYING ROLES:
## A DYADIC APPROACH

For some educators and researchers, bullying is considered a dyadic process involving one bully and one victim. This research perspective predominantly focuses on peer nomination and/or teacher report whereby children and/or teachers are asked to identify which individuals are the bullies and which individuals are the victims. For example, Marsh *et al.* (2001) used the terms *troublemaker* and *victim*. The troublemaker was described as the individual not following rules, getting into physical fights, and picking on others. On the other hand, the victim was characterized as the child who did not feel safe at school due to receipt of threats and/or real physical harm by someone at his or her school.

Ramirez (2001) studied 315 students between the ages of 10 to 15 years and found distinct personality characteristics between bullies and victims. Bullies scored significantly higher on psychoticism and leadership measures while victims scored significantly higher on anxiety and shyness scales. Other distinctions within this dyadic interaction have also been reported. Olafsen and Viemero (2000) reported significant differences between the two groups in regards to physical strength, attitudes toward violence, extroversion, and self-esteem with bullies scoring higher than victims on all of these dimensions.

Olweus (1978) expanded the dyadic view and identified two types of bullies: the *aggressive bully* and the *anxious bully*. He claimed that the aggressive bully was active, impulsive, assertive, strong, and easily provoked. The aggressive bully takes the lead in initiating the aggression and often seeks for another bully to follow his or her instructions. These bullies are skilled at avoiding blame and feel no remorse or empathy for their victims. They are most likely to use direct and indirect verbal aggression, such as hurtful words, gestures, and stares (Olweus, 1993). According to Olweus (1993), most bullies fall into this category.

The anxious bully, on the other hand, rarely initiates the bullying. He or she usually works alongside an aggressive bully. The anxious bully is characterized with low self-esteem, lack of confidence, and disruptive temper tantrums. Olweus (1978) indicated that the anxious bully most likely follows the aggressive bully to compensate for inadequate feelings about him or herself. Thus, anxious bullies desperately seek approval from aggressive bullies.

## CLASSIFICATION OF BULLYING ROLES: A GROUP APPROACH

According to Sutton and Smith (1999), bullying should not be viewed exclusively as a dyadic process. Instead, bullying needs to be viewed as a group phenomenon. Most children are directly or indirectly involved in the bullying that occurs in their school (Hawkins, Pepler, & Craig, 2001). Pepler and Craig (1995) found that peers were present in 85% of bullying situations; thus, these incidences impact not only the bully and victim but also individuals who witness the bullying and individuals who hear about the occurrence. Salmivalli *et al.* (1996) argued that all the children in a given class or school where bullying occurs are somehow involved in the bullying process. Although they may not be actively participating in the bullying behavior, their response to the bullying may impact whether it will be repeated. Research indicates that the majority of children report a negative or neutral attitude toward bullying (Boulton & Underwood, 1992; Whitney & Smith, 1993); however, many will end up reinforcing the bully (Bjorkqvist, Ekman, & Lagerspetz, 1982). Whether an individual cheers, laughs, or observes the bullying and does nothing, these actions or "nonactions" reinforce bullying behavior and increase the likelihood that it will occur again. Moreover, other children may not directly observe the bullying but may hear about it from their peers. In all cases, these individuals are exposed to the bullying occurrence at some level.

Many research studies have been conducted to investigate the various roles involved in bullying. Karatzias, Power, and Swanson (2002) studied 425 Scottish middle school-aged students and identified the following participant categories in bullying: *bully, victim, bully-victim,* and *uninvolved*. Menesini, Fonzi, and Sanchez (2002) investigated 91 youth residents of Italy and divided the students into status groups of *bullies, victims, outsiders,* and *defenders*. They described outsiders as individuals who were not directly involved in the bullying episode. Defenders were students who tried to aid the victim in some way. Both studies reported significant differentiation between the various roles of bullying.

Viewing bullying as a social phenomenon was also emphasized in research conducted by Salmivalli and her colleagues (1996). They investigated almost 600 Finnish sixth grade students and had them evaluate how well each child in their class, including themselves, fit 50 behavioral descriptions involving bullying episodes. From the 50 descriptions, the researchers were able to identify the following six subscales describing various participant roles in a bullying situation: *ringleader bully, assistant of the bully, reinforcer of the bully, defender of the victim, outsider,* and *victim.* The ringleader bully took an active role in initiating the bullying. The assistant bully was as active in the bullying process but was more of a follower to the ringleader bully. (These classifications seem somewhat parallel to Olweus's (1978) *aggressive bully* and *anxious bully* descriptions.) The reinforcer acted in ways to encourage the bullying behavior. These reinforcers displayed such behaviors as laughing, coming to watch the episode, and remaining during the bullying episode to provide an "audience" for the bully. The defender of the victim engaged in behaviors to protect and help the victim as well as to discourage the bully from continuing. The outsider did nothing and stayed away from the bullying episodes. The victim was bullied but placed into the category only if he or she were nominated by at least one-third of the same-sex classmates. Salmivalli *et al.* (1996) were able to assign 87% of the students to one of the above-mentioned participant roles, lending support to the notion that most children are directly or indirectly involved in bullying situations occurring in their schools.

Sutton and Smith (1999) used a shortened adaptation to the Salmivalli *et al.* (1996) Participant Role Scale and reported similar results with children in England. Interestingly, they found that children tend to downplay their active participation in bullying and emphasize their activity in defending victims and remaining outsiders to the bullying situation.

In addition, McKinnon (2001) argued that bullying encompasses multiple roles. After conducting extensive, structured interviews with 153 children (mean age 11 years), five specific roles were identified. She concluded that *bullies, victims, guardians, henchme,* and *active bystanders* are all part of the bullying process. Guardians were those individuals who befriended the victim. Henchmen were the loyal followers of the bully, and active bystanders witnessed the event. Interestingly, results revealed a relationship between classroom group membership and participation in bullying episodes. McKinnon (2001) found that children who belonged to a prominent classroom group and held prominent leadership roles were most likely to take on bully or guardian roles. Children who were members of the prominent classroom group but did not hold leadership roles were most likely to serve as active bystanders in a bullying situation. Last, children who did not belong to a classroom social group were most likely to be victims in a bullying situation. Thus, group dynamics appear to play a central role on bullying.

Moreover, Olafsen, and Viemero (2000) identified multiple roles in bullying. Their study involved more than 500 fifth and sixth graders from 17 elementary schools in Finland. Their results revealed five roles in the bullying process: the *bully*, the *bully victim*, the *victim of direct bullying*, the *victim of indirect bullying*, and the *individuals not involved*. They reported that 76% of the students fell into the "not involved" category, 4.1% were considered bullies, 2.2% labeled as bully-victims, and 17% were victims. Victims of indirect bullying were the most common of the types of victims studied.

Overall, the research literature indicates that bullying is being viewed more often as a group phenomenon as opposed to a dyadic interaction. Although many children and youth may not be playing the "predominant" roles of the bully and/or the victim, they do play a role in the process. Whether their role involves defending the victim, encouraging the bully, and/or remaining an outsider to the situation, they are being impacted by the bullying. They are influencing how the bullying is affecting others and whether the bullying will continue to occur.

## THEORETICAL PERSPECTIVES OF BULLYING

Many researchers and educators have been challenged to explain *theoretically* the phenomenon of bullying. Thus, numerous perspectives have been used to try to make sense out of why individuals choose to engage in bullying.

According to Sutton (2001), bullying is strongly regulated by social cognition and environmental factors. Recently, experts in the field have focused on these factors to develop theoretical frameworks to explain why bullying occurs. In particular, two theories have been strongly emphasized: the social information processing theory and the theory of the mind framework. A third theoretical approach, moral development theory, will also be discussed.

### Social Information Processing Theory

The social information processing theory (SIP) was originally developed by Dodge in 1986 and redefined by Crick and Dodge in 1994. The reformulated theory involves six sequential stages of processing social information. In step one, the individual encodes sensory information being taken into the "system." Second, the individual attempts to make sense or interpret the sensory information. Next, clarification of the information and goal setting occurs. Fourth, the individual seeks ideas for possible responses or develops unique ones on his or her own. Fifth, a decision about which response is most appropriate occurs. Last, the individual follows through with the behavioral response.

Using this model, Crick and Dodge (1994) claimed that bullying occurs as a result of social information processing biases or deficits at one or more of the six stages. Research findings have supported their ideas. For example,

Camodeca *et al.* (2003) reported that bully-victims exhibit deficits in the second stage of processing (clarification/interpretation) and the fifth stage of processing (response decision making). In addition, Berkowitz (1977) found significant differences among individuals in how they interpret situational cues during conflict. Moreover, Camodeca *et al.* (2003) reported that bullies and victims display lower social competence than children not directly involved in the bullying episode. They concluded that the necessary social knowledge may have been available to the children but that bullies and victims did not always apply it successfully.

Randall (1997) argued that individuals who exhibit bullying are doing so because they do not process social information accurately. They exhibit what he termed *social blindness* in that they are lacking skills to understand other people's perspectives. That is, bullies have little awareness of what others are thinking of them and display a deficient ability to empathize. Evidence suggests that these deficits result from environmental influences (McKeough, Yates, & Marini, 1994). Children who are exposed to neglect or other inadequate experiences are likely to develop internal working models of human relationships that are not healthy or normal. Thus, social incompetence results. The popular stereotype of a bully who is a social outcast and lacks social insight is implied by the SIP theoretical framework.

## Theory of the Mind Framework

Recently, the SIP perspective on bullying has been challenged (Sutton *et al.*, 1999). Instead of explaining bullying behavior as a result of social incompetence, Sutton and his colleagues claim that some bullies actually possess a "superior" theory of the mind. Sutton (2001) described the theory of the mind (TOM) framework as "the ability of individuals to attribute mental states to themselves and others in order to explain and predict behavior." That is, individuals who possess well-developed TOM skills will be more equipped to read and understand the feelings and emotions of other people. Thus, they do not lack social competence as implied by the SIP framework but instead have an advanced ability at "reading" other people.

Sutton and his colleagues (1999) argued that successful bullying may be a result of superior TOM skills. Being able to understand the mental states of others and to predict their behaviors can be utilized to manipulate the minds of others. This could be a potentially useful skill in all aspects of bullying, particularly with indirect aggression such as spreading rumors, excluding victims from social groups, and avoiding getting caught in a bullying episode. For instance, for a bully to socially exclude his or her victim, the bully needs to understand the feelings of others in the social context to manipulate others to make the victim feel "left out."

Children begin to exhibit more fine-tuned TOM skills as they develop beyond 6 years of age (Sutton *et al.*, 1999). As indicated by research, older bullies are more likely to use indirect types of bullying, while younger bullies exhibit more direct methods (Rivers & Smith, 1994). In addition, indirect bullying is more likely to occur with girls than with boys (Bjorkqvist *et al.*, 1992), and TOM studies indicate that girls exhibit more sophisticated TOM skills than do boys (Baron-Cohen & Hammer, 1996). These findings imply that engaging in indirect methods of bullying requires a well-developed TOM framework. However, some critics of the TOM framework argue that having advanced TOM skills can not only lead to various types of bullying but can also lead to highly prosocial behavior; thus, "having a superior TOM says nothing about how that knowledge will be utilized" (Arsenio & Lemerise, 2001).

Sutton (2001) claimed that prior research provides support for the TOM perspective. When Sutton categorized students into one of the six participant roles in bullying (as discussed earlier in this chapter), they also assessed the participants' understanding of cognitive false beliefs and emotions based on false beliefs. They claimed that this research was measuring the children's TOM skills. Results revealed that a bully's scores were significantly higher than those of the assistants of the bully, reinforcers of the bully, defenders of the victim, outsiders, and victims. In addition, results indicated a positive correlation between bullying and social cognition. Bjorkqvist *et al.* (2000) also reported a significant positive correlation between social intelligence and indirect aggression. Hence, these findings support the notion that bullies possess more advanced TOM skills than the other "players" in the bullying episode.

## Moral Development Theory

In response to the debate between Crick and Dodge (1999) and Sutton *et al.* (1999), Arsenio and Lemerise (2001) argued that bullying cannot be fully understood without considering the moral aspects involved in the phenomenon. They claimed that such issues as fairness, individuals' welfare, and sacrifice need to be addressed. It appears that the SIP and TOM theoretical perspectives do not adequately include this aspect of bullying and victimization. Guerra, Nucci, and Huesmann (1994) indicated that the gap between the study of bullying and the study of moral reasoning is unsettling. A common element exists within the two areas, and experts in the field of bullying would be remiss not to include this theoretical framework in the study of bullying.

One theory of moral development that seems to link social cognition and bullying behavior is Rest's four-component model of morality (Rest, 1983). Using Piaget's (1932) and Kohlberg's (1969) theories of moral development, Rest proposed a four-component model of morality that involves four separate aspects of moral understanding. In this cognitive-developmental model, Rest theorized that moral development consists of moral sensitivity (being aware that a moral problem exists), moral judgment (deciding on a moral action), moral motivation (staying committed to one's values and prioritizing a moral action), and moral character (implementing and following through on the moral action). This model supports the notion that developmental differences in moral understanding exist partially because of the strong cognitive component of moral development.

Rest's model of moral development adds an additional element to the study of morality that most other moral developmental theories leave out: a behavioral component. The first two components (moral sensitivity and moral judgment) tap into the social cognition capabilities of the individual. These components integrate ideas proposed by the SIP and TOM perspectives. That is, one's ability to identify a moral problem and consider various possible moral actions requires social information processing skills (SIP) as well as the ability to understand and predict feelings and behaviors of other people (TOM).

The other two components of the model (moral motivation and moral character), however, address the behavioral component to morality. This behavioral component can be directly related to bullying behavior. Once an individual assesses the social situation and considers all possible responses to the situation, he or she may or may not commit to the response and may or may not make a cognitive decision to respond in an aggressive manner. These components basically determine whether the individual will choose to exhibit actual bullying behavior. Without considering all four components of Rest's model, the complete bullying phenomenon is not fully explained. A person's moral developmental understanding must be taken into account. Researchers, educators, and parents need not only understand how the bully is processing the social information and how the bully is reading others' feelings and emotions, but they must also seek to explain why certain behavioral outcomes occur as a response to the social cognition.

Further research in this area is needed to reveal how moral development theories can add to the understanding of bullying behavior. Although Sutton (2001) argued against incorporating moral behavior into the study of bullying, the author suggests that an attempt may prove to be worthwhile. Why is it that some children choose to resort to bullying behavior as their "moral" action, whereas other children choose not to? An individual's sense of "right" and "wrong" certainly plays an important role in the process. Thus, more investigation into this area of human development is warranted.

## CONCLUSIONS

Bullying is a common and persistent problem in society, particularly in schools. Overall, a large number of children and youth will experience some type of bullying during their educational experience. Bullying has been identified as a problem in many countries, including the United States,

Canada, Japan, Australia, New Zealand, Germany, Belgium, Italy, Spain, Portugal, France, Switzerland, England, Ireland, and Finland (Ross, 2002; Smith, Morita, Junger-Tas, Olweus, Catalano, & Slee, 1999) and has taken a front seat in the research arena in many of these countries (Smith *et al.*, 1999).

Considerable debate surrounds the definition of bullying. What does it mean to say someone has been "bullied?" Experts in the field agree that a worldwide-accepted definition of bullying is needed. The literature on the subject carries a variety of operational definitions for the phenomenon, and these discrepancies allow for weaknesses in the research. Thus, more effort in creating a solid operational definition is needed.

In the past, bullying was predominantly considered a dyadic interaction. Most of the research tried to identify and investigate only the bully and the victim. Recently, more emphasis has been placed on viewing bullying as a group process. Many research studies have identified various roles in the bullying phenomenon. The bully and the victim are not the only individuals who are influencing and who are being influenced by bullying episodes. Research indicates that nearly 90% of children or youth in a school setting are easily categorized as "players" in bullying situations (Salmivalli et al., 1996). Thus, research needs to be broadened to emphasize the study of all the roles.

Last, the social information processing (SIP) theory and theory of the mind (TOM) have helped experts explain the bullying phenomenon. The SIP perspective claims that bullying occurs because the bully has deficits or biases in processing social information. Advocates of the TOM perspective, on the other hand, argue that some bullies actually possess "superior" skills in understanding the feelings and emotions of others. This allows them to successfully predict others' behaviors and manipulate them. Theorists from both camps have challenged each other claiming that their perspective is correct.

It is suggested that an "eclectic" theoretical approach needs to be taken to explain bullying behavior. In addition to using the SIP and TOM approaches, researchers, practitioners, and educators need to include theories of moral development to grasp a richer understanding of this serious phenomenon.

## References

Arsenio, W. F., & Lemerise, E. A. (2001). Varieties of childhood bullying: Values, emotion processes and social competence. *Social Development*, 10(1), 59–73.

Baron-Cohen, S., & Hammer, J. (1996). Is autism an extreme form of the male brain? *Cognition*, 21, 37–46.

Beale, A. V., & Scott, P. C. (2001). "Bullybusters": Using drama to empower students to take a stand against bullying behavior. *Professional School Counseling*, 4(4), 300–305.

Berkowitz, L. (1977). Situational and personal conditions governing reactions to aggressive cues. In D. Magnusson & N. S. Endler (Eds.), *Personality at the crossroads: Current issues in interactional psychology* (p. 165–171). New York: Wiley.

Bjorkqvist, K., Ekman, K., & Lagerspetz, K. M. J. (1982). Bullies and victims: Their ego picture, ideal ego picture and normative ego picture. *Scandanavian Journal of Psychology*, 23, 307–313.

Bjorkqvist, K., Lagerspetz, K. M. J., & Kaukiainen, A. (1992). Do girls manipulate and boys fight? Developmental trends in regard to direct and indirect aggression. *Aggressive Behavior*, 18, 117–127.

Boulton, M. J. (1997). Teachers' views on bullying: Definitions, attitudes, and ability to cope. *British Journal of Educational Psychology*, 67, 223–233.

Boulton, M. J., & Underwood, K. (1992). Bully/victim problems among middle school children. *British Journal of Developmental Psychology*, 62, 73–87.

Camodeca, M., Goossens, F. A., Schuengel, C., & Terwogt, M. M. (2003). Links between social information processing in middle childhood and involvement in bullying. *Aggressive Behavior*, 29, 116–127.

Carney, A. G., & Merrell, K. W. (2001). Bullying in schools: Perspectives on understanding and preventing an international problem. *School Psychology International*, 22(3), 364–383.

Charach, A., Pepler, D. J., & Ziegler, S. (1995). Bullying at school: A Canadian perspective. *Education Canada*, Spring.

Crick, N. R., & Dodge, K. A. (1996). Social information processing mechanisms in reactive and proactive aggression. *Child Development*, 67, 993–1002.

Crick, N. R., & Dodge, K. A. (1999). Superiority in the eye of the beholder: A comment on Sutton, Smith, and Swettenham. *Social Development*, 8(1), 128–131.

Dodge, K. A. (1986). A social information processing model of social competence in children. In M. Perlmutter (Ed.), *The Minnesota symposium on child psychology*, Vol. 18. Hillsdale, NJ: Erlbaum.

Dodge, K. A. (1991). The structure and function of reactive and proactive aggression. In D. J. Pepler & K. H. Rubin (Eds.), *The development and treatment of childhood aggression*. Hillsdale, NJ: Erlbaum.

Dupper, D. R., & Meyers-Adams, N. (2002). Low-level violence: A neglected aspect of school culture. *Urban Education*, 37(3), 350–364.

Farrington, D. P. (1993). Understanding and preventing bullying. In M. Tonry (Ed.), *Crime and justice*, vol. 17. Chicago: The University of Chicago Press.

Guerra, N. G., Nucci, L., & Huesmann, L. R. (1994). Moral cognition and childhood aggression. In L. R. Huesmann (Ed.), *Aggressive behavior: Current perspectives* (pp. 13–33). New York: Plenum Press.

Hawkins, D. L., Pepler, D. J., & Craig, W. M. (2001). Naturalistic observations of peer interventions in bullying. *Social Development*, 10(4), 512–527.

Hazler, R. J. (1992). What kids say about bullying. *Executive Educator*, 14, 20–22.

Hazler, R. J., Carney, J. V., Green, S., Powell, R., & Jolly, L. S. (1997). Areas of expert agreement on identification of school bullies and victims. *School Psychology International*, 18, 3–12.

Hughes, T. (1857). *Tom Brown's schooldays*. London: MacMillan.

Karatzias, A., Power, K. G., & Swanson, V. (2002). Bullying and victimization in Scottish secondary schools: Same or separate entities? *Aggressive Behavior*, 28(1), 45–61.

Kawabata, N. (2001). Adolescent trauma in Japanese schools: Two case studies of Ijime and school refusal. *Journal of the American Academy of Psychoanalysis*, 29(2), 85–103.

Kirksey, J. (2003, February 7). Harrassment chases teen from school. *The Denver Post*, p. B1.

Kohlberg, L. (1969). Stage and sequence: The cognitive-developmental approach to socialization. In D. Goslin (Ed.), *Handbook of socialization theory and research*. Chicago: Rand McNally.

Ma, X. (2001). Bullying and being bullied: To what extent are bullies also victims? *American Educational Research Journal*, 38(2), 351–370.

Marsh, H. W., Parada, R. H., Yeung, A. S., & Healey, J. (2001). Aggressive school troublemakers and victims: A longitudinal model examining the pivotal role of self-concept. *Journal of Educational Psychology*, 93(2), 411–419.

McCudden, L. (2001). Bullying—A teenager's perspective. *Clinical Child Psychology*, 6(4), 609–611.

McKinnon, J. E. (2001). An examination of bullying from a group-dynamic perspective: The third-party role of peers in bullying incidents. *Dissertation Abstracts International*, 62 (6-B). (University Microfilms No. 2991).

Menesini, E., Fonzi, A., & Sanchez, V. (2002). Attribution of emotion of responsibility and moral disengagement in a bullying scenario: Differences between bullies, victims, outsiders, and defenders. *Eta Evolutiva*, 71(1), 76–83.

Merrick, J., Kessel, S., & Morad, M. (2002). Trends in school violence. *International Journal of Adolescent Medicine and Health*, 14(1), 77–80.

Morita, Y., Soeda, H., Soeda, K., & Taki, M. (1999). Japan. In P. K. Smith, Y. Morita, J. Junger-Tas, D. Olweus, R. Catalono, & P. Slee (Eds.), *The nature of school bullying: A cross-national perspective*. New York: Routledge.

Nansel, T. R., Overpeck, M., Pilla, R. S., Ruan, W. J., Simons-Morton, B., & Scheidt, P. (2001). Bullying behavior among United States youth: Prevalence and association with psychosocial adjustment. *Journal of the American Medical Association* 285(16), 2094–2100.

Olafsen, R. N., & Viemero, V. (2000). Bully/victim problems and coping with stress in school among 10–12 year old pupils in Aland, Finland. *Aggressive Behavior*, 26, 57–65.

Olweus, D. (1978). *Aggression in schools: Bullies and whipping boys*. Washington, DC: Hemisphere.

Olweus, D. (1993). *Bullying at school: What we know and what we can do*. Cambridge, MA: Blackwell.

Olweus, D., & Alsaker, F. D. (1991). Assessing change in a cohort cohort-Longitudinal study with hierarchical data. In D. Magnusson, L. R. Bergman, G. Rudinger, & B. Rorestad (Eds.), *Problems and methods in longitudinal research: Stability and change*. Cambridge, UK: Cambridge University Press.

Pepler, D. J., & Craig, W. M. (1995). A peek behind the fence: Naturalistic observations of aggressive children with remote audiovisual recording. *Developmental Psychology*, 31, 548–553.

Piaget, J. (1932). *The moral judgment of the child*. New York: The Free Press.

Rivers, I., & Smith, P. K. (1994). Types of bullying behaviour and their correlates. *Aggressive Behavior*, 20, 359–368.

Ramirez, F. C. (2001). Personality variables associated to bullying in 10-to-15-year-old schools. *Anales de Psicologia*, 17(1), 37–43.

Randall, P. (1997). *Adult bullying: Perpetrators and victims*. London: Routledge.

Rest, J. R. (1983). Morality. In J. Flavell & E. Markham (Eds.) Vol. 3: *Cognitive development* (pp. 556–629). New York: Wiley.

Ross, D. M. (1996). *Childhood bullying and teasing: What school personnel, other professionals, and parents can do*. Alexandria, VA: American Counseling Association.

Ross, D. M. (2002). Bullying. In J. Sandoval (Ed.), *Handbook of crisis counseling, intervention, and prevention in schools* (pp. 105–135). Mahwah, NJ: Erlbaum.

Salmivalli, C., Lagerspetz, K., Bjorkqvist, K., Osterman, K., & Kaukiainen, A. (1996). Bullying as a group process: Participant roles and their relations to social status within the group. *Aggressive Behavior*, 22, 1–15.

Salmivalli, C., & Nieminen, E. (2002). Proactive and reactive aggression among school bullies, victims, and bully/victims. *Aggressive Behavior*, 28(1), 30–44.

Sharp, S. (1995). How much does bullying hurt? The effects of bullying on the personal well-being and educational progress of secondary-aged students. *Educational and Child Psychology*, 12(2), 81–88.

Sharp, S., & Smith, P. K. (1991). Bullying in UK schools: The DES Sheffield bullying project. *Early Childhood Development and Care*, 77, 47–55.

Sharp, S., Thompson, D., & Arora, T. (2000). How long does it hurt? An investigation into long-term bullying. *School Psychology International*, 21(1), 37–46.

Shields, A., & Cicchett, D. (2001). Parental maltreatment and emotion dysregulation as a risk factor for bullying and victimization in middle childhood. *Journal of Clinical Child Psychology*, 30(3), 349–363.

Siris, K. (2001). Using action to alleviate bullying and victimization in the classroom. *Dissertation Abstracts International*, 62 (2-A). (University Microfilms No. 463).

Smith, P. K., & Brain, P. (2000). Bullying in schools: Lessons from two decades of research. *Aggressive Behavior*, 26, 1–9.

Smith, P. K., Morita, Y., Junger-Tas, J., Olweus, D., Catalono, R., & Slee, P. (Eds.), *The nature of school bullying: A cross-national perspective.* New York: Routledge.

Smith, P. K., & Sharp, S. (Eds). (1994). *School bullying: Insights and perspectives.* London: Routledge.

Smith, P. K., & Thompson, D. (1991). Dealing with bully/victim problems in the UK. In P. K. Smith & D. Thompson (Eds.), *Practical approaches to bullying.* London: David Fulton.

Sutton, J. (2001). Bullies: Thugs or thinkers? *The Psychologist,* 14(10), 530–534.

Sutton, J., & Smith, P. K. (1999). Bullying as a group process: An adaptation of the participant role approach. *Aggressive Behavior,* 25, 97–111.

Sutton, J., Smith, P. K., & Swettenham, J. (1999). Socially undesirable need not be incompetent: A response to Crick and Dodge. *Social Development,* 8(1), 132–134.

Tanaka, T. (2001). The identity formation of the victim of shunning. *School Psychology International,* 22(4), 463–476.

Treml, J. N. (2001). Bullying as a social malady in contemporary Japan. *International Social Work,* 44(1), 107–117.

Whitney, I., & Smith, P. K. (1993). A survey of the nature and extent of bullying in junior/middle and secondary schools. *Educational Research,* 35, 3–25.

APPENDIX

# A

# Most Prevalent Characteristics of Bullies as Indicated by Experts in the Field

- Control others through verbal threats and physical actions
- Are quicker to anger and use force sooner than others
- Tend to have little empathy for the problems of others in the victim-bully relationship
- Have often been exposed to models of aggressive behavior
- Chronically display aggressive behavior
- Inappropriately perceive hostile intent in the action of others
- Are angry and revengeful
- Have parents who are poor role models for getting along with others
- Are likely to have contact with aggressive groups
- Have parents who are poor role models for constructively solving problems
- See aggression as the only way to preserve their self-image
- Have inconsistent discipline procedures at home
- Think physical image is important for maintaining a feeling of power or control
- Focus on angry thoughts
- Have many more family problems than usual
- Have parents who often do not know their whereabouts
- Suffer physical and emotional abuse at home
- Create resentment and frustration in a peer group
- Exhibit obsessive or rigid actions

Source: Hazler, Carney, Green, Powell, & Jolly (1997)

# Most Prevalent Characteristics of Victims as Indicated by Experts in the Field

- Believe that they cannot control their environment
- Have ineffective social skills
- Have poor interpersonal skills
- Are less popular than others
- Have underlying fears of personal inadequacy
- Blame themselves for their problems
- Are given labels suggesting inadequacy
- Feel socially isolated
- Are afraid of going to school
- Are physically younger, smaller, and weaker than peers
- Have limited skills for gaining success and acceptance
- Lack of communication capabilities during high-stress incidents
- Have a poor self-concept
- Show physical mannerisms associated with depression
- Have frequent feelings of personal inadequacy
- Perform self-destructive actions
- Believe others are more capable of handling various situations
- Have difficulty relating to peers
- Have family members who are overinvolved in their decisions and activities
- Perceived progressive failures cause them to put forth less effort with each presenting opportunity
- Feel external factors have more of an impact on them than internal control

Source: Hazler, Carney, Green, Powell, & Jolly (1997)

# CHAPTER 2

# Who Are the Victims?

XIN MA

*University of Kentucky*

In their review of school bullying, Ma, Stewin, and Mah (2001) regarded Besag's (1989) definition of bullying as a good representation of the major components of bullying. They explain that bullying is a repeated action, rather than a one-time occurrence. Bullying also takes multiple forms that can be characterized as physical, verbal, psychological, and social. In addition, bullying is characterized by two conflicting parties that are imbalanced in power, physically and/or mentally. Finally, the results of bullying are empowerment and gratification for one party and suffering and distress for the other.

A student who is a repeated target of another student's coercive behavior becomes a victim of bullying (Olweus, 1993). Coercive behaviors can be physical, such as hitting, pushing, holding, and hostile gesturing; verbal, such as threatening, humiliating, degrading, teasing, name-calling, and taunting; psychological, such as staring, sticking out the tongue, eye-rolling, and ignoring; and social, such as manipulating friendships and ostracizing (Batsche & Knoff, 1994; Clarke & Kiselica, 1997; Remboldt, 1994a, 1994b). Sexual harassment in words or in actions has been added recently as another distinct bullying category: Coercive behaviors can also be sexual (Lipson, 2001).

# CLASSIFICATIONS OF VICTIMS

Researchers have long realized that victims of bullying vary substantially in their characteristics. In other words, victims demonstrate different academic, social, mental, physical, and interpersonal characteristics. For this reason, there are a variety of classifications of victims in current literature. Taking a classical approach, Olweus (1978) distinguished between *passive victims* and *provocative victims*. Passive victims feel insecure and helpless and appear cautious, sensitive, and nervous on the surface. In later research, Olweus (1997) also labeled passive victims as submissive because these victims submit to attacks and insults without retaliation. Although provocative victims are also anxious, they are defensive, unlike passive victims. More important, provocative victims' irritable hyperactive behavior and provocative quick temper frequently get them into trouble. Carney and Merrell (2001) described these victims as "the least liked of their peer group" (p. 368). Approximately one in five victims is provocative (Olweus, 1984).

Perry, Kusel, and Perry (1988) proposed two classifications for victims. Their first classification is based on behavior. They classified victims into *low-aggressive* and *high-aggressive* groups. To some extent, low-aggressive victims resemble passive victims, and high-aggressive victims resemble provocative victims. There are approximately as many high-aggressive victims as low-aggressive victims (Perry *et al.*, 1988). For the second classification, Perry *et al.* (1988) employed the three critical elements of bullying (i.e., victimization, aggression, and peer rejection) to categorize victims into three heterogeneous groups: victims who are rejected by peers for their victimization, victims who are rejected by peers for their aggression, and victims who are rejected by peers for both their victimization and their aggression. Perry *et al.* (1988) noted that students in the last group are both bullies and victims at the same time. Table 1 summarizes the variety of schemes regarding victimization.

**TABLE 1**
**Classification of Victimization**

| Author | Classification | Characteristics |
|---|---|---|
| Olweus (1978, 1997) | Passive (or submissive) victims | Display insecurity, helplessness, cautiousness, sensitivity, nervousness, and submissiveness |
|  | Provocative victims | Are anxious, defensive, hyperactive, and provocative |
| Perry et al. (1988) | Low-aggressive victims | Resemble passive (or submissive) victims |
|  | High-aggressive victims | Resemble provocative victims |
| Perry et al. (1988) | Victimization victims | Are peer rejected for victimization |
|  | Aggression victims | Are peer rejected for aggression |
|  | Victimization and aggression victims | Are peer rejected for both victimization and aggression |

## INDIVIDUAL CHARACTERISTICS OF VICTIMS

Most studies of school bullying have concentrated on identifying individual characteristics of victims and bullies from various aspects of students' family and school life. With a focus on victims of school bullying, this section categorizes individual characteristics of victims as academic, social, mental (emotional), physical, and interpersonal.

### Academic Characteristics

Academically, victims appear to be less intelligent than non-victims (Perry *et al.*, 1988; Roland, 1989). Sweeting and West (2001) reported that bullies target victims with poor academic performance in school. More important, victims often have inferior social intelligence, social cognition, and, in particular, mental skills compared to bullies (Kaukiainen *et al.*, 1999; Sutton, Smith, & Swettenham, 1999a, 1999b). This situation often gives bullies an advantage by allowing them to smartly inflict suffering on victims without being blamed (Ma *et al.*, 2001). It appears, however, that the victim-bully is not likely to target victims who are doing a worse job academically or who seem less intelligent (Ma, 2001).

### Social Characteristics

Socially, victims tend to have close relations with their parents (especially mothers in the case of passive male victims) (Olweus, 1978). In contrast, families of bullies tend to struggle with financial and social problems, lack family structure (including parental conflict), and have a cold emotional environment, all of which distance bullies from their parents (Oliver, Young, & LaSalle, 1994). Parents of victims are often both responsive (which keeps children from giving up on their relationship with parents) and repulsive (which teaches them how to be victims), according to Troy and Sroufe (1987). Troy *et al.* (1987) explained that parents being both responsive and repulsive can cause victims to continue to interact with their bullies, because responsive parents keep their parents from giving up relations with them and repulsive parents teach their children to be victims. In contrast, parents of bullies are often authoritarian, hostile, and rejecting (Batsche & Knoff, 1994).

Although victims, particularly passive victims, do not have friends in school, they are sensitive to peer comments and peer evaluations (Slee, 1994). Female victims typically experience social distress and social avoidance (Slee, 1994). Bullies, on the other hand, are popular with their peers (Olweus, 1993, 1994).

### Mental Characteristics

Mentally (or emotionally), victims see themselves as dull, stupid, and worthless. Their self-esteem is low, and their social anxiety is high (Hoover & Juul,

1993; Lane, 1989; Slee, 1994). Victims lack effective emotional problem-solving strategies to prevent, de-escalate, and resolve conflicts in peer interactions (Andreou, 2001; Mahady-Wilton, 1997). Once victimized, they lack effective emotional coping skills to ease stresses of negative emotions from frustration, failure, and trauma (Mahady-Wilton, 1997). In addition, victims often have depressive and suicidal thoughts (Roland, 2002). Worrying, depression, and psychosomatic symptoms are quite common among victims (also among bullies) (Kaltiala-Heino, Rimpela, Rantanen, & Rimpela, 2000).

## Physical Characteristics

Physically, victims are weak, and bullies take advantage of their physical weaknesses (Besag, 1989; Olweus, 1997). Bullies often target victims for other physical disadvantages as well. Bullies frequently target victims who are disabled, overweight, or physically unattractive (Sweeting & West, 2001). Victims can also be the younger students in the student population. Olweus (1991a) reported that 11% of students in elementary school grades are victims of bullying, compared with 5% of students in junior high school grades.

Moreover, gender plays a part in victimization. Male victims are usually bullied by male bullies, whereas female victims can be bullied by both male and female bullies (Clarke & Kiselica, 1997). Overall, 80% of male victims are bullied by male bullies, 60% of female victims are bullied by male bullies, and 15 to 20% of female victims are bullied by both male and female bullies (Olweus, 1991a). Male victims are more likely to suffer from direct, physical abuse, whereas female victims are more likely to suffer from indirect, verbal abuse (Eron, Husemann, Dubow, Romanoff, & Yarmel, 1987; Hoover, Oliver, & Hazler, 1992; Olweus, 1991a).

## Interpersonal Characteristics

Interpersonally, though longing for social approval, victims rarely initiate prosocial activities (Bernstein & Watson, 1997; Troy & Sroufe, 1987). Victims often receive inadequate support to develop effective interpersonal relationships (Champion, 1997). Unfortunately, social distress and social avoidance as well as fear of peer comments and peer evaluations (see Slee, 1994) often prevent victims from seeking support. Furthermore, educators are tempted to concentrate on changing behaviors of bullies and, as a result, give less attention to victims (Boulton & Underwood, 1992). Many victims often do not report bullying incidents partly because they perceived or experienced inadequate support from educators in the past (Olweus, 1994; Roberts & Coursel, 1996). This situation makes it difficult for educators to identify victims and help them improve their interpersonal skills.

In sum, Slee (1994) concluded that "victimization is associated with poor physical, social, and psychological well-being" (p. 100). Researchers believe that victims often exhibit behaviors (physical, mental, social, or interpersonal behaviors) that invite and reinforce bullying (Egan & Perry, 1998; Hodges, Malone, & Perry, 1997).

## Update in Research

In a recent data analysis of sixth- and eighth-grade students, Ma (2002) attempted to identify critical student-level characteristics of victims and bullies. Student-level variables included in the analysis were gender, family socioeconomic status (SES), number of parents (measuring family structure), number of siblings (measuring family size), academic condition (an average achievement measure from four achievement tests including mathematics, science, reading, and writing), affective condition (largely a measure of self-esteem), and physical condition (largely a measure of general health).

Ma (2002) characterized victims in the sixth grade as being male, coming from wealthy families, performing well academically, and having affective or physical weakness. Gender and physical condition were the most important characteristics. Meanwhile, Ma (2002) characterized victims in the eighth grade as being male and having poor academic, affective, and physical conditions. Once again, gender and physical condition turned out to be the most important characteristics. Ma (2002) concluded that bullies particularly targeted physically weak male students in the sixth and eighth grades, showing therefore that salient student-level characteristics of victims were fairly consistent in both grades.

The secondary student-level characteristic poor affective condition was consistently found in victims of both the sixth and eighth grades. This finding is in line with the research literature suggesting that victims have low self-esteem (Hoover & Juul, 1993; Lane, 1989; Slee, 1994). Other secondary student-level characteristics changed from grade to grade. In the sixth grade, bullies targeted students with good academic performance, whereas in the eighth grade, bullies targeted students with poor academic performance. This situation fits well into the theory that victims have inferior mental skills compared to bullies as briefly discussed earlier (Kaukiainen *et al.*, 1999; Sutton *et al.*, 1999a, 1999b). Poor academic status is not a disadvantage for students in elementary school because students have more or less the same social-cognitive maturity. At the secondary school level, however, the social-cognitive gap becomes large among students due to differences in social-cognitive maturity, and a student with poor academic performance becomes a bully's target.

Finally, Ma (2001) concluded that students from wealthy families were more likely to be victims in the sixth grade, but that wealth was not a factor for those in the eighth grade. Given the strong relationship between SES and academic achievement as abundantly shown in the research literature, this finding can also be appreciated from the theory of a victim's inferior mental skills. At the secondary school level, the large gap in academic achievement between students of high and low SES implies that students with high SES have superior social-cognitive skills that prevent them from being targeted by bullies. The parental involvement theory (Edwards & Young, 1992) in which parents with high SES pay much attention to their children's education is also relevant to this finding. Parents who are aware of their children's victimization in elementary schools are much more likely to choose favorable secondary schools for their children and actively monitor what happens in these schools.

## SCHOOL-LEVEL CHARACTERISTICS OF VICTIMS

Surprisingly, victimization happens in school rather than on the way to or from school (Olweus, 1991a, 1993, 1994; Whitney, Nabuzoka, & Smith, 1992). Therefore, it is important to identify characteristics of schools where bullying occurs. Although research has not focused on this topic, it is appropriate to identify elements of school context and climate that encourage (or discourage) victimization. *School context* often refers to the physical characteristics of a school, such as enrollment size, location, and socioeconomic composition. *School climate* refers to the inner workings of school life, such as the way that students are organized for instruction; the academic values that teachers, administrators, and parents hold for their students; and the way that schools are operated and managed.

Contextually, researchers have found that victimization is more likely to happen in large city schools than in small town schools (Olweus, 1991a, 1993, 1994; Whitney & Smith, 1993). Researchers also witness more victimization in schools that serve students from disadvantaged socio-economic backgrounds (Whitney & Smith, 1993). Climatically, victimization is not likely in schools where parents are involved in their children's education (Banks, 1997; Foltz-Gray, 1996; Horne & Socherman, 1996), where school counselors proactively intervene in cases of bullying incidents (Clarke & Kiselica, 1997; Roberts & Coursol, 1996), where intensive supervision is practiced (Barone, 1997), and where there are antibullying measures or programs for students and teachers (Barone, 1997; Cartwright, 1995).

Ma (2002) also attempted to identify critical school-level characteristics of victims (and bullies). School-level contextual variables included in the analysis were school enrollment size, school location (either urban or rural), and school mean SES (measuring school socioeconomic composition). School-level climatic variables were the disciplinary climate of a school, the academic expectations of peers and teachers, and the extent that parents get involved in their children's schooling.

Ma (2002) reported that victims came from schools with poor disciplinary climate in the sixth and eighth grades. Measures of disciplinary climate emphasized school disciplinary rules as well as student compliance and staff reinforcement. This finding suggests that victimization is a natural consequence of disciplinary rules, compliance, and reinforcement. It calls schools to develop, monitor, and reinforce a clear antibullying policy, with the involvement of students, teachers, and parents to ensure fairness. This consistent finding across grade levels adds support to previous findings that call for intensive supervision of student activities and antibullying regulations for students and teachers (Barone, 1997; Cartwright, 1995) that will improve and maintain a positive school disciplinary environment.

Ma (2002) also reported that in schools where parental involvement was strong, students with weak affective condition were less likely to be victimized; in schools where parental involvement was weak, students with weak affective condition were more likely to be victimized. Therefore, strong parental involvement compensates for a student's affective weakness and reduces victimization of students with weak affective condition. Although this finding may not come as a surprise in light of the parental involvement theory (as introduced earlier), it does call for strong cooperation between teachers and parents. In other words, parental involvement is an indispensable part of any school's effort to combating bullying.

## REACTIONS OF VICTIMS

The most common reaction of victims to bullying is withdrawal. Victims learn to avoid certain places at school, such as the school playground, for fear of being bullied. Some victims avoid going to school for a period of time to stay away from bullies or even drop out of school altogether (Berthold & Hoover, 2000). Partly due to their avoidance behaviors, victims experience decline or even failure in academic performance (Hazler, Hoover, & Oliver, 1992; Olweus, 1978). Perhaps the most unfortunate reaction of victims is that they often blame themselves for what has happened, which reinforces their self-perception of being stupid and worthless. At home, victims often lash out their frustrations at their parents who are not aware of the victimization (Ambert, 1994). This unfortunate reaction often results in deterioration of family relationships.

Reactions of some victims can become dangerous and harmful. Lane (1989) and Olweus (1991a, 1991b) have documented cases of suicide committed by victims. These victims are usually targets of long-term, severe bullying. Victims can also react violently to bullies by shooting and killing them (Greenbaum, 1988). Carney and Merrell (2001, p. 368) stated that:

Victims are far more likely than non-bullied children to bring weapons to school to
protect themselves. In rare cases, victims have been so tormented by their aggressor
that they plan and sometimes carry out acts of retribution. This retribution sometimes
occurs when the children are still in school, but has also been documented years after
the bullying.

In general, however, victims rarely adopt criminal ways of retribution, and
even as adults, their criminal record is shorter than a bully's record (Olweus,
1997). In fact, as a result of bullying, victims continue to suffer in adulthood.
They often have low self-esteem, experience high stress levels, are depressed, have psychosocial problems, and experience psychosexual difficulties
(Carney and Merrell, 2001).

## DURATION OF VICTIMIZATION

Victims usually do not report bullying incidents for fear of retaliation and
because of inadequate support from adults (Roberts & Coursel, 1996). Some
victims refuse to report bullies because of self-shame. Smith and Shu (2000)
noticed that 30% of victims never inform anyone of their victimization.
Olweus (1991a, 1993, 1994) reported that 40% of elementary school children
and 60% of junior high school children complain about teachers not taking
action when victims report bullying incidents. Victims sometimes even
receive less attention from teachers than do bullies (Boulton & Underwood,
1992).

Because victims are reluctant to report bullying incidents, bullies often
victimize the same student more than once. As a result, a student can be
victimized for a long time. Pellegrini and Bartini (2000) reported that aggressive victimization often continues over time. Sharp, Thompson, and Arora
(2000) used the term *long-term bullying* to describe a small percentage of
students who are bullied for a fairly long period of time. Specifically, Olweus
(1991a, 1993, 1994) found that most male victims at age 13 are still victims at
age 16. Slee (1994) reported that 28% of victims are bullied for a period of a
few months to more than 6 months. Boulton and Underwood (1992) found
that many victims are bullied for two consecutive school terms. Perry *et al.*
(1988) concluded that once bullied, victims are likely to be consistently
harrassed, and "a stable propensity to be victimized is established by the
time children reach middle school" (p. 182).

The duration of victimization has not yet drawn much attention from
researchers and educators. This is unfortunate because victims who take
extreme reactive measures, such as committing suicide, are chronic victims
of bullying (Greenbaum, 1988; Lane, 1989; Olweus, 1991a). Chronic victims
are expected to react to bullying (as discussed earlier) in a much stronger
manner. Therefore, the duration of victimization warrants more attention
from researchers and educators. Educators should be aware of a potential

chronic history of victimization and note instances that suggest continued victimization of a student. This approach therefore demands that educators frequently meet with victims and follow up on their current situation. Such a comprehensive approach can also help teachers collect evidence and discipline chronic bullies.

## THE BLURRED BOUNDARY BETWEEN VICTIMS AND BULLIES

In their recent review of bullying in school, Ma *et al.* (2001, pp. 255–256) emphasized the existence of a victim-bully cycle that has not received adequate attention from either researchers or educators. They used the following evidence to illustrate this victim-bully cycle:

> Floyd (1985) and Greenbaum (1988) have labeled bullying as an "intergenerational" problem. That is, bullies in school are often victims at home (Floyd, 1985; Greenbaum, 1988; Horne & Socherman, 1996). These researchers imply a victim-offender cycle which is quite common in social violence. Perry *et al.* (1988) made this point more explicit. They studied the relationship between victimization and aggression, claiming that the two elements are orthogonal. That is, some of the most extreme victims of bullying are also some of the most aggressive bullies.

Recently, more researchers have started to notice this victim-bully cycle. For example, Glover *et al.* (2000) identified four behavior patterns among students: *bullies, bully-victims, victims,* and *nonparticipants,* recognizing that there is a group of victims who also bully. Haynie *et al.* (2001) also considered victims who bully as a distinct and important group.

However, empirical studies that investigate the existence of this victim-bully cycle are lacking, and there has not been much research about student-level and school-level characteristics that contribute to this victim-bully cycle. Recently, Ma (2001) examined this issue using a sophisticated statistical model with the same data in Ma (2002) discussed earlier. This is the first empirical research that has examined the victim-bully cycle and identified student-level and school-level characteristics that contribute to the cycle of bullying in schools. Ma (2001) supported the significance of the victim-bully cycle. Extending the knowledge about the cycle of bullying, Ma (2001) showed that gender, affective condition, and physical condition contributed to the victim-bully cycle in both the sixth and eighth grades, whereas SES, number of parents, and academic condition did not contribute in a notable way to the cycle of bullying at either grade level. The number of siblings contributed to the victim-bully cycle for students in the eighth grade but not for those in the sixth grade.

Specifically, Ma (2001) demonstrated that for sixth- and eighth-grade students, gender played a role in who became a bully. That is, a boy is a lot more likely to bully others than to be bullied by them. In disagreement with

Lane (1989) who claimed that boys bully for social power and dominance, Ma (2001) argued that boys bully for "indirect compensation" in that they take revenge on innocent others rather than on their bullies. More important, this phenomenon was twice as common in the sixth grade as in the eighth grade, implying that older boys are less likely than younger boys to excise indirect compensation for their victimization. A student's moral values may explain this difference: Older students become more aware that indirect compensation is morally wrong.

Affective condition was also more a characteristic of bullies than victims in the sixth and eighth grades. This indicates that a student with poor affective condition is a lot more likely to bully others than to be bullied by others. More important, this phenomenon was almost twice as common in the eighth grade as in the sixth grade. For older students with poor affective condition, it appears that victimization is a more serious blow to their already poor affective condition, which promotes a stronger desire to "win back" their affective dignity by bullying (or gaining gratification from) innocent others. Overall, this finding does not support Rigby and Slee (1991), who reported that bullies do not have low self-esteem.

On the other hand, poor physical condition was more a characteristic of victims than bullies. A student with poor physical condition is a lot more likely to be victimized by others than to bully others. More important, this phenomenon is more than twice as common in the sixth grade as in the eighth grade. This implies that when students are young, those with weaker physical condition are more likely to be victimized. But when students grow older, poor physical condition becomes less a reason for being bullied.

The finding that a student from a large family was more likely to become a bully than a victim is explained by Ma (2001) as a *carry-over effect*. Ma argued that students from large families experience more "sibling bullying" than those from small families, and long-term exposure to sibling bullying encourages students to internalize bullying behaviors as normal and acceptable. These students then carry this experience over to their schools and bully others.

Ma (2001) also suggested that the cycle of bullying was evident in several aspects of school life. Specifically, school enrollment size and disciplinary climate contributed to the victim-bully cycle in both the sixth and eighth grades. Parental involvement contributed to the cycle of bullying in the sixth grade, whereas academic expectation (of peers and teachers) contributed to the cycle of bullying in the eighth grade. On the other hand, school mean SES did not contribute to the victim-bully cycle in either grade.

School enrollment size (small school) was a characteristic that affected the actions of bullies than victims. That is, students in small schools are a lot more likely to bully others than to be bullied by others. Based on this finding, Ma (2001) suggested that victims in small schools can be repeatedly victimized because it is difficult for bullies to find different victims. Another implication is that bullying is usually done in private rather than in front of a large crowd. Ma (2001) argued that large schools have fewer bullying incidents than small schools because bullying in private is less likely in large crowded schools. To some extent, this situation indicates that many students are aware that bullying is not socially acceptable.

One of the most important findings in Ma (2001) is that all three school climate variables contributed to the victim-bully cycle. This is encouraging news because administrators, teachers, and parents can control school climate rather than school context. In other words, school climate (e.g., disciplinary climate) is changeable through educational policies and practices, whereas school context (e.g., school location) is difficult to change.

Specifically, Ma (2001) reported that disciplinary climate helped victims and discouraged bullies to the same extent in both the sixth and eighth grades. In the sixth grade, parental involvement discouraged bullies from victimizing. Ma (2001) argued that parents have close contacts with their children and are in a good position to prevent or discourage their children's involvement in bullying in school. In the eighth grade, academic expectation also discouraged bullies from picking on others. Ma (2001) believed that the reason for this change in behavior is that most students in schools with intense academic pressure are too busy academically to look around for victims. Overall, Ma (2001) concluded that improvement in disciplinary climate and parental involvement reduces bullying in the early grades of middle school, whereas improvement in disciplinary climate and academic expectation reduces bullying in the later grades of middle school.

## THEORETICAL EXPLANATION OF THE VICTIM-BULLY CYCLE

Many researchers believe that bullying is a learned social behavior. Slee and Rigby (1994) stated that parents who employ power-assertive discipline strategies in their parenting effectively teach their children aggressive ways to deal with other persons. As shown earlier, many studies claim that bullies in school are often victims at home (Floyd, 1985; Greenbaum, 1988; Horne & Socherman, 1996). For example, Schwartz, Dodge, Pettit, and Bates (1997) reported that aggressive victims often experience punitive, hostile, and abusive treatment at home.

Lorber, Felton, and Reid (1984), Matson (1989), and Sobsey (1994) explained that social learning theory holds the key to explaining the cycle of social violence (including bullying in school). They found that abuse victims are more likely to be violent, aggressive, and disruptive than non-abuse controls and accounted for this situation as a result of socially learned behavior. Social learning theory can also help explain the finding that some of the most extreme victims of bullying are also some of the most aggressive bullies (Perry *et al.*, 1988).

Social learning theory forms a theoretical foundation to explain the victim-bully cycle in Ma (2001). For example, boys who were most likely to enter the victim-bully cycle were victims of bullying. They learned to treat others in the same way they were treated. Students with poor physical or affective condition were also likely to enter the victim-bully cycle. For example, victims with poor physical condition learned to take physical advantage of even weaker victims just as their bullies took physical advantage of them.

In addition, Ma (2001) found that the extent of victimization and the extent of aggression were not necessarily equivalent. For example, students with poor affective condition were victims, but they also bullied others to a greater extent than they were bullied. On the other hand, students with poor physical condition bullied others, but they were victimized more often than they bullied. These unbalanced circles of school bullying need to be taken into account when working with victim-bullies.

## OVERCOMING VICTIMIZATION

With a focus on victims, research implications for prevention and intervention have been offered in various places in this chapter. Still, there are quite a few other things that school staff can do to help students overcome victimization. Bullock (2002, p. 132) suggested that:

> When teachers observe an incident of bullying, they can intervene by asking the bully to consider the consequences of his or her actions and think about how others feel. By talking calmly, yet firmly, to the bully, the teacher can make it clear that such behavior is unacceptable. Teachers can show the bully alternate ways to talk, interact, and negotiate; at the same time, they can encourage victims to assert themselves.

Currently, teachers are mainly working with bullies, but such actions are important for victims to witness. Victims should realize that immediate measures are being taken to stop bullying in schools, which indicates to victims that teachers are behind them and are always ready to help them.

Citing research evidence (Kochenderfer & Ladd, 1997; Ladd, Kochenderfer, & Coleman, 1996), Bullock (2002) argued that teachers need to help victims "form ties with peers who can offer protection, support, security, and safety, thus helping to reduce children's exposure to bullying" (p. 133). Indeed, peer mediation is becoming a popular recommendation to reduce bullying in school (or help students overcome victimization) (Cunningham *et al.*, 1998).

Once victimized, students will often need to be enrolled in a treatment program, and school counselors are in a particularly important position to help these victims (Clarke & Kiselica, 1997; Roberts & Coursol, 1996). Passive victims often benefit from programs that work on building assertiveness and a stronger visual profile (Batsche & Knoff, 1994). Provocative victims often benefit from treatments that focus on interpreting hostile bias and assertive but less aggressive solutions to threat (Dodge, Coie, Pettit, & Price, 1990).

Finally, Crick and Grotpeter (1995) suggested that school counselors work closely with victims to improve their social-psychological adjustments. Changes in social affiliations are also important to minimize victimization (Pellegrini & Bartini, 2000). All these efforts in prevention and intervention work better when parents get involved (Peterson & Skiba, 2001).

Abundant literature exists on direct preventions and interventions for bullying in school, but a lack of literature exists on indirect preventions and interventions. Ma (2001) has shown that improving school climate helps reduce bullying in school. This call for improvement in school climate as a measure to reduce bullying in school is certainly not alone. Peterson and Skiba (2001) also argued that violence and misbehavior in school can be prevented directly or indirectly through improving school social climate by encouraging parent and community involvement, character education, violence prevention, conflict resolution curricula, and peer mediation. These are effective programs that can help improve school social climate, which in turn discourages bullying in school.

The blurred boundary between victims and bullies has important policy implications. The cycle of bullying in school may reflect the ineffectiveness of many bullying prevention or intervention programs that see victims and bullies as two separate groups of individuals. As a result, a bully can victimize right after being counseled as a victim. This victim-bully cycle needs to be taken into account in any prevention or intervention program.

## References

Ambert, A. M. (1994). A qualitative study of peer abuse and its effects: Theoretical and empirical implications. *Journal of Marriage and the Family, 56*, 119–130.

Andreou, E. (2001). Bully/victim problems and their association with coping behavior in conflictual peer interactions among school-age children. *Educational Psychology, 21*, 59–66.

Banks, R. (1997, March). Bullying in schools. *ERIC Digest.*

Barone, F. J. (1997). Bullying in school. *Phi Delta Kappan, 79*, 80–82.

Batsche, G. M., & Knoff, H. M. (1994). Bullies and their victims: Understanding a pervasive problem in the schools. *School Psychology Review, 23*, 165–174.

Bernstein, J. Y., & Watson, M. W. (1997). Children who are targets of bullying. *Journal of Interpersonal Violence, 12*, 483–498.

Berthold, K. A., & Hoover, J. H. (2000). Correlates of bullying and victimization among intermediate students in the Midwestern USA. *School Psychology International, 21*, 65– 78.

Besag, V. E. (1989). *Bullies and victims in schools.* Milton Keynes, UK: Open University Press.

Boulton, M. J., & Underwood, K. (1992). Bully/victim problems among middle school children. *British Journal of Educational Psychology, 62*, 73–87.

Bullock, J. R. (2002). Bullying among children. *Childhood Education, 78*, 130–133.

Carney, A. G., & Merrell, K. W. (2001). Bullying in schools: Perspectives on understanding and preventing an international problem. *School Psychology International*, 22, 364–382.

Cartwright, N. (1995). Combating bullying in a secondary school in the United Kingdom. *Journal for a Just and Caring Education*, 1, 345–353.

Champion, K. M. (1997). Bullying in middle school: Exploring the individual and interpersonal characteristics of the victim (Doctoral dissertation, University of Kansas, 1997). *Dissertation Abstracts International*, 59 (1362A).

Clarke, E. A., & Kiselica, M. S. (1997). A systemic counseling approach to the problem of bullying. *Elementary School Guidance and Counseling*, 31, 310–315.

Crick, N. R., & Grotpeter, J. K. (1995). Relational aggression, gender and social-psychological adjustment. *Child Development*, 66, 710–722.

Cunningham, C., Cunningham, L., Martorelli, V., Tran, A., Young, J., & Zacharias, R. (1998). The effects of primary division, student-mediated conflict resolution programs on playground aggression. *Journal of Child Psychology and Psychiatry*, 39, 653–662.

Dodge, K. A., Coie, J. D., Pettit, G. S., & Price, J. M. (1990). Peer status and aggression in boys' groups: Developmental and contextual analyses. *Child Development*, 61, 1289–1309.

Edwards, P. A., & Young, L. S. (1992). Beyond parents: Family, community, and school involvement. *Phi Delta Kappan*, 74, 72–80.

Egan, S. K., & Perry, D. G. (1998). Does low self-regard invite victimization? *Developmental Psychology*, 34, 299– 309.

Eron, L. D., Husemann, L. R., Dubow, E., Romanoff, R., & Yarmel, P. W. (1987). Aggression and its correlates over 22 years. In D. H. Crowell & I. M. Evans (Eds.), *Childhood aggression and violence: Sources of influence, prevention, and control* (pp. 249–262). New York: Plenum.

Floyd, N. M. (1985). Pick on somebody your own size! Controlling victimization. *Pointer*, 29, 9–17.

Foltz-Gray, D. (1996). The bully trap: Young tormentors and their victims find ways out of anger and isolation. *Teaching Tolerance*, 5(2), 18–23.

Glover, D., Gough, G., Johnson, M., & Cartwright, N. (2000). Bullying in 25 secondary schools: Incidence, impact and intervention. *Educational Research*, 42, 141–156.

Greenbaum, S. (1988). What can we do about schoolyard bullying? *Principal*, 67(2), 21–24.

Haynie, D. L., Nasel, T., Eitel, P., Crump, A. D., Saylor, K., Yu, K., & Simons-Morton, B. (2001). Bullies, victims, and bully/victims: Distinct groups of at-risk youth. *Journal of Early Adolescence*, 21, 29–49.

Hazler, R. J., Hoover, J. H., & Oliver, R. (1992). What kids say about bullying. *Executive Educator*, 20–22.

Hodges, E. V. E., Malone, M. J., & Perry, D. G. (1997). Individual risk and social risk as interacting determinants of victimization in the peer group. *Development Psychology*, 33, 1032–1039.

Hoover, J. H., & Juul, K. (1993). Bullying in Europe and the United States. *Journal of Emotional and Behavioral Problems*, 2, 25–29.

Hoover, J. H., Oliver, R., & Hazler, R. J. (1992). Bullying: Perceptions of adolescent victims in the Midwestern USA. *School Psychology International*, 13, 5–16.

Horne, A. M., & Socherman, R. (1996). Profile of a bully: Who would do such a thing. *Educational Horizons*, 74, 77–83.

Kaltiala-Heino, R., Rimpela, M., Rantanen, P., & Rimpela, A. (2000). Bullying at school: An indicator of adolescents at risk for mental disorders. *Journal of Adolescence*, 23, 661–674.

Kaukiainen, A., Bjorkqvist, K., Lagerspetz, K. M. J., Osterman, K., Salmivalli, C., Forsblom, S., & Ahlbom, A. (1999). The relationships between social intelligence, empathy, and three types of aggression. *Aggressive Behavior*, 25, 81–89.

Kochenderfer, B., & Ladd, G. (1997). Victimized children's responses to peers' aggression: Behaviors associated with reduced versus continued victimization. *Development and Psychopathology*, 9, 59–73.

Ladd, G. W., Kochenderfer, B. J., & Coleman, C. (1996). Friendship quality as a predicator of young children's early school adjustment. *Child Development*, 67, 1103–1118.

Lane, D. A. (1989). Bullying in school. *School Psychology International*, 10, 211–215.

Lipson, J. (2001). Hostile hallways: Bullying, teasing, and sexual harassment in school. *American Journal of Health Education*, 32, 307–309.

Lorber, R., Felton, D. K., & Reid, J. B. (1984). A social learning approach to the reduction of coercive process in child abuse families: A molecular analysis. *Advances in Behavior Research and Therapy*, 6, 29–45.

Ma, X. (2001). Bullying and being bullied: To what extent are bullies also victims? *American Educational Research Journal*, 38, 351–370.

Ma, X. (2002). Bullying in middle school: Individual and school characteristics of victims and offenders. *School Effectiveness and School Improvement*, 13, 63–90.

Ma, X., Stewin, L. L., & Mah, D. L. (2001). Bullying in school: Nature, effects, and remedies. *Research Papers in Education*, 16, 247–270.

Mahady-Wilton, M. M. (1997). *Emotional regulation and display in classroom victims and bullies: Characteristics expressions of affect, coping styles and relevant contextual factors.* Unpublished master's thesis, Queen's University: Kingston, Canada.

Matson, J. L. (1989). *Social learning approaches to the treatment of emotional problems.* Toronto: Lexington Books.

Oliver, R. L., Young, T. A., & LaSalle, S. M. (1994). Early lessons in bullying and victimization: The help and hindrance of children's literature. *School Counselor*, 42, 137–146.

Olweus, D. (1978). *Aggression in the schools: Bullies and whipping boys.* Washington, DC: Hemisphere.

Olweus, D. (1984). Aggressors and their victims: Bullying at school. In N. Frude & H. Gault (Eds.), *Disruptive behavior disorders in schools* (pp. 57–76). New York: Wiley.

Olweus, D. (1991a). Bully/victim problems among school children: Basic facts and effects of a school-based intervention program. In D. J. Pepler & K. H. Rubin (Eds.), *The development and treatment of childhood aggression* (pp. 411–448). Hillsdale, NJ: Erlbaum.

Olweus, D. (1991b). Victimization among school children. In R. Baenninger (Ed.), *Targets of violence and aggression* (pp. 45–102). Holland: Elsevier Science.

Olweus, D. (1993). *Bullying at school: What we know and what we can do.* Oxford: Blackwell.

Olweus, D. (1994). Bullying at school: Long-term outcomes for the victims and an effective school-based intervention program. In L. R. Huesmann (Ed.), *Aggressive behavior: Current perspectives* (pp. 97–130). New York: Wiley.

Olweus, D. (1997). Bully/victim problems in school: Knowledge base and an effective intervention program. *Irish Journal of Psychology*, 18, 170–190.

Pellegrini, A. D., & Bartini, M. (2000). A longitudinal study of bullying, victimization, and peer affiliation during the transition from primary school to middle school. *American Educational Research Journal*, 37, 699–725.

Perry, D. G., Kusel, S. J., & Perry, L. C. (1988). Victims of peer aggression. *Developmental Psychology*, 24, 807–814.

Peterson, R. L., & Skiba, R. (2001). Creating school climates that prevent school violence. *Clearing House*, 74, 155–163.

Remboldt, C. (1994a). *Solving violence problems in your school: Why a systematic approach is necessary.* Minneapolis, MN: Johnson Institute.

Remboldt, C. (1994b). *Violence in schools: The enabling factor.* Minneapolis, MN: Johnson Institute.

Rigby, K., & Slee, P. T. (1991). Bullying among Australian school children: Reported behavior and attitudes toward victims. *Journal of Social Psychology*, 131, 615–627.

Roberts, W. B., Jr., & Coursol, D. H. (1996). Strategies for intervention with childhood and adolescent victims of bullying, teasing, and intimidation in school settings. *Elementary School Guidance and Counseling*, 30, 204–212.

Roland, E. (1989). Bullying: The Scandinavian research tradition. In D. P. Tattum & D. A. Lane (Eds.), *Bullying in schools* (pp. 21–32). London: Trentham Books.

Roland, E. (2002). Bullying, depressive symptoms and suicidal thoughts. *Educational Research*, 44, 55–67.

Schwartz, D., Dodge, K., Pettit, G. S., & Bates, J. E. (1997). The early socialization of aggressive victims of bullying. *Child Development*, 68, 665–675.

Sharp, S., Thompson, D., & Arora, T. (2000). How long before it hurts? An investigation into long-term bullying. *School Psychology International*, 21, 37–46.

Slee, P. T. (1994). Situational and interpersonal correlates of anxiety associated with peer victimization. *Child Psychology and Human Development*, 25, 97–107.

Slee, P. T., & Rigby, K. (1994). Peer victimization at school. *Australian Journal of Early Childhood*, 19, 3–10.

Smith, P. K., & Shu, S. (2000). What good schools can do about bullying: Findings from a survey in English schools after a decade of research and action. *Childhood*, 7, 193–212.

Sobsey, D. (1994). *Violence and abuse in the lives of people with disabilities: The end of silent acceptance?* Baltimore: Paul H. Brookes.

Sutton, J., Smith, P. K., & Swettenham, J. (1999a). Bullying and 'theory of mind': A critique of the 'social skills deficit' view of anti-social behavior. *Social Development*, 8, 117–127.

Sutton, J., Smith, P. K., & Swettenham, J. (1999b). Social cognition and bullying: Social inadequacy or skill manipulation? *British Journal of Developmental Psychology*, 17, 435–450.

Sweeting, H., & West, P. (2001). Being different: Correlates of the experience of teasing and bullying at age 11. *Research Papers in Education*, 16, 225–246.

Troy, M., & Sroufe, L. A. (1987). Victimization among preschoolers: Role of attachment relationship history. *Journal of the American Academy of Child and Adolescent Psychiatry*, 26, 166–172.

Whitney, I., Nabuzoka, D., & Smith, P. K. (1992). Bullying in schools: Mainstream and special needs. *Support for Learning*, 7, 3–7.

Whitney, I., & Smith, P. K. (1993). A survey of the nature and extent of bullying in junior/middle and secondary schools. *Educational Research*, 35, 3–25.

# CHAPTER 3

# A Theoretical Review of Bullying: Can It Be Eliminated?

ADRIENNE NISHINA

*University of California, Los Angeles*

This chapter provides a theoretical framework for thinking about bullying. The framework uses a social-biological perspective that suggests bullying behavior may serve specific social and evolutionarily adaptive functions. Although this concept may sound nihilistic or fatalistic at times, it does not sanction bullying. That is, such a view of bullying does *not* suggest that its occurrence cannot be reduced, nor does it assert that nothing can (or should) be done for the individual who is the target of peer aggression. Rather, the chapter places bullying within a theoretical framework that will help schools and interventionists anticipate potential barriers to the implementation of bullying prevention and intervention measures.

This chapter is divided into three sections. First, some general information about peer bullying is presented with a brief review of research that illustrates why schools in particular should be concerned about bullying. Second, the bulk of the chapter provides a social-biological perspective about the occurrence of bullying and presents evidence in the literature that supports this perspective. Third, the discussion focuses on what challenges a social-biological concept might create for bullying prevention and intervention programs.

## WHAT IS BULLYING?

Bullying, commonly known in the research literature as *peer victimization* or *peer harassment*, is a form of social interaction that many children and adolescents encounter (Hoover, Oliver, & Hazler, 1992). *Bullying* (a term subsequently used in this chapter interchangeably with peer victimization and peer harassment) typically refers to a form of social exchange in which there is: (a) a *difference in power* such that the target is less able to defend against experienced hostility and (b) an *intent* to cause physical or psychological harm/discomfort to the target (see Schuster [1996] for a review). There are several points to note about this definition. First, incidents of bullying can include interactions between specific bully-victim dyads, between one aggressor and several victims, between several aggressors and one victim, or between several aggressors and several victims. Second, bullying can include aggressive exchanges between friends. Third, this definition specifically describes social interactions and not the particular participants within the interaction. Thus, an individual could play the role of the bully in one social interaction and the victim in another. In fact, there is a growing literature on children and adolescents who are considered *aggressive-victims* (or *bully-victims*) and are perceived by peers as being both aggressive toward others and frequently victimized by peers (Schwartz, Proctor, & Chien, 2001). Finally, when classifying youth into types (e.g., *victims, bullies, bully-victims*) rather than describing the behavior of these youth, the constraint of recurrence is often added. That is, students are considered victims of peer aggression when they have been targeted "repeatedly and over time" (Olweus, 1991).

The second part of the peer victimization definition specifies an "intent to harm" and therefore excludes social exchanges that are clearly playful teasing and perceived as such by all individuals involved. However, it is often the case that the recipients of the negative peer attention perceive the incident to be harassment, whereas the aggressor contends that he or she was "just teasing" or "didn't really mean anything by it" (Boxer & Cortés-Conde, 1997; Kowalski, 2000; Pellis & Pellis, 1996). Pellis and Pellis (1996) further suggest that it can be particularly difficult to determine the intent of the aggressor—that is, whether the aggressor is "play fighting" or actually attempting to engage in more harmful aggression. In these cases, whether bullying has occurred depends on whom one asks and what types of outcomes are of interest.

In summary, bullying is a common type of social experience that students refer to as "getting picked on." Conceptualized this way, the phenomenon extends beyond the one or two students in the class who are frequently and chronically targeted by peers to include a wider range of students. Although in some cases, peer harassment has escalated into more serious forms of violence resulting in injuries requiring medical attention or homicide (National School Safety Center, 2000), for the purpose of this review, peer victimization is also distinguished from these extreme forms of violence (Dahlberg, 1998).

## "KIDS WILL BE KIDS":
## HOW COMMON IS PEER HARASSMENT?

Peer harassment is a form of social interaction that many schoolchildren experience. Self-reports are the most common method of assessment. With this method, youth are asked to indicate how frequently they experience various forms of harassment within a given time frame (e.g., in the last month or last year) or rate their subjective feelings of being a victim of peer harassment (Neary & Joseph, 1994). Self-report methodology generally yields a wide range of prevalence estimates, with as many as 75% of youth reporting being the target of peer harassment at least occasionally (Hoover *et al.*, 1992; Juvonen, Nishina, & Graham, 2000; Kaufman *et al.*, 1999; Nansel, Overpeck, Pilla, Ruan, Simons-Morton, & Scheidt, 2001; Olweus, 1978; Slee, 1993).

In a recent daily report study, two different samples of sixth-grade middle-school students were asked about their peer harassment experiences and negative affect on four or five randomly selected school days during a 2-week period (Nishina & Juvonen, 2003). On each day, students were asked whether they had personally experienced or witnessed peer harassment earlier that day. During the 2 weeks, approximately 50% of the students in both samples reported experiencing peer harassment on at least one of the data collection days. Furthermore, across the two samples, 37 to 66% of the students reported that they had witnessed a fellow classmate become the target of peer aggression that day. These responses are expected to be reasonably accurate estimates given that students were asked to describe a concrete event that had occurred earlier the same day. Thus, the estimate is less likely to be inflated by memory biases.

Other methods of assessment include peer reports, adult reports (e.g., parent or teacher), and observational techniques (see Pellegrini [2001] for a more in-depth review). Peer reports of harassment are typically assessed through peer nominations that ask students to name individuals in their class who are often targets of peer harassment (Graham & Juvonen, 1998; Lagerspetz, Björkqvist, Berts, & King, 1982; Perry *et al.*, 1988). Based on peer reports of victimization, estimates range from 5 to 15%. When adults (e.g., teachers, parents) are used as informants, estimates typically range from 10 to 20% (Kumpulainen, Räsänen, & Hentonen, 1999; Perry, Kusel, & Perry, 1988; Siann, Callaghan, Lockhart, & Rawson, 1993). Relatively few studies rely on observational methods to study the phenomenon of peer harassment (Atlas & Pepler, 1998; Boulton, 1999; Cadigan, 2003; Eder, 1995; Evans & Eder, 1993; Pepler & Craig, 1995). One study using observational methodology (focusing only on 27 teacher-nominated aggressive or nonaggressive children) found that harassment incidents occurred at a rate of approximately two times per hour (Atlas & Pepler, 1998).

Finally, the phenomenon of peer victimization has now been studied extensively worldwide, including the United States, Great Britain, Australia, Canada, Japan, China, and Scandinavia (Boivin, Hymel, & Bukowski, 1995; Boulton & Underwood, 1992; Kumpulainen et al., 1998; Matsui, Kakuyama, Tsuzuki, & Onglatco, 1996; Olweus, 1978; Österman, Björkqvist, Lagerspetz, Kaukiainen, Huesmann, & Fraczek, 1994; Perry et al., 1988; Rigby & Slee, 1991; Schwartz, Chang, & Farver, 2001). While cultural variants in the presentation of peer victimization are sometimes observed, all studies have found that a sizable portion of school-aged children have experienced peer harassment at least occasionally during their education.

## Forms of Bullying

Peer harassment manifests itself in different forms. In addition to physical and direct verbal aggression (i.e., name-calling, "put-downs," etc.), threats, destruction of property, invasion of physical space, gestures (e.g., holding one's nose when someone walks by), and indirect aggression (e.g., rumors or exclusion) are also considered forms of peer harassment (Crick & Grotpeter, 1996; Mynard & Joseph, 2000; Nishina & Juvonen, 2003; Owens, Shute, & Slee, 2000; Rivers & Smith, 1994; Shute, Owens, & Slee, 2003; Smith et al., 2002). Studies comparing the relative frequencies of different types of harassment find that verbal aggression occurs more often than do physical or indirect forms of aggression, and it is common for different types of aggression to be used within the same interaction (Nansel et al., 2001; Nishina & Juvonen, 2003).

The lay perception of peer harassment is that physical forms of aggression are more detrimental to students' well-being than other forms of victimization (e.g., verbal, indirect, gestures). As a result, schools may be much more likely to intervene when the peer harassment is physical in nature. Although some suggest that different types of peer victimization may have different implications in terms of adjustment, this understanding is cursory and speculative at best (Crick & Grotpeter, 1996; Hawker & Boulton, 2001). Data on students' daily experiences with peer harassment in school suggest that students are equally bothered and distressed by experiences of peer victimization, regardless of whether they are verbal, physical, indirect forms or are multiple forms of peer aggression within the same incident (Nishina & Juvonen, 2003). As will be discussed in the upcoming section, depending on the outcome measures being evaluated, bullying can be viewed as a mental health concern, a public health concern, and a school adjustment concern—all of which have implications for students' ability to learn in school—for youth from a wide range of age groups and cultures.

## Bullying in School: What is the Potential Cost?

Why should there be an interest in the occurrence of peer harassment in the first place? Previous research suggests that not only are students who are directly involved in peer harassment incidents at risk for a host of adjustment difficulties, but even bystanders and onlookers who witness such harassment events can be negatively affected. The following section provides a very brief overview of some of the adjustment difficulties that are associated with bullying in school.

A large body of literature focuses on aggressive students and suggests that aggressive children and adolescents may be at risk for a host of negative outcomes (Boivin, Hymel, & Hodges, 2001; Coie & Dodge, 1998; Loeber, Green, Lahey, & Kalb, 2000; Moffitt, 1993). These studies have found that aggressive youth experience more peer rejection and exhibit higher levels of delinquency, psychosocial maladjustment, and lower levels of school performance than do socially adjusted youth. Aggression is not only limited to externalizing forms of maladjustment but has also been associated with increased internalized symptoms such as depression (Angold, Erkanli, Loeber, & Costello, 1996). Mize and Juvonen (2003) found that students labeled as aggressive by their peers are likely to have negative feelings about school fairness (which can lead to disengagement) compared to their nonaggressive counterparts.

Similarly, targets of peer aggression are also at concurrent and long-term risk for a host of psychological and social adjustment difficulties, including depression, social anxiety, low self-esteem, and peer rejection (Card, 2003a; Hawker & Boulton, 2000). At the daily level, on days in which students personally experience peer harassment at school, they also report increases in daily negative mood (Nishina & Juvonen, 2003). Additional research has found that students who frequently experience peer harassment are more likely to report physical symptoms—both psychosomatic and otherwise—than their more socially adjusted counterparts (Kumpulainen et al., 1998; Nishina, Juvonen, Witkow, & Federoff, 2003; Rigby, 1999; Williams, Chambers, Logan, & Robinson, 1996). Finally, both direct and indirect links have been found between peer harassment and indicators of school functioning, including decreased appreciation of school, lower GPAs, and increased absenteeism (Juvonen et al., 2000; Kochenderfer & Ladd, 1996; Nishina et al., 2003; Slee, 1994). In a study of elementary- and middle-school youth, Slee (1994) found that approximately 10% of the student sample admitted to staying away from school because they were bullied. Almost one third said that they thought about not attending school.

An emerging body of research has now begun to examine the adjustment of *bully-victims*: students who are considered to be both aggressive toward peers and also frequent targets of peer aggression (Schwartz, Proctor, et al., 2001). Although bully-victims are a relatively small subset of students, they appear to be the most maladjusted group of students (Haynie et al., 2001;

Kumpulainen *et al.*, 1998; Kumpulainen, Räsänen, & Henttonen, 1999; Mize & Juvonen, 2003; Schwartz, 2000; Schwartz, Proctor, *et al.*, 2001; Xu, Farver, Schwartz, & Chang, 2003). Kumpulainen *et al.* (1999) found that bully-victims were the most likely group of students to remain chronically involved in bullying years later. Furthermore, comparisons of bully-victims to "pure" bully and pure victim groups showed that bully-victims demonstrated the psychological, social, and scholastic adjustment difficulties associated with bullies and victims, but they experienced none of the social rewards—such as the popularity—of some aggressive students (Haynie *et al.*, 2001; Juvonen, Graham, & Schuster, 2003; Xu *et al.*, 2003).

Potential negative consequences are associated with bullying for students who do not fall into the roles of bullies, victims, or bully-victims. Perceptions of high peer victimization levels within a school have been found to be associated with more negative perceptions of school climate, which in turn have been related to decreased school engagement (Astor, Benbenishty, Zeira, & Vinokur, 2002; Dupper & Meyer-Adams, 2002). Witnessing peer harassment at school has also been associated with an increase in daily feelings of anxiety and school aversion (Nishina & Juvonen, 2003). Thus, even when students are not directly involved in bullying, they may be negatively impacted in ways that can impede the learning process.

In sum, previous research indicates that there are negative psychosocial and academic consequences associated with being a bully, a victim, or a bully-victim. In addition, students who simply witness these aggressive social interactions may experience adverse consequences. Schools with a high prevalence of peer victimization may consequently have students who are less engaged, less able to concentrate in school, and more prone to school avoidance. Given that peer harassment appears to be a common and universal form of behavior, what might explain its occurrence? The next section highlights a social-biological/evolutionary explanation for the occurrence of peer harassment.

## IS IT OUR NATURE: A SOCIAL-BIOLOGICAL/ EVOLUTIONARY VIEW OF PEER HARASSMENT

A big-picture conceptualization of the phenomenon has been lacking from the peer harassment literature. Development of a good theory explaining why bullying occurs can help to create working hypotheses for research as well as inform the development of prevention and intervention approaches.

### Previously Proposed Theories

Theories about the occurrence of peer harassment have been proposed but they do not take a social-biological approach. These explanations often make comparisons between aggressors and targets of peer aggression. For example, Bukowski and Sippola (2001) view peer harassment from a group dynamics perspective. They maintain that some children are actively rejected (i.e., victimized and excluded) from the peer group because they do not contribute to—or are believed to block the attainment of—group goals, such as cohesion, homogeneity, and evolution (i.e., the group's ability to change and adapt to the environment as needed). Specifically, they suggest that children who get excluded from the peer group are often withdrawn and anxious and *choose* to be socially isolated. Bukowski and Sippola further assert that similar victimization and rejection occurs with *aggressive* children because they also threaten group cohesion, homogeneity, and evolution, though they do so in different ways.

One flaw with the application of group dynamics theory to explain peer harassment is that it dichotomizes individuals into either facilitating or impeding group goals. In reality, the process may not be that simple. For example, it would appear that aggressive children are more of a threat to the group than anxious and/or withdrawn children. A "passively withdrawn" child might be expected to "go with the flow" in terms of group dynamics, neither facilitating goals nor impeding them. In addition, if these children "choose" not to participate in the group, there would be no direct threat to the group, and thus there should be no need to waste energy and resources by attempting to push them out of the group.

On other hand, given the group dynamics rationale, aggressive children might be expected to actively threaten group goals (e.g., cohesion) by being disruptive and aggressive toward other group members. Consequently, aggressive children should have more peer problems than withdrawn children. However, this is not the case in the literature. Hawley (1999) suggests that at a very early age (before prosocial and coercive strategies are fully differentiated), toddlers and preschool-aged children who are aggressive seem to be liked, watched, and imitated by their peers. According to a growing body of literature, aggressive children and adolescents appear to remain "socially central." Although there is evidence that peers reject aggressive adolescents (though often less so than victimized children), aggressive children also tend to be viewed as leaders and considered among the more popular individuals within the peer group (Rigby & Slee, 1991; Rodkin, Farmer, Pearl, & Van Acker, 2000; Salmivalli, Lagerspetz, Björkqvist, Österman, & Kaukiainen, 1996). For example, Rodkin *et al.* (2000) collected self- and peer-report data from a sample of fourth- through sixth-grade boys. They found that aggressive boys perceived themselves as "cool," and these perceptions were confirmed by peer nomination data.

One should note, however, that peer nominations for different social and behavioral attributes may not come from the same nominator. It may be that in studies finding positive associations between peer aggression and peer rejection, the rejection nominations are derived mainly from the specific children against whom bullies aggress. One should also recall that the subset of aggressive children and adolescents who are also bullied may be the most maladjusted social group (Mize & Juvonen, 2003; Schwartz, Proctor, et al., 2001). Thus, the empirical data suggest that being aggressive is not uniformly socially beneficial nor always detrimental. The following section discusses this subgroup of students in more detail.

While aggressive children may enjoy some positive attention from a group of peers, research on observers' attitudes about peer harassment suggests that cross-culturally there is a substantial subgroup of students who do not sympathize with victims, who believe that some kids deserve to get picked on, and who admire bullies (Menesini et al., 1997; Oliver, Hoover, & Hazler, 1994; Perry, Williard, & Perry, 1990; Rigby & Slee, 1991; Teräsahjo & Salmivalli, 2003). In a recent qualitative study of elementary school-aged children, Teräsahjo and Salmivalli (2003) found that many students offered explanations that seemed to justify bullying. In particular, students underestimated the prevalence and frequency of bullying among classmates, suggested that the victim had done something to deserve the peer aggression, or pointed out that the victim was somehow deviating from peer group norms. Moreover, these attitudes may increase during adolescence to be held by the majority of students. One study of seventh- through twelfth-grade students (N = 207) found that 61% of the students believed victims were responsible for the peer harassment and that such harassment "helps the person by making them tougher" (Oliver et al., 1994). Moreover, 48% felt that they would lose social status if they had a victim as a friend.

Hawker and Boulton (2001) present a different explanation for peer harassment using concepts from social rank theory. They propose that aggressive individuals—whether physically or verbally aggressive—actually hold a great deal of power within a social group. Thus, to the extent that power is valued, aggressive behavior may be reinforced. On the other hand, they suggest that being the target of peer aggression damages an individual's sense of belonging (a highly valued human experience) or hold of power within a group. As is discussed later, feelings of belongingness may indeed serve as one of the functions of bullying. While this theoretical approach primarily attempts to explain how peer harassment might lead to psychological adjustment difficulties, it focuses less on explaining why peer harassment exists.

One commonality that Bukowski and Sippola (2001) and Hawker and Boulton (2001) present is that bullying has to do with group processes. In fact, peer victimization may serve several different social functions, which may explain why it appears to be so prevalent among school-aged youth: (1) the need to establish a hierarchy and maintain social order within a group (which would explain within-group bullying) and (2) the need to distinguish the "in-group" from the "out-group" and foster feelings of connectedness among in-group members (which would explain peer victimization between members from different social groups). Research supports both of these functions, and schools may provide structure that either promotes or limits within-group and between-group forms of bullying.

## SOCIAL DOMINANCE THEORY APPLIED TO BULLYING BEHAVIORS

A social-biological or evolutionary perspective offers yet another view of peer harassment (see Hawley [1999] for a somewhat different take on social dominance and the evolutionary perspective). Is it something about a bully-victim interaction that is part of human nature? As discussed previously, numerous cross-cultural studies suggest that peer harassment is a universal phenomenon. These cross-cultural studies have found similar correlates (e.g., social withdrawal, submissiveness, and physical weakness) of being a target of peer aggression (Olweus, 1978; Schwartz, Farver, Chang, & Lee-Shin, 2000; Schwartz, Dodge, & Coie, 1993). Rather than group members pushing these withdrawn and submissive children out of the group (Bukowski & Sippola, 2001), group members may push them to the bottom of the group. Social dominance theory (Sidanius, 1993; Sidanius & Pratto, 1999), which seeks to explain prejudice and aggression among members of larger societies, may provide an explanation for the occurrence of peer aggression. Social dominance theory states that human beings are predisposed to create social dominance hierarchies. According to the theory, these strivings would be favored in evolutionary processes because clearly established hierarchies can serve to minimize conflict within a group. Furthermore, groups with clear hierarchies are more organized and thus better able to attack other groups to procure additional resources or defend themselves from attack by outsiders, thereby increasing the likelihood of an individual's survival. In this way, human beings have evolved to feel more at ease when hierarchies have been clearly established.

Drawing from the concept of social dominance theory and the notion that establishing social hierarchies within groups may be an adaptive behavior, one can begin to understand both the occurrence of peer harassment among classmates and peer harassment among friends. Here, the definition of the social group is broadly defined and depends on the particular context in which bullying might occur. For example, within-group aggression can take place in the context of the school as a whole, a grade within a school, a particular classroom within a grade, or a friendship group.

One clear method of establishing social hierarchies and status within groups is through the use of aggression. Perhaps aggressive children are admired by their peers (i.e., more popular) because rather than threatening group cohesion (Bukowski & Sippola, 2001), they actually promote a clear hierarchical organization within the group. Hawley (1999) suggests that both socially coercive and socially prosocial children may be seen as leaders, holding high rank within a hierarchy, though "bistrategic controllers" who use both approaches may enjoy the best outcomes. Further, Hawley proposes that either type of child (coercive or bistrategic) may have access to more resources, which might explain why they are admired by others (Hawley, 2002; Hawley & Little, 1999; Hawley, Little, & Pasupathi, 2002). Similarly, Salmivalli (2001) maintains that bullies are by definition the "ring-leaders" of the aggressive social interaction.

A recent ethnographic study of middle school students also found that peer victimization helps the aggressor establish his or her place in a social hierarchy (Cadigan, 2003). Cadigan asserts that students can demonstrate their social status by (successfully) aggressing against other students. Those who aggressed against others but were unsuccessful at it, however, were not likely to hold the top positions in the status hierarchy. In a novel study, Card, Isaacs, and Hodges (2000) asked adolescents to indicate which specific students in their class victimized them and which students they personally bullied. In addition, they collected the typical peer nomination data asking students to list those in their class who were victims or bullies. They found that nonvictimized (or "pure") aggressors were validated by their targets (i.e., the victimized students confirmed that they were indeed bullied by those individuals). However, aggressive-victims' reports about who they bullied were less often validated.

Research with primates by Sapolsky and colleagues has found that groups with clearly dominant males tend to have well-defined social hierarchies (Sapolsky & Ray, 1989). Moreover, this research suggests that successfully aggressive, dominant males tend to enjoy both social and physiological benefits compared to lower ranking males (Ray & Sapolsky, 1992; Sapolsky & Ray, 1989; Sapolsky & Share, 1994; Virgin & Sapolsky, 1997). The aggressive/dominant individuals enjoy greater access to females for mutual grooming and consorts. They also have lower levels of basal stress hormones and quantitatively different physiological reactions to stress than low-ranking individuals. Other primate researchers, however, suggest that some of the negative physiological consequences of being a low-ranking individual may be attenuated when hierarchies are stable and when there are infrequent attempts to knock the dominant male out of power (Barrett, Shimizu, Bardi, Asaba, & Mori, 2002; Stavisky, Adams, Watson, & Kaplan, 2001). In other words, when a hierarchy is stable, there may be little need for aggression among members because group members know their relative status in the group. Alternatively, when hierarchies are unstable and certain individuals (e.g., aggressive-victims) are competing for higher ranking positions, this unpredictable social environment may have negative consequences for group members.

This theoretical approach also sheds some light on why the aggressive-victim group of students is so disliked and rejected by classmates. These are the students who have the capacity to destabilize the hierarchy, thus making individual group members feel uncomfortable. For example, some research suggests that unlike Hawley's (1999) bistrategic controllers, aggressive-victims do not appear to be as aware of their social status in comparison to others (Hodges & D'Elena, 2003). Aggressive-victims have been found to attack both weaker and stronger individuals, whereas "pure" bullies most frequently bully weaker individuals. Although these individuals may remain in the middle of the dominance hierarchy and not actually move up in status, their potential to disrupt the hierarchy's stability by aggressing so indiscriminately may be enough to elicit feelings of dislike from peers.

Social dominance theory provides rationale for the occurrence of peer harassment across the lifespan. However, an evolutionary/developmental approach to this theory can explain why using peer harassment as a means to establish social hierarchies might be especially prevalent and important during early adolescence. Early adolescence is marked by a number of transitions. For example, the period is marked by a daily social behavior that begins to change. Adolescents begin to spend much more time with peers and much less time with family members (Larson & Richards, 1991; Larson, Richards, Moneta, Holmbeck, & Duckett, 1996). Increased time spent with peers increases the probability that an adolescent will experience peer aggression.

Furthermore, adolescence is a life stage marked by puberty. At least in the evolutionary past, this is a time when individuals would start establishing their social status and competing for potential mates. Thus, social and physiological changes may predict increases in bullying. Consistent with this prediction, Anderman and Kimweli (1997) found that during middle school years, peer harassment appeared to be the most prevalent. Two large nationally representative United States studies have found that peer victimization appears to peak in sixth grade and decline steadily thereafter (Kaufman et al., 1999; Nansel et al., 2001). Although this developmental transition may lead to increased aggression among youth overall, the likelihood of becoming the target of peer aggression and experiencing its negative consequences may be particularly high when pubertal timing is different relative to that of peers (Craig, Pepler, Connolly, & Henderson, 2001; Nadeem & Graham, 2003).

The application of social dominance theory to predict the establishment of social hierarchies also provides an explanation for why peer harassment occurs among friends. As will be discussed in the following paragraphs, it is not necessarily surprising that having friends may protect students from victimization or from the negative consequences of bullying (Cadigan, 2003; Hodges et al., 1999; Nansel et al., 2001; Nishina, 2003). However, friendship groups can experience peer victimization as well (Crick & Grotpeter, 1996). It may be that peer harassment also serves to help establish hierarchies within friendship groups. Alternatively, peer victimization may be used as a method of socialization among friends, thereby promoting greater similarities (or homogeneity) among in-group members.

## Bullying as Socialization Process Within Groups

As youth begin to spend more time with their peers during early adolescence, peers' views become more powerful in influencing their adjustment (Daniels & Moos, 1990; Harter, 1998). For example, Harter (1998) suggests that adolescents perceive peers' opinions of them as more "objective" than their friends' opinions. As such, peer (e.g., classmate) approval is a stronger predictor of self-esteem than approval from close friends. Harris (1995) asserts that the strong influence of the peer group's opinions may serve as a socialization agent for the individual. Bullying as a socialization process within a group has also been observed by a number of qualitative studies (see Cadigan, 2003; Eder, 1995; Teräsahjo & Salmivalli, 2003). It is important to note that the most common explanation elementary students offered for bullying was that the victim was deviant in some way, such as in behavior, appearance, or nationality (Teräsahjo & Salmivalli, 2003). Cadigan (2003) and Eder (1995) both observed that bullying was used as a form of "gender policing" (i.e., gender socialization) among their respective samples of middle school students. Thus, during a time of developmental change and instability, peer harassment may be particularly important in facilitating the development of hierarchies and promoting a sense of stability as well as socializing group members. The next section reviews several functions of between-group aggression (i.e., peer victimization that occurs between members of different groups).

## Establishing the In-Group by Defining the Out-Group

In the evolutionary past, it was important for survival to know which people in one's social world could be considered friends and which were enemies (Trivers, 1971). Even in the present, it is beneficial to know who is a likely aggressor and who could be trusted as an aid. Youth differentiate between in-group and out-group members in their social worlds and may use social aggression to solidify these distinctions. Like the definition of the social group above, the in-group and out-group can be situation-specific. For instance, in-group/out-group distinctions can refer to those in one's friendship group versus those who are not part of that group, those in one's grade versus students in other grades, or students in one's school versus students from a different school, and so forth.

Researchers in the classic Robbers Cave experiment found that distinctions made between in-groups and out-groups could develop quickly (Sherif, Harvey, White, Hood, & Sherif, 1961). In this study, two groups of boys (very similar on a multitude of demographic variables) were brought to summer camp and neither was aware that there was another group. Eventually, the two groups were introduced to one another and, facilitated by intergroup competition, a rivalry soon followed. Members of each group developed strong negative beliefs about boys in the other group. Subsequently, the boys from both groups engaged in interactions—such as name-calling and physical aggression—that could be construed as peer harassment. These negative interactions occurred despite the fact that prior to camp, some of the boys in the opposing groups had been friends. Instead, the boys within each group began showing more loyalty to their own group members. The researchers found that the intergroup rivalry escalated and proved to be more difficult than expected to reduce. Certainly one can see this type of in-group cohesion while attending a sporting event between rival schools. In these situations, within-group animosity (e.g., peer harassment among classmates) may be decreased in favor of higher order between-group rivalries (i.e., rooting for one's school and not the opposing team).

Research, such as the Sherif *et al.* (1961) study described in the preceding paragraph, illustrates that youth designate out-groups in their social worlds. Recent literature has started to examine this differentiation in the form of *mutual antipathies* (or *enmities* in their most extreme form). Mutual antipathies are characterized as social relationships in which there is mutual or reciprocated dislike among classmates (Abecassis, Hartup, Haselager, Scholte, & Van Lieshout, 2003; Hodges & Card, 2003). Anywhere from 15 to 65% of children and adolescents (across all sociometric status groups) have been found to have at least one mutual antipathy (Hartup & Abecassis, 2002; Pope, 2003). Moreover, the existence of mutual antipathies—and bullying in general—appears to continue into adulthood (Holt, 1989; Schuster, 1996). Peer victimization may be more likely among mutual antipathies than among friendships or neutral peers (Card, 2003b) and may also serve as a strategy by which students make sense of their social worlds by defining in-groups and out-groups. Although Card (2003b) found that involvement in mutual antipathies predicts increases in students' maladjustment over time, Abecassis (2003) points out that mutual antipathies may have the additional benefit of strengthening friendships and solidifying ties with in-group members.

## Belongingness as Motivation

Understanding who is a member of one's in-group may play an important role in successfully eliciting aid. Abecassis (2003) and Cadigan (2003) hypothesize that bullying others—either directly or indirectly—can serve to establish, maintain, and reinforce in-group bonds and differentiate in-group from out-group members. At the same time, it has been proposed that this shared or group aggression against others might foster feelings of belongingness among in-group members. Creating feelings of belongingness can be a strong motivational force for bullying (Baumeister & Leary, 1995; Newman &

Newman, 2001). Hawker and Boulton (2001) placed a strong emphasis on the role of belongingness in peer victimization experiences, and Bukowski and Sippola (2001) highlighted the importance of group cohesion. To have a group and feel a sense of belonging to it, there must be at least two groups. In other words, to have an in-group and feel like one is part of it, there needs to be an out-group in which people feel they are *not* a member. Teräsahjo and Salmivalli (2003) found that children, when talking about frequent targets of peer aggression, would often underestimate similarities between themselves and the victim. Generally these social comparisons are not favorable to the victim and such downward comparisons have been found to boost self-esteem and adjustment (Gibbons, 1986; Gibbons & Gerrard, 1989; Gibbons & McCoy, 1991; Taylor, Aspinwall, & Giuliano, 1994).

Another way in which bullying may foster feelings of belongingness is through the roles that group members play in the social exchange. Salmivalli and colleagues (Salmivalli, 2001; Salmivalli et al., 1996; Salmivalli, Huttunen, & Lagerspetz, 1997) maintain that bullying is a group process in which all group members have defined roles. They suggest that there are at least six distinct roles (*bully, assistant, reinforcer, defender, victim,* and *outsider-bystander*) in which students can fall during bullying episodes. Three of these roles are distinctly related to the bully side of the interaction and likely serve to reinforce the occurrence of bullying. Bullies are viewed as the "ringleaders" who are responsible for instigating the aggression against the target(s). Assistants are considered followers who go along with the bully and engage in aggression against peers. Reinforcers are those peers who provide attention to the bully and positive feedback about the bully's aggressive behavior. Students who occupy these roles establish their place in the social hierarchy and reinforce the occurrence of bullying. Having an established role may also increase feelings of belongingness. On the other hand, two roles are considered to be related to the victim side of the interaction. Victims are students who are targets of peer aggression, and defenders try to help the victim or make him or her feel better. Thus, just as bonds are likely to form among bullies, assistants, and reinforcers, bonds may also form between victims and defenders.

## "Birds of a Feather": Similarities Among In-Group Members

That such peer aggression can serve to reinforce in-group bonds by making in-group/out-group distinctions and fostering a sense of belongingness among in-group members is difficult to test empirically. It is unlikely that youth are aware of and able to articulate these benefits as functions of peer harassment. There are, however, a few studies that appear to support these notions.

Research has found that children and adolescents with similar behavioral tendencies are likely to interact with one another and that aggressive behaviors are maintained and may increase if they are reinforced by the peer group (Romero, Card, & Hodges, 2001; Salmivalli *et al.*, 1997). For example, Romero *et al.* (2001) collected peer nomination data on mutual friendships (i.e., when two individuals both nominated the other as a friend) and specific bully-victim dyads. That is, rather than asking students to name classmates who were frequently aggressive toward peers or bullied by peers, they asked students to name the classmates that *they specifically* aggressed against and who specifically aggressed against them. Romero *et al.* found that mutual friends are likely to target the same specific individuals for peer aggression. In these cases, it may be that friends who pick on others do so to strengthen in-group bonds and create clear out-group boundaries (Bukowski & Sippola, 2001). At the same time, when friends are picked on as part of a group, it is possible that it may serve as a bonding experience—albeit an unpleasant one—as part of a shared plight. Further, bonds between friends might be strengthened if support were provided during the course of the experience—for example, this would be the case if the friend helped or intervened on behalf of the victim during the event or tried to make the friend feel better afterward.

A few studies support the notion that having close ties to friends can protect students against both actual occurrences of victimization as well as some of the psychological consequences of being the target of peer aggression (Cadigan, 2003; Hodges, Vitaro, & Bukowski, 1999; Nishina, 2003). In a daily report study of peer harassment, students who had witnessed peer harassment were asked to indicate whether they had helped the target of peer aggression (Nishina, 2003). Students were significantly more likely to report helping the target either during or after the incident if the target was perceived to be a friend (57% of the time), rather than an acquaintance (22% of the time) or stranger (3% of the time). In a study of fourth and fifth graders, Hodges *et al.* (1999) found that merely having a mutual friend protected victimized students against internalizing symptoms.

Conversely, potential exposure to bullying may explain why aggressive-victims are the least liked and most rejected of their peer groups (Haynie *et al.*, 2001; Schwartz, 2000; Xu *et al.*, 2003). Being friends with someone who is a frequent target of peer aggression may be risky for the friend because he or she may be bullied by association. Moreover, if the aggressive-victim is also frequently aggressive toward peers, the friend might place him or herself at risk for being targeted by the aggressive-victim as well.

In summary, students' aggressive behavior may be rewarded by the peers whose opinions mean the most to them (i.e., their friends) by generating feelings of belongingness and highlighting group membership. At the same time, the larger peer group may reward engaging in peer victimization. Members may actively reinforce the behavior by laughing or joining in or passively reinforce the behavior by not standing up for the target of the aggression. Given that peer harassment is likely to be reinforced by a number of others, it is important to take these sources of reinforcement into consideration when thinking about designing prevention and intervention programs.

## NOW WHERE DO WE GO: CHALLENGES FOR PREVENTION AND INTERVENTION

Taking a social-biological view of peer harassment presumes that such harassment is a fairly common and sometimes adaptive form of human (and primate) social behavior. This view of bullying supports the notion that peer aggression serves certain social functions such as establishing hierarchies and reinforcing feelings of stability and affiliation. The final section of this chapter will relate the functions of bullying to specific challenges that schools may encounter when developing and implementing bullying prevention and intervention measures. First, it reviews how the structure and organization of schools may reinforce status differences among students. Next, it compares the social reinforcement derived from bullying to the typical school practice of punishing aggressive behavior. Finally, it presents a special case of introducing a new student into an existing social group and describes the implications associated with this introduction.

### The Social Hierarchy

As discussed above, social dominance theory posits that individuals strive to form social hierarchies because it is evolutionarily advantageous to do so. Cross-cultural studies support this notion, as peer harassment appears to be a universal phenomenon. Similar social aggression and dominance hierarchies are found in primate groups as well. Taken together, these findings would suggest that it is difficult, if not impossible, to *completely* eliminate peer harassment. The social dominance perspective predicts that attempts to eliminate peer victimization would promote unstable hierarchies. In turn, these unstable hierarchies would cause individuals within the group to feel uncomfortable and seek other ways of establishing social stratification (e.g., resorting to more covert forms of peer harassment).

Assessments of most intervention programs appear to support this notion. Evaluation studies have mainly found changes in attitudes about peer harassment or the intervention itself on face valid measures (Naylor & Cowie, 1999). Further, some of these studies may pull for positive answers (e.g., "In what ways do you think the program has helped?"). Even then, there is evidence that the observed improvements might be short-lived (Stevens, Van Oost, & de Bourdeaudhuij, 2000). Evaluations regarding actual behavior change are not very encouraging—generally few changes are found (Nishina, Juvonen, & Leiner, 2001; Peterson & Rigby, 1996).

While establishing clear social hierarchies may be *evolutionarily* adaptive, the process can negatively affect personal adjustment. What may be adaptive for the group as a whole does not necessarily benefit all individuals in the group. As noted above, students experience negative consequences from being the target of peer aggression. Thus, while such events may serve to establish the aggressor's place in the hierarchy, the behavior does not benefit the aggressor's targets.

Social dominance theory does not predict that interpersonal or intergroup aggression *cannot* be reduced. Sidanius (1993) maintains that countries vary in the degree to which there are differences between ethnic groups and intergroup conflict. Most cultures have laws or proscriptions against certain forms of interpersonal aggression (e.g., murder, rape, sexual harassment). Ethnographic studies have also found evidence that violence and aggression can be reduced. For example, among the Trobrianders of Papua New Guinea, symbolic competition was introduced by British missionaries in the form of the game of cricket. Though the game was subsequently greatly modified, it provided an alternative form of intergroup competition which reduced (but did not eliminate) the occurrence of warfare between indigenous tribes (Leach & Kildea, 1974; Weiner, 1988). Alternatively, in communities where gangs are prevalent, a community's involvement in monitoring and a lack of tolerance for gang activity has been found to effectively reduce the occurrence of gang violence (Jankowski, 1991).

As Cadigan (2003) notes, a school's structure and climate may serve to reinforce the notion of hierarchical status within its student population. For instance, in Cadigan's ethnography, she points out that schools in general tend to be stratified by age/grade and a certain amount of status may be afforded to older students (e.g., student council positions). Moreover, Cadigan observes that status hierarchies are further established and maintained between students and adults within the school and among adults that make up the school personnel (e.g., principal, teachers, aides, janitors). The mere existence of hierarchies does not necessarily mean that bullying is rampant within a school. In fact, to some extent, having a hierarchy and understanding how it works may provide a certain sense of order to students, particularly if in general, individuals feel more comfortable in well-defined hierarchies. Understanding the time-limited nature of this type of stratification may ameliorate some of the negative consequences when grade-based bullying occurs. For example, sixth graders within a middle school may not enjoy being allowed fewer privileges than older students, but they may be reassured by the fact that this part of their social status is grade-based and that eventually their status will improve as they advance to older grades.

Cadigan (2003) provides a salient example in her ethnography of how the structure of a school can serve to promote status hierarchies. Of the school in her study, Cadigan notes that seventh and eighth graders were allowed to eat anywhere during lunch, whereas those in the sixth grade were confined to a specific part of the schoolyard. In fact, *all* seventh and eighth graders ate in the area that was off-limits to sixth graders and actively prohibited the younger students from entering this restricted area. In this way, Cadigan suggests that the grade hierarchy within the school was made especially salient by this physical and psychological distinction.

This school policy may have been a practical measure to limit crowding and congestion in certain areas of the school. Alternatively, it may have been a conscious act on the part of school personnel to protect the younger students from bullying by separating them from older students who might target them. By providing an institutional hierarchy, some aggression—especially during lunchtime—may have been limited. Unfortunately, this protocol also appears to have had the unanticipated effect of highlighting which students were sixth graders and making them targets at other times of the school day. Nevertheless Cadigan found that many sixth graders looked forward to advancing to the next grade and reaping some of the benefits that this advancement would afford them in school.

In other instances, an imposed social structure within a school can have a decidedly negative impact on students. For example, the degree of privileges afforded to individuals (both adults and students) of different status may reinforce hierarchy-based bullying within a school. The school climate and social stratification created by adults of the school—both in their treatment of one another and in their treatment of students—may affect the overall prevalence and impact of bullying within a school. That is, bullying may be more likely and frequent in schools in which adults are socially aggressive to one another and schools in which adults use their higher social status in ways that demean students (e.g., teachers putting down students in front of the class; office staff assuming that students are "up to no good"; aids and security guards using their authority to boss around students or let some students break the rules while reinforcing the rules with others). School-based solutions therefore point to comprehensive, systemic approaches that address bullying (Olweus, 1993; Olweus, 1997; Rigby, 1996). In sum, social dominance theory suggests that limiting peer aggression when it serves the purpose of establishing and maintaining social hierarchies should be difficult but not impossible to accomplish. Social aggression can either be reduced or exacerbated by the types of social structures that schools externally impose.

## Positive Reinforcement of the Bully

The typical measures that schools use to limit bullying are punitive responses to aggressive students. In many cases, these prohibitions solely target physical aggression (e.g., fighting) and only very specific forms of verbal aggression (i.e., sexual harassment and racial slurs). However, given the particular functions of bullying outlined in the previous paragraphs, there is reason to expect that these measures alone may not be sufficient in greatly reducing the occurrence of bullying in schools.

As noted above, bullying goes beyond the bully-victim dyad. Acts of aggression between students do not occur in a vacuum. Salmivalli's work (Salmivalli, 2001; Salmivalli *et al.*, 1996; Salmivalli *et al.*, 1997; Teräsahjo & Salmivalli, 2003) illustrates that other students are often around when the bullying occurs and fill other roles within the victimization event (e.g., reinforcer, assistant, defender, bystander). If this is the case, targeting the bully would do little to limit the aggression between other students involved in the incident (e.g., victim-defender and reinforcer-assistant). Punishment of the bully does not address the roles that other students may have played and does not address the positive social reinforcement (e.g., acceptance, belongingness, admiration) the bully may receive from other students such as the reinforcers, assistants, and bystanders. Recall that many students are likely to side with the bully and express little sympathy for the victim (Oliver *et al.*, 1994; Teräsahjo & Salmivalli, 2003). Thus, the positive social reinforcement for students involved in bullying may outweigh any negative consequences doled out by school personnel. In addition, punishing the aggressor does not address the possibility that the aggression serves to establish or maintain a hierarchy. Subsequently, other members of the bully's group (e.g., reinforcer, assistant) may attempt to assume a new role (i.e., bully) if the former bully is removed.

## Inconsistency of Interventions

Additional contextual factors further complicate the picture. First, adults are rarely present during the majority of bullying incidents—particularly the more subtle forms of bullying (e.g., overt aggression, name calling, subtle gestures). For example, in daily reports of peer harassment experiences, students report that adults are present in only 5% of the personally experienced (and mostly physical) victimization incidents reported (Nishina, 2003). In a different study of high school students, Astor, Meyer, & Behre (1999) found that peer victimization most often occurred during unsupervised times and at unsupervised locations. Developmental changes can also make catching bullying behavior more difficult. As students develop cognitively, they may become more skilled and discreet about how and when they aggress against others (Nishina *et al.*, 2001). For example, students may learn that directing overt physical or verbal aggression toward others may place them at risk for retaliation from the victim (or defender) and punishment by adults, whereas spreading rumors about another could serve the same purpose with less risk involved.

Second, it is often the case that punishment for bullying is inconsistently imposed. This inconsistency is played out because adults only witness bullying some of the time and also because of differential punishment based on victimization type. For example, suppose that adults were privy to all bullying incidents within a school. Consider what most schools would do in response to a student (a) punching and kicking another classmate, (b) calling a classmate a "slut," (c) calling a classmate "fat and ugly," or (d) rolling his or her eyes and holding his or her nose as a classmate walks by. Most schools would not assess these four incidents to be equal in severity or magnitude. Rather, most would likely only intervene in one or two of the cases, even though recent research has found that students do not tend to differentiate between different forms of bullying when reporting distress (Nishina & Juvonen, 2003). Students report being equally distressed, regardless of the type of bullying they experience.

Thus, consistent punishment of bullying behavior is probably an unrealistic goal given that adults are not always present when such behavior occurs, some forms of bullying are extremely subtle and difficult to observe, and students may become more sophisticated about carrying out bullying behavior as they get older. This again underscores the importance of systemic, whole-school approaches to violence prevention. In addition, it points to the need for providing students with adaptive coping strategies should they become the target of peer aggression, which will now be discussed in more detail.

## Targeting the Victim

Interventions that target the bully do not necessarily help the individual victim by reducing the likelihood or negative consequences of peer harassment. In a recent study, sixth graders' social perceptions (i.e., perceived frequency of personal experiences of peer victimization, prevalence of bullying occurring to classmates, and characterological self-blame) were measured prior to collecting daily reports of peer harassment and negative affect (Nishina, 2003). These social perceptions moderated the relationship between daily peer victimization experiences and negative affect. That is, the social perceptions predicted greater reactivity to daily encounters with peer harassment: On days in which students experienced peer victimization, those students who started out with higher than average perceptions of victimization frequency, prevalence, and characterological self-blame reported even stronger increases in negative affect than did students who were average or below average on those social perception measures. For these students, there was almost a 100% increase in some negative affect composites above and beyond the effect of experiencing peer victimization.

Preventive interventions that target students' maladaptive social perceptions by teaching more adaptive coping strategies would help bullied students not only in social interactions that take place in school but also in difficult social situations they encounter outside of school. Moreover, there are a variety of cognitive and behavioral coping strategies in response to victimization, some of which can buffer against negative outcomes and elicit more favorable responses from onlookers (Kochenderfer & Skinner, 2002; Scambler, Harris, & Milich, 1998). It is important to remember that such preventive interventions should not necessarily target the most chronically victimized students. Targeted approaches would likely serve to further stigmatize the victim. Moreover, these approaches would also likely overlook a substantial portion of occasionally victimized students such as those who happen to hold maladaptive social perceptions (described previously). Kochenderfer-Ladd and Ladd (2001) suggest that it is not necessarily the frequency of peer victimization experiences but the personal perceptions of the experiences that will determine students' subsequent psychological adjustment.

In sum, intervention measures that only target aggressive students may not be powerful enough to reduce or eliminate bullying, given that aggression sometimes gains a student higher social status (e.g., popularity, visibility among peers, reputation as a leader). Social aggression can be further reinforced by peer approval and feelings of belongingness. Moreover, targeting the bully is not very realistic because although students appear to be equally distressed by all forms of peer harassment, certain forms of bullying are very difficult for school staff to detect and address (e.g., gestures, rumors). Developmental changes also bring about challenges to prevention and intervention. As students get older, (1) they may become more savvy about who they target, where they aggress against others, and what forms of aggression they use, and (2) adults become less aware of and involved in negative social interactions between students that do not involve immediate physical harm. Thus, systemic, school-wide prevention approaches and the promotion of adaptive coping strategies are likely to best address bullying in schools.

## The New Kid on the Block

One final consideration involves new students who are introduced to an existing social environment. Depending on the particular student, such an introduction has the potential to increase the prevalence of peer aggression within a classroom or an entire school. The student may attempt to establish him or herself within an existing social hierarchy, thus clashing with other students and destabilizing the hierarchy. At the same time, students may try to fit the newcomer into the existing schemas of their social world. Existing groups need to determine whether this individual should be invited to be part of their in-group or should be regarded as an out-group member (see Cadigan [2003] for an excellent example of the potential impact of a new student and the subsequent instability within the social hierarchy). If the newcomer is to become part of the in-group, he or she must demonstrate similarities with in-group members while accentuating differences from out-group members. Part of this demonstration could take the form of peer harassment. Alternatively, if certain group members feel threatened by the appearance of the new student, they may direct aggression toward the newcomer in an attempt to maintain in-group and out-group boundaries. Thus, schools should be prepared for the possible impact a new student might have on other students and expect that peer harassment might increase—at least temporarily—as the existing social hierarchy adjusts to accommodate the newcomer.

## SUMMARY

The occurrence of bullying among school-aged youth may serve a number of functions. These functions, in turn, can explain why reducing peer aggression among youth can be a difficult task for schools. For instance, peer aggression within social groups may serve the purpose of establishing and maintaining social hierarchies that at least in the evolutionary past were likely to increase the chances of survival of individuals within these groups. Moreover, social aggression within groups can work to establish and reinforce norms for behavior. Between-group aggression may also serve a number of social functions. For example, peer aggression may assist in forming in-groups and distinguishing out-group boundaries, provide youth with feelings of belongingness, and be reinforced by in-group approval for aggression directed toward out-group members. These numerous functions of peer aggression make it difficult—but not impossible—to reduce or limit the occurrence of bullying in schools. Understanding the functions of peer aggression will provide schools with insight into the types of preventions and interventions that would be successful with their students and suggest that global, systemic approaches are warranted.

## References

Abecassis, M. (2003). I hate you just the way you are: Exploring the formation, maintenance, and need for enemies. In E. V. E. Hodges & N. A. Card (Eds.), *Enemies and the darker side of peer relations*. San Francisco: Jossey-Bass.

Abecassis, M., Hartup, W. W., Haselager, G. J. T., Scholte, R. H. J., & Van Lieshout, C. F. M. (2002). Mutual antipathies and their significance in middle childhood and adolescence. *Child Development*, 73, 1543–1556.

Anderman, E. M., & Kimweli, D. M. S. (1997). Victimization and safety in schools serving early adolescents. *Journal of Early Adolescence*, 17, 408–438.

Angold, A., Erkanli, A., Loeber, R., & Costello, E. J. (1996). Disappearing depression in a population sample of boys. *Journal of Emotional & Behavioral Disorders*, 4, 95–104.

Astor, R. A., Benbenishty, R., Zeira, A., & Vinokur, A. (2002). School climate, observed risky behaviors, and victimization as predictors of high school students' fear and judgments of school violence as a problem. *Health Education and Behavior*, 29, 716–736.

Astor, R. A., Meyer, H. A., & Behre, W. J. (1999). Unowned places and times: Maps and interviews about violence in high schools. *American Educational Research Journal*, 36, 3–42.

Atlas, R. S., & Pepler, D. J. (1998). Observations of bullying in the classroom. *Journal of Educational Research*, 92, 86–99.

Barrett, G. M., Shimizu, K., Bardi, M., Asaba, S., & Mori, A. (2002). Endocrine correlates of rank, reproduction, and female-directed aggression in male Japanese macaques (*Macaca fuscata*). *Hormones and Behavior*, 42, 85–96.

Baumeister, R. F., & Leary, M. R. (1995). The need to belong: Desire for interpersonal attachments as a fundamental human motivation. *Psychological Bulletin*, 117, 497–529.

Boivin, M., Hymel, S., & Bukowski, W. M. (1995). The roles of social withdrawal, peer rejection, and victimization by peers in predicting loneliness and depressed mood in childhood. *Development and Psychopathology*, 7, 765–785.

Boivin, M., Hymel, S., & Hodges, E. V. (2001). Toward a process view of peer rejection and harassment. In J. Juvonen & S. Graham (Eds.), *Peer harassment in school: The plight of the vulnerable and victimized* (pp. 265–289). New York: Guilford Press.

Boulton, M. J. (1999). Concurrent and longitudinal relations between children's playground behavior and social preference, victimization, and bullying. *Child Development*, 70, 944–954.

Boulton, M. J., & Underwood, K. (1992). Bully/victim problems among middle school children. *British Journal of Educational Psychology*, 62, 73–87.

Boxer, D., & Cortés-Conde, F. (1997). From bonding to biting: Conversational joking and identity display. *Journal of Pragmatics*, 27, 275–294.

Bukowski, W. M., & Sippola, L. K. (2001). Groups, individuals, and victimization: A view of the peer system. In J. Juvonen, & S. Graham (Eds.), *Peer harassment in school: The plight of the vulnerable and victimized* (pp. 355–377). New York: Guilford Press.

Cadigan, R. J. (2003). Scrubs: An ethnographic study of peer culture and harassment among sixth graders in an urban middle school. *Dissertation Abstracts International*, 63 (7A), pp. 2597. (University Microfilms No. 3058487)

Card, N. A. (2003a, April). Victims of peer aggression: A meta-analytic review. In N. A. Card & A. Nishina (Chairs), *Whipping boys and other victims of peer aggression: Twenty-five years of research, now where do we go?* Symposium presented at the biennial meeting of the Society for Research in Child Development: Tampa, FL.

Card, N. A. (2003b, April). Victimization from friends, mutual antipathies, and neutral peers: Associations with risk factors and psychosocial adjustment. In N. A. Card & A. Nishina (Chairs), *Whipping boys and other victims of peer aggression: Twenty-five years of research, now where do we go?* Symposium presented at the biennial meeting of the Society for Research in Child Development: Tampa, FL.

Card, N. A., Isaacs, J., & Hodges, E. V. (2000, March). Dynamics of interpersonal aggression in the school context: Who aggresses against whom? In J. Juvonen & A. Nishina (Chairs), *Harassment across diverse contexts*. Symposium presented at the biennial meeting of the Society for Research in Adolescence: Chicago.

Coie, J. D., & Dodge, K. A. Aggression and antisocial behavior. In W. Damon, & N. Eisenberg (Eds.), *Handbook of child psychology* (pp. 779–862). New York: Wiley.

Craig, W. M., Pepler, D., Connolly, J., & Henderson, K. (2001). Developmental context of peer harassment in early adolescence: The role of puberty and the peer group. In J. Juvonen, & S. Graham (Eds.), *Peer harassment in school: The plight of the vulnerable and victimized* (pp. 242–261). New York: Guilford Press.

Crick, N. R., & Grotpeter, J. K. (1996). Children's treatment by peers: Victims of relational and overt aggression. *Development and Psychopathology*, 8, 367–380.

Dahlberg, L. L. (1998). Youth violence in the United States: Major trends, risk factors, and prevention approaches. *American Journal of Preventive Medicine*, 14, 259–272.

Daniels, D., & Moos, R. H. (1990). Assessing life stressors and social resources among adolescents: Applications to depressed youth. *Journal of Adolescent Research*, 5, 268–289.

Dupper, D. R., & Meyer-Adams, N. (2002). Low-level violence: A neglected aspect of school culture. *Urban Education*, 37, 350–364.

Eder, D. (1995). *School talk: Gender and adolescent culture.* New Brunswick, New Jersey: Rutgers University Press.

Evans, C., & Eder, D. (1993). "No exit": Processes of social isolation in the middle school. *Journal of Contemporary Ethnography, 22,* 139–170.

Gibbons, F. X. (1986). Social comparison and depression: Company's effect on misery. *Journal of Personality and Social Psychology, 51,* 140–148.

Gibbons, F. X., & Gerrard, M. (1989). Effects of upward and downward social comparison on mood states. *Journal of Social and Clinical Psychology, 8,* 14–31.

Gibbons, F. X., & McCoy, S. B. (1991). Self-esteem, similarity, and reactions to active versus passive downward comparison. *Journal of Personality and Social Psychology, 60,* 414–424.

Graham, S., & Juvonen, J. (1998). Self-blame and peer victimization in middle school: An attributional analysis. *Developmental Psychology, 34,* 587–538.

Harris, J. R. (1995). Where is the child's environment? A group socialization theory of development. *Psychological Review, 102,* 458–489.

Harter, S. (1998). The development of self-representations. In N. Eisenberg & W. Damon (Eds.), *Handbook of Child Psychology: Vol 3, Social, Emotional, and Personality Development* (pp. 553–617). New York: Wiley.

Hartup, W. W., & Abecassis, M. (2002). Friends and enemies. In P. K. Smith & C. H. Hart (Eds.), *Handbook of childhood social development* (pp. 286–306). Malden, MA: Blackwell.

Hawker, D. S. J., & Boulton, M. J. (2001). Subtypes of peer harassment and their correlates: A social dominance perspective. In J. Juvonen & S. Graham (Eds.), *Peer harassment in school: The plight of the vulnerable and victimized* (pp. 378–397). New York: Guilford Press.

Hawker, D. S. J., & Boulton, M. J. (2000). Twenty years' research on peer victimization and psychosocial maladjustment: A meta-analytic review of cross-sectional studies. *Journal of Child Psychology and Psychiatry and Allied Disciplines, 41,* 441–455.

Hawley, P. H. (1999). The ontogenesis of social dominance: A strategy-based evolutionary perspective. *Developmental Review, 19,* 97–132.

Hawley, P. H. (2002). Social dominance and prosocial and coercive strategies of resource control in preschoolers. *International Journal of Behavioral Development, 26,* 167–176.

Hawley, P. H., & Little, T. D. (1999). On winning some and losing some: A social relations approach to social dominance in toddlers. *Merrill-Palmer Quarterly, 45,* 185–214.

Hawley, P. H., Little, T. D., & Pasupathi, M. (2002). Winning friends and influencing peers: Strategies of peer influence in late childhood. *International Journal of Behavioral Development, 26,* 466–474.

Haynie, D. L., Nansel, T., Eitel, P., Crump, A. D., Saylor, K., Yu, K., & Simons-Morton, B. (2001). Bullies, victims, and bully/victims: Distinct groups of at-risk youth. *Journal of Early Adolescence, 21,* 29–49.

Hodges, E. V. E., & Card, N. (in press). *Enemies and the darker side of peer relations, New directions for child and adolescent development.* San Francisco: Jossey-Bass.

Hodges, E. V. E., Boivin, M., Vitaro, F., & Bukowski, W. M. (1999). The power of friendship: Protection against an escalating cycle of peer victimization. *Developmental Psychology, 35,* 94–101.

Hodges, E. V. E., & D'Elena, P. (2003, April). Do aggressive victims and aggressive nonvictims differ in social cognitive evaluations toward varying target types? In D. Schwartz (Chair), *Children who are concurrently bullied and aggressive: New directions in research on a vulnerable subgroup.* Symposium presented at the biennial meeting of the Society for Research in Child Development: Tampa, FL.

Holt, R. R. (1989). College students' definitions and images of enemies. *Journal of Social Issues, 45,* 33–50.

Hoover, J. H., Oliver, R., & Hazler, R. J. (1992). Bullying: Perceptions of adolescent victims in the midwestern USA. *School Psychology International, 13,* 5–16.

Jankowksi, M. S. (1991). *Islands in the street: Gangs and American urban society.* Berkeley, CA: University of California Press.

Juvonen, J., Graham, S., & Schuster, M. (in press). Bullying among young adolescents: The strong, the weak, and the troubled. *Pediatrics*.

Kaufman, P., Chen, X., Choy, S. P., Ruddy, S. A., Miller, A. K., Chandler, K. A., Chapman, C. D., Rand, M. R., & Klaus, P. (1999). *Indicators of school crime and safety*. (NCES 1999-057/NCJ-178906). Washington, DC: Departments of Education and Justice.

Kochenderfer, B. J., & Ladd, G. W. (1996). Peer victimization: Cause or consequence of school maladjustment? *Child Development, 67*, 1305–1317.

Kochenderfer-Ladd, B., & Ladd, G. W. (2001). Variations in peer victimization: Relations to children's maladjustment. In J. Juvonen & S. Graham (Eds.), *Peer harassment in school: The plight of the vulnerable and victimized* (pp. 25–48). New York: Guilford Press.

Kochenderfer-Ladd, B., & Skinner, K. (2002). Children's coping strategies: Moderators of the effects of peer victimization? *Developmental Psychology, 38*, 267–278.

Kowalski, R. M. (2000). "I was only kidding!": Victims' and perpetrators' perceptions of teasing. *Personality and Social Psychology Bulletin, 26*, 231–241.

Kumpulainen, K., Räsänen, E., & Henttonen, I. (1999). Children involved in bullying: Psychological disturbance and the persistence of the involvement. *Child Abuse & Neglect, 23*, 1253–1262.

Kumpulainen, K., Räsänen, E., Henttonen, I., Almqvist, F., Kresanov, K., Linna, S.-L., Moilanen, I., *et al.* (1998). Bullying and psychiatric symptoms among elementary school-age children. *Child Abuse and Neglect, 22*, 705–717.

Lagerspetz, K. M., Björkqvist, K., Berts, M., & King, E. (1982). Group aggression among school children in three schools. *Scandinavian Journal of Psychology, 23*, 45–52.

Larson, R., & Richards, M. H. (1991). Daily companionship in late childhood and early adolescence: Changing developmental contexts. *Child Development, 62*, 284–300.

Larson, R. W., Richards, M. H., Moneta, G., Holmbeck, G. C., & *et al.* (1996). Changes in adolescents' daily interactions with their families from ages 10 to 18: Disengagement and transformation. *Developmental Psychology, 32*, 744–754.

Leach, J. W., & Kildea, G. (1974). *Trobriand cricket: An ingenious response to colonialism* [Motion picture]. (Available from University of California Extension Media Center, 2223 Fulton Street, Berkeley, CA 94720)

Loeber, R., Green, S. M., Lahey, B. B., & Kalb, L. (2000). Physical fighting in childhood as a risk factor for later mental health problems. *Journal of the American Academy of Child and Adolescent Psychiatry, 39*, 421–428.

Matsui, T., Kakuyama, T., Tsuzuki, Y., & Onglatco, M. L. (1996). Long-term outcomes of early victimization by peers among Japanese male university students: Model of a vicious cycle. *Psychological Reports, 79*, 711–720.

Menesini, E., Eslea, M., Smith, P. K., Genta, M. L., Giannetti, E., Fonzi, A., & Costabile, A. (1997). Cross-national comparison of children's attitudes towards bully/victim problems in schools. *Aggressive Behavior, 23*, 245–257.

Mize, J., & Juvonen, J. (2003, April). The plight of aggressive victims: The worst of all worlds? In D. Schwartz (Chair), *Children who are concurrently bullied and aggressive: New directions in research on a vulnerable subgroup*. Symposium presented at the biennial meeting of the Society for Research on Child Development: Tampa, FL.

Moffitt, T. E. (1993). Adolescence-limited and life-course-persistent antisocial behavior: A developmental taxonomy. *Psychological Review, 100*, 674–701.

Mynard, H., & Joseph, S. (2000). Development of the multidimensional peer-victimization scale. *Aggressive Behavior, 26*, 169–178.

Nadeem, E., & Graham, S. (2003). Pubertal development and peer victimization among urban, minority adolescents. *Manuscript Under Review*.

Nansel, T. R., Overpeck, M., Pilla, R. S., Ruan, W. J., Simons-Morton, B., & Scheidt, P. (2001). Bullying behaviors among us youth: Prevalence and association with psychosocial adjustment. *Journal of the American Medical Association, 285*, 2094–2100.

National School Safety Center. (2000). *School associated violent deaths*. Retrieved April 17, 2000, from: http://www.nssc1.org/savd/savd.htm

Naylor, P., & Cowie, H. (1999). The effectiveness of peer support systems in challenging school bullying: The perspectives and experiences of teachers and pupils. *Journal of Adolescence*, 22, 467–479.

Neary, A., & Joseph, S. (1994). Peer victimization and its relationship to self-concept and depression among schoolgirls. *Personality and Individual Differences*, 16, 183–186.

Newman, B. M., & Newman, P. R. (2001). Group identity and alienation: Giving the we its due. *Journal of Youth and Adolescence*, 30, 515–538.

Nishina, A., & Juvonen, J. (2003). Daily reports of peer harassment and daily affects in middle school. *Manuscript Under Review*.

Nishina, A., Juvonen, J., & Leiner, W. (2001, April). Coping with peer harassment: Insights from a safe school evaluation project. In M. Prinstein (Chair), *Children's responses to peer victimization: Moderators of Psychological Adjustment*. Symposium presented at the biennial meeting of the Society for Research on Child Development: Minneapolis, MN.

Nishina, A., Juvonen, J., Witkow, M., & Federoff, N. (2003, April). Victimized by peers and feeling sick: Implications for school adjustment difficulties. In B. Kochenderfer-Ladd (Chair), *Mediators and moderators of the effects of peer victimization on children's adjustment*. Symposium presented at the biennial meeting of the Society for Research in Child Development: Tampa, FL.

Nishina, A. R. (2003). Peer victimization in school: Implications for mental health, physical symptoms, and school adjustment. *Dissertation Abstracts International*, 64 (01B), pp. 427. (UMI No. 3076598)

Oliver, R., Hoover, J. H., & Hazler, R. (1994). The perceived roles of bullying in small-town midwestern schools. *Journal of Counseling and Development*, 72, 416–420.

Olweus, D. (1978). *Aggression in the schools: Bullies and whippings boys*. Washington, DC: Hemisphere.

Olweus, D. (1991). Bully/victim problems among schoolchildren: basic facts and effects of a school based intervention program. In D. J. Pepler & K. H. Rubin, *The development and treatment of childhood aggression* (pp. 411–448). Hillsdale, NJ: Lawrence Erlbaum Associates.

Olweus, D. (1993). *Bullying at school: What we know and what we can do*. Malden, MA: Blackwell Publishers.

Olweus, D. (1997). Bully/victim problems in school: Facts and intervention. *European Journal of Psychology of Education*, 12, 495–510.

Österman, K., Björkqvist, K., Lagerspetz, K. M. J., Kaukiainen, A., Huesmann, R., & Fraczek, A. (1994). Peer and self-estimated aggression and victimization in 8-year-old children from five ethnic groups. *Aggressive Behavior*, 20, 411–428.

Owens, L., Shute, R., & Slee, P. (2000). "Guess what I just heard": Indirect aggression among teenage girls in Australia. *Aggressive Behavior*, 26, 67–83.

Pellegrini, A. D. (2001). Sampling instances of victimization in middle school: A methodological comparison. In J. Juvonen & S. Graham (Eds.), *Peer harassment in school: The plight of the vulnerable and victimized* (pp. 125–144). New York: Guilford Press.

Pellis, S. M., & Pellis, V. C. (1996). On knowing it's only play: The role of play signals in play fighting. *Aggression & Violent Behavior*, 1, 249–268.

Pepler, D. J., & Craig, W. M. (1995). A peek behind the fence: Naturalistic observations of aggressive children with remote audiovisual recording. *Developmental Psychology*, 31, 548–553.

Perry, D. G., Kusel, S. J., & Perry, L. C. (1988). Victims of peer aggression. *Developmental Psychology*, 24, 807–814.

Perry, D. G., Williard, J. C., & Perry, L. C. (1990). Peers' perceptions of the consequences that victimized children provide aggressors. *Child Development*, 61, 1310–1325.

Peterson, L., & Rigby, K. (1999). Countering bullying at an Australian secondary school with students as helpers. *Journal of Adolescence*, 22, 481–492.

Pope, A. W. (2003). Developmental risk associated with mutual dislike in elementary school children. In E. V. E. Hodges & N. A. Card (Eds.), *Enemies and the darker side of peer relations*. San Francisco: Jossey-Bass.

Ray, J. C., & Sapolsky, R. M. (1992). Styles of male social behavior and their endocrine correlates among high-ranking wild baboons. *American Journal of Primatology*, 28, 231–250.

Rigby, K. (1996). *Bullying in schools—And what to do about it.* Melbourne, Australia: ACER.

Rigby, K. (1999). Peer victimisation at school and the health of secondary school students. *British Journal of Educational Psychology, 69,* 95–104.

Rigby, K., & Slee, P. T. (1991). Bullying among Australian school children: Reported behavior and attitudes toward victims. *Journal of Social Psychology, 131,* 615–627.

Rivers, I., & Smith, P. K. (1994). Types of bullying behaviour and their correlates. *Aggressive Behavior, 20,* 359–368.

Rodkin, P. C., Farmer, T. W., Pearl, R., & Van Acker, R. (2000). Heterogeneity of popular boys: Antisocial and prosocial configurations. *Developmental Psychology, 36,* 14–24.

Romero, P. A., Card, N. A., & Hodges, E. V. E. (2001, April). *Common targets of aggression among reciprocated friends, unilateral friends, and neutral peers.* Poster session presented at the biennial meeting of the Society for Research in Child Development: Minneapolis, MN.

Salmivalli, C. (2001). Group view on victimization: Empirical findings and their implications. In J. Juvonen & S. Graham (Eds.), *Peer harassment in school: The plight of the vulnerable and victimized* (pp. 398–419). New York: Guilford Press.

Salmivalli, C., Huttunen, A., & Lagerspetz, K. M. J. (1997). Peer networks and bullying in schools. *Scandinavian Journal of Psychology, 38,* 305–312.

Salmivalli, C., Lagerspetz, K., Björkqvist, K., Österman, K., & Kaukiainen, (1996). Bullying as a group process: Participant roles and their relations to social status within the group. *Aggressive Behavior, 22,* 1–15.

Sapolsky, R. M., & Ray, J. C. (1989). Styles of dominance and their endocrine correlates among wild olive baboons (*Papio anubis*). *American Journal of Primatology, 18,* 1–13.

Sapolsky, R. M., & Share, L. J. (1994). Rank-related differences in cardiovascular function among wild baboons: Role of sensitivity to glucocorticoids. *American Journal of Primatology, 32,* 261–275.

Scambler, D. J., Harris, M. J., & Milich, R. (1998). Sticks and stones: Evaluations of responses to childhood teasing. *Social Development, 7,* 234–249.

Schuster, B. (1996). Rejection, exclusion, and harassment at work and in schools. *European Psychologist, 1,* 293–309.

Schwartz, D. (2000). Subtypes of victims and aggressors in children's peer groups. *Journal of Abnormal Child Psychology, 28,* 181–192.

Schwartz, D., Chang, L., & Farver, J. M. (2001). Correlates of victimization in Chinese children's peer groups. *Developmental Psychology, 37,* 520–532.

Schwartz, D., Dodge, K. A., & Coie, J. D. (1993). The emergence of chronic peer victimization in boys' play groups. *Child Development, 64,* 1755–1772.

Schwartz, D., Farver, J. M., Chang, L., & Lee-Shin, Y. (2002). Victimization in South Korean children's peer groups. *Journal of Abnormal Child Psychology, 30,* 113–125.

Schwartz, D., Proctor, L. J., & Chien, D. H. (2001). The aggressive victim of bullying: Emotional and behavioral dysregulation as a pathway to victimization by peers. In J. Juvonen & S. Graham (Eds.), *Peer harassment in school: The plight of the vulnerable and victimized.* New York: Guilford Press.

Sherif, M., Harvey, O. J., White, B. J., Hood, W. R., & Sherif, C. W. (1961). *Intergroup cooperation and competition: The Robbers Cave experiment.* Norman, OK: University Book Exchange.

Shute, R., Owens, L., & Slee, P. (2002). "You just stare at them and give them daggers": Nonverbal expressions of social aggression in teenage girls. *International Journal of Adolescence and Youth, 10,* 353–372.

Siann, G., Callaghan, M., Lockhart, R., & Rawson, L. (1993). Bullying: Teachers' views and school effects. *Educational Studies, 19,* 307–321.

Sidanius, J. (1993). The psychology of group conflict and the dynamics of oppression: A social dominance perspective. In S. Iyengar & W. J. McGuire (Eds.), *Explorations in Political Psychology* (pp. 183–219). Durham, NC: Duke University Press.

Sidanius, J., & Pratto, F. (1999). *Social dominance: An intergroup theory of social hierarchy and oppression.* New York: Cambridge University Press.

Slee, P. T. (1993). Bullying: A preliminary investigation of its nature and the effects of social cognition. *Early Child Development and Care, 87*, 47–57.

Slee, P. T. (1994). Situational and interpersonal correlates of anxiety associated with peer victimisation. *Child Psychiatry and Human Development, 25*, 97–107.

Smith, P. K., Cowie, H., Olafsson, R. F., Liefooghe, A. P. D., Almeida, A., Araki, H., Del Barrio, C., *et al.* (2002). Definitions of bullying: A comparison of terms used, and age and gender differences, in a fourteen-country international comparison. *Child Development, 73*, 1119–1133.

Stavisky, R. C., Adams, M. R., Watson, S. L., & Kaplan, J. R. (2001). Dominance, cortisol, and behavior in small groups of female Cynomolgus monkeys (*Macaca fascicularis*). *Hormones and Behavior, 39*, 232–238.

Stevens, V., Van Oost, P., & de Bourdeaudhuij, I. (2000). The effects of an anti-bullying intervention programme on peers' attitudes and behaviour. *Journal of Adolescence, 23*, 21–34.

Taylor, S. E., Aspinwall, L. G., & Giuliano, T. A. (1994). Emotions as psychological achievements. In S. H. M. van Goozen & N. E. Van de Poll (Eds.), *Emotions: Essays on emotion theory* (pp. 219–239). Hillsdale, NJ: Lawrence Erlbaum Associates.

Teräsahjo, T., & Salmivalli, C. (2003). "She is not actually bullied." The discourse of harassment in student groups. *Aggressive Behavior, 29*, 134–154.

Trivers, R. L. (1971). The evolution of reciprocal altruism. *The Quarterly Review of Biology, 46*, 35–57.

Virgin, C. E., & Sapolsky, R. M. (1997). Styles of male social behavior and their endocrine correlates among low-ranking baboons. *American Journal of Primatology, 42*, 25–39.

Weiner, A. B. (1988). *The Trobrianders of Papua New Guinea.* Orlando, FL: Holt, Rinehard, and Winston.

Williams, K., Chambers, M., Logan, S., & Robinson, D. (1996). Associations of common health symptoms with bullying in primary school children. *British Medical Journal, 313*, 17–19.

Xu, Y., Farver, J. A. M., Schwartz, D., & Chang, L. (2003). Identifying aggressive victims in Chinese children's peer groups. *International Journal of Behavioral Development, 27*, 243–252.

## Author's Note

Portions of this chapter are based on a doctoral dissertation by Adrienne Nishina completed at the University of California, Los Angeles. Preparation of this chapter was supported in part by a NSRA from the National Institute of Mental Health (2T32MH18372) and a Charles Scott Fellowship. I am especially grateful to Jaana Juvonen, Amy Bellmore, Noel Card, Sandra Graham, and Melissa Witkow for providing helpful insight and suggestions on earlier versions of this chapter.

CHAPTER

4

# In the Looking Glass: A Reciprocal Effects Model Elucidating the Complex Nature of Bullying, Psychological Determinants, and the Central Role of Self-Concept

HERBERT W. MARSH, ROBERTO H. PARADA, RHONDA
G. CRAVEN, & LINDA FINGER
*Self Research Center University of Western Sydney Australia*

## INTRODUCTION

This chapter addresses the multidimensional self-concepts and other personality characteristics of bullies and victims. We begin with a focused review, emphasizing the Marsh, Parada, Yeung, & Healey (2001) study based on the large, nationally representative National Education Longitudinal Study (NELS) 88 U.S. database that included the eighth, tenth, and twelfth grades. Using this literature review, we demonstrate the complex relations between self-concept, other personality characteristics, being a bully, and being a victim of bullying. Based on our previous research, we developed new, psychometrically stronger measures of bullying and victimization and revealed new attitudes toward these behaviors. In a large-scale, longitudinal study we relate our new measures of bullying and victimization as well as new related attitudes to multiple dimensions of self-concept and to measures of depression, locus of control, and coping styles. We then evaluate how the pattern of relations varies with gender and age (12 to 18 years of age).

Capitalizing on the longitudinal nature of our study, we pursue longitudinal causal modeling studies in which we attempt to disentangle the order of causality of bullying and victimization with other self-concept and personality constructs considered in our research. Intriguing questions include:

- Are bullies and victims more alike than different?
- Does a student's low self-concept and depression make him or her vulnerable to bullying or are these merely by-products of being a victim?
- Do school bullies successfully use bullying behaviors as a strategy to enhance their self-concepts and reduce depression?

## BACKGROUND

### The Nature of Bullying

Bullying is a growing and significant problem in many schools around the world (Olweus, 1997). Bullying is a deliberate act designed to inflict physical and psychological harm. It involves a person's or group's intentional, hurtful action directed toward one person or more than one person and involves a complex interplay of dominance and social status (Sutton, Smith, & Swettenham, 1999). Bullying incorporates a wide range of aggressive and social behaviors such as name-calling, extortion, physical violence, slander, group exclusion, damage to property, and verbal intimidation (Smith & Sharp, 1994). Whereas aggression may involve a singular action by individuals or groups against each other and tends to be time-limited (Feshbach & Zagrodzka, 1997), bullying is typically repetitive in nature, whereby bullies continue to bully victims for extended periods of time (Rigby, 1996). Bullying also involves a power imbalance between the bully and victim characterized by a victim's inability to defend him or herself against the bully (Olweus, 1997). The imbalance of power might, but does not necessarily, include physical superiority over the victim (Lagerspetz et al., 1982). The imbalance can also be caused by group membership or affiliation (i.e,. the bully may belong to a gang, a group with intellectual superiority, or a group with a racial or ethnic composition different to that of the victim). An imbalance can also exist if the victim holds certain attitudes and beliefs. For example, victims may be scared of a bully, or victims may hold beliefs that prevent them from resorting to violence to defend themselves (Parada, 2002). The key factor is that bullies, for their own benefit, exploit this imbalance of power to dominate the victim repeatedly in an unwelcome way such that the victim does not welcome this domination and is harmed or disadvantaged in some way.

At least one in six Australian students are bullied on a weekly basis at school (Rigby, 1996). Similar figures have been found in schools in Canada, Scandinavia, Ireland, and England (Smith et al., 1999). Research regarding bullying rates in the United States has been limited by the fact that representative surveys have largely concentrated on violence and aggression in schools and have to some extent ignored other typical components of bullying. Studies that have attempted to look at the incidence of bullying in the United States provide bullying rates ranging from 10% for third through sixth graders to 29% for middle school students who self-reported engaging in bullying behavior in the previous 30 days (Harachi, Catalano & Hawkins, 1999). Nansel *et al.* (2001) reported on results from a stratified nationally representative sample of 15,686 U.S. students in the sixth through tenth grades. This survey differed from most available prevalence estimates in the United States because it was nationally representative and it contained items specifically designed to measure bullying rates. Questions were preceded with a definition of bullying in which key aspects of the bullying phenomenon were outlined (*viz, repetition, harm*, and *imbalance of power*) and students were asked to respond thinking about their current school term. Overall, 8.5% of students reported being victimized at least on a weekly basis, and 8.8% of the sample reported bullying others at the same frequency. Minor differences in frequency of bullying and no significant differences in the frequency of being bullied were observed among youth from urban, suburban, town, and rural areas. Bullying was more prevalent among males than females and among middle school than high school students in the United States. Nansel *et al.* concluded "bullying is a serious problem for U.S. youth" (p. 5) with a national estimate of more than 1.5 million students bullying and being bullied at least on a weekly basis.

Based on research examining gender and developmental differences in children's aggressiveness (Bjöerkqvist, Lagerspetz, & Kaukiainen, 1992) bullying behaviors have been classified into two distinct categories: *direct* and *indirect bullying* (Rivers & Smith, 1994). Direct bullying is characterised by behaviors that involve hitting, kicking, pinching, taking money or belongings, name-calling, teasing, taunting, and threatening (Wolke, Woods, Bloomfield, & Karstadt, 2000). Crick and Grotpeter (1995) define indirect bullying/aggression as mainly peer relational in kind. Indirect bullying is characterized by the hurtful manipulation of peer relationships/friendships to inflict harm on others through behaviors such as social exclusion and rumor spreading. The direct or indirect nature of bullying is therefore primarily defined by which method is used to bully the target, whereas direct methods are characterized by overt behaviors (e.g., verbal and physical bullying).

Based on these categories, many studies have also suggested the indirect/direct typology may be further differentiated into distinct subcategories of bullying behaviors. At least three have been suggested: *physical, verbal, anti-social/relational* (Björkqvist, *et al.* 1992; Crick *et al.*, 2001; Rigby & Slee, 1999; Salmivalli, Kaukiainen, & Lagerspetz, 2000). Mynard and Joseph (2000) reported on the development of a multidimensional peer-victimization self-report scale that was intended to evaluate direct and indirect forms of bullying. Participants were 812 children, aged 11 to 16 years, in secondary school in England. Students responded on a three-point scale (0 = Not at all, 1 = Once, and 2 = More than once) to 45 items describing different forms of bullying acts (e.g., "called me names," "punched me," and "told a lie about me"). Exploratory factor analysis, after excluding 29 of the original items, revealed four factors: *physical, verbal, social manipulation*, and *attacks on property*. Mynard and Joseph's study suggests that it may be possible that a direct/indirect conceptualization of bullying may be composed of additional subtypes, making bullying behaviors multidimensional in nature. However, other studies have not made any advances on this important issue. This is particularly frustrating considering the widespread practice in other areas of inquiry (e.g., self-concept, intelligence, and personality research) for verifying underlying constructs through the use of strong statistical methods such as confirmatory factor analysis. Such analyses would help to elucidate the nature and structure of these constructs, serve to inform theory, and underpin the development of appropriate measurement and research.

## The Consequences of Bullying

A substantial body of evidence has documented the array of detrimental long-term negative effects of bullying on victims and perpetrators (Bernstein & Watson, 1997; Nansel *et al.*, 2001). Involvement in school bullying has been empirically identified as a contributing factor to peer rejection (Deater-Deckard, 2001), delinquent behavior (Rigby & Cox, 1996), criminality (Eron *et al.*, 1987), psychological disturbance (Kumpulainen, Räsäen, & Henttonen, 1999), further violence in the school (Galinsky & Salmond, 2002), depression (Kaltiala-Heino *et al.*, 1999), and suicidal ideation (Rigby & Slee, 1999). These effects have been found to continue into adulthood for both the perpetrators of bullying and victims of those perpetrators (Olweus, 1993). Research has also found that male adolescents who report being frequent victims of bullying are more likely than others to approve of husbands abusing their wives (Rigby, Black, & Whish, 1993).

Engaging in bullying also has adverse consequences for bullies. A link between bullying behaviors at school and future criminality, poor mental health, and diminished school performance has been identified. The mental health problem most commonly associated with school bullying is depression. In addition, high levels of engagement in peer bullying have been associated with delinquent behavior (Rigby & Cox, 1996). International studies examining the onset of criminal behavior patterns have demonstrated that antisocial and criminal acts begin early in adolescence and are extremely stable over time (Farrington, 1995). Hence, bullies may be more likely to engage in teenage delinquent behavior, suffer from depression, have a diminished ability to perform at full potential in school, and engage in criminal behaviors after leaving school. For example, Eron *et al.* (1987) showed that aggressive bullies identified by age eight had about a 1 in 4 chance of having a criminal record by age 30 compared to other children who had 1 in 20 chance. Similarly, Olweus (1991) reported that 60% of boys identified as bullies in the sixth through ninth grades had at least one conviction at age 24, and 35 to 40% had three or more convictions.

Bullying also impacts schools and communities. Schools where bullying takes place are often characterized by (a) students feeling unsafe at school, (b) a sense of not belonging and unconnectedness to the school community, (c) distrust among students, (d) formation of formal and informal gangs as a means to either instigate bullying or protect the group from bullying, (e) legal action being taken against the school by students and parents, (f) low reputation of the school in the community, (f) low staff morale and higher occupational stress, (g) and a poor educational climate (Glover, Cartwright, & Gleeson, 1998; Hoover & Oliver, 1996). Approximately 14% of students believed that being exposed to bullying has a severe impact on their lives (Hoover, Oliver, & Hazler, 1992).

## Gender Differences in Bullying

Gender differences have been observed in school bullying. An extensive body of literature suggests that boys are more likely than girls to be bullies as well as victims (Nansel et al. 2001; Boulton & Smith, 1994; Boulton & Underwood, 1992). Although "maleness" itself is probably not a causal factor as some have suggested (Egger, 1995), the social and situational forces that combine with masculinity may well be. Thus school bullying, in particular, seems to be more frequent among boys than girls and among younger than older students. For example, Rigby and Slee (1993) identified 10% of 201 boys aged 7 to 13 compared to 6% of 211 girls as victims of school bullying. Girls, however, may engage in more covert forms of indirect bullying behaviors such as spreading rumors, social rejection, and exclusion (Crick & Grotpeter, 1995; Björkqvist et al., 1992; Crick, Bigbee, & Howes, 1996) making the actual rates of bullying/victimization attributed to girls possibly underestimated. Wolke and colleagues (2000) have reported that young boys are equally or more likely to be involved in relational bullying. They contend that gender differences in previous research may have been the result of methodological artifacts. They explain that different methodologies and instruments have been used to assess the incidence of bullying behavior types. This claim is supported by Tulloch (1995) who found that boys used excluding and ignoring tactics more than girls. Establishing whether gender differences make a person more prone to bullying is of great importance as there may be a need to differentially administer, evaluate, and monitor bullying based on these differences.

## Who Are the Victims and the Bullies?

Factors that promote aggressive and victimizing behaviors within school have been the focus of only a few studies. These studies found that in contrast to commonly held beliefs, bullying is not a result of large or small class sizes or academic competition, and although a student has personal characteristics that deviate markedly from the norm may contribute to making that person a target of bullying, their contribution is not significant. The only physical characteristic that has been associated with victimization is physical strength (Olweus, 1997). Victims tend to be physically weaker than their bullies. Demographic characteristics such as age and gender have been consistently associated with victimizing others. Boys tend to bully more than girls, and there seems to be a decline in victimization with an increase of age (Rigby, 1996). Psychological or cognitive explanations about why particular students engage in bullying have largely concentrated on cognitive deficit theories. The general consensus has been that bullies are deficient in social information processing or may be intellectually disadvantaged (Besag, 1989). Advocates of this view have generally referred to the aggression and conduct disorder literature to justify their claims. Much of the work in this area has stemmed from Crick and Dodge (1994) who proposed a social cognition model that explains responses to social situations as being mediated by a filtering process. This "cognitive filter" is biased in aggressive individuals, interpreting neutral or ambiguous cues as hostile and therefore making them more likely to engage in aggressive behaviors. Bosworth, Espelage, and Simon (1999), for example, found in a sample of adolescent high school students that misconduct, anger, and beliefs supportive of violence were significantly related to bullying behaviors. Pellegrini, Bartini, and Brooks (1999), studying a sample of primary school students, found that proactive aggression (aggression that is used instrumentally to achieve some end) and reactive aggression (aggression used as a response to provocation or used after losing control) were both related to engagement in bullying.

Sutton *et al.* (1999), however, have questioned the assumption that all bullies are cognitively deficient decoders of peer interactions. They have argued that although bullying is an aggressive act, this does not imply that bullies and aggressive or conduct-disordered individuals are a homogenous group. Sutton and colleagues pointed out that bullying is in fact always an interaction that occurs within a complex social environment. Bullies are part of highly structured social groups that require of them the ability to negotiate and attribute mental states to themselves and others to explain or predict their behavior, otherwise referred to as *theory of mind*. This is exemplified by the types of bullying in which students engage, particularly indirect bullying such as exclusion. A bully employing exclusion needs an understanding of who is a safe target, who will join them in excluding the target, what kind of reasons peers will consider justifiable to engage in excluding other students, and mobilizing such cognitions to incite other students to exclude the target. Such sophisticated cognitions contravene the notion that bullies are cognitively inept or simple in their interactions with peers (Sutton *et al.*, 1999). Further research is therefore needed to examine the contributing factors that lead students to victimize others.

The factors that predict victimization are also elusive. Olweus has found no support for other physical factors such as weight, wearing glasses, type of clothing, or the way the victim speaks as reliably predicting victimization. Ultimately, any explanation of how bullying behaviors come to be maintained must be able to reconcile students' individual attributes and the fact that bullying occurs within a complex social setting. To date, research has largely concentrated on an individualistic, mainly pathological, understanding of the origin of bullying (Sullivan, 2000; Rigby, 1996; Besag, 1989) and has to a large extent neglected how social aspects of peer interactions may be responsible for initiating and/or maintaining bullying dyads or groups. This is particularly relevant when evidence drawn from large-scale interviews with children in the United States has highlighted that the reasons for victimizing a student may not be rational but relational (Glover *et al.*, 1998). A victim may therefore be targeted for numerous reasons. It is likely that being a victim has as much to do with the social milieu in which the students find themselves as it does to their personal characteristics.

### Rethinking Bipolar Classification Schemes and Dichotomizing Bully and Victim Variables

The measurement of bullying and victimization in schools has largely been dominated by the use of simple surveys. Typically, intervention studies have used questionnaires based on a single item to define the various bullying constructs such as direct, indirect, verbal, or physical bullying and victimization (Rigby, 1996; Smith & Sharp, 1994). Based on their review research examining victimization and mental health studies from 1980 to 2000, Hawker and Boulton (2000) concluded that the complexity of the bullying phenomenon has been largely ignored in measuring bullying. In studies looking at the link between victimization and depression, for example, "only one study measured relational or indirect victimization, and this study did not include verbal victimization [and] only one study used more than one item to assess peer-reported victimization" (p. 447). Bosworth *et al.* (1999) have highlighted several shortcomings of recent international efforts to measure bullying in the school. These include studies that have concentrated on the extreme ends of what may very well be a continuum of bullying behaviors by excluding students who report low and moderate levels of bullying or by collapsing participants into categories of students who are at the extreme of bullying/victimization archetypes. Shortcomings also include presenting students with a definition of bullying prior to asking them to self-report their engagement in such behavior, which might increase social desirability bias, particularly when the definition contains negative connotations. Bosworth and colleagues therefore advocate a continuum approach to the measurement of bullying, recommending that it may be more appropriate to "simply ask students about the frequency of specific behaviors such as teasing and hitting" (Bosworth *et al.*, 1999, p. 343).

Problems in the classification and measurement of bullying and being bullied are due in part to historical tendencies to classify students as bullies or victims. We now know that this is inappropriate for a variety of reasons. It is important to note that this simplistic classification schema is based on an implicit model that treated being a bully and being a victim was mutually exclusive or bipolar opposite patterns of behaviors. However, a growing body of research—including our own—shows that the two tend to be positively correlated. Whereas there is ongoing debate about the size, nature, and underlying processes associated with this positive correlation, the correlation is clearly not the $-1.0$ correlation that would be consistent with the mutually exclusive or bipolar classification schemes. This underlying assumption has led to another inappropriate and more common practice of dichotomizing the bully and victim continuums. This practice is typically based on overly simplistic classification schemes or misguided attempts to simplify statistical analyses. In some cases, measures used to classify students only result in a dichotomous bully (i.e., bully/not bully) and victim scores. More frequently, however, researchers devise dubious cut-off values to classify students with scores that vary along an underlying continuum of being a bully or a victim. Although this practice has been broadly recognized as largely inappropriate in psychological research for more than a quarter of a century, the practice is still widespread. MacCallum *et al.* (2002) highlighted problems associated with dichotomizing continuous variables which include reduced effect sizes and statistical significance, differences between variables that existed prior to dichotomization to be considered as equal when dichotomized, distortion of effects, and the potential of researchers to overlook nonlinear relationships.

The positive correlation between bullying and being bullied has been observed in many studies around the world (Harachi *et al.*, 1999); however, there have been few attempts to explain the correlation. Besag (1989) followed the dichotomizing tradition and suggested that these "provocative victims" were another subgroup of victim types. We believe that this positive correlation suggests that these might be mutually reinforcing roles whereby prior bullying behavior may lead to later victimization, and prior victimization may lead to later bullying behavior. In some students, therefore, being a victim makes them more likely to be *bullies* while some bullies may fall prey to even bigger bullies, thus becoming victims themselves. This suggests, perhaps, a dynamic pattern of reciprocal relations in which students drop in and out of bully-victim roles over time. Testing causal hypotheses of this type requires, at a minimum, longitudinal models. In terms of research and theory, longitudinal causal findings would implicate the way in which those who bully and those who are victimized are viewed. Hence, bully and victim roles would not be seen as separate entities, but rather as mutually reinforcing roles that co-occur for those involved. Viewing bullying and victimization as mutually reinforcing roles and explaining the causal relations between being a bully and being a victim can help explain how certain characteristics are more likely to instigate bullying behavior or becoming victimized. The explanation can also shed light on how bullying and victimization directly—negatively and/or positively—affect psychological factors, specifically self-concept.

## SELF-CONCEPT AND ITS ROLE IN BULLYING RESEARCH

### A Multidimensional Perspective on Self-Concept

Historically, self-concept research has suffered in that "everybody knows what it is" so that researchers have not felt compelled to provide a theoretical basis or psychometric evaluation of their self-concept measures. In an attempt to remedy this problem, Shavelson, Hubner, and Stanton (1976) developed a multifaceted, hierarchical model of self-concept in which general self-concept was divided into specific domains (e.g., *social*, *physical*, *emotional*, and *academic*). These domains were further subdivided into specific facets (e.g., *relations with same/opposite sex*, *relations with parents*, *math self-concept*, and *physical abilities self-concept*). This theoretical model was so important that it provided the blueprint for the development of a new generation of multidimensional self-concept instruments that are the basis of considerable advances in the quality of self-concept research due to the development of stronger theoretical models (Marsh & Shavelson, 1985), improved methodology, and stronger interventions (e.g., Craven, Marsh, & Debus, 1991; Marsh & Craven, 1997). Our research program (at the Self-Concept Enhancement and Learning Facilitation (SELF) Research Center) has contributed to important advances in self-concept research. These include (1) critical tests of the Shavelson model and its subsequent refinement (e.g., Marsh, 1993; Marsh & Shavelson, 1985; Marsh, Byrne, & Shavelson, 1988), (2) the development of the Self-Description Questionnaire (SDQ) instruments that are internationally regarded as the strongest multidimensional measures for school-aged students (Boyle, 1994; Byrne, 1996; Hattie, 1992; Wylie; 1989), (3) innovative self-concept enhancement interventions (Craven, 1996; Craven, *et al.* 1991), and (4) new methodologies for evaluating self-concept interventions (Marsh, & Craven, 1997; Craven, Marsh, & Burnett, 2003).

### Self-Concept of Bullies and Victims

The role of self-concept in bullies and victims might provide insights into why students engage in bullying and why they remain victims. Staub (1999) proposed that bullies might not have the socially valued means to gain a positive self-concept through competence and good performance at school. Therefore, bullies organize their self-esteem around strength, power, and physical superiority over others. Harming others may become a way of reaffirming self-identity and of compensating for frustration in other areas, such that students engage in behaviors to protect and enhance their self-concept. Behaviors that enhance students' self-concepts and that are re-inforced by fellow students and teachers are more likely to be repeated. Hay (2000) examined the self-concepts of high school students who had been suspended from their schools for persistent behavior problems (e.g., in-class disruption and verbal or physical aggression). Total self-concept scores using the Self-Description Questionnaire II (Marsh, 1988) for both boys and girls were low compared to norms, suggesting that school troublemaking is associated with an overall low self-concept. Overall, bullies' self-concepts may be low, which may serve as a motivating factor for bullies to enhance aspects of their self-concept by engaging in bullying behaviors. Hence, bullies might achieve a personal sense of power as a consequence of their victimization behaviors and might receive social reinforcement from peers for bullying.

Salmivalli et al. (1999) measured peer and self-evaluated self-esteem among 14- to 15-year-olds and found no evidence to suggest bullies have anything other than a slightly above average self-esteem, combined with narcissistic and self-grandiose tendencies. However, just because bullies may perceive themselves to be well-liked does not mean they actually are. Randall (1995) suggested that people who use bullying behaviors see themselves as superior and powerful, but that this belief may not be a true reflection of what others really think of them. Using bullying behaviors may get children what they want because others are afraid of them, not because they are respected or liked. A study of 12- to 13-year-old children by Salmivalli et al. (1996) found bullies were not popular (but not as unpopular as victims), contradicting self-perceptions they may hold of themselves. Comparatively, Luthar and McMahon (1996) found peer popularity to be linked to both prosocial and aggressive behavior in adolescence. Aggressive children (including bullies) tend to overestimate their competencies, and children who overestimate their peer acceptance are more likely to be nominated by their peers as aggressive (Bowker & Woody, 1993; Juvonen, Nishina & Graham, 2001).

Empirical findings to support the suggestion that bullies have positive perceptions of themselves have been somewhat inconsistent; findings suggest that more aggressive individuals can have either high or low self-concepts). For example, Salmivalli (1998) reported adolescent bullies had high social and physical self-concepts, but more negative self-perceptions in other areas, such as in academic self-concept (Salmivalli, 2001). These results suggest that bullies' social and physical self-concepts are reinforced by engaging in bullying while other aspects of self-concept remain low. In this same study, victims had low scores in most self-concept domains. There was, however, a group of victimized students who still reported high self-concept in the areas of family-related and behavioral self-concept. Hence, evidence suggests that the role of self-concept in relation to bullying and victimization is a complex phenomenon that could be further disentangled by taking into consideration the multidimensionality of self-concept.

To date, there have been a number of studies that looked at self-concept in relation to victimization. A consistent negative correlation was found between being bullied and global self-concept (Neary & Joseph, 1994; Rigby & Cox, 1996; Stanley & Arora, 1998). Studies that have looked at specific aspects of self-concept, such as social self-concept, have generally found that victims tend to have negative self-views regarding their social competency or being well accepted by their peers (Callaghan & Stephen, 1995; Hawker & Boulton, 2000). This offers evidence supporting a downward spiral for victims of bullying, which may help to perpetuate their victim status. Investigating this spiral further, Egan and Perry (1998) tested two hypotheses in relation to self-regard and victimization. First, they studied whether low self-regard contributed over time to victimization by peers. Second, they analyzed whether high or low self-regard had any protective function in children with personal characteristics such as physical weakness, anxiousness, and poor social skills. Egan and Perry's results supported the view that low self-concept leads to further victimization over time. In addition, among children with undesirable social characteristics, children with high self-concept were less likely to become caught up in victimization over time.

Marsh *et al.* (2001) found that aggressive school troublemaker factors (getting into physical fights, getting into trouble, being labeled troublemakers, and being punished for getting into trouble) and victim factors (being threatened, not feeling safe) were related to three components of self-concept (*general self-esteem, same sex relations,* and *opposite sex relations,* adapted from the SDQ II) based on the large North American representative National Education Longitudinal Study (NELS). Longitudinal structural equation models for the same students in the eighth, tenth, and twelfth grades showed that the *troublemaker* and *victim* constructs were reasonably stable over time and positively correlated. This offers further support for the finding that many students are both troublemakers and victims (Forero *et al.,* 1999). Whereas the *aggressive-troublemaker* factor was also correlated somewhat negatively with self-concepts, the troublemaker factor had small positive effects on subsequent self-concept. This suggests that low self-concept may trigger troublemaking behavior in a possibly successful attempt to enhance subsequent self-concept. Bullies in particular may achieve a personal sense of power and may receive social reinforcement from their peers for engaging in bullying behaviors that result in the intimidation of their victims. Although boys had higher troublemaker and victim scores than girls, the effects of these constructs on subsequent self-concept were similar for boys and girls. Victims also tended to have negative social self-concepts in terms of seeing themselves as socially competent or accepted by their peers. A downward spiral existed for victims of bullying whereby being bullied led to lower self-concepts and perpetuated their victim status within the group or school. It seems therefore that the effect of being bullied on self-concept is clearly a negative one. Although bullying may serve to increase the self-concept of bullies, being bullied decreases the self-concept of victims.

The Marsh *et al.* (2001) study was an important application of structural equation modeling based on longitudinal data for a large nationally representative sample, but it suffered several potential weaknesses that the present investigation addresses. Because the study was based on existing data from a large generic survey, the authors were limited to available data. In particular, there was not a fully adequate measure of bullying that could be considered, and so the researchers used a somewhat different construct that they called "troublemaking." Whereas measures of general self-concept were collected at all three waves, the measures of same sex and opposite sex self-concepts were only available in the second wave. Finally, there might have been more active or passive reinforcement of bullying in the late 1980s and early 1990s, providing a basis for bullies to enhance their self-concept. Hence, it is important to replicate, refine, and expand on the Marsh *et al.* (2001) research.

In summary, research suggests that being a victim is negatively correlated with self-concept and may lead to further declines in the victim's self-concept. Less clear is the causal role of a high self-concept in protecting students from being bullied. The nature and role of self-concept for bullies is even more complex and less well understood. There is no consistent support for the direction of the correlation between self-concept and bullying, which might vary depending on the particular component of self-concept. Some support exists for the suggestion that low self-concept causes students to bully so that they may enhance self-concept or that bullying may become a way of reaffirming self-identity and compensate for frustration in other areas. There is, however, limited research on the causal role of self-concept and bullying. Available studies have generally been cross-sectional, examining relations among variables at a single point in time. Research has also relied upon constructs derived from large-scale surveys not specifically designed to measure bullying or victimization or from psychometrically weak measures of bully-victim constructs. More generally, previous research has been plagued with a lack of theory, a lack of appropriate measures with demonstrated reliability and construct validity, weak research designs, and weak statistical analyses. Theory, research, methodology, and practice are all inextricably intertwined so that problems in any one area will adversely affect the others.

# THE PRESENT INVESTIGATION

The present investigation is part of an ongoing research program designed to decrease bullying in schools. Here we consider responses from a large sample of approximately 4000 students in the seventh through eleventh grades (ages 12 to 18) from eight urban nongovernment schools located in Western Sydney collected on three occasions during a single school year. Teachers received training on the administration of instrumentation. The extensive survey instrument (see Appendix for a summary of scales, scale reliabilities, and sample items) was specifically designed to measure bullying and being bullied (the bully and victim subscales of The Adolescent Peer Relations Instrument, Parada, 2000), associated attitudes and behaviors, multiple dimensions of self-concept (based on a new short version of the SDQ II [Marsh, 2000]) and relevant personality correlates. Preliminary confirmatory factor analyses of responses to 190 items provided clear support for *a priori* factors that the battery of measures was designed to measure (see Appendix).

The present investigation aims to address issues relevant to understanding bullies and victims by (a) developing and testing the psychometric properties of an instrument specifically designed to measure bullying and victimization and associated attitudes and behaviors; (b) testing the effects of age and gender in relation to bullying and victims; (c) evaluating relations between measures of bullying and victims, multiple dimensions of self-concept, and other personality correlates; (d) using structural equation models of longitudinal data to disentangle the causal processes underlying the positive correlation between being a bully and a victim; and (e) elucidating the role of self-concept by extending these causal ordering models of longitudinal data to include measures of self-concept and depression.

## Results

### The Factor Structure of a New Instrument to Assess Bullies and Victims

Confirmatory factor analyses (CFAs) were conducted on responses to the 36 items of the Adolescent Peer Relations Instruments (APRI) that were designed to measure six *a priori* scale factors. Reliabilities were acceptable for the three bully factors (*physical-bully*, *verbal-bully*, and *social-bully*; alpha coefficients .82 to .92, see Appendix) and for the three corresponding victim factors (*physical-victim*, *verbal-victim*, and *social-victim*; alpha coefficients .87 to .93, see Appendix). We tested a highly restrictive CFA model in which each item was allowed to load on only the factor it was designed to measure (see Figure 1a). This model (see Table 1) provided an exceptionally good fit to the data (TLI = .98, RMSEA = .05). Each of the items loaded substantially on the

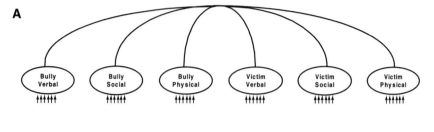

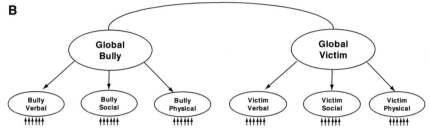

**FIGURE 1.**

First-Order Bully and Victim Factors (A), and Higher-Order
Bully and Victim Factors (B).

**TABLE 1**
**Confirmatory Factor Analysis of Bully-Victim Scales**

|  | Bully | | | Victim | | | |
|---|---|---|---|---|---|---|---|
|  | Verb | Soc | Phys | Verb | Soc | Phys | UNIQ |
| Factor Loadings |  |  |  |  |  |  |  |
| Bully |  |  |  |  |  |  |  |
| Verb1 | .74 |  |  |  |  |  | .46 |
| Verb2 | .80 |  |  |  |  |  | .37 |
| Verb3 | .75 |  |  |  |  |  | .44 |
| Verb4 | .74 |  |  |  |  |  | .45 |
| Verb5 | .70 |  |  |  |  |  | .51 |
| Verb6 | .81 |  |  |  |  |  | .34 |
| Soc 1 |  | .67 |  |  |  |  | .55 |
| Soc 2 |  | .70 |  |  |  |  | .51 |
| Soc 3 |  | .62 |  |  |  |  | .62 |
| Soc 4 |  | .71 |  |  |  |  | .50 |
| Soc 5 |  | .66 |  |  |  |  | .57 |
| Soc 6 |  | .61 |  |  |  |  | .62 |
| Phys1 |  |  | 73 |  |  |  | .47 |
| Phys2 |  |  | 71 |  |  |  | .50 |
| Phys3 |  |  | 60 |  |  |  | .64 |
| Phys4 |  |  | 72 |  |  |  | .48 |
| Phys5 |  |  | 76 |  |  |  | .42 |
| Phys6 |  |  | 69 |  |  |  | .52 |

**TABLE I**

| | | Bully | | | Victim | | |
|---|---|---|---|---|---|---|---|
| | Verb | Soc | Phys | Verb | Soc | Phys | UNIQ |
| **Victim** | | | | | | | |
| Verb1 | | | | .78 | | | .38 |
| Verb2 | | | | .81 | | | .35 |
| Verb3 | | | | .84 | | | .30 |
| Verb4 | | | | .79 | | | .38 |
| Verb5 | | | | .81 | | | .34 |
| Verb6 | | | | .85 | | | .28 |
| Soc 1 | | | | | .73 | | .47 |
| Soc 2 | | | | | .69 | | .52 |
| Soc 3 | | | | | .78 | | .39 |
| Soc 4 | | | | | .73 | | .46 |
| Soc 5 | | | | | .76 | | .42 |
| Soc 6 | | | | | .74 | | .45 |
| Phys1 | | | | | | .74 | .45 |
| Phys2 | | | | | | .76 | .42 |
| Phys3 | | | | | | .77 | .41 |
| Phys4 | | | | | | .75 | .43 |
| Phys5 | | | | | | .77 | .40 |
| Phys6 | | | | | | .75 | .43 |
| **Factor Correlations** | | | | | | | |
| Bull | Verb | 1.00 | | | | | |
| Bull | Soc | .72 | 1.00 | | | | |
| Bull | Phys | .83 | .73 | 1.00 | | | |
| Vict | Verb | .27 | .17 | .21 | 1.00 | | |
| Vict | Soc | .14 | .18 | .13 | .84 | 1.00 | |
| Vict | Phys | .27 | .22 | .34 | .81 | .83 | 1.00 |
| **Higher-Order Factor Loadings** | | | | | | | |
| Bully | | .90 | .80 | .91 | | | |
| Victim | | | | | .90 | .92 | .90 |

Note: All parameter estimates, based on Time 1 responses, are presented in completely standardized format. Factor loadings, uniquenesses, and factor correlations are based on Model M1 positing six first-order factors. Model M1 provided a good fit to the data (N = 3512, df = 579, RMSEA = .05, TLI = .98, CFI = .98). The higher-order factor loadings are based on Model M2 positing that relations among the six first-order factors in Model M1 can be explained in terms of two higher-order factors. Model M2 provided a good fit to the data (N = 3512, df = 587, RMSEA = .05, TLI = .98, CFI = .98). The correlation between the two higher-order factors in Model M2 was .27. (N = sample size, df = degrees of freedom, RMSEA = root mean square error of approximation, TLI = Tucker-Lewis index, CFI = comparative fix index.)

factor it was designed to measure. As expected, factor correlations among the three bullying scales (ranging from .72 to .83) and among the three victimization scales (ranging from .81 to .84) were all very high, suggesting the possibility of *higher-order bully* and *victim* factors. The statistically signifi- cant (but small) positive correlations between specific facets of victimization and bullying behaviors (ranging from .13 to .34) demonstrate that some persons may participate in bullying behaviors as well as become victimized by others who take on such behaviors.

We then pursued a higher-order CFA (see Figure 1b) with two higher-order factors: a *higher-order bully factor* (defined by the first-order physical-bully, verbal-bully, and social-bully factors) and a *higher-order victim factor* (defined by the first-order physical-victim, verbal-victim, and social-victim factors). As discussed previously, higher-order factors were hypothesized to contain the three components of bullying/victimization behaviors hypothesized by previous research (physical, verbal, and social bullying). The higher-order model also resulted in an excellent fit (TLI = .98, RMSEA = .05) and a well-defined factor structure. Parameter estimates demonstrated first-order factors substantially loaded onto the two higher-order factors (bully: ranging from .80 to .91; victim: ranging from .90 to .92). The correlation between these higher-order bully and victim factors ($r = .27$) was consistent with results based on the first-order factor structure. These results support the *a priori* higher-order factor structure consistent with the design of the instrument.

## Gender and Age Effects on Bullying and Being Bullied

CFA based on responses at Time 1 was used to evaluate the effects of gender, age (linear and quadratic components), and their interaction with the bully and victim factors (Table 2; also see Appendix). There were systematic effects of gender and age for all six measures of bullying (physical-bully, verbal-bully, and social-bully) and victimization (physical-victim, verbal-victim, and social-victim). Males had significantly higher scores than females for all six bully and victim scales (see Table 2). Contrary to expectations, females did not have higher scores than males for the social-relations scales, although the gender differences on these factors were substantially smaller than for the verbal and particularly the physical scales. Our results support findings of previous studies in which boys have been found to both bully and be bullied to a greater extent than girls. We extend these findings by showing that this is the case for all three (verbal, social, and physical) forms of bullying and being bullied. We would like to highlight that, contrary to expectations, boys also used social means of bullying (e.g., excluding others, spreading rumors, and manipulating friendships) to a greater extent than girls. There was also a gradual increase with age in the use of social bullying by boys, whereas for girls there was a decline in the senior high school years.

Our results also indicate that for all three bullying scales, there were statistically significant linear and quadratic effects of age on bullying behaviors: Bullying increased during the early high school years and then tended to level out in later high school years (see Figure 2). Most important, however, there was no decrease in bullying during these high school years. For the three victim scales, the linear effects were small, but the quadratic effects were substantial. In particular, there was a substantial increase for all three

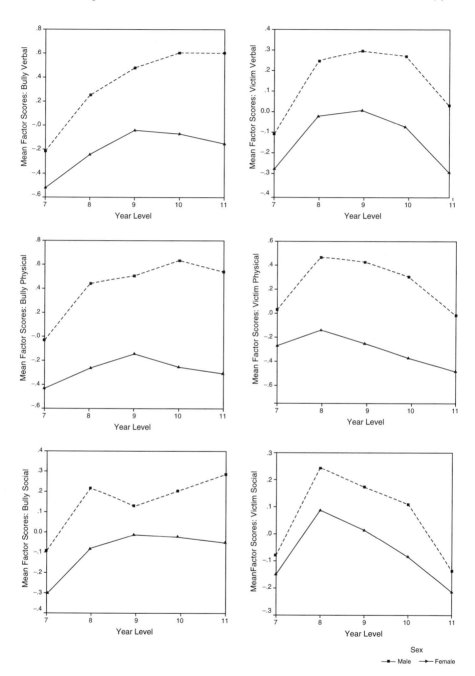

**FIGURE 2.**
Gender and Age (Year in School) Differences in Bully and Victim Factors.

**TABLE 2**
**Factor Correlations Relating Bully and Victim Factors to Other Constructs**

| | Bully Factors | | | Victim Factors | | |
|---|---|---|---|---|---|---|
| | Verbal | Social | Phys | Verbal | Social | Phys |
| Year in School & Gender | | | | | | |
| Sex (1=Male, 2=Female) | −.26* | −.09* | −.36* | −.13* | −.05* | −.26* |
| Year-linear | .23* | .08* | .11* | .07* | −.01 | .01 |
| Year-quadratic | −.13* | −.08* | −.10* | −.14* | −.12* | −.12* |
| Year x sex interaction | −.05* | .04 | −.06* | −.02 | −.01 | −.02 |
| Bullying Attitudes | | | | | | |
| Pro-bully | .54* | .47* | .53* | .09* | .06* | .14* |
| Pro-victim | −.36* | −.31* | −.41* | .01 | .01 | −.07* |
| Participant Roles | | | | | | |
| Active reinforcer | .55* | .55* | .57* | .12* | .12* | .19* |
| Passive reinforcer | .47* | .38* | .39* | .07* | .01 | .07* |
| Ignore/Disregard | −.11* | −.07* | −.13* | −.03 | .02 | −.01 |
| Advocate for victim | −.36* | −.24* | −.28* | .00 | .05* | −.03 |
| Coping Styles | | | | | | |
| Avoidance | .13* | .19* | .13* | .30* | .36* | .29* |
| Problem solving | −.13* | −.05* | −.12* | −.04 | −.02 | −.04 |
| Seek social support | −.15* | −.01 | −.20* | −.05* | −.02 | −.11* |
| Locus of Control | | | | | | |
| Internal | −.12* | −.18* | −.18* | −.04* | −.08* | −.09* |
| External | .18* | .19* | .13* | .26* | .28* | .27* |
| Anger Expression | | | | | | |
| Control | −.24* | −.19* | −.23* | −.13* | −.09* | −.12* |
| Internalize | .00 | .03 | −.06* | .34* | .35* | .24* |
| Externalize | .33* | .27* | .31* | .16* | .14* | .16* |
| Childhood Depression | | | | | | |
| Depression | .11* | .12* | .07* | .41* | .42* | .32* |
| Stressful Life Events | | | | | | |
| Life | .14* | .14* | .09* | .23* | .20* | .21* |
| Self-Concept Scales | | | | | | |
| Physical | −.05* | .00 | .02 | −.11* | −.05* | −.05* |
| Appearance | −.01 | .03 | .07* | −.13* | −.08* | −.02 |
| Opposite sex relations | .11* | .09* | .12* | −.17* | −.16* | −.13* |
| Same sex relations | −.06* | −.03 | −.03 | −.40* | −.43* | −.36* |
| Parent relations | −.22* | −.19* | −.15* | −.14* | −.13* | −.10* |
| Honesty/Trustworthiness | −.50* | −.41* | −.42* | −.18* | −.14* | −.21* |
| Emotional stability | .03 | −.06* | .07* | −.24* | −.27* | −.17* |
| Academic-Math | −.10* | −.09* | −.06* | −.07* | −.08* | −.05* |
| Academic-Verbal | −.21* | −.15* | −.24* | −.09* | −.09* | −.09* |
| Academic-School | −.22* | −.20* | −.24* | −.13* | −.13* | −.13* |
| General Self-Esteem | −.19* | −.13* | −.14* | −.18* | −.16* | −.13* |

Note: Correlations were based on a large CFA conducted on responses to 190 items collected at Time 1 that represented all the constructs included in this table. The goodness of fit for this model was good, particularly given the extremely large number of different constructs. For present purposes, we focus on relations with the three bully scales and the three victim scales that are the focus of this chapter.

scales from the seventh- to eighth-grade years (when victimization peaked), followed by a gradual decline in the experience of being a victim (see Figure 2). Although there were small interactions between gender and age for two of the six scales, the general pattern of age effects was similar for males and females. As suggested by Smith *et al.* (1999), bullies may be more likely to target younger students and, with increasing age, some of the victims may learn strategies to counter bullying.

In summary, our findings confirm that boys are bullied and bully more than girls. This trend is evident across all grade levels. Boys are also more likely than girls to use indirect methods of bullying as well as verbal and physical means. We observed an increased rate of bullying in the early years of high school followed by a decline. This finding in particular attests to the strong validity of our instrument, both in its multidimensional nature and its sensitivity to developmental trends in bullying that have been independently observed.

## Psychological Correlates of Bullying and Being Bullied: Self-Concept and Other Personality Constructs

Confirmatory factor analysis based on responses at Time 1 was used to evaluate the relations between the bully and victim factors, the multiple dimensions of self-concept, and other personality constructs (Table 2; also see Appendix). Hence, factors representing each construct inferred on the basis of multiple constructs are optimally weighted combinations of the items designed to measure the construct and are corrected for unreliability.

### Bully Attitudes

*Pro-bully* and *pro-victim* attitudes were each measured by 6-point scales (see Appendix). The two factors were negatively correlated ($-.50$). Overall, pro-bullying attitudes *increased* with age, whereas pro-victim attitudes decreased. Girls tended to hold more pro-victim attitudes than boys, and these gender differences were similar across ages. Relations between bully and victim factors and attitudes toward bullying and being bullied generally supported our expectations, but also offered a few surprises (see Table 2). Not surprisingly, bullying was strongly related to endorsing pro-bullying attitudes and negatively related to pro-victim attitudes. More interesting, however, was the finding that victims had a similar (although weaker) pattern of relationships. The victim factors were weakly but *positively* related to pro-bully attitudes and were nearly unrelated to pro-victim attitudes. The lack of pro-victim attitudes by victims reflects the negative feelings that these students have for themselves. The positive relation between the victim factor and pro-bully factors is also consistent with the suggestion that victims may subsequently become bullies.

## Participant Roles

Four *participant role* scales were each based on six-item scales in which students were asked to state their reaction to witnessing a bully situation (*active bully reinforcer, passive bully reinforcer, ignore/disregard*, and *victim advocate*; see Appendix). They were asked, for example, whether they would encourage the bully actively by joining in or passively watching or whether they would ignore the incident or help the victim. Particularly advocating for the victim decreased with age, whereas active and particularly passive reinforcement of the bully tended to increase with age. Whereas girls were more likely to advocate for the victim, boys were more likely to take the active or passive reinforcer role when confronted with a bully situation; the nature of these gender differences was consistent with age.

The relations between the bully factors and the four participant role scales were as expected. Bullies were substantially more likely to reinforce the bully—to actively and passively encourage the bullying behaviors. In contrast, bullies were less likely to ignore the situation and were particularly less likely to become an advocate for the victim. Again, the pattern of results for the victim factors was somewhat surprising and disturbing. The victim factors were somewhat positively correlated with taking the role of an active or passive reinforcer of the bully but were essentially unrelated to ignoring or disregarding the situation or actively advocating for the victim. Hence, victims were more likely to be active or passive reinforcers of the bully.

## Coping Styles

Three *coping style* scales were based on responses to a total of 15 items asking students how they cope with a problem or stressful situation (*avoidance, problem solving*, or *seek support*; see Appendix). It is important to note that the measure did not assess coping with bullying—rather, students were asked how they cope with general difficulties. Both bullies and (particularly) victims were more likely to use avoidance coping strategies (e.g., "I avoid the problem by watching television") and less likely to problem solve or seek social support. However, victims were much more likely than bullies to use avoidance. Whereas the bully factors were negatively correlated with problem solving and seeking social support factors, the victim factors were nearly unrelated to these coping styles.

## Locus of Control

*Internal and external locus of control* scales were each based on responses to six items (see Appendix). We expected the pattern of responses between these two locus of control scales to be very different for bullies and victims. Surprisingly, however, the patterns were similar (Table 2). Both the bully and victim factors were positively related to external locus of control, with size of the correlations being somewhat more positive for the victim factors. Both bully and victim factors were negatively related to internal locus of control, although the correlations were somewhat more negative for the bully factors. The pattern of high external and low internal scores is not surprising for victims, but this finding is not the expected pattern for bullies. Indeed, bullies have even lower internal control scores than do victims. The results, however, do reinforce the conclusion that bullies and victims are similar to each other in many respects.

## Anger Expression

Three *anger expression* scales were each based on responses to four items asking students how they cope with anger (*control, internalize, externalize*; see Appendix). Both bullies and victims have difficulties in controlling their anger, particularly when it comes to verbal or physical bullying and victimization respectively. A clear pattern emerges, however, in which bullies are more likely to deal with anger by externalizing means (e.g., "I let it all out") and in which victims are more likely to internalize their angry feelings (e.g., "No one can tell I am furious inside").

## Depression

Depression measurement was based on responses to a 10-item *childhood depression* scale (see Appendix). A substantial body of literature attests to the negative consequences of victimization (Hawker & Boulton, 2000). Our results, however, indicate that both bullies and victims report depressed affect, although victims do so to a much larger extent.

## Stressful Life Events

*Stressful life event* measurement was based on responses to 17 items asking students whether they had experienced any of a series of stressful life events and how much they had been bothered by those experiences. Interestingly, these stressful life events did not specifically include bully and victim situations. Both bullies and victims reported a significant number of stressful life events, although the number was greater for victims. Considering that the questionnaire used for the purposes of this study did not include being bullied as part of the life event list, this difference cannot be explained by a victim's different roles.

## Multiple Dimensions of Self-Concept

A total of 11 *self-concept* scales were based on responses to 51 items from the short version of the SDQ II (*physical, appearance, opposite sex relations, same sex relations, parent relations, honesty/trustworthiness, emotional stability, general self-esteem, academic-math, academic-verbal, academic-school;* see Appendix). Based on previous research, we expected that the victim factors would be consistently and negatively correlated with multiple dimensions of self-concept. These expectations were clearly supported. Previous research did not provide such clearly defined expectations in terms of expected correlations between the bully factors and the multiple dimensions of self-concept. Although most of these correlations were negative, the correlations were close to zero for the two physical scales, for the two peer-relationship (same-sex and opposite-sex) scales, and for the emotional stability scale. Interestingly, however, general self-esteem is negatively correlated with both bully and victim factors, and the sizes of these negative correlations are very similar. Hence, neither bullies nor victims seem to have particularly good self-concepts.

Despite the generally negative correlations of self-concept with both the bully and victim factors, there are some clear distinctions in the patterns of relations. Particularly notable and consistent with the Marsh *et al.* (2001) study of U.S. students, the bully factors are positively correlated with self-concept associated with opposite sex relations. Bullies perceive themselves to get along well with members of the opposite sex. For victims, the most negative area of self-concept is same sex relations—more negative than other areas of self-concept for victims and more negative than those experienced by bullies. Victims also fare worse than bullies in terms of emotional stability self-concept, which is consistent with finding on the depression scores discussed earlier. For bullies, the most negative area of self-concept is honesty/trustworthiness. This suggests that bullies realize they are not doing the right thing when they bully other people. Generally, bullies fare worse than victims with moderate to strong negative correlations between bullying factors and honesty/trustworthiness, parent relations academic-verbal, and academic-school self-concepts. In summary, bullies and victims both have self-concepts that are below average in most areas. Again, although there are qualitative differences between bullies and victims, the results suggest that there are many similarities between bullies and victims.

## Summary of Correlates of Bullying

Bullies, not surprisingly, are likely to have more positive pro-bully (and more negative pro-victim) attitudes and are more likely to actively or passively reinforce bullies when confronted with a bullying situation. What we found surprising, as well as worrisome, was that victims showed a somewhat similar pattern of results for these variables. Bullies and victims were also more likely to use avoidance coping strategies to deal with stressful situations, although bullies were also less likely to use problem solving or seek social support as coping strategies. Both bullies and victims tended to be high on the external locus of control and low on the internal locus of control.

Both bullies and victims tended to be depressed, although depression was greater for victims. Both bullies and victims had difficulty controlling their anger, although bullies are more likely to externalize their anger and victims are more likely to internalize it. Both bullies and (particularly) victims report high levels of life stress. There were a few marked differences between bullies and victims: Bullies were particularly low on the scale for honesty/trust-worthiness and nearly average for parent relations, physical, appearance, and emotional stability self-concepts; victims were particularly low on the scale for same sex relationships and emotional stability. Nevertheless, both bullies and victims had lower levels of self-concept for most of the 11 components of self-concept. In particular, bullies and victims both had equally low levels of general self-esteem. In summary, across the wide variety of psychological correlates considered here, there was a remarkable degree of similarity between bullies and victims as well as some striking differences.

## CAUSAL ORDERING OF BULLYING
## AND BEING BULLIED

There is now a growing body of literature showing that bully status and victim status are not antithetical—the two tend to be positively correlated, as shown in Table 1. We now pursue the more complicated question of how bulling and being bullied on one occasion influences subsequent bully and victim status. Because the correlations in Table 1 were based on a single wave of data, they provide no clear basis for concluding that either bullying leads to being bullied or that being bullied leads to being a bully. To disentangle the causal ordering of these constructs, we now consider struc-tural equation models of bullying and victim responses collected on three occasions (see Figure 3a and Table 3). More specifically, we test the hypo-thesis that bullying and being a victim are associated with a pattern of reciprocal effects in which they mutually reinforce each other over time.

For purposes of these analyses, we focus on global bully factors inferred from the three components of bullying (*verbal*, *social-relational*, and *physical*) and on global victim factors inferred from the three corresponding victim sub-scales. Separate bully and victim factors are posited for Time 1 (T1, early in the school year), Time 2 (T2, middle of the school year), and Time 3 (T3, end of the school year). All six factors (bully and victim at each of three times) are well defined in that factor loadings are substantial (varying from .72 to .91) and the *a priori* model provides a good fit to the data (TLI = .97).

Factor correlations indicate that both bully and victim scales are reason-ably stable over time. Thus, for example, correlations between T1 and T2 and between T2 and T3 are approximately .7 for both bully and victim scales. Importantly, these analyses again indicate that the global bully and global victim factors are positively correlated—students who are bullies are also

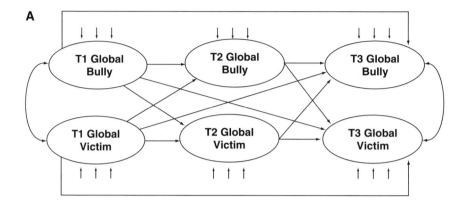

A

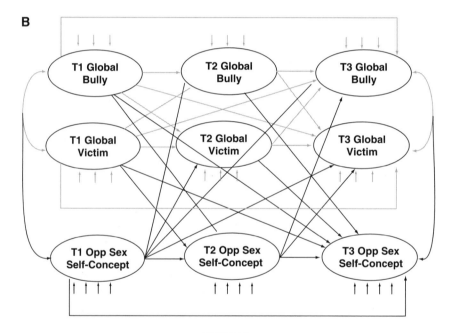

B

**FIGURE 3.**
**Causal Order Models of Relations Between Bully and Victim Factors**
(Figure 3a; also see Table 3) **Between Bully, Victim, and Opposite**
**Sex Self-Concept Factors** (Figure 3b; also see Table 4) **at Times 1, 2, and 3,**
**First-and Higher-Order Bully and Victim Factors**. The two path models
differ in that Opposite Sex self-concept Factors for Times 1, 2 and 3 were
included in the second path model (new path coefficients associated
with the added self-concept factors are dark lines). Separate path models
like that in Figure 3b were evaluated for each of the 11 self-concept
factors and for depression.

**TABLE 3**
**Reciprocal Effects of Bully and Victim: Structural Equation Model of**
**Responses at Times 1, 2, and 3**

| | Time 1 | | Time 2 | | Time 3 | | |
|---|---|---|---|---|---|---|---|
| | Bully | Vict | Bully | Vict | Bully | Vict | UNIQ |
| Factor loadings | | | | | | | |
| T1BVerb | .86** | | | | | | .30 |
| T1BSoc | .72** | | | | | | .44 |
| T1BPhys | .84** | | | | | | .29 |
| T1VVerb | | .87** | | | | | .26 |
| T1VSoc | | .84** | | | | | .27 |
| T1VPhys | | .86** | | | | | .27 |
| T2BVerb | | | .88** | | | | .28 |
| T2BSoc | | | .75** | | | | .39 |
| T2BPhys | | | .88** | | | | .22 |
| T2VVerb | | | | .87** | | | .25 |
| T2VSoc | | | | .86** | | | .24 |
| T2VPhys | | | | .88** | | | .24 |
| T3BVerb | | | | | .88** | | .26 |
| T3BSoc | | | | | .82** | | .30 |
| T3BPhys | | | | | .91** | | .17 |
| T3VVerb | | | | | | .88** | .25 |
| T3VSoc | | | | | | .90** | .18 |
| T3VPhys | | | | | | .91** | .18 |
| Factor Correlations | | | | | | | |
| t1bull | 1.00 | | | | | | |
| t1vict | .28** | 1.00 | | | | | |
| t2bull | .73** | .24** | 1.00 | | | | |
| t2vict | .25** | .73** | .35** | 1.00 | | | |
| t3bull | .58** | .20** | .68** | .24** | 1.00 | | |
| t3vict | .25** | .56** | .33** | .70** | .46** | 1.00 | |
| Path Coefficients | | | | | | | |
| t1bull | | | | | | | |
| t1vict | | | | | | | |
| t2bull | .64** | .06** | | | | | |
| t2vict | .06** | .67** | | | | | |
| t3bull | .21** | .04* | .47** | .00 | | | |
| t3vict | .01 | .15** | .11** | .51** | | | |
| Total Effects | | | | | | | |
| t1bull | | | | | | | |
| t1vict | | | | | | | |
| t2bull | .64** | .06** | | | | | |
| t2vict | .06** | .67** | | | | | |
| t3bull | .51** | .06** | .47** | .00 | | | |
| t3vict | .11** | .50** | .11** | .51** | | | |

*(continues)*

**TABLE 3**

(*continued*)

|  | Time 1 | | Time 2 | | Time 3 | | |
|---|---|---|---|---|---|---|---|
|  | Bully | Vict | Bully | Vict | Bully | Vict | UNIQ |
| Factor Residual Var/Covar | | | | | | | |
| t1bull | 1.00 | | | | | | |
| t1vict | .28** | 1.00 | | | | | |
| t2bull | | | .56** | | | | |
| t2vict | | | .16** | .53** | | | |
| t3bull | | | | | .59** | | |
| t3vict | | | | | .24** | .55** | |

Note: All parameter estimates are presented in completely standardized format based on a structural equation (causal ordering) model relating bully and victim responses at Times 1, 2, and 3. As shown in the results, T1 constructs were posited to affect T2 and T3 constructs, whereas T2 constructs were posited to affect T3 constructs. Bullying and victim constructs collected at the same time were posited to be correlated. Path coefficients are the direct effects of each construct on subsequent constructs, whereas the total effects are the combination of direct and indirect (mediated) effects. Model M3 provided a good fit to the data (chi-sq = 1990.0, df = 102, RMSEA = .04, TLI = .97, CFI = .98). N is 3613, students who completed the survey on at least two of the three occasions. $p < .05$, **$p < .01$.

more likely to be victims and vice versa. Interestingly, the correlation between these two factors grew stronger over time (.28 at T1, .35 at T2, and .46 at T3).

Path coefficients and the total effects are particularly important (see Figure 3a). Path coefficients are the direct effects relating earlier variables to subsequent variables in the causal ordering (e.g., T1 scores to T2 and T3 scores; see Figure 3a). Total effects are the sum of direct and indirect (mediated) effects. Path coefficients and total effects are necessarily the same for the effects of T1 variables on T2 variables and for T2 variables on T3 variables. Because no variables come between T1 and T2 variables or between T2 and T3 variables, in the causal ordering there are no mediated effects. Hence, total and direct effects are the same. However, for the effects of T1 variables on T3 variables, there are both direct and mediated effects (e.g., the direct effect of T1 variables on T3 variables and the effects of T1 variables that are mediated by T2 variables). Hence, the total effects and direct effects typically differ. Because much of the effects of T1 variables on T3 variables are likely to be mediated by T2 variables, we focus primarily on the total effects.

The largest effect for each T2 and T3 outcome is the same variable from the previous occasion. As noted earlier, the test-retest correlation is about .70 for both the bully and victim factors. However, the most important effects in relation to the *a priori* hypothesis are the effects of previous bully scores on subsequent victim scores and the effects from previous victim scores to subsequent bully scores. Importantly, the total effects of T1 bully on T2 and T3 victim scores are positive. Similarly, the total effects of T1 victim on T2 and T3 bully scores are positive. This indicates that there is a pattern of reciprocal effects in which bullying and being bullied are both positive causes and positive effects of each other (i.e., prior bullying leads to being a victim and being a victim leads to being a bully). However, at least for T3 outcomes, the effect of T1 bullying on T3 victim scores is stronger than the effect of T1 victim scores on T3 bully scores. Similarly, the effect of T2 bullying on T3 victim scores is significant, whereas the effects of T2 victim scores on T3 bullying scores are not. This suggests some asymmetry in the pattern of reciprocal effects in which the effects on a bully becoming a victim stronger than those on a victim becoming a bully.

In summary, the results indicate that being a bully may lead an individual to become victimized in the future, and being a victim may lead an individual to be a bully in the future. This important and previously unidentified finding illustrates the bully and victim roles are mutually reinforcing patterns of behavior such that the occurrence of one leads to the other. These results have important implications for better understanding the nature of bullies and victims, for interventions that aim to decrease bullying in schools, and for future research.

## THE ROLE OF MULTIPLE DIMENSIONS OF SELF-CONCEPT AND DEPRESSION IN THE CAUSAL ORDERING OF BULLYING AND BEING A VICTIM

What is the causal pattern of effects relating bullying and being a victim to multiple dimensions of self-concept and depression? In this section, we broaden the causal ordering analyses (see Table 3 and Figure 3b) to include multiple dimensions of self-concept and depression. Our earlier results (see Table 2) indicate that both bullies and victims tend to have lower levels of self-concepts and higher levels of depression. For victims, the pattern of lower self-concepts is reasonably consistent across different areas of self-concept, although their self-concepts are particularly low for same sex relations and emotional stability self-concepts. For bullies, the pattern is more varied across different areas of self-concept with average self-concepts in terms of physical, parent relations, and emotional stability scales. Interestingly, however, general self-esteem is negatively related to both bully and victim factors to about the same extent. Although these correlations have important implications for understanding the nature of bullies and victims, they are not particularly useful in disentangling the causal ordering of these constructs. In this section, we pursue causal ordering models with our longitudinal data to disentangle the pattern of causal effects in relation to bullying, victimization, self-concept, and depression. We determine whether bullying and being a victim are causes of self-concept and depression changes or are consequences of them or both (i.e., the effects are reciprocal).

Beginning with the causal model for the global bully and victim factors already discussed (Table 3; also see Figure 3a), we evaluated 12 causal ordering models. In each model, we added responses to one of the 11 self-concept factors or to depression (see Figure 3b). We also added responses to items used to infer one of the self-concept or depression factors on each of three occasions. Consistent with earlier analyses, we evaluated a "full-forward" structural equation path model in which all the T1 constructs (bully, victim, and self-concept) were posited to influence all T2 and T3 constructs, and all T2 constructs were posited to influence all T3 constructs. In Figure 3b we have shown only one of these 12 models (for opposite sex relation self-concept), but the design of each of the 12 models was similar. All 12 models were well-defined in that factor loadings were substantial and the fit statistics were very good (e.g., TLIs were all greater than .95). As in earlier analyses, our main focus is on the pattern of total effects relating T1 constructs to those at T2 and T3 and relating the T2 construct to those of T3 (see summaries in Table 4; also see Table 2 for correlations among the constructs at T1).

## Effects of Bullying on Self-Concept and Depression

Does being a bully lead to higher or lower levels of self-concept and depression? The T1 bully factor was generally negatively correlated with T1 self-concept (except for opposite sex relations, physical, appearance, and emotional stability scales where some of the relations were positive; see Table 2) and positively related to depression. The results of the causal modeling provide a reasonably consistent pattern of small effects of prior bullying on subsequent self-concept across all 11 components of self-concept and depression.

The effects of prior levels of bullying were typically negative or nonsignificant for different areas of self-concepts and significantly positive for depression. Thus, higher prior levels of bullying led to lower subsequent levels of general self-esteem, same sex relations, parent relations, honesty/trustworthiness, academic-math, academic-verbal, and academic-school self-concepts and to higher levels of depression. However, the effects of prior bully factors were all nonsignificant for opposite sex relations, physical, and appearance self-concepts. The only exception to this pattern of results was the very small positive effect of T1 bully on T2 emotional stability self-concept (the effects of T1 and T2 bully on T3 emotional stability self-concept were not statistically significant).

In summary, being a bully tended to have small effects on subsequent levels of self-concept, and the direction of these effects was generally unfavorable (lower levels of self-concept and higher levels of depression). There

**TABLE 4**
**Tests of Causal Ordering: Total Effects Of T1, T2, and T3 constructs**

**Opposite Sex Self-Concept**

|        | T1bull | T1vict | T1osex | T2bull | T2vict | T2osex |
|--------|--------|--------|--------|--------|--------|--------|
| T2bull | .64*   | .06*   | .01    |        |        |        |
| T2vict | .06*   | .67*   | −.01   |        |        |        |
| T2osex | .00    | −.06*  | .78*   |        |        |        |
| T3bull | .51*   | .06*   | .03*   | .47*   | .00    | .01    |
| T3vict | .12*   | .49*   | −.02   | .11*   | .50*   | −.06*  |
| T3osex | .00    | −.06*  | .69    | .01    | −.06*  | .64*   |

**Same Sex Self-Concept**

|        | T1bull | T1vict | T1ssex | T2bull | T2vict | T2ssex |
|--------|--------|--------|--------|--------|--------|--------|
| T2bull | .64*   | .05*   | −.01   |        |        |        |
| T2vict | .06*   | .65*   | −.04*  |        |        |        |
| T2ssex | −.02   | −.09*  | .68*   |        |        |        |
| T3bull | .51*   | .07*   | .03    | .48*   | .01    | .04    |
| T3vict | .12*   | .46*   | −.09*  | .10*   | .48*   | −.07*  |
| T3ssex | −.07*  | −.06*  | .62*   | .02    | −.04   | .57*   |

**Physical Self-Concept**

|        | T1bull | T1vict | T1phys | T2bull | T2vict | T2phys |
|--------|--------|--------|--------|--------|--------|--------|
| T2bull | .64*   | .05*   | .03*   |        |        |        |
| T2vict | .06*   | .67*   | .01    |        |        |        |
| T2phys | −.01   | −.03*  | .84    |        |        |        |
| T3bull | .51*   | .06*   | .04*   | .48*   | −.01*  | .08*   |
| T3vict | .11*   | .50*   | .00    | .11*   | .51*   | .07*   |
| T3phys | .01    | −.04*  | .77*   | .00    | −.03   | .63*   |

**Appearance Self-Concept**

|        | T1bull | T1vict | T1appr | T2bull | T2vict | T2appr |
|--------|--------|--------|--------|--------|--------|--------|
| T2bull | −.64*  | −.05*  | −.00   |        |        |        |
| T2vict | −.05*  | −.67*  | −.01   |        |        |        |
| T2appr | −.02   | −.03^  | −.75   |        |        |        |
| T3bull | −.51*  | −.06*  | −.02   | −.47*  | −.00   | −.07*  |
| T3vict | −.11*  | −.50*  | −.01   | −.11*  | −.51*  | −.03   |
| T3appr | −.00   | −.03*  | −.64*  | −.02   | −.02   | −.66*  |

**Parent Self-Concept**

|        | T1bull | T1vict | T1prnt | T2bull | T2vict | T2prnt |
|--------|--------|--------|--------|--------|--------|--------|
| T2bull | .63*   | .05*   | −.06*  |        |        |        |
| T2vict | .05*   | .66*   | −.05*  |        |        |        |
| T2prnt | −.03*  | −.03*  | .80*   |        |        |        |
| T3bull | .50*   | .05*   | −.06*  | .46*   | −.01   | −.05   |
| T3vict | .10*   | .49*   | −.05*  | .09*   | .50*   | −.14*  |
| T3prnt | −.05*  | −.03*  | .71*   | −.04*  | −.02   | .59*   |

**Honesty/Trustworthiness Self-Concept**

|        | T1bull | T1vict | T1hons | T2bull | T2vict | T2hons |
|--------|--------|--------|--------|--------|--------|--------|
| T2bull | .59*   | .05*   | −.11*  |        |        |        |
| T2vict | .05*   | .67*   | −.02   |        |        |        |
| T2hons | .00    | −.01   | .79*   |        |        |        |
| T3bull | .43*   | .05*   | −.15*  | .44*   | .00    | −.07*  |

*(continues)*

**TABLE 4**
(*continued*)

| | | | | | | |
|---|---|---|---|---|---|---|
| T3vict | .09* | .50* | −.03 | .12* | .51* | .05 |
| T3hons | −.04* | −.01 | .70* | −.06* | .03 | .61* |

**Emotional Stability Self-Concept**

| | T1bull | T1vict | T1emot | T2bull | T2vict | T2emot |
|---|---|---|---|---|---|---|
| T2bull | .64* | .06* | .03 | | | |
| T2vict | .06* | .67* | −.01 | | | |
| T2emot | .03* | .00 | .82* | | | |
| T3bull | .50* | .08* | .10* | .47* | .00 | .02 |
| T3vict | .11* | .49* | −.02 | .11* | .50* | −.09* |
| T3emot | .00 | .01 | .77* | .00 | −.06* | .58* |

**Academic-Math Self-Concept**

| | T1bull | T1vict | T1math | T2bull | T2vict | T2math |
|---|---|---|---|---|---|---|
| T2bull | .64* | .05* | −.02 | | | |
| T2vict | .06* | .67* | −.01 | | | |
| T2math | −.04* | .03* | .81 | | | |
| T3bull | .51* | .06* | .01 | .47* | −.01 | −.03 |
| T3vict | .11* | .50* | −.01 | .11* | .51* | .00 |
| T3math | −.02 | .00 | .74* | −.01 | −.01 | .69* |

**Academic-Verbal Self-Concept**

| | T1bull | T1vict | T1verb | T2bull | T2vict | T2verb |
|---|---|---|---|---|---|---|
| T2bull | .63* | .05* | −.03 | | | |
| T2vict | .05* | .67* | −.02 | | | |
| T2verb | .00 | −.03* | .78* | | | |
| T3bull | .50* | .05* | −.06* | .47* | −.01 | −.02 |
| T3vict | .10* | .50* | −.03* | .10* | .51* | −.08* |
| T3verb | −.03* | −.02 | .70* | −.02 | .01 | .66* |

**Academic-School Self-Concept**

| | T1bull | T1vict | T1schl | T2bull | T2vict | T2schl |
|---|---|---|---|---|---|---|
| T2bull | .63* | .05* | −.04* | | | |
| T2vict | .05* | .67* | −.01 | | | |
| T2schl | −.04* | .02 | .80* | | | |
| T3bull | .50* | .05* | −.04* | .47* | .00 | −.04 |
| T3vict | .10* | .49* | −.04* | .10* | .51* | −.06* |
| T3schl | −.04* | .01 | .76* | −.06* | .01 | .62* |

**General Self-Esteem Self-Concept**

| | T1bull | T1vict | T1gen | T2bull | T2vict | T2gen |
|---|---|---|---|---|---|---|
| T2bull | .64* | .06* | −.01 | | | |
| T2vict | .05* | .67* | −.01 | | | |
| T2gen | −.03* | −.03* | .78* | | | |
| T3bull | .50* | .07* | −.04* | .47* | .00 | .04 |
| T3vict | .11* | .50* | −.03 | .11* | .49* | −.07* |
| T3gen | −.06* | −.01 | .70* | −.03 | −.01 | .61* |

**Depression**

| | T1bull | T1vict | T1depr | T2bull | T2vict | T2depr |
|---|---|---|---|---|---|---|
| T2bull | .64* | .04* | .02 | | | |
| T2vict | .05* | .64* | .07* | | | |

**TABLE 4**

| | | | | | | |
|---|---|---|---|---|---|---|
| T2depr | .04* | .00 | .74 | | | |
| T3bull | .51* | .05* | .00 | .48* | .00 | −.02 |
| T3vict | .11* | .46* | .07* | .10* | .45* | .16* |
| T3depr | .04* | −.01 | .64* | .07* | .05* | .64* |

Note: A total of 12 structural equation (causal ordering) models were evaluated relating bullying and victim responses at Times 1, 2, and 3 with responses to each of the self-concept scales and to depression. Shown are the total effects of each T1 and T2 construct on subsequent T2 and T3 constructs that are the main focus of this chapter.

was no support for the suggestion that bullies are able to enhance their self-concept or reduce depression through bullying other students.

## Effects of Self-Concept and Depression on Being a Bully

What are the effects of prior levels of self-concept and depression on changes in bullying behaviors? At T1, bully factors tended to be negatively correlated with multiple dimensions of self-concept and positively related to higher levels of depression. Across the 12 causal models, the effects of prior self-concept and depression on subsequent bully factors were mostly small or statistically nonsignificant. The statistically significant effects of prior self-concept on subsequent bullying were negative for six scales (parent relation, honesty/trustworthiness, appearance, academic-school, academic-verbal, and general self-esteem) but were positive for three other self-concept factors (opposite sex relations, physical, and emotional stability). The largest effects were the negative effects of parent relations and honesty/trustworthiness on subsequent bullying. Hence, particularly for these self-concept factors, students with higher levels of self-concept were less likely to be bullies; self-concept acted as a deterrent to subsequent bullying behaviors.

## Effects of Being a Victim on Self-Concept and Depression

Does being a victim lead to higher levels of self-concept and depression? T1 victim scores were consistently negatively related to all 11 areas of self-concept and positively related to depression (Table 2). These correlations were particularly large for same sex relationships, emotional stability, and depression. The results of the causal modeling analyses indicated that being a victim tended to have further negative effects—beyond those experienced at T1—leading to further declines in multiple dimensions of self-concept and increased levels of depression.

Effects of prior victim factors were significantly negative in 8 of the 11 self-concept models (general self-esteem, opposite sex relations, same sex relations, physical, appearance, parent relations, emotional stability, academic-verbal, academic-school) and significantly positive for depression. Exceptions to this pattern were for academic-school and honesty/trustworthiness scales where all the effects of prior victimization were nonsignificant and for academic-math self-concept where there was a very small positive effect of T1 victim on T2 math self-concept (the effects of T1 and T2 victim on T3 self-concept were not statistically significant). In summary, being a victim tended to lead to further declines in self-concept and increased depression.

## Effects of Self-Concept and Depression
## on Being a Victim

What are the effects of prior levels of self-concept and depression on subsequently being a victim? Across the 12 causal models, the effects of prior self-concept and depression on subsequent victim factors were mostly negative or statistically nonsignificant. For many of the self-concept factors (parent relations, opposite sex relations, same sex relations, general esteem, emotional stability, academic-school, academic-verbal), lower prior levels of self-concept led to higher subsequent levels of being a self beyond what could be explained in terms of prior levels of the victim factor. Similarly, higher levels of prior depression led to higher subsequent levels of being a victim.

Interestingly, physical self-concept provided a pattern of results that was somewhat different from the other self-concept factors. In particular, higher prior levels of T2 physical self-concept led to increased—not lower—T3 victim scores (although the effects of T1 physical self-concept on T2 and T3 victim factors were nonsignificant). These results were, however, consistent with the finding that prior physical self-concept also had positive effects on subsequent bullying behaviors that in turn had positive effects on victims.

## Summary

We began this section with the ambitious task of disentangling the causal ordering of self-concept, depression, being a bully, and being a victim. Particularly given the relatively high levels of stability for each of these factors and the relatively short time period considered (less than one school year), changes in these constructs were not large. There was, however, a reasonably consistent pattern of results across the different self-concept and depression factors.

Being a bully and being a victim both tended to lead to lower levels of self-concept and to higher levels of depression. However, the negative effects of being a victim tended to be larger and more consistent than the negative effects of being a bully. Hence, being a bully and particularly being a victim were not effective strategies for enhancing self-concept or reducing depression.

Higher levels of self-concept (and lower levels of depression) typically led to lower levels of both being a victim and being a bully. However, this pattern of results was more consistent for the effects of self-concept and depression on being a victim than being a bully. The main exception to this pattern of results was physical self-concept, which had positive effects on both the bully and victim factors. In general, however, students who had more positive feelings about themselves were less likely to be either bullies or victims.

## GENERAL DISCUSSION

We commenced this chapter with a series of intriguing questions. We then presented our results based on a series of sophisticated analyses. In this section, we more fully discuss the significance of the results for theory, research, and practice in the context of the questions posed and the implications thereof.

### The Development of a New Theoretical Model to Explain the Nature of Bullying

In the beginning of this chapter, we proposed that bullies and victims may be more alike than different. We surmised that the positive correlation between bullying and being bullied evidenced in previous research suggests that these might be mutually reinforcing roles. We also set out to test this proposition in the context of a causal hypothesis based on longitudinal models. In addition, we aimed to identify some of the psychological correlates of bullying and more fully elucidate the causal relation of self-concept to bullying and victimization.

The results presented throughout this chapter and discussed further below have led us to the juncture whereby we proposed a new theoretical model that can help to elucidate the nature of bullying. Given this model facilitates the interpretation and the implications of the results pertaining to the present investigation, we present an overview of this model here. The results emanating from this study suggest that being a bully leads to being a victim, and being a victim subsequently leads to being a bully. Hence, the bully and victim roles cannot be seen as separate entities but rather as mutually reinforcing roles that co-occur. To encapsulate these phenomena we propose a reciprocal effects model for the nature of bullying, postulating that:

a) Bullying and victimization factors will co-occur as is demonstrated by positive relations between these latent variables;

b) Engaging in bullying and being subjected to bullying will be mutually reinforcing, as is demonstrated by causal models whereby prior bullying will have a causal positive relation to both subsequent bullying and subsequent victimization, and prior victimization will have a causal positive relation to both subsequent victimization and subsequent bullying such that reciprocal effects are evidenced;

c) Causal relations between an array of psychological constructs, bullying, and victimization need to be interpreted in the context of reciprocal effects regarding the nature of bullying whereby the causal relation of a psychological construct is tested by juxtaposition with both bullying and victimization factors to allow for full interpretation of causal relations; and

d) Self-concept, bullying, and being bullied will have reciprocal effects on each other such that self-concept is both a contributor to and an outcome of bullying and being bullied.

The reciprocal effects model is a potentially significant contribution of the present study to the extant literature examining bullying. It offers a theoretical basis for explaining more fully the complex nature of bullying. It also has the potential to inform and underpin our understanding of the causal relations between bullying, victimization, and a wide array of psychological determinants. As such, the reciprocal effects model offers a basis from which to further extend and inform theory, research, policy, and practice. As will be seen in the following discussion of results emanating from the present investigation, the reciprocal effects model can serve to explain complex phenomena and offers a theoretical basis for providing fresh insights on the nature of bullying.

## The Development of New Psychometrically Sound Instrumentation

Fundamental to the present investigation and the reciprocal effects model was the development of new, psychometrically sound measures of bullying and being a victim. The creation of these measures is an important contribution to further advancing bullying research. Based on previous theory and research, we posited that bullying behaviors and the experience of victims could both be divided into three categories: verbal, social-relational, and physical. In support of these predictions, we found clear support for the six *a priori* factors that our new instrument was designed to measure. However, correlations among the three bullying factors and among the three victim factors were substantial. Hence, we also evaluated a higher-order factor model in which the three bully factors defined a higher-order bully factor and the three victim factors defined a higher-order victim factor. This higher-order model was well-defined and able to fit the data very well.

The confirmatory factor analyses of the bully and victim responses were also important because they confirmed that the factors of being a bully and being a victim were moderately positively correlated. Thus, for example, the higher-order bully factor correlated .27 with the higher-order victim factor. These results indicate that some bullies are also victims and that some victims are also bullies. This result is consistent with previous research and underpins the first component of the reciprocal effects model in that bullying and victimization factors co-occur, as is demonstrated by positive relations between these latent variables. However, although the instrument seems to be a significant improvement over most instruments used in this area of research, more research is needed to determine whether responses to this instrument are best summarized in terms of six lower-order factors or two higher-order factors. At least in the present investigation, the different bully factors and the different victim factors were so highly correlated that the factors necessarily had limited discriminant validity. However, because there is theoretical as well as some empirical support for the retention of the six-factor structure, we recommend that researchers retain the six factors and also consider the higher-order factors. To evaluate how generalizable this support is for the first component of the reciprocal effects model, we also recommend that researchers continue to examine the correlation between bully and victim factors with diverse participants, settings, and contexts.

## Causal Ordering of Bullying and Being Bullied

The positive correlation between bully and victim factors based on a single wave of data is informative and heuristic, but it does not say much about the underlying mechanisms that result in this positive correlation. Hence, an important contribution of our research was to use structural equation models of longitudinal data to disentangle the causal relations of prior bully and victim factors on subsequent bully and victim factors. Although there is a long history concerning the use of such models in other areas of research (e.g., Marsh, Byrne & Yeung, 1999), we are not aware of prior applications in bullying research. The results of these causal models were reasonably clear, with important implications for theory, research, and practice. Prior experience of being a bully is likely to contribute to being a victim in the future and previous experience of being a victim is likely to contribute to being a bully in the future. Hence, there is a pattern of reciprocal effects between the bully and victim factors such that each factor contributes to the other.

These findings led to the development of the second component of the reciprocal effects model whereby it is postulated that engaging in bullying and being subjected to bullying will be mutually reinforcing. We recommend that this aspect of the model needs to be tested in the context of diverse participant groups, settings, and contexts to further test the external validity of the proposed model. The results also contribute to the growing recognition of the inappropriateness of treating bullies and victims as solely separate groups in the context either of research or of the classroom. Clearly, many bullies are likely to be victims, and many victims are likely to be bullies. These findings have important implications for theory, research, policy, practice, and intervention design: The nature of bullying cannot be adequately understood if the reciprocal relation between engaging in bullying and being a victim is not considered simultaneously.

## Gender and Age Differences in Bullying and Being Bullied

Gender and age are important demographic variables in bullying research. As expected, we found that overall levels were systematically higher for males than females across all types of bullying and victimization. Clearly males are more likely to engage in all three types of bullying behaviors measured and are more likely to experience all three types of victimization in comparison to girls. Whereas these gender differences were largest for the physical scale it is interesting to note that males had higher scores for even the social-relation type of both bullying and victimization. Given there is a widespread belief that females are more likely than boys to both engage in and be subjected to social bullying, these results were surprising. The bully and victim factors also varied with age. There were initial increases of bullying behavior in early years and then the behavior leveled out during later high school years. On the other hand, victimization initially increased in early years, peaked during early high school years, and then declined. These results imply that preventive interventions addressing bullying and victimization may need to be implemented both prior to and at transition to the secondary school for the age group considered in this study. However, the gender differences of bullies and a victims did not vary much with age. This general pattern of age and gender differences was also evident in attitudes toward bullying and participant roles when confronted with a bullying situation. Boys were more likely to provide active or passive reinforcement to the bully and to have pro-bully attitudes, whereas girls were more likely to advocate for the victim and to have pro-victim attitudes. In summary, whereas bullying—particularly of the social-relation type—is evident in girls, our results show traditional gender stereotypical differences in these bully and victim constructs in that boys are more likely to reinforce, engage in, and also be subjected to bullying than girls.

## Relations Between Bullying, Being Bullied, and Psychological Correlates

We also examined the patterns of relations between bully and victim factors and a wide variety of other self-concept and psychological constructs. Some of the constructs were logically related to being a bully or being a victim. Thus, for example, students rated their attitudes toward bullies and victims and indicated the role that they would assume if confronted with a situation involving bullying. Whereas some of these relations were expected, some were also surprising. As expected, bullies had higher pro-bully attitudes and lower pro-victim attitudes than other students. Surprisingly, however, victims also had higher pro-bully attitudes than other students and did not have higher pro-victim attitudes. These results suggest that victims have negative feelings toward themselves (as victims) or that they identified themselves more as being bullies rather than victims. It is important to note that both bullies and—to a lesser extent—victims indicated that if confronted by a bullying situation, they would be more likely to actively or passively reinforce the bullying behaviors than to ignore the situation or be an advocate for the victim. Clearly, victims are likely to reinforce bullying behaviors and not serve as an advocate for the victim. While these results seem counterintuitive at first glance, they are consistent with understanding the nature of bullying in the context of our reciprocal effects model. Victims and bullies are clearly much more alike than they are different. Overall, we were first struck by the similarity between responses by bullies and victims on a wide range of psychological constructs. For example, bullies and victims were both more likely to endorse pro-bullying behaviors, actively or passively reinforce bullying, use avoidance coping strategies, hold an external locus of control, have difficulties in controlling their anger, be depressed, experience a significant amount of stressful life events, and have negative self-concepts in most areas. In addition, bullies and victims were less likely to ignore a bullying situation, problem solve, seek social support, and hold an internal locus of control.

These similarities between bullies and victims are consistent with our finding that bullying leads to being a victim and vice versa and are consistent with the logic inherent in our reciprocal effects model. As such, the strength, pattern, and similarity of these relations across such a wide range of psychological constructs offers further support for the reciprocal effects model that underpins the nature of bullying. These results also led to developing the third component of the reciprocal effects model, whereby we proposed that causal relations between an array of psychological constructs, bullying, and being a victim need to be interpreted in the context of reciprocal effects to be fully understood.

## Causal Ordering of Bullying and Being Bullied with Self-Concept and Depression

We also extended our causal modeling analyses of our longitudinal data to include the 11 self-concept scales and depression. The aim of these analyses was to determine whether being a bully or a victim led to higher or lower self-concepts and depression and also whether self-concept influenced subsequent levels of bullying and being a victim. Again, we were struck by the similarities in results for bullies and victims more than the differences. Both bullying and victim factors at Time 1 (T1) typically led to lower self-concepts and higher levels of depression. Whereas these negative consequences were somewhat larger and more consistent for victims than bullies, the overall pattern of results was similar. Higher levels of self-concept and lower levels of depression at T1 typically resulted in lower levels of subsequent bullying and being a victim, although the reduced levels of being a victim were larger and more consistent. Physical self-concept was the main exception to these results in that higher physical self-concepts at T1 led to somewhat higher levels of bullying and victimization. Nevertheless, students who felt more positively about themselves were typically less likely to be either bullies or victims.

The results for parent relations and honesty/trustworthiness self-concepts were particularly noteworthy. Good relations with parents (as expressed in positive parent relations self-concept) and good moral values (as expressed in honesty/trustworthiness self-concept) led to significant reductions in the likelihood of a student becoming a bully or a victim. Furthermore, being a bully led to reduced levels of parent relations and honesty/trustworthiness self-concept factors. This pattern of results suggests that students who have good parent relations and good moral values are antithetical to both bullying and victimization. Hence, interventions designed to counter the negative consequences of being a bully and being a victim need to involve parents and emphasize good moral values. In addition, such interventions should feature a focus on enhancing students' self-concepts as the results of this study clearly indicate that a student with high self-concept is less likely to be a bully or a victim. The latter is important because the results of this study imply that high self-concept may serve as a psychological tool that produces adaptive psychological responses and resiliency to being either a bully or a victim. Furthermore, the results emanating from this part of the present investigation led to the development of the final component of the reciprocal effects model. Considering the importance of a good self-concept in of itself and the role of self-concept in positively impacting a range of desirable outcomes, we would encourage researchers to continue to investigate the causal relations of self-concept, being a bully, and being a victim in the context of the predictions of the reciprocal effects model.

## IMPLICATIONS AND SUMMARY

In the introduction, we posed three heuristic and provocative questions that we intended to address. Like many "big picture" questions with important implications for future research and policy, we can only provide tentative answers based on our research that must be viewed in relation to potential limitations of our research.

- Are bullies and victims more alike than different?

There are some obvious differences between bullies and victims, and these were not surprising. What was more striking, however, was the similarity between bullies and victims on a wide variety of psychological constructs: attitudes toward bullying, reactions to a bullying situation, strategies for coping with problems, inability to control anger, depression, life event stress, low self-concept, and general self esteem. Whereas these similarities seem surprising from a historical, bipolar perspective of bullies and victims, they are readily encapsulated in our reciprocal effects model. Apparently, a historical theoretical model, whereby being a bully and being a victim has been assumed to be bipolar, has clouded interpretations of the structure and nature of bullying as well as the elucidation of psychological determinants. Bullies tend to be victims of bullying, and victims tend to be bullies. Our causal modeling also revealed that bullying leads to subsequent victimization whereas previously it was believed that bullying led only to more bullying behavior. Thus, when results are interpreted from the fresh perspective of our reciprocal effects model, it is not surprising that bullies and victims are similar on a variety of psychological constructs.

- Do low self-concepts and depression lead to victimization, or are these merely byproducts of being a victim?

Our results provide reasonably clear evidence that low self-concepts and high levels of depression do cause a student to become a victim. Thus, positive self-perceptions provide a strategic approach to developing psychological tools and a resiliency that serves to protect students from becoming victims. However, by drawing on our reciprocal effects model, our results also extend these findings by demonstrating that positive self-perception also protects students from becoming bullies.

- Do school bullies successfully use bullying behaviors as a strategy to enhance their self-concepts and reduce depression?

Our results provide reasonably clear evidence that there are no benefits to being a bully in terms of increased levels of self-concept or lowered levels of depression. However, even if the use of bullying for this purpose is not a successful strategy, it is still possible that the strategy remains a motivation for students to become bullies. For this reason, the school community of students, teachers, administrators, and parents should reinforce that bullying behaviors are unacceptable so that students cannot delude themselves into thinking that such socially inappropriate behaviors can result in enhanced social status and self-perceptions, real or self-perceived.

Our research also has some potentially important implications for interventions. Bullies have particularly low self-concepts on the honesty/trustworthy, parent relations, and academic-school scales. This suggests that interventions aimed at building moral values associated with home and school may provide a deterrent to bullying behaviors. Interestingly, these are three of the self-concept scales where victims scored higher than bullies. In contrast, victims had lower self-concepts than bullies particularly on the two peer-relationship (same-sex and opposite-sex) scales. This supports interventions designed to improve the social skills particularly of victims. Whereas both bullies and victims were low on the anger control scale, victims tended to internalize anger and bullies tended to externalize it. Bullies and particularly victims tended to use avoidance to deal with potentially stressful situations. Thus, anger control and effective coping strategies may be important ingredients in intervention programs. Whereas both bullies and victims tended to be depressed, victims were much more depressed than bullies. Finally, a successful intervention must be able to alter the pattern of positive pro-bully and negative pro-victim attitudes.

Finally, in searching for the answers to the above questions, we had to rethink historical theoretical approaches that have characterized bullies and victims as bipolar latent variables. We found the latter theoretical model wanting in the light of recent research evidence and results emanating from this investigation. We set out to find answers to some intriguing questions, and we discovered that our results could underpin the development of a new theoretical model that has the potential to make a real difference in strengthening and driving research and practice in this area. Theory, research, and practice are all intertwined; neglect in any one area will undermine the others. The time is ripe for researchers and practitioners to capitalize on stronger theoretical models, sound instrumentation, and interventions underpinned by advances in theory and research. Bullying is a social issue of our time that results in dire consequences for bullies, victims, and society and, as such, needs to be urgently addressed. We trust that the results of this study will contribute to making a difference.

## References

Amirkhan, J. H. (1990). A factor analytically derived measure of coping: The coping strategy indicator. *Journal of Personality and Social Psychology*, 59(5), 1066–1074.

Bernstein, J. Y., & Watson, M. W. (1997). Children who are targets of bullying: a victim pattern. *Journal of Interpersonal Violence*, 12(4), 483–499.

Besag, V. E. (1989). *Bullies and victims in schools: A guide to understanding and management*. Philadelphia: Open University Press.

Boyle, G. J. (1994). Self-Description Questionnaire II: A review. *Test Critiques*, 10, 632–643.

Björkqvist, K., Lagerspetz, K. M. J., & Kaukiainen, A. (1992). Do girls manipulate and boys fight? Developmental trends in regard to direct and indirect aggression. *Aggressive Behavior*, 18, 117–127.

Bosworth, K., Espelage, D. L., & Simon, T. R. (1999). Factors associated with bullying behavior in middle school students. *Journal of Early Adolescence*, 19(3), 341–362.

Boulton, M. J., & Smith, P. K. (1994). Bully/victim problems in middle-school children: Stability, self-perceived competence, peer perceptions and peer acceptance. *British Journal of Developmental Psychology*, 12, 315–329.

Boulton, M. J., & Underwood, K. (1992). Bully/victim problems among middle school children. *British Journal of Educational Psychology*, 62, 73–87.

Byrne, B. (1996). *Measuring self-concept across the life span: Issues and instrumentation.* Washington, DC: American Psychological Association.

Callaghan, S., & Stephen, J. (1995). Self-concept and peer victimization among school children. *Journal of Personality and Individual Differences*, 18(1), 161–163.

Craven, R. G. (1996). Enhancing academic self-concept: A large-scale longitudinal study in an educational setting. Doctoral thesis submitted to the University of Sydney, Sydney, New South Wales, Australia.

Craven, R. G., Marsh, H. W., & Burnett, P. C. (2003). Cracking the self-concept enhancement conundrum: A call and blueprint for the next generation of self-concept enhancement research. In H. W. Marsh, R. G. Craven, & D. M. McInerney (Eds.), *International Advances in Self Research* (Vol. 1, pp. 67–90). Greenwich, Connecticut: Information Age.

Craven, R. G., Marsh, H. W., & Debus, R. L. (1991). Effects of internally focused feedback and attributional feedback on enhancement of academic self-concept. *Journal of Educational Psychology*, 83(1), 17–27.

Crick, N. R., Bigbee, M. A., & Howes, C. (1996). Gender differences in children's normative beliefs about aggression: How do I hurt thee? Let me count the ways. *Child Development*, 67, 1003–1014.

Crick, N. R., & Dodge, K. A. (1994). A review and reformulation of social-information-processing mechanisms in children's social adjustment. *Psychology Bulletin*, 115, 74–101.

Crick, N. R., & Grotpeter, J. K. (1995). Relational aggression, gender, and social-psychological adjustment. *Child Development*, 66(3), 710–722.

Crick, N. R., Nelson, D. A., Morales, J. R., Cullerton-Sen, C., Casas, J. F., & Hickman, S. E. (2001). Relational victimization in childhood and adolescence: I hurt you through the grapevine. In J. Juvonen, A. Nishina & S. Graham (Eds.), *Peer harassment in school: The plight of the vulnerable and victimized* (pp. 196–214). New York: Guilford.

Deater-Deckard, K. (2001). Annotation: Recent research examining the role of peer relationships in the development of psychopathology. *Journal of Child Psychology and Psychiatry*, 42(5), 565–579.

Egan, S. K., & Perry, D. G. (1998). Does low self-regard invite victimization? *Developmental Psychology*, 34(2), 299–309.

Egger, S. (1995). An overview of violence in Australia. In D. Chappell & S. Egger (Eds.), *Australian violence: Contemporary perspectives II* (pp. 271–280). Canberra: Australian Institute of Criminology.

Eron, L. D., Huesmann, R. L., Dubow, E., Romanoff, R., & Yarmel, P. W. (1987). Childhood aggression and its correlates over 22 years. *Childhood Aggression and Violence*. New York: Plenum.

Farrington, D.P. (1995). The Twelfth Jack Tizard Memorial Lecture: The development of offending and antisocial behavior from childhood: Key findings from the Cambridge Study in delinquent development. *Journal of Child Psychology and Psychiatry*, 36, 929–964.

Feshbach, S., & Zagrodzka, J. (Eds.). (1997). *Aggression: Biological, developmental, and social perspectives.* New York: Plenum.

Forero, R., McLellan, L., Rissel, C., & Bauman, A. (1999). Bullying behavior and psychosocial health among school students in New South Wales, Australia: Cross sectional survey. *British Medical Journal*, 319(7206), 344–348.

Galinsky, E., & Salmond, K. (2002). Ask the children youth and violence: Students speak out for a more civil society. *The Ask the Children Series*. The Colorado Trust, Families, and Work Institute. Retrieved 2003 from: http://www.familiesandwork.org/summary/yandv.pdf

Glover, D., Cartwright, N., & Gleeson, D. (1998). *Towards bully-free schools: Interventions in action*. Philadelphia: Open University Press.

Harachi, T. W., Catalano, R. F., & Hawkins, D. J. (1999). United States. In P. K. Smith & Y. Morita & J. Junger-Tas & D. Olweus & R. F. Catalano & P. T. Slee (Eds.), *The nature of school bullying: A cross national perspective*. London: Routledge.

Hattie, J. (1992). *Self-concept*. Hillsdale, NJ: Erlbaum.

Hawker, D. S. J., & Boulton, M. J. (2000). Twenty years' research on peer victimization and psychosocial maladjustment: A meta-analytic review of cross-sectional studies. *Journal of Child Psychology and Psychiatry*, 41(4), 441–445.

Hay, I. (2000). Gender self-concept profiles of adolescents suspended from high school. *Journal of Child Psychology and Psychiatry*, 41(3), 345–352.

Hoover, J. H., & Oliver, R. (1996). *The Bullying prevention handbook: A guide for principals, teachers and counselors*. Bloomington, IN: National Educational Service.

Hoover, J. H., Oliver, R., & Hazler, R. J. (1992). Bullying: Perceptions of adolescent victims in the Midwestern USA. *School Psychology International*, 13(1), 5–16.

Hymel, S., Bowker, A., & Woody, E. (1993). Aggressive versus withdrawn unpopular children: Variations in peer and self-perceptions in multiple domains. *Child Development*, 64, 879–896.

Juvonen, J., Nishina, A., & Graham, S. (2001). Self views vs. peer perception of victim status among early adolescents. In J. Juvonen, A. Nishina, & S. Graham (Eds.), *Peer harassment in school: The plight of the vulnerable and victimized* (pp. 105–124). New York: Guilford.

Kaltiala-Heino, R., Rimpela, M., Marttunen, M., Rimpela, A., & Rantanen, P. (1999). Bullying, depression, and suicidal ideation in Finnish adolescents: School survey. *British Medical Journal*, 319, 348–351.

Kovacs, M. (1992). *Children's depression inventory (CDI) manual*. Multi Health Systems, Toronto, Canada.

Kumpulainen, K., Räsänen, E., & Henttonen, I. (1999). Children involved in bullying: Psychological disturbance and the persistence of the involvement. *Child Abuse and Neglect*, 23(12), 1253–1262.

Lagerspetz, K. M. J., Björkqvist, K., Berts, M., & King, E. (1982). Group aggression among school children in three schools. *Scandinavian Journal of Psychology*, 23, 45–52.

Luthar, S. S., & McMahon, T. J. (1996). Peer reputation among inner-city adolescents: Structure and correlates. *Journal of Research on Adolescence*, 6(4), 581–603.

MacCallum, R. C., Zhang, S., Preacher, K. J., & Rucker, D. D. (2002). On the practice of dichotomization of quantitative variables. *Psychological Methods*, 7(1), 19–40.

Marsh, H. W. (1988). *Self-Description Questionnaire: A theoretical and empirical basis for the measurement of multiple dimensions of preadolescent self-concept: A test manual and a research monograph*. San Antonio, TX: The Psychological Corporation.

Marsh, H. W. (2000) *Self-Description Questionnaire (SDQ) II-Short: A theoretical and empirical basis for the measurement of multiple dimensions of adolescent self-concept: An interim test manual and a research monograph*. Sydney, Australia: Publication Unit, Self-Concept Enhancement and Learning Facilitation (SELF) Research Center, University of Western Sydney.

Marsh, H. W. (1993). Academic self-concept: Theory, measurement, and research. In J. M. Suls (Ed.), *The self in social perspective. Psychological perspectives on the self*, Vol. 4 (pp. 59–98). Hillsdale, NJ: Lawrence Erlbaum Associates.

Marsh, H. W., Byrne, B. M., & Shavelson, R. J. (1988). A multifaceted academic self-concept: Its hierarchical structure and its relation to academic achievement. *Journal of Educational Psychology*, 80(3), 366–380.

Marsh, H. W., Byrne, B. M., Yeung, A. S. (1999). Causal ordering of academic self-concept and achievement: Reanalysis of a pioneering study and revised recommendations. *Educational Psychologist*, 34, 155–167.

Marsh, H. W., & Shavelson, R. (1985). Self-concept: Its multifaceted, hierarchical structure. *Educational Psychologist*, 20(3), 107–123.

Marsh, H. W., & Craven, R. (1997). Academic self-concept: Beyond the dustbowl. In G. D. Phye (Ed.), *Handbook of classroom assessment: Learning, achievement, and adjustment. Educational psychology series* (pp. 131–198). San Diego: Academic Press.

Marsh, H. W., Parada, R. H., Yeung, A. S. & Healey, J. (2001). Aggressive school troublemakers and victims: A longitudinal model examining the pivotal role of self-concept. *Journal of Educational Psychology*, 93(2), 411–419.

Mynard, H., & Joseph, S. (2000). Development of the multidimensional peer-cictimization scale. *Aggressive Behavior*, 26, 169–178.

Nansel, T. R., Overpeck, M., Pilla, R. S., Ruan, J. W., Simons-Morton, B., & Scheidt, P. (2001). Bullying behaviors among U.S. youth: Prevalence and association with psychosocial adjustment. *JAMA*, 285(16), 2094–2100.

Neary, A., & Joseph, S. (1994). Peer victimization and its relationship to self-concept and depression among schoolgirls. *Personality and Individual Differences*, 16(1), 183–186.

Olweus, D. (1997). Bully/victim problems in school: Facts and intervention. *European Journal of Psychology of Education*, 12, 495–510.

Olweus, D. (1993). Bully/victim problems among schoolchildren: Long-term consequences and an effective intervention program. In S. Hodgins (Ed.), *Mental disorder and crime* (pp. 317–349). Newbury Park, CA: Sage.

Olweus, D. (1991). Bully/victim problems among schoolchildren: Basic facts and effects of a school-based intervention program. In D. J. Pepler & K. H. Rubin *et al.* (Eds.), *The development and treatment of childhood aggression* (pp. 411–448). Hillsdale, NJ: Erlbaum.

Parada, R. (2002). *Beyond bullying secondary schools program: Consultant's handbook*. Sydney, Australia: Publication Unit, Self-Concept Enhancement and Learning Facilitation (SELF) Research Center, University of Western Sydney.

Parada, R. (2000). *Adolescent Peer Relations Instrument: A theoretical and empirical basis for the measurement of participant roles in bullying and victimization of adolescence: An interim test manual and a research monograph: A test manual*. Sydney, Australia: Publication Unit, Self-Concept Enhancement and Learning Facilitation (SELF) Research Center, University of Western Sydney.

Pellegrini, A. D. (2002). Bullying, victimization, and sexual harassment during the transition to middle school. *Educational Psychologist*, 37(3), 151–163.

Pellegrini, A. D., Bartini, M., & Brooks, F. (1999). School bullies, victims, and aggressive victims: factors relating to group affiliation and victimization in early adolescence. *Journal of Educational Psychology*, 91(2), 216–224.

Randall, P. (1995). A factor study on the attitudes of children to bullying. *Educational Psychology in Practice*, 11(3), 22–26.

Rigby, K. (1996). *Bullying in schools—And what to do about it*. Melbourne: ACER.

Rigby, K., Cox, L. (1996). The contribution of bullying at school and low self-esteem to acts of delinquency among Australian teenagers. *Personality and Individual differences*, 21(4), 609–612.

Rigby, K., Black, G., & Whish, A. (1993, 15–18 June 1993). *School children's perceptions of wife abuse*. Paper presented at the Australian Institute of Criminology second national conference on violence: Canberra, Australia.

Rigby, K., & Slee, P. T. (1999). Suicidal ideation among adolescent school children, involvement in bully-victim problems, and perceived social support. *Suicide and Life-Threatening Behavior*, 29(2), 119–130.

Rigby, K., & Slee, P. T. (1993). Dimensions of interpersonal relation among Australian children and implications for psychological well-being. *The Journal of Social Psychology*, 133, 33–42.

Rivers, I., & Smith, P. K. (1994). Types of bullying behavior and their correlates. *Aggressive Behavior*, 20(5), 359–368.

Salmivalli, C. (2001). Feeling good about oneself, being bad to others? Remarks on self-esteem, hostility, and aggressive behavior. *Aggression and Violent Behavior*, 6, 375–393.

Salmivalli, C. (1998). Intelligent, attractive, well-behaving, unhappy: The structure of adolescents' self-concept and its relations to their social behavior. *Journal of Research on Adolescence*, 8(3), 333–354.

Salmivalli, C., Kaukiainen, A., Kaistaniemi, L., & Lagerspetz, K. M. J. (1999). Self-evaluated self-esteem, peer-evaluated self-esteem, and defensive egotism as predictors of adolescents' participation in bullying situations. *Personality & Social Psychology Bulletin*, 25(10), 1268–1278.

Salmivalli, C., Kaukiainen, A., & Lagerspetz, K. M. J. (2000). Aggression and sociometric status among peers: Do gender and type of aggression matter? *Scandinavian Journal of Psychology*, 41(1), 17–24.

Salmivalli, C., Lagerspetz, K. M. J., Björkqvist, K., Österman, K., & Kaukiainen, A. (1996). Bullying as a group process: Participant roles and their relations to social status within the group. *Aggressive Behavior*, 22, 1–15.

Shavelson, R. J., Hubner, J. J., & Stanton, G. C. (1976). Validation of construct interpretations. *Review of Educational Research*, 46, 407–441.

Smith, P. K., & Sharp, S. (Eds.). (1994). *School bullying: Insights and perspectives*. London: Routledge.

Smith, P. K., Madsen, K. C., & Moody, J. (1999). What causes the age decline in reports of being bullied at school? Towards a developmental analysis of risks of being bullied. *Educational Research*, 41, 267–285.

Smith, P. K., Morita, Y., Junger-Tas, J., Olweus, D., Catalano, R. F., & Slee, P. (Eds.). (1999). *The nature of school bullying: A cross-national perspective*. London: Routledge.

Staub, E. (1999). The roots of evil: Social conditions, culture, personality and basic human needs. *Personality and Social Psychology Review*, 3, 179–192.

Stanley, L., & Arora, T. (1998). Social exclusion amongst adolescent girls: Their self-esteem and coping strategies. *Educational Psychology in Practice*, 14, 94–100.

Sullivan, K. (2000). *The Anti-Bullying Handbook*. Auckland, New Zealand: Oxford University Press.

Sutton, J., Smith, P. K., & Swettenham, J. (1999). Bullying and 'theory of mind': a critique of the 'social skills deficit' view of anti-social behavior. *Social Development*, 8(1), 117–127.

Tomada, G., & Schneider, B. H. (1997). Relational aggression, gender, and peer acceptance: Invariance across culture, stability over time, and concordance among informants. *Developmental Psychology*, 33, pp. 601–609.

Tulloch, M. (1995). Gender differences in bullying experiences and attitudes to social relationships in high school students. *Australian Journal of Education*, 39, 279–293.

Wolke, D., Woods, S., Bloomfield, L., & Karstadt, L. (2000). The association between direct and relational bullying and behavior problems among primary school children. *Journal of Child Psychology and Psychiatry*, 41(8), 989–1002.

Wylie, R. C. (1989). *Measures of self-concept*. Lincoln, NE: University of Nebraska Press.

# Appendix:
# Scales Considered in the Present Investigation: Description, Reliability, and Length

## Instrument Description

The Adolescent Peer Relations Instruments (APRI) are multidimensional measures that were specifically developed for this study to measure interpersonal relationships between high school students (Parada, 2000). The APRI-BT measures bully and victim (targets of bullying) behaviors (*verbal, physical,* and *social*). The first section asks students to state how often on a 6-point Likert scale (1 = Never to 6 = Everyday) they engage in a series of behaviors against other students. The second section asks how often they have been a victim of these behaviors. The APRI-PR, which measures participant roles (*active reinforcer, passive reinforcer, victim advocate,* and *disregard/ ignore*), offers a list of reactions to the witnessing of a bullying situation. Students are asked to rate how true these reactions are to their own reactions on a 6-point Likert scale (1 = False to 6 = True). The APRI-A, the bullying attitude scale (pro-bullying or pro-victim), asks students to rate on a 6-point Likert scale how much they agree or disagree (1 = Completely Disagree to 6 = Agree) with a series of statements reflecting pro-victim or pro-bully ideals.

A Coping Strategies Questionnaire based on Amirkhan's (1990) work was used to measure three coping strategies commonly used by adolescents when faced with difficulties: *active problem solving, social support seeking,* or *problem avoidance.* The stem statement "When I have a problem . . ." preceded 15 items describing various ways of dealing with problems. Students rated on a 6-point Likert scale (1 = Never to 6 = Always) how they react when they face difficulties.

A Locus of Control Scale (LOC) was specifically developed to measure the extent to which students attribute their success or failures in day-to-day living to internal (e.g., effort) or external (e.g., luck) factors. Students were asked to show how much they agreed or disagreed with eight statements about life on a 6-point Likert scale (1 = Completely to Disagree 6 = Agree).

The Anger Expression Index–Adolescent (AEI-A) instrument consists of 12 items developed to measure 3 components of anger expression that are relevant to this study: internalizing feelings of anger, externalizing feelings of anger, and controlling feelings of anger in appropriate ways. The stem statement "When I am angry..." precedes items describing various ways of reacting to anger. Students were asked to rate on a 6-point Likert scale (1 = Never to 6 = Always) how they react when they are angry.

The short version of the Child Depression Inventory (CDI) (Kovacs, 1992), one of the most widely used assessment tools for both clinical and nonclinical populations, was used to assess depressive symptoms in the students. Each of the 10 items consists of 3 statements expressing different levels of a depressive symptom. Students are asked to indicate which statement is the truest for them by placing a tick ( ) next to their choice.

The Brief Life Event Inventory for Adolescents (LEI-A) consists of 17 items describing adverse life events such as a death in the family. Students are asked to state whether the situation has happened to them (by circling "Yes" or "No") and, if yes, how much it bothered them on a 4-point response scale. Items were scored on a 1 to 5, in which 1 represented an event that had not happened to them and 5 represented an event that had happened to them and bothered them a lot.

The self-concept measure was derived from the Self-Description Questionnaire (SDQ) II (Marsh, 1990; Marsh, 2000), an Australian instrument with local norms and widely regarded internationally to be the best available self-concept instrument for this age group (Boyle, 1994; Byrne, 1996; Hattie, 1992). The 102 items yield 11 subscales, each measuring a distinct component of self-concept. A shorter 51-item version has been developed specifically for this study. This shorter version retains the 11 subscales and strong psychometric properties of the longer version of the instrument and is particularly suitable for this large-scale study.

## INSTRUMENT RELIABILITIES AND ITEM SAMPLES

### APRI Bully Scales

Bully verbal (.89, .90, .92); 6 items (e.g.: I teased them by saying things to them.)
Bully social (.82, .86, .90); 6 items (e.g.: I got my friends to turn against a student.)
Bully physical (.85, .87, .90); 6 items (e.g.: I got into a physical fight with a student because I didn't like her.)

### APRI Victim (Target of Bullying) Scales

Victim verbal (.92, .92, .93); 6 items (e.g.: I was teased by students saying things to me.)
Victim social (.87, .91, .92); 6 items (e.g.: A student wouldn't be friends with me because other people didn't like me.)
Victim physical (.89, .89, .92); 6 items (e.g.: I was threatened to be physically hurt or harmed.)

### APRI-PR Participation Roles

Role active reinforcer (.78, .86, .87); 6 items (e.g.: I would join in myself.)
Role passive reinforcer (.88, .90, .91); 6 items (e.g.: I would stay to watch what happens.)
Role ignore (.87, .89, .91); 6 items (e.g.: I would pay no attention to it.)
Role victim advocate (.89, .91, .92); 6 items (e.g.: I would get my friends to help me stop it.)

### APRI-A Bully Attitudes

Pro-bully (.64, .68, .74); 6 items (e.g.: It's okay to bully others if others are doing it.)
Pro-victim (.68, .74, .79); 6 items (e.g.: People who are bullied deserve our help.)

# Coping Style

Cope avoidance (.75, .79, .83); 6 items (e.g.: I avoid the problem by spending more time alone.)

Cope problem solving (.85, .87, .89); 5 items (e.g.: I develop a plan about how to solve the problem before doing anything.)

Cope seek support (.90, .91, .92); 4 items (e.g.: I go to a friend for advice on how to solve the problem.)

# Locus Of Control

LOC internal (.75, .81, .85); 4 items (e.g.: My own efforts and actions are what will determine my future.)

LOC external (.71, .75, .78); 4 items (e.g.: External things mostly control my life.)

# AEI: Anger Expression

Anger control (.85, .87, .88); 4 items (e.g.: I stay steady and in control.)

Anger internalize (.67, .69, .75); 4 items (e.g.: No one can tell, but I am furious inside.)

Anger externalize (.66, .68, .71); 4 items (e.g.: I let people see just how angry I am.)

# CDI-Short: Childhood Depression

Depression (.83, .85, .76); 10 Items (e.g.: I am sad once in a while, I am sad many times, and I am sad all the time.)

# Stressful Life Events

Event (.64, .65, .67); 17 items (e.g.: Someone very close to me died.)

# SDQ II Short: Self-Concept

Physical (.83, .84, .84); 4 items (e.g.: I enjoy things like sports, gym and dance.)

Appearance (.87, .88, .89); 4 items (e.g.: I have a nice looking face.)

Opposite sex relations (.85, .84, .85); 4 items (e.g.: I am not very popular with members of the opposite sex.)

Same sex relations (.79, .82, .83); 5 items (e.g.: It is difficult to make friends with members of my own sex.)

Parent relations (.84, .86, .85); 4 items (e.g.: I get along well with my parents.)

Honesty/Trustworthiness (.79, .81, .81); 6 items (e.g.: I am honest.)

Emotional stability (.81, .83, .85); 5 items (e.g.: I worry more than I need to.)

General self-esteem (.82, .84, .85); 6 items (e.g.: Overall, I have a lot to be proud of.)

Academic math (.90, .90, .90); 4 items (e.g.: Mathematics is one of my best subjects.)

Academic verbal (.89, .90, .91); 5 items (e.g.: I am hopeless in English classes.)

Academic school (.84, .86, .86); 4 items (e.g.: I get bad marks in most school subjects.)

---

Note: For each scale, the coefficient *alpha* estimates of reliability are presented for responses at Times 1, 2, and 3 respectively (in parentheses) along with the number of items and sample items from the scales.

CHAPTER

5

# The Bully in the Family: Family Influences on Bullying

JAMES R. HOLMES
*Center for Psychological Services*

HEATHER A. HOLMES-LONERGAN
*Metropolitan State College of Denver*

The purpose of this chapter is to review family influences on the development of bullies. One of the difficulties in reviewing research on bullying is that there is little agreement about how the concept of a bully is formulated. More specifically, the literature on bullying does not contain a comprehensive, generally accepted formulation of the concept of bullying. Hence, before reviewing the literature on bullies in families, this chapter presents an alternate, and we believe more coherent, framework for understanding the concept of a bully and the behavior of bullies.

## THE FRAMEWORK OF DESCRIPTIVE PSYCHOLOGY

Because this discussion uses parts of the descriptive psychology framework, a brief introduction to this framework is necessary. Descriptive psychology is a set of concepts delineated by Peter G. Ossorio (1979, 1995) and applied by Ossorio and his colleagues to a wide range of problems both within and outside the domain of traditional psychology over the past 40 years. One way to understand descriptive psychology is to think of it as a map. In this case, it is a map of the concepts of persons, behavior, language, and the world. As a map, it is not a theory anymore than a map of Florida is a theory about Florida. However, once you have a map of Florida or any other territory, you can begin to systematically explore the various parts of the territory and to map the different features and the relationships between those features. You can systematically map things like towns, roads, rivers, lakes, hills, and the coastline and also systematically assess populations of plants and animals, water supplies, air quality, commerce, and so forth.

You cannot have a theory about something unless and until you have some idea of what the theory is a theory of. You cannot have a theory about elephants unless you have the concept of an elephant. The proverbial tale of the three blind men and the elephant each holding a part of the elephant's body and loudly proclaiming that the trunk, tail, or leg is what an elephant is illustrates the difficulty in developing a theory or engaging in empirical research without first being able to systematically say what a theory is a theory about.

Descriptive psychology delineates the concepts of a person and behavior, which inturn enables a systematic investigation of questions about why people do what they do, what the differences are among people, and how people develop. It provides a framework for keeping track of what we know and do not know about people and their behavior. For the purposes of this chapter, it is best to view descriptive psychology as an organizing framework in which we represent systematically what we do as psychologists. We can represent all of our current theories and our efforts to answer empirical questions that we develop from those theories in descriptive psychology. We can describe our efforts to change people and their behavior through therapeutic and educational programs. We can also distinguish conceptual questions that cannot be answered by empirical research from empirical questions that can only be answered by observation.[1]

This chapter presents parts of the descriptive psychology framework to delineate the concept of bullying in a way that will facilitate future attempts to develop empirical research and a better understanding of the bullying phenomenon.

## HOW DO WE DEFINE BULLYING? LET US COUNT THE WAYS

A number of researchers have attempted to define bullying behavior. For example:

- Tattum and Tattum (1992) explain that "bullying is the willful, conscious desire to hurt another and put him/her under stress."

---

[1] Because descriptive psychology is a framework within which we can represent all of the facts about persons and their behavior and therefore all the facts about everything else, the framework can be used to represent all of human knowledge (Ossorio, 1998).

- Rigby (1996) defines bullying as "the repeated oppression, psychological, or physical, of a less powerful person by a more powerful person or group of persons."
- Griffiths (1997) describes bullying as a repetitive attack that causes distress not only at the time of attack but also by the threat of future attack. It may be verbal, physical, social, or psychological.
- Smith (2000) says that bullying is the systematic abuse of power.
- Farrington (1993) defines bullying as "a physical, verbal, or psychological attack or intimidation intended to cause fear, distress, or harm to the victim, with a more powerful person oppressing a less powerful one."
- The U.S. Justice Department (Ericson, 2001) describes bullying as the following:

> Bullying encompasses a variety of negative acts carried out repeatedly over time. It involves a real or perceived imbalance of power, with the more powerful child or group attacking those who are less powerful. Bullying can take three forms: physical (hitting, kicking, spitting, pushing, taking personal belongings); verbal (taunting, malicious teasing, name calling, making threats); and psychological (spreading rumors, manipulating social relationships, or engaging in social exclusion, extortion, or intimidation).

Other definitions focus on what happens to the victim in school settings:

- "A person is being bullied when he or she is exposed, repeatedly over time, to negative actions on the part of one or more other students" (Olweus, 1993, p. 9).
- "A student is being bullied or picked on when another student says nasty and unpleasant things to him or her. It is also bullying when a student is hit, kicked, threatened, locked inside a room, sent nasty notes, and when no one ever talks to him" (Smith & Sharp, 1994, p. 1).

In the above definitions, bullying is seen as a type of desire, a type of oppression, an attack, or an abuse of power. The definitions include a wide range of negative physical, verbal, and psychological behaviors. Others have defined bullying in terms of what happens to the victim. These definitions are quite different, confusing, and sometimes contradictory. Moreover, they are not helpful in adding to our understanding of bullies and bullying because:

- To describe what a bully does as oppression or as a repetitive attack on another does not distinguish those actions from other forms of oppression or other types of attacks, and it does not tell us what the bully gains from being oppressive.
- Although a bully might want to hurt or put his victim under stress, it is by no means clear what the bully would gain from such an interaction. There are ways of causing stress that have little to do with bullying.

- Defining bullying as an abuse of power does not give us access to what the bully actually does and does not distinguish between bullying as an abuse of power and other types of abuses of power.

We are left with the conclusion that the bully engages in some form of behavior that is harmful to others in some way, but these definitions do not allow us to distinguish bullying from other types of abuse, and they do not contribute to our understanding of what makes an aggressive or negative behavior a case of bullying.

Definitions that focus on the victim and what happens to the victim also do not shed light on the bully or his behavior. Such definitions focus on the victim. To say that a victim is being bullied when he is being hit, kicked, locked-out, or taunted tells us little about what makes those behaviors instances of bullying as opposed to some other form of aggression or violence. The list of the types of mistreatment is so extensive that one begins to wonder whether it is just that, a list of the ways in which a person can be mistreated on a regular basis in schools, work settings, or families. As such, this list does not distinguish the acts of a bully from other forms of neglect or abuse.

## BULLYING FROM A DESCRIPTIVE PSYCHOLOGY STANDPOINT

What is needed here is not a better definition of bullying but a better understanding of the concepts of bullying and being a bully. Previous formulations of bullying have not recognized that the statement "Butch[2] is bullying Bill" is a criticism or an appraisal of Butch's behavior. In saying this, we are saying that Butch's actions were in some way inappropriate and we are criticizing his behavior, but we are not directly identifying what Butch did. There is a wide range of behaviors that we would appraise as being cases of bullying. For example, Butch may be kicking or pushing Bill around, taking his lunch money, chasing him off the playground, threatening to break his arm, harassing him as he walks down the hall, or putting his face in the mud. Moreover, Butch's use of certain behavior could in turn be a way of achieving another goal. Butch could be kicking Bill to prove he's "king of the hill," to punish Bill for some transgression, or to get money to buy cigarettes. Butch could also be emulating his father

---

[2] In this paper, we will use "Butch" as our generic title for someone we would view as a bully; therefore, we will often use masculine pronouns. We are certainly aware that there are girls and women who are viewed as bullies, but males are more likely to be bullies than females, and Butch allows us to avoid awkward language. Moreover, we want to keep open the possibility that Butch may be engaged in a variety of other behaviors. Our apologies to the Butch's of the world who do not engage in any of these behaviors.

who kicks his mother on a regular basis. We might characterize all of these actions as being cases of bullying. In doing so, we are making an appraisal of Butch's actions.

As with any behavior, a number of intended and unintended results may occur as a result of Butch's behavior. For example, adults may punish Butch, or Bill's friends may gang up on him. One of the other unintended results of Butch's behavior may be that observers and critics judge his behavior as bullying behavior. He is then classified as a "bully."

It is important to note that children do not typically set out to bully others aspire to become a bullies. Children whose behavior is appraised as bullying are reported to offer the following explanations for what they were doing (Rigby, 2002):

"Because they annoyed me."
"To get even."
"For fun."
"Because others were doing it."
"Because they were wimps."
"To show how tough one is."
"To get things or money from them."

From the above comments, it does not appear that these children would describe themselves as being bullies or as engaged in bullying behaviors. As actors, they describe themselves as having very different goals in mind. As critics, we might describe their behavior somewhat differently. We would not necessarily expect actor descriptions of a behavior to be the same as critic descriptions of the same behavior. Being aware of and understanding the difference between the kinds of descriptions that we as actors and as critics[3] would give of the same behavior is essential to understanding the behavior in question. Learning what a bully intends to achieve through his or her behavior is an important step in any attempt to investigate systematically what bullies are doing or to develop prevention or treatment programs for bullying. This is not to say that these children are behaving in ways that are acceptable or that sanctions for their actions are not warranted. However, for a critic to simply say that the child is engaged in bullying may not provide us with a scientifically or pragmatically useful way to approach the phenomenon in question.

The way we have described and tried to understand bullying as explained in the previous pages is an example of a fairly common kind of error that we make in trying to describe and understand the behavior of children and adults. That is, we identify some state of affairs that result from a person's behavior and conclude that this particular state of affairs is what the person wanted and was trying to achieve. This is the difference between a *behavior*

---

[3] The concepts of actor and critic will be delineated more fully later on, but here they can be viewed as different perspectives that we can take with regard to behavior.

*description* (what the person wanted and was trying to achieve) and an *achievement description* (the state of affairs that resulted from the person's behavior).

In other cases, identifying the results of a behavior is confused with identifying the person's intentions. For example, when a teacher says that "Joe is a troublemaker" or that "He is causing problems in the classroom," it may sound as though she is describing Joe's behavior. However, the teacher's description does not explain what Joe did or why he did it. The teacher's description *does* tell us that Joe's behavior has resulted in making the teacher believe Joe is behaving inappropriately and creating a problem. Joe may be starting a spitball fight, teasing a girl he likes, or making funny sounds that entertain his friends. Although his actions may cause trouble for the teacher, he is probably not trying to cause trouble; Joe may simply be having fun or goofing around.

For a parent to say of a child, "He's driving me crazy!" means that the parent is not identifying what the child is doing but saying that the child's behavior has caused frustration. Notice that upon hearing that the child has been driving the mother crazy, we are likely to ask the parent to tell us what the child has been doing. The answer, "driving me crazy," expresses the mother's state of mind but does not tell us what the child is trying to achieve. Children seldom wake up and say, "I think I will drive Mom crazy today" or "I am going to disrupt Mrs. Jones's classroom."

Hence, we may say that Joe is disturbing the classroom, but we probably are not identifying what Joe is doing. We are identifying one of the results of Joe's behavior and offering a criticism of Joe. The criticism may tell us where the teacher stands, but it also tells us a little about what it is that Joe is doing in the classroom. Joe may be engaged in one or more of a wide range of behaviors that have the effect of creating a disturbance in the classroom, but it is unlikely that Joe wants or even knows that his behavior is having that result.

## ACHIEVEMENT DESCRIPTIONS AS PARTIAL BEHAVIOR DESCRIPTIONS: UNDERSTANDING THE BEHAVIOR OF THE BULLY

At this point, the reader might ask, "So why is it important to distinguish between achievement descriptions and behavior descriptions?" When we, as parents, educators, and researchers, do not recognize that we are incorrectly identifying what a child is trying to accomplish, we are very likely to overlook or misunderstand the significance of what the child is doing. As a result, we are likely to be ineffective in stopping or preventing the behavior. For example, the teacher or parent who appraises the child as being a "troublemaker" and who describes the child's behavior as "making trouble" is likely to misunderstand what the child is doing and consequently is unlikely to be effective in working with the child. Likewise, attempts to conduct research on the causes of troublemaking or disruptive behavior are also unlikely to be productive because it is not clear what behavioral phenomena are being investigated.

## Other Research on Achievement Descriptions Versus Behavior Descriptions

Little research on human behavior has been conducted concerning achievement versus behavior descriptions. Davis (2002), however, has shown that describing someone as a stalker does not identify the stalker's motivation or the significance of what it is that the stalker is trying to do. Davis then proceeds to develop a description of the stalker's behavior that includes the motivation for and significance of what the stalker does. More specifically, the actions of stalkers can be understood as attempts to act on the status that the stalker has assigned to the victim. The stalker has assigned the victim the status of his or her beloved and is engaging in behaviors that express that relationship. The victim can be a person who has had a previous relationship with the stalker or someone whom the stalker has never met but someone to whom the stalker has assigned the status of "my beloved". The perpetrator will send letters, give gifts, make phone calls, and be constantly preoccupied with his or her beloved. The victim may well be terrified by the perpetrator's actions. Obviously, the person who is the object of these actions no longer has and may never have had a love relationship with the perpetrator and may well be terrified by the perpetrator's actions. To say, however, that the perpetrator is stalking the victim is to offer a criticism (and one that may be warranted from a legal standpoint), but it does not offer an account of what the stalker is doing that is useful scientifically, nor does it provide an understanding for effectively dealing with the actions of the perpetrator.

## Forms or Parameters of Behavior Description

To illustrate the distinction between a behavior description and an achievement description, it is useful to discuss what is involved in identifying a behavior and identifying the results of a behavior. In describing what a person is doing, we make a commitment to a range of facts about the person and the behavior in question:

- *Want*: If we say that Sally is going to get a drink of water so she can take her medicine, we are saying that Sally is reason or motive for getting a drink of water is to take her medicine.
- *Knowledge*: We are also saying that Sally has the concepts and facts needed to perform the behavior. She has concepts regarding medicine, the pill, water, sources of water, and facts about where the water is located.

- *Know-how*: Sally also has the skill for getting the water, drinking from a container, and swallowing a pill.
- *Performance*: We are also saying that Sally engages in an observable performance such as walking to the cabinet and getting a glass.
- *Achievement*: There is likely to be more than one result of Sally's performance. If she is successful, she gets a drink. However, there may be unintended results of the behavior, such as Sally dropping the glass, spilling the water on the floor, and getting cut picking up the glass.
- *Personal characteristics*: We are also saying that Sally's behavior is an expression of one or more of her personal characteristics, such as she is self-reliant and likes to take care of her medication by herself.
- *Significance*: Finally, we are saying that Sally is participating in one or more of the social practices of her community. In this example, she is taking medication to treat an illness.

Whenever we identify what a person is doing, we are making a commitment to all of these aspects of behavior. Notice how little sense it would make to say that Sally went to get a drink of water but had no reason to do so or could not distinguish water from other things. Engaging in the performance of getting a drink would not be possible if Sally had not mastered the necessary range of concepts and skills, as any parent knows. Also, it would make no sense to say that the behavior had no result even if the result was an unintended minor disaster. We would not know what to make of the statement "Sally engaged in a behavior that did not reflect her knowledge, values, abilities, or other personal characteristics." Finally, we would not understand Sally's actions if we could not recognize that her behavior was one of the things we as members of our community do and that she performed it in a familiar way.

The aspects of behavior illustrated above are parameters of behavior in that they are the ways in which one behavior can be similar to or different from another behavior. If we change the values of any one of the parameters, we will be identifying a different behavior. A simple case is that the same performance can be a way of accomplishing two different behaviors if the want or motivation parameter is different in the two behaviors. For example, I can clean the house because I want a clean house, or I can clean the house because I am afraid someone will be angry with me if I do not clean the house. The performances are the same although the motivation I am acting on may be quite different. As a result, my behavior can be described as cleaning the house in the first case and as avoiding someone's anger in the second case.

Because the parameters of behavior (*want, knowledge, know-how, performance, achievement, personal characteristics*, and *significance*) represent the ways in which one behavior can be similar to or different from another behavior, every instance of behavior will include all of the parameters. In describing what a person is doing, we are assigning values to all of the parameters. However, there are a number of reasons why we might refrain from assigning values to one or more of the parameters and, in doing so, we give less than a complete description of the behavior. One obvious reason for restricting ourselves in assigning values to particular parameters is that we do not know what the values of the parameters are for a particular behavior. I may observe my friend wandering around the house but not know why he is engaged in this performance.

## Behavior Description Versus Activity Description

To say that "Butch is bullying Bill" sounds like a description of Butch's behavior. It is at best, however, an *activity description*. An activity description is a limited behavior description that does not specify what the person wants or achieves and does not indicate the significance of the behavior. As we have seen, we do not know what Butch wants, is trying to achieve, or is doing by bullying Bill. The description "Butch is bullying Bill" also does not identify what performance Butch is engaged in. There is a wide range of performances that Butch might be engaged in that would count as bullying.

Most of the research that has been done on bullying has focused on activities such as hitting, shoving, making threats, and taking money or possessions. Little attention has been given to fact that the activities we evaluate as being instances of bullying are quite different, and there is a very real possibility that the significance of those behaviors may be quite different as well. The behavior of two children who are pushing or hitting younger children on the playground could be appraised as bullying, but the motivation for and significance of their behaviors might be very different. For example, one child may be trying to get money from the younger children, while the other child may be trying to show them who is boss. Questions about the significance of behaviors have generally not been addressed in empirical research on bullying. As a result, our understanding of bullies and their behavior has been limited.

## Achievement Descriptions Revisited

*Achievement descriptions* are states of affairs that are the result of a behavior or a series of behaviors. Examples of achievement descriptions include:

"Sam got a 100% on the exam."
"Tom ticked him off."
"Mary frustrated the heck out of me."
"Her ex-boyfriend is stalking Helen."
"Butch bullied Bill."

Each of these descriptions identifies a particular state of affairs that is achieved as the result of some performance. However, it should be noted that an achievement description is a very limited description because we are not making any commitment regarding the want, knowledge, know-how, performance, significance, or personal characteristic parameters of the behavior. As a result, we do not know the person's performance or how the behavior was accomplished. Sam may have cheated to get a 100% on the test. Further, we do not know what the person wanted or what concepts or skills the person was acting on. Tom may have unknowingly angered the person in question, and Mary may simply not have understood what I was trying to say. Similarly, Butch may be trying to get others to accept him and have no idea that he was bullying Bill because that was not his intention. Others, such as Butch's parents or teachers, may say that Butch's behavior clearly qualifies as bullying. Butch, however, would probably not recognize bullying Bill as something he was trying to do or wanted to do.

## ACTOR, OBSERVER, CRITIC: THREE WAYS TO UNDERSTAND THE BEHAVIOR OF BULLIES

To better understand this kind of difference in what Butch and others would say about what Butch is doing, we will need to introduce the three logical roles that we can have with regard to behavior. The three roles are *actor, observer-describer,* and *critic-appraiser.* These three roles are not metaphysical entities but simply three kinds of jobs in which we all engage. Since actor, observer, and critic are logical roles or jobs that a person can have with regard to behavior, they can be occupied or carried out by the same person or by different people. Thus, I can function as an actor and be an observer and critic of my own behavior, or I can be an observer and/or critic of the behavior of other people. I can be an actor and others can function as observers and/or critics of my behavior.

The actor, observer, and critic (AOC) diagram presented in Figure 1 is a convenient way of illustrating the dynamics of these three logical roles. In general, the AOC diagram represents how we function as self-regulating persons. That is, as actors, we do what comes naturally. We act on our

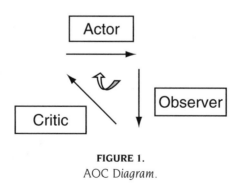

**FIGURE 1.**
AOC *Diagram.*

reasons to do something. As actors, we are spontaneous, creative, and value giving. As observer-describers of behavior, our job is to be aware of what we are doing, to note what is happening, to understand is the case, and to note how things are. Our task as critic-appraisers is to act in the interest of the actor. We do this by deciding whether things are going satisfactorily and appreciating that things are going well if that is the case. If things are not satisfactory, our job as critic is to figure out what has gone wrong and prescribe ways to make things go better for the actor. If self-criticism is effective, we, as actors, are able to make things go better. For example, I was driving down the road, I was aware of what I was doing, and I took corrective action when I noticed the car in front of me weaving from one lane to another.

These three jobs are an essential part of being a person. Imagine if you will an individual being unable to do any one of these three jobs. An individual who could not act spontaneously and do what comes naturally would be, at best, a pathological person and, at worst, a machine making motions or an individual living the life of a vegetable. A person who acts but has no idea what he or she is doing would be considered to be a potential menace, and we would restrain his or her freedom to act in the world. A person who could not function as a critic would be unable to recognize when his or her behavior was inappropriate or take corrective action to make things go better. This individual would have difficulty surviving or being treated as a full-fledged person.

Part of a critic's job is to notice and be able to say how things have gone wrong. Thus, the language of the critic tends to be evaluative and to focus on how well the actor has done. The language of the actor tends to focus on the state of affairs that the actor wants or is trying to achieve. In saying that Butch is a bully or that he is engaged in bullying Bill, we are functioning primarily as critics. We are not primarily identifying what Butch wanted or was trying to achieve. We are evaluating how appropriately he has behaved.

One of the ways that we can go wrong as observers and critics of persons and their behavior is to assume that the various states of affairs that occur as a result of a person's behavior are what the person was trying to achieve. As we shall see, this kind of error has restricted efforts in understanding and preventing the kinds of behaviors that we appraise as bullying.

## BULLYING AND STATUS: HOW TO GET IT AND HOW TO KEEP IT

When we discussed stalkers earlier, we said that the stalker is someone who is acting on an assumed relationship. He is treating the object of his attention as his beloved. He is not eligible to have a relationship with the person he designates as his beloved, so his behavior is inappropriate and may be illegal, but his behavior does make sense. The formulation by Davis

(2002) helps us to make sense out of "stalking" behaviors and to better understand what stalkers are trying to achieve.

It may be the case that the people we identify as bullies are similarly enacting a certain kind of relationship or status[4] with whom they are interacting. All behaviors that are viewed as bullying seem to be ways of degrading another person and, as such, may be ways of affirming that a bully is someone who has a higher status than a victim. When Butch is hitting Bill, taking his personal belongings, calling him names, and intimidating him in other ways, he is not doing these things for their own sake. Butch is engaging in these activities to establish or maintain a particular relationship or status with regard to Bill or other victims.

More specifically, Butch may be doing these things to show that he is someone who has a special status or place in the community. One of the ways in which people can increase their status is by successfully degrading others. As we have seen, there are a large number of behaviors that we would view as instances of bullying. All of these behaviors can be seen as ways of degrading others. Even actions such as demanding the victim's money can be a way of degrading the victim, especially if the bully's intention in taking the money is to show that he or she can force the victim to do the bully's bidding. Unfortunately, Butch achieves or maintains his status by degrading others who are unable to defend themselves. Butch has some status (e.g., older child, boss, or parent) or some other personal characteristic (usually size or strength) that allows him to take unfair advantage of others who do not have the status or personal characteristics that would enable them to defend themselves. This description of Butch's behavior is one way to make sense of the behaviors of those we regard as bullies. We can now view these behaviors as attempts by the bully to achieve or maintain an elevated status or position in the community by means of degrading others. Whether the behavior of Butch and other bullies has this kind of significance is an empirical question. However, this formulation of the significance of Butch's behavior does, as we shall see, allow us to understand much of the behavior that we appraise as bullying as well as better understand the results of research on bullying. With this conceptual framework in hand, we can now turn to a discussion of the research concerning family influence on bullying.

## THE BULLY IN THE FAMILY

Family influences on bullying have been explored by correlating appraisals that a child is a bully or is frequently engaged in bullying behaviors with a

---

[4] By status, we do not mean social prestige but one's place or position in a community. The community in question may be the neighborhood playground, a classroom, or a corner where kids hang out.

variety of family conditions and characteristics. Several studies have examined the impact of the overall conditions of the family, such as single-parent, divorced families, or socioeconomic status, on bullying (Farrington, 1993; Olweus, 1980). Other studies have examined the connection between parenting styles or discipline practices and children who engage in bullying (Baldry & Farrington, 1998, 2000; Curtner-Smith, 2000; Lowenstein, 1978; Olweus, 1980; Roland & Galloway, 2002; Stevens, De Bourdeaudhuij, & Van Oost, 2002). Still others have focused on children's perceptions of cohesion within the family or relationships with parents and how those perceptions relate to bullying (Berdondini & Smith, 1996; Bowers, Smith, & Binney, 1992; Espelage, Bosworth, & Simon, 2000; Říčan, 1995; Říčan, Klicperová, & Koucká, 1993; Rigby, 1993, 1994).

The literature has not concentrated as much on generating explanations for the relationship between the family and bullying behaviors, but a few researchers have addressed this issue (Loeber & Hay, 1997; Patterson, DeBaryshe, & Ramsey, 1989; Rigby, 1994; Smith, Bowers, Binney, & Cowie, 1993). Their explanations have dealt with attachment theory, family systems theory, and interactive models that examine the interplay between characteristics of the child and family or community variables.

Oliver, Oaks, and Hoover (1994) created a list of six characteristics that families of bullies tend to have:

1. "Cool-to-cold emotional environment" (p. 200) with lack of involvement from the primary caregiver

2. Permissive parenting style—few rules or limits for behavior, little family structure

3. Isolation of family from the community, and active social life or social involvement of family is lacking

4. Conflict between parents, and disharmony within the family

5. In appropriate use of discipline—parents fail to punish or may even reinforce aggression and fail to reward or may even punish prosocial behavior

6. Authoritarian parenting with high use of controlling and punitive discipline—parents try to maintain order with rigid household standards and rules

Batsche and Knoff (1994) add to this list of characteristics by stating that families of bullies are sometimes simultaneously hostile and permissive. They suggest that parents of bullies do not monitor or supervise their children very often or very closely (and, in particular, do not set limits with respect to their children's aggressive behavior), but when they do, they tend to use harsh, punitive methods of discipline (Greene, 2000). Further, Batsche and Knoff state that parents of bullies "have poor problem-solving skills" and "teach their children to strike back at the least provocation" (p.166).

Neufeld (2002), in a paper on ethics that addresses the impact of families on bullying, cites some of the messages that children might hear in the home. These include "Being bullied is just a part of growing up," "You need to stand up for yourself," "Boys will be boys," and "You need to toughen up. Don't be so sensitive" (p. 207).

## Family Characteristics of Bullies

These descriptions paint a picture of a family environment that is hostile, negative, and lacking in warmth and affection. Greene (2000) states that parents of bullies feel detached from their children and that "not surprisingly, these children do not feel particularly close to their parents" (p. 79). Further, parents of bullies more often use power-assertive discipline to maintain order within the household. It is quite likely that children who become bullies have learned at home what kinds of behaviors will enable them to maintain or increase their status by degrading the status of others. We will return to this point later in the chapter.

A number of studies have clearly shown that parenting styles and discipline practices are related to bullying behavior. Much of the research literature has focused on specific parenting practices or methods of discipline and their relationship to bullying behavior. In general, these studies indicate that more authoritarian and punitive styles of parenting are positively correlated with bullying (Baldry & Farrington, 1998, 2000; Curtner-Smith, 2000; Lowenstein, 1978; Olweus, 1980; Roland & Galloway, 2002; Stevens, De Bourdeaudhuij, & Van Oost, 2002). In one of the earliest studies to examine parents' perceptions of their discipline techniques and their relationship to bullying, Olweus (1980) interviewed mothers about their attitudes toward their children, their use of power-assertive methods of discipline, and their attitudes toward aggression in their children. He found mothers who had more negative attitudes toward their children, who used more physical punishment, and who permitted higher levels of aggression in their children were more likely to have children who were more aggressive. One of the difficulties here, however, is that it is not clear how or whether aggressiveness in children is related to bullying. Children who are aggressive may be successful in a wide range of acceptable ways and may not use their aggression to degrade others.

Baldry and Farrington (1998) measured authoritative versus authoritarian parenting, parental involvement in school matters and parental support, and parental agreement. In addition, they measured parental use of punitive punishment. Bullies had parents who were more authoritarian, more punitive, who disagreed more often, and who were less supportive. In a second study, Baldry and Farrington (2000) measured parental practices, which included parenting style, agreement between parents, and agreement between the child and the parents. The parenting style items assessed the degree to which parents used an authoritarian versus a supportive style.

Again, they found that bullies were more likely to have parents who used an authoritarian parenting style and who more often disagreed with one another and with the child.

Curtner-Smith (2000) asked mothers to rate the following: marital satisfaction, disciplinary practices, levels of social support, temperament, levels of depression, degree of parent-child involvement, and perceptions of sons' friendships. Sons' perceptions of how closely their mothers monitored their behavior were assessed as well. Boys who had higher ratings of bullying behavior had mothers who were less satisfied with their marriages, used inappropriate methods of discipline (e.g., hitting, nagging, locking the child out of the house), and had little social support from others. Mothers who reported that they often felt angry or depressed had boys who were more likely to engage in bullying. Low family involvement also was positively correlated with bullying. Curtner-Smith argues these measures indicate that in families with bullies, mothers are modeling poor relationship skills for their sons and the family climate of bullies is angry, hostile, and generally negative.

In a study of aggressive victims (who can sometimes also be bullies), Schwartz, Dodge, Pettit, and Bates (1997) conducted interviews with mothers who were asked to discuss the harshness and frequency of their discipline, how often children were exposed to physical violence in the home or the community, and the degree of marital conflict in the home. The mothers completed a written questionnaire on how family members resolved conflicts, and interviewers observed mother-child interaction during the visit. The interviewer assessed how likely it was that a child had experienced physical abuse. Interviewers rated how often a mother expressed hostility and warmth to the child during the visit. Family Socioeconomic Status (SES) was also assessed. Aggressive victim status of the children was assessed three to four years later. Boys who became aggressive victims came from homes where they were exposed to violence. Physical punishment and abuse were common. Mothers tended to be harsh and restrictive, and high degrees of conflict in the home were reported.

## Bullies' Perceptions of Their Families

Another approach to research concerning family influences on bullying has been to ask children to give their perceptions of their relationships with their parents. Several studies have shown that children who bully perceive their parents to be more authoritarian, and they rate their families as less cohesive than do victims or control children (Berdondini & Smith, 1996; Bowers, Smith, & Binney, 1992; Espelage, Bosworth, & Simon, 2000; Říčan, 1995; Říčan et al., 1993; Rigby, 1993, 1994). Some of the seminal studies on this aspect of family influences on bullying (Berdondini & Smith,1996; Bowers et al., 1992; Smith, Bowers, Binney, & Cowie, 1993) used the Family System Test (FAST) to assess children's perceptions of cohesion within the family. The test requires children to place wooden figures, each of which represents a family member, on a wooden board. The distances between the figures are then measured to determine the children's perceptions of how close family members are to one another. Blocks under the figures indicate how much power family members are perceived to have. All three studies indicated that cohesion scores were lower for bullies than for comparison groups. Two of the studies (Bowers *et al.*, 1992; Smith *et al.*, 1993) indicated that bullies perceived their siblings as quite powerful. In one study (Bowers *et al.*, 1992), bullies and victims had higher power scores for fathers than for mothers, but the effects were not very strong.

In a similar vein, Rigby (1993, 1994) used the Family Functioning in Adolescence Questionnaire, which measures adolescents' perceptions of cohesion, affective expressiveness, communication, democratic methods of discipline, transmission of ethical standards, and the permeable boundaries within the family. Rigby (1993) also used the Attitude Toward Parents Scale, which consists of a set of adjectives that are applied to both the mother and the father. These adjectives are *friendly, fair, understanding, helpful, affectionate, dependable, critical, sarcastic, unkind, bossy, selfish,* and *suspicious.* Finally, Rigby assessed adolescents' relationships to their parents by asking them to state how close versus distant, how warm versus cold, and how positive versus negative they felt those relationships were. Children who had greater tendencies to bully had lower scores on the Family Functioning Scale (Rigby, 1993, 1994) as well as less positive attitudes toward their parents and less positive relationships with their parents (1993).

Espelage and colleagues (2000) asked young adolescents to rate the kinds of messages they received from their families about violence, what kinds of discipline were used in their homes, and how much time they spent with their families. Adolescents from families who used more physical discipline were more likely to engage in bullying behavior as were adolescents who spent less time with their family members and those who received fewer messages about using nonviolent means of conflict resolution. Flouri and Buchanan (2003) also found that children who perceived a high degree of involvement between themselves and their parents were less likely to engage in bullying. In a study by Ma (2001), children who stated that their parents were more involved in their schooling were less likely to bully others.

Finally, Říčan and colleagues (Říčan, 1995; Říčan, *et al.*, 1993) have investigated this issue as well. Říčan conducted a factor analysis on The Family Principles Questionnaire, which is designed to assess the transmission of values from parent to child. He measured the association between scores on this questionnaire and bullying. Children who espoused values such as "We should try to help suffering people" and "If you see somebody being hurt, defend him!" were less likely to be bullies. Říčan and colleagues asked children to complete questionnaires regarding their relationships with their parents. Fathers' positive attitude was negatively associated with bullying (for girls only), and fathers' hostility was positively associated with bullying (for both boys and girls). Fathers' encouragement of autonomy was negatively correlated with bullying. For mothers, only their hostility in their relationships with their sons was positively associated with bullying.

Still other studies have assessed family relationships from the points of view of both parent and child. Stevens *et al.* (2002) measured the quality of family functioning using a Dutch version of the Family Environment Scale. This scale includes seven subscales: *cohesion, expressiveness, conflict, organization, control, moral emphasis,* and *social orientation.* Parenting practices were assessed using the Child-Rearing Inventory. This inventory includes three subscales that measure parents' use of punishment, the degree to which children experience a warm and attached relationship with their parents, and the degree to which parents encourage children to be autonomous. On these scales, bullies perceived less cohesion, expressiveness, organization, control, and social orientation and experienced more conflict within their families than victims or control children. On the parenting measure, parents of bullies reported using more punishment, and bullies perceived that more punishment occurred at home than did control children. Control children reported a more personal relationship with their parents than did bullies.

## Sibling Influences

There is evidence to suggest that there are sibling, as well as parental, influences on bullying. Duncan (1999) found that children who bullied their peers were also likely to bully their siblings. Ma (2001) related family size to bullying behavior and found that children from larger families were more likely to become bullies than victims. The author speculates that these children are more likely to experience more bullying from siblings and that there is a "carry-over effect" to their relations with peers. Greene (2000) also cites evidence that children who are bullies are more concerned with the power differentials between themselves and their siblings than are children who are not bullies.

## Direct Influences of Family Relationships on Bullying

When we move from describing the patterns of behavior that occur in the families of bullies to attempting to explain why the correlations between parent-child interactions and bullying exist, several different theoretical perspectives have been proposed. First, a number of researchers have suggested that the connection between parental discipline practices and child bullying behavior is direct (Baldry & Farrington, 1998; Espelage *et al.*, 2000, Olweus, 1980; 1993). In other words, parents tolerate aggression in their children, display aggression through the use of an authoritarian parenting style and through the use of punitive physical punishment, and fail to show warmth and affection toward their children (Olweus, 1993). These behaviors directly shape the behavior of children in the family, so children learn that aggression is the way to achieve status because that has been modeled for them by their parents. Further, in these kinds of families, an aggressive intrusion by a family member that is met with an aggressive response by the child will often stop the family member's intrusion. Therefore, the child learns within the context of the family that aggression helps them to deflect unwanted interactions with others (Patterson & Yoerger, 1993).

In addition, the combination of a lack of parental supervision with the use of power-assertive methods of discipline may be especially potent in terms of its contribution to bullying behavior. Baldry and Farrington (1998) state that this kind of parent-child relationship makes children have a high need for power and status within the peer group and have fewer inhibitions toward aggression. Therefore, bullying is a natural consequence of their particular set of family influences.

## Indirect Family Influences—From Attachment to Family Systems Theory

Other researchers believe a broader view of the family environment is neces-sary (Patterson, et al., 1989; Rigby, 1994; Smith et al., 1993). In this view, it is important to consider how families developed such maladaptive patterns of behavior to begin with. For example, attachment theory has been discussed as a possible explanation for the negative family climates described above (Loeber & Hay, 1997; Smith & Myron-Wilson, 1998; Smith et al., 1993). Attachment theorists argue that the infant-mother attachment relationship serves as an internal working model for later relationships. There is evidence to suggest that children with an insecure attachment to their mothers have difficulty with later peer relationships (Turner, 1991; Troy & Sroufe, 1987). One study (Troy & Sroufe, 1987) showed that bullies were more likely to have had an avoidance attachment to their caregivers, whereas victims were more likely to have had an anxious attachment history.

To understand how an avoidance attachment history might develop, it is necessary to look more closely at the characteristics of the parents of bullies. According to Smith et al. (1993), parents who do not feel emotionally close to their children and/or who experience ambivalence about their roles as parents may be setting the stage for an avoidance attachment to develop. These parents have difficulty expressing positive emotions toward their children and may avoid interacting with them. The child, in turn, learns that the parent cannot be trusted to respond appropriately and learns to avoid the parent.

How would a parent develop these characteristics? A number of factors could be involved. Parents who suffer from psychological disorders, most notably depression, may be at risk (Loeber & Hay, 1997). Single parenthood, marital conflict, and divorce also have been associated with aggressive behavior, particularly in boys (Curtner-Smith, 2000; Loeber & Hay, 1997, Lowenstein, 1978, Patterson *et al.*, 1989). Other studies have not found these relationships (Espelage *et al.*, 2000, Loeber & Hay, 1997). SES and unemployment are family stressors that may contribute to bullying (Farrington, 1993; Patterson, *et al.*, 1989). Some studies, however, find no connection between SES and bullying (e.g., Olweus, 1980). Farrington (1993) assessed intergenerational transmission of bullying behavior specifically and found that there was a relationship. In other words, boys who bullied others as adolescents were more likely in their 30s to have children who were bullies.

The intergenerational effects of poor family management and discipline can also extend to grandparents. Having antisocial parents and grandparents is even more predictive of antisocial behavior in adolescence (Patterson *et al.*, 1989).

It has been suggested that the connection of family variables such as SES, divorce, single parenthood, and parental psychopathology with child aggression is not necessarily a direct one. Rather, the relationship is mediated by parental discipline practices and family management skills (Patterson *et al.*, 1989; Rigby, 2002; Smith *et al.*, 1993). In addition, Loeber and Hay (1997) delineated a list of characteristics that were associated with aggressive behavior of a child. These include temperament, intelligence, attention problems (e.g., ADHD), deficits in social problem-solving skills, and issues with self-esteem. Several of these characteristics also have been discussed in relation to bullying *per se* (Farrington, 1993; Olweus, 1980, 1993).

Some of these characteristics, most notably temperament and intelligence, are viewed as having a genetic component. Therefore, it could be argued that parents may influence these characteristics through their genetic contributions to their children. In addition, children contribute to the family environment partly in terms of their status on these various characteristics. Therefore, the family must be considered as a unit to understand why the child might become a bully (Rigby, 1994; Smith *et al.*, 1993).

Rigby (1994) believes that family systems theory provides a more coherent explanation for the relation between family influences and bullying than studying specific behaviors that occur between parents and children. In this theory, family patterns might predispose children toward bullying. According to Patterson *et al.* (1989), family stressors have a disruptive effect on parenting skills, which then puts the child at risk for adjustment problems. Smith *et al.* (1993) state that certain developmental pathways may lead to bullying. For example, an infant who has a difficult temperament may develop an avoidance attachment to his or her caregiver because the caregiver lacks the skills to deal effectively with the child's temperament. This parent might also be experiencing other stressors (Patterson *et al.*, 1989) that interfere with the parent's ability to be sensitive and responsive to the infant. If the family remains under stress, then it is likely that the family's management skills will continue to be less than optimal. The child then continues to be at increased risk for behavior and adjustment problems. One possible outcome of this developmental pathway could be bullying (Smith *et al.*, 1993).

## THE BULLY'S STATUS IN THE FAMILY

The most significant difficulty in approaching research on the ways in which families influence the development of bullies is that, as we noted earlier, there is no coherent or comprehensive formulation of the concept of bullying. Currently, we use the term *bullying* as a *criticism* of what someone is doing rather than as a way of *identifying* what the person is doing or why he or she is doing it. Thus we use the term to identify one of the states of affairs that may result from what someone does and not as a way of identifying a type of behavior. Consequently, the question of how families influence the development of bullying behavior becomes a question about how families influence the development of people who are later criticized for behaving inappropriately.

This kind of question is formally similar to the question of how families influence the development of children or adults with poor manners or children who do not play by the rules. Studies presented in the preceding review showed that bullying is associated with families in which people do not treat each other with respect or families in which children are not taught to respect the rights of others. In this view, bullying is viewed as a failure in socialization. One of the obvious questions here is why one child in such a family becomes a bully but others do not.

Some researchers suggest that children are socialized to be bullies. That is, they learn bullying by seeing other members of their family engage in bullying behaviors and simply emulate what they have learned (Baldry & Farrington, 1998; Espelage *et al.*, 2000, Olweus, 1980, 1993). Identifying someone as a bully is a negative status assignment, suggesting that the bully is somewhat cowardly and unable to compete with others who have status and are able to defend themselves. Why anyone would want to achieve the status of being a bully is not clear. As we have seen, it is not clear that Butch or any other person we designate as being a bully sets out to be or intends to be a bully.

In general, numerous studies correlate family characteristics with being designated as a bully. It appears that there is a positive correlation between being designated as a bully and coming from a family in which members are not accepted, respected, or loved and in which discipline is harsh and unpredictable. However, these studies do not describe *how* or *why* someone would become a bully in a particular family or type of family. The difficulty that researchers encounter in trying to understand bullies and how their behavior develops in certain family environments is that they are not focus-ing on the significance of what a bully is actually doing. For example, recall Butch and Bill's bullying situation described at the beginning of this chapter. These researchers are not asking what Butch is doing by acting in ways that are socially inappropriate, that violate the rights of others, and that in some cases are illegal. How does it make sense for Butch to become a person whom others do not respect and would avoid if possible?

To say that Butch is trying to increase or maintain his status by degrading others is to focus on the *significance* of what Butch is doing. In focusing on the significance of his behavior, we are asking the question, "What is he doing by pushing, shoving, taking money, chasing, and taunting Bill or other victims?" The values of the significance parameter of behavior are the other behaviors that are accomplished at one and the same time. For example, saying, "That was a stupid thing to do" is to engage in a verbal behavior, but it is also a way of insulting someone. Both behaviors are accomplished at one and the same time by means of the same performance.

The first thing to notice is that given this formulation, we can see how the many different types of behavior that bullies engage in make sense. All behaviors make sense as ways of one person degrading another. For example, taking a younger child's money, hitting the child, treating the child as a wimp, and intimidating the child all make sense as ways of degrading the child. Rather than seeing these behaviors as a more or less random list of bullies' actions, we can see how they are related as ways in which one person could degrade another. If Butch is able to successfully degrade Bill or others in his community, then Butch, in his view, has a higher position or status than those he has degraded. Asking the question, "What is Butch doing by doing the things that we see as bullying?" makes Butch's behavior more understandable and more accessible to scientific inquiry.

As Olweus (1993) has discussed, bullies are often speculated to be inse-cure underneath their "tough" exterior. Olweus states that the opposite, in fact, appears to be true. Bullies do not seem to lack self-confidence. If bullying behaviors are ways of increasing or maintaining Butch's status, then it is not surprising that Butch would report being self-confident. It is important to keep in mind, however, that bullies behave like persons with low self-confidence are expected to behave. Bullies seldom compete with others who are of equal status, age, strength, or size. Bullies typically pick targets who cannot or will not stand up to the bully. Therefore, it is possible that earlier research has not been able to determine the true nature of the bully's self-esteem. Further, the status that Butch achieves is therefore somewhat hollow because it is achieved by degrading others who are younger, weaker, and so forth.

Given this kind of significance description, we can begin to ask how a child would develop a pattern of achieving status by degrading others who are younger, weaker, or otherwise unable to stop the degradation. We also can begin to make sense out of the research on family influences on bullying. If the bully comes from a family in which other members degrade one another as a way to increase or maintain status, then it may be likely that the child will choose to behave in the same way outside the family. What kind of family would this be? Quite possibly this is a family that is lacking in warmth and affection, that uses authoritarian styles of discipline and power-assertive methods of punishment, and is lacking in cohesion. Our conceptual formulation, therefore, gives us a new way of examining the results of the research. Rather than focusing on what the parent is doing, such as the specific behaviors the parent is engaged in (e.g., yelling, spanking, etc.), it is more important to focus on the *significance* of what the parent is doing. In other words, if the parent in the course of dealing with the child is doing things that degrade the child's status, then the child (1) feels degraded and, because he or she is not able to increase his or her status at home, may choose to degrade him or her peers as a way of increasing status outside of the home and/or (2) learns that this behavior enables him or her to get what he or she wants.

It is important to note once again that the child is not waking up in the morning and saying, "I'm going to go and bully some other kids today." However, the child *is* in the position of having been degraded either directly or indirectly by the lack of acceptance and affection in the family. In general, a child is not able to successfully challenge the status parents assign to him or her. One way to gain the status he or she does not get at home is to degrade others: "I cannot hit my mother or father, but I can dish it out to the kid down the street."

A parent who lacks confidence in his or her parenting abilities, who does not feel close to his or her child, and who has learned to use punitive methods of punishment as a way to not only maintain order in the household but also to increase or maintain his or her own status is likely to make choices in dealing with his or her child that are degrading to the child. On the other hand, the fact that a child grows up in an authoritarian family (or a poor family, a single-parent family, etc.) does not mean that the child is necessarily degraded or disciplined in an arbitrary and harsh manner, which explains why children from these types of families do not always become bullies.

In addition, different children will solve the problems they face growing up in a family in different ways. One child will seek to emulate a parent while another will seek to be the opposite of the same parent. In dealing with neglectful, cold, harsh, and degrading parents, one child will move toward finding affection and acceptance from others while another child in the same family will seek to gain status through abusing and dominating others.

The task at this point is to determine what kinds of studies can be done that investigate family influences on bullying from this new vantage point.

Merely asking parents (or children) to complete a survey about parenting practices and determining whether the children engage in bullying will not help us to answer the questions raised in this chapter. What we need are studies that examine a parent's behavior in a way that allows us to see whether the parent is degrading the child in the course of discipline and whether that degradation of status is related to the child's bullying. This research would require observers who are able to understand the significance of what the parents and children in the family are doing. It would also require obtaining samples of how parents interact with and understand the behavior of their child (Smith & Myron-Wilson, 1998).

In terms of prevention and treatment of bullying, efforts should also focus on the status degradation that occurs in the course of bullying. In particular, attempts to prevent and treat bullying should concentrate on understanding how the bully might have been degraded and/or learned to degrade others. It is possible that bullies have a continuing sense of uncertainty about their status based on their family history. This may be one reason why they persist in bullying others. Research efforts might also explore whether there are variations in the kinds of status that bullies are trying to achieve. The child who states that he or she bullies "Because they annoyed me" or "To get even" may be trying to achieve a different sort of status than the bully who gives a justification such as "To get things or money from them" (Rigby, 2002). Another interesting empirical question would be whether bullies engage in more frequent or more severe degradations of others in their community when their status is threatened by an adult or a peer. The primary emphasis, however, should be on finding ways to help bullies increase their status by means other than bullying.

## References

Baldry, A. C., & Farrington, D. P. (1998). Parenting influences on bullying and victimization. *Legal and Criminological Psychology, 3*, 237–254.

Baldry, A. C., & Farrington, D. P. (2000). Bullies and delinquents: Personal characteristics and parental styles. *Journal of Community and Applied Social Psychology, 10*, 17–31.

Batsche, G. M., & Knoff, H. M. (1994). Bullies and their victims: Understanding a pervasive problem in the schools. *School Psychology Review, 23*, 165–174.

Berdondini, L., & Smith, P. K. (1996). Cohesion and power in the families of children involved in bully/victim problems at school: An Italian replication. *Journal of Family Therapy, 18*, 99–102.

Bowers, L., Smith, P. K., & Binney, V. (1992). Cohesion and power in the families of children involved in bully/victim problems at school. *Journal of Family Therapy, 14*, 371–287.

Curtner-Smith, M. E. (2000). Mechanisms by which family processes contribute to school-age boys' bullying. *Child Study Journal, 30*, 169–186.

Davis, K. E. (2002, September). *Stalkers and their worlds.* Paper presented at the annual meeting of the Society for Descriptive Psychology: Estes Park, CO.

Duncan, R. D. (1999). Peer and sibling aggression: An investigation of intra-and extra-familial bullying. *Journal of Interpersonal Violence, 14*, 871–886.

Ericson, N. (2001, June). *Addressing the problem of juvenile bullying* (OJJDP Fact Sheet #27). Washington, DC: U.S. Department of Justice.

Espelage, D. L., Bosworth, K., & Simon, T. R. (2000). Examining the social context of bullying behaviors in early adolescence. *Journal of Counseling and Development*, 78, 326–333.

Farrington, D. P. (1993). Understanding and preventing bullying. In M. Tonry (Ed.), *Crime and justice: A review of research*, Vol. 17 (pp. 381–458). Chicago: University of Chicago Press.

Flouri, E., & Buchanan, A. (2003). The role of mother involvement and father involvement in adolescent bullying behavior. *Journal of Interpersonal Violence*, 18, 634–644.

Greene, M. B. Bullying and harassment in schools. In R. S. Moser & C. E. Frantz (Eds.), *Shocking violence: Youth perpetrators and victims—A multidisciplinary perspective* (pp. 72–101). Springfield, IL: Charles C. Thomas.

Loeber, R., & Hay, D. (1997). Key issues in the development of aggression and violence from childhood to early adulthood. *Annual Review of Psychology*, 48, 371–410.

Lowenstein, L. F. (1978). Who is the bully? *Bulletin of the British Psychological Society*, 31, 147–149.

Ma, X. (2001). Bullying and being bullied: To what extent are bullies also victims? *American Education Research Journal*, 38, 351–370.

Neufeld, P. J. (2002). School violence—Family responsibility. *The Journal: Counseling and Therapy for Couples and Families*, 10, 207–209.

Oliver, R., Oaks, I. N., & Hoover, J. H. (1994). Family issues and interventions in bully and victim relationships. *The School Counselor*, 41, 199–202.

Olweus, D. (1980). Familial and temperamental determinants of aggressive behavior in adolescent boys: A causal analysis. *Developmental Psychology*, 16, 644–660.

Olweus, D. (1993). Bully/victim problems among schoolchildren: Long-term consequences and an effective intervention program. In S. Hodgins (Ed.), *Mental disorder and crime* (pp. 317–349). Thousand Oaks, CA: Sage.

Olweus, D. (1993). *Bullying at school: What we know and what we can do*. Oxford, UK: Blackwell.

Ossorio, P. G. (1979). *"What actually happens": The representation of real-world phenomena*. Columbia, SC: The University of South Carolina Press.

Ossorio, P. G. (1981). Notes on behavior description. In K. E. Davis (Ed.), *Advances in Descriptive Psychology*, Vol. 1 (pp. 13–36). Greenwich, CT: JAI Press.

Ossorio, P. G. (1995). *The collected works of Peter G. Ossorio: Vol. 1. persons*. Ann Arbor, MI: Descriptive Psychology Press.

Ossorio, P. G. (1998). What there is, how things are. In H. J. Jeffrey & R. M. Bergner (Eds.), *Advances in descriptive psychology*, Vol. 7 (pp. 7–32). Ann Arbor, MI: Descriptive Psychology Press.

Patterson, G. R., & Yoerger, K. (1993). Developmental models for delinquent behavior. In S. Hodgins (Ed.), *Mental disorder and crime* (pp. 140–172). Newbury Park, CA: Sage.

Patterson, G. R., DeBaryshe, B. D., & Ramsey, E. (1989). A developmental perspective on antisocial behavior. *American Psychologist*, 44, 329–335.

Říčan, P. (1995). Family values may be responsible for bullying. *Studia Psychologica*, 37, 31–36.

Říčan, P., Klicperová, M., & Koucká, T. (1993). Families of bullies and their victims: A children's view. *Studia Psychologica*, 35, 261–265.

Rigby, K. (1993). School children's perceptions of their families and parents as a function of peer relations. *The Journal of Genetic Psychology*, 154, 501–513.

Rigby, K. (1994). Psychosocial functioning in families of Australian adolescent schoolchildren involved in bully/victim problems. *Journal of Family Therapy*, 16, 173–187.

Rigby, K. (2002). Bullying in childhood. In P. K. Smith & C. H. Hart (Eds.), *Blackwell handbook of child social development* (pp. 549–587). Oxford, UK: Blackwell.

Roland, E., & Galloway, D. (2002). Classroom influences on bullying. *Educational Research*, 44, 299–312.

Schwartz, D., Dodge, K. A., Pettit, G. S., & Bates, J. E. (1997). The early socialization of aggressive victims of bullying. *Child Development*, 68, 665–675.

Shideler, M. M. (1988). *Persons, behavior, and the world: The descriptive psychology approach*. Lanham, MD: University Press of America.

Smith, P. K., & Myron-Wilson, R. (1998). Parenting and school bullying. *Clinical Child Psychology and Psychiatry*, 3, 405–417.

Smith, P. K., & Sharp, S. (1994). *School bullying: Insights and perspectives.* London: Routledge.

Smith, P. K., Bowers, L., Binney, V., & Cowie, H. (1993). Relationships of children involved in bully/victim problems at school. In S. Duck (Ed.), *Learning about relationships* (pp. 184–237). Newbury Park, CA: Sage.

Stevens, V., De Bourdeaudhuij, I., & Van Oost, P. (2002). Relationship of the family environment to children's involvement in bully/victim problems at school. *Journal of Youth and Adolescence, 31,* 419–428.

Tattum, D., & Tattum, E. (1992). *Social education and personal development.* London: David Fulton.

Troy, M., & Sroufe, A. (1987). Victimization among preschoolers: Role of attachment relationship history. *Journal of the American Academy of Child and Adolescent Psychiatry, 26,* 166–172.

Turner, P. J. (1991). Relations between attachment, gender, and behavior with peers in preschool. *Child Development, 62,* 1475–1488.

CHAPTER

# 6

# Peer Influences

HELEN COWIE
*University of Surrey*

## CHILDREN'S NEEDS AND RIGHTS: INTRODUCTION

Most children appear to deal with the problems they encounter in the course of growing up. They may experience separation from friends through moving or changing schools, sadness about the death of a pet, discouragement about setbacks in their academic achievement, jealousy of an older sibling, or anxiety about their physical rate of growth in comparison to peers. They will undoubtedly experience difficulties as well as joys in the relationships that they build with their peers. Most will experience or observe bullying at school. The majority, however, learn from these ups and downs and make the most of their abilities and talents while guided by the support that they receive from their families, friends, and communities.

Children's needs and rights are of central importance in any discussion of bullying in the school context. Adults play a clearly significant role in meeting children's needs, but as this chapter explains, children also potentially play a part in addressing their own needs and overcoming the difficulties and injustices they experience in relationships. By helping others overcome interpersonal problems in peer relationships, children and adolescents can gain enormously in confidence and self-esteem and can begin the long process of learning to be good citizens in their own communities. I begin this chapter by examining the fundamental needs of children for

*Implications for the Classroom*

healthy emotional, social, and cognitive development to take place. Next, with particular focus on the issue of bullying, I look at the broader issue of children's rights.

## Children's Needs

A number of researchers have summarized children's needs to guide educators and policymakers (Adcock & White, 1985; Coleman & Warren-Adamson, 1992; Dalrymple & Hough, 1995). Here I relate each of the fundamental needs to the specific issue of bullying. The following aspects are perceived as essential:

- **Basic physical care**: Children need to be provided with warmth, shelter, food and rest; they need to be kept clean. It is no coincidence that bullies regularly target these basic needs by, for example, extorting lunch money, stealing snacks, and pushing victims to the ground during recess.
- **Protection**: Children have to be kept safe and be protected from danger, including the risk of sexual abuse and violence. A bullied child lacks this sense of protection.
- **Security, guidance, support, and control**: It is also important for children to have a sense of continuity of care and the expectation that the family unit will remain stable. Routines and predictable patterns of care, reasonable sets of rules, and consistent monitoring facilitate this sense of security. Children need to be in a context where there is consistent, firm guidance on acceptable social behavior and where adults act as "good enough" role models. Where bullying goes unchecked and unchallenged and where antibullying policies are inadequate, bullies learn that their antisocial behavior is accepted or even admired; bullied children learn that the adults are too busy or too afraid to help them.
- **Love, affection, and respect**: Children require affectionate, respectful physical contact; to be comforted when in distress; to be held with tenderness; to be listened to; to be taken seriously; to be given opportunities for challenge, exploration, and the growth of a sense of competence; and to be encouraged to share feelings, including those that express anger, bewilderment, and hurt. If bullying is not challenged, bullied children discover that their distress is overlooked and ignored; they often learn to hide their feelings and to stay silent about their suffering.
- **Stimulation to learn and access to schooling**: Throughout the preschool years, children need to explore their world at their own pace; to have stimulating materials, playthings, and books; and to have their questions answered. Once at school, they need to have access to appropriate educational opportunities in contexts where there is a concern to provide them with resources to help them learn and realize their potential. Bullied children are often too afraid to go to school and so suffer the loss of education. Even

when they are in class, they may find it impossible to concentrate on their studies through fear of intimidation and derision on the part of bullies and bystanders.

• **Autonomy and responsibility**: Last, children and adolescents must gain the experience of taking responsibility for themselves and others in age-appropriate ways; for example, children should put away toys, help with household chores, and manage their pocket money. They need to be given helpful information on a variety of topics, such as sexual matters and making informed and reasoned decisions that affect themselves, families, and friends. This information should not be weighted with value-laden judgements. They should have opportunities to deal with ethical dilemmas and interpersonal conflicts and to live with the consequences, whatever these may be. Schools that take the problem of bullying seriously can provide an opportunity for children to help peers in distress and to be rewarded for their sense of responsibility. They can also help to create caring communities that set good examples for the children's and adolescents' future roles in adult society.

## Children's Rights

The United Nations (UN) Convention on the Rights of the Child (United Nations, 1991) proposes an international perspective on the rights of children to life itself and to a reasonable quality of life. This document gives nations the opportunity to define human rights standards for children, to identify gaps in the provision for those rights, and to set this in the context of an international binding agreement. In addition to protection from abuse and violence and provision of state services for care, education, social security, and health, the UN document emphasizes the need for active participation by children and adolescents in decision making on matters affecting them. Legislation in the United Kingdom (UK) (DfES, 1992) states that children should be educated for active citizenship and that schools should provide a balance between rights and expectations on the one hand and responsibilities on the other. But there is still much to be done in terms of facilitating greater participation on the part of children in the decisions that affect their lives and in resolving the problems that many of them experience or observe daily in their lives.

Children also have rights. Increasingly, society acknowledges an obligation to establish a basic set of children's rights that it is unacceptable or even illegal to contravene. The concept of children's rights can be a contentious one since adults find it hard to agree on the extent to which they should be prepared to share power with children in ways that provide safety for the child and enable the child to make responsible decisions—even decisions that may be wrong. However, there are currently strong movements to promote children's rights through peer support systems, school councils, and youth parliaments. The issue of bullying provides a platform from which to develop these initiatives since it is a problem that most children will have experienced or observed during their years at school.

## THE ROLE OF THE BYSTANDER IN
## SCHOOL BULLYING

In the UK today, around 30% of school children who are the victims of bullying are suffering in silence. Being bullied can leave emotional scars that last into adulthood and, as newspaper headlines attest, the strain can drive some children to suicide. But bullying does not happen in a vacuum. The bystander can play a crucial role by reinforcing those who bully—or by defending those at risk of being bullied.

A key aim in school antibullying interventions is to change the behavior of children who bully and to offer coping strategies to bullied children to empower them in bullying situations. At the same time, researchers and practitioners recognize the difficulties involved in effecting such change. Programs of intervention can result in change in the short term, but unless they are reinforced over a longer period, it is likely that the changes will not be sustained. Furthermore, in some school contexts where the bullying rates are high, the task facing school staff in counteracting the problem is likely to be especially difficult (Cowie & Olafsson, 2000).

The authors of the UK Elton Report (DES, 1989) argued that *school ethos* is a critical factor in the process of challenging antisocial behavior and stressed the important function of schools in creating an atmosphere in which staff consistently encouraged pro-social values and where there were clear sanctions against bullying behavior. A key aspect of this process is the part to be played by the peer group itself, in particular on the part of bystanders (Pepler & Craig, 1995; Pepler, 2003; Rigby & Slee, 1991). Hazler (1996) comments on the fact that professionals involved in antibullying work typically ignore the potential contribution of the bystanders. Bystanders see what is happening but are likely to have limited insight into their own emotional response to bullying and have not learned the skills of responsible and appropriate social intervention.

Hazler suggests that bystanders fail to take action for one of the following basic reasons: They do not know what to do, they are fearful of becoming the brunt of the bullies' attacks, and they might do the wrong thing and cause even more problems. The safest line of action in these circumstances is likely to be nonintervention. There are consequences arising from the failure to take action when faced with a peer in distress. Children and adolescents become desensitized to others' suffering the longer they are exposed to situations during which intervention does not take place. Although such desensitization reduces anxiety about being personally attacked or ridiculed, or about causing further distress to the victim (e.g., through retaliation), Hazler argues that it can give bystanders a sense of powerlessness similar to that being experienced by the victim. The victim's loss of self-esteem within the peer group is clear to perpetrators and those who played a less active part. But the consequences for bystanders are also negative (Hazler, 1996, p. 15):

> An *adrenaline* rush may well come with watching someone be victimized, but there is no pride or self-respect in knowing you are an ineffective bystander in someone else's tragic situation. Regaining the self-respect and confidence that goes with feeling in control does not have to come by accident. It can also be conscientiously fostered by counselors, educators, and parents.

Talamelli and Cowie (2001) report on the successful and unsuccessful strategies that bullied pupils have adopted in attempts to deal with the problem. Those that were perceived to be most effective included:

- **Telling someone**: By reporting a bullying incident to someone, the victim takes the first step toward dealing with the problem and finding a solution. This is not a sign of weakness, though domineering peers may say that it is. It is helpful for schools to create a climate in which it is acceptable to talk about issues of concern.
- **Having a friend**: Having at least one friend at school is a fundamental resource for the prevention of bullying. It can also be a real strategy when the victimized pupil starts a process of getting new friends to cope with the bullying.
- **Nonchalance**: Victims giving the impression that they do not care about the bullying can be an effective strategy, especially if the bullied pupils have an inner sense that bullying is unjust and wrong. This strategy is quite different from passively accepting the situation.

Strategies that Talamell and Cowie (2001) reported as unsuccessful included:

- **Acting in a submissive way**: Bullied children respond differentially to bullying behavior depending on whether they are nonaggressive or aggressive victims. Nonaggressive victims are submissive in the face of attack and easily capitulate by, for example, letting bullies extort money or other resources from them. These young people are more likely to have ineffective social skills for dealing with the problem. This means that they reward the attackers for their aggressive behavior by, for example, crying or showing signs of fear and anxiety. Unfortunately, such responses can lead to further rejection from the peer group.
- **Counter aggression**: Aggressive victims try to counterattack when they are bullied. Their disruptive and argumentative responses can antagonize members of the peer group. The victimized pupils' anger seems to be ineffective since they typically have difficulty in regulating their emotions and tend to be overwhelmed by their anger. By actively engaging an already hostile bully, it seems that these young people simply prolong the episodes

only to lose through their exaggerated displays of unregulated anger and distress, responses that in turn are satisfying to the bullies.

- **Helplessness**: A sense of helplessness can be a direct consequence of social exclusion and loneliness and indicates a passive attitude toward the problem. Both helplessness and counter aggression in the case of girls and solely counter aggression in the case of boys appear to encourage further bullying.
- **Staying silent**: The information that emerged from this research suggests that a proportion of bullied children live in fear of retaliation from bullies and shame over peers' perceptions of them. Very often, bullied children do not tell anyone what is going on. Their attempts to cope alone seldom alter the stance of peers (whether bullies or bystanders) toward this type of aggressive behavior even if the bullying stops spontaneously. Bullies continue to perpetrate acts of violence thanks to this wall of silence.

Children and adolescents face strong peer pressures regarding bystander apathy in the face of bullying: fear of retaliation by bullies, lack of confidence in their supportive skills, embarrassment at being rebuffed, anxiety about saying the wrong thing, relief at not being the target, or even enjoyment at someone else's misfortune. Bystanders may find it easier to turn away and pretend they did not notice anything. However, if members of the peer group do offer comfort to the bullied classmate or express in some way that they are not happy about this kind of negative behavior, then attitudes can shift. Defending the victim takes courage, and there are pitfalls along the way, but this behavior results in enormous benefits for the whole school community. The next section explores some of the ways in which systems of peer support can make a difference and offers some explanations about why this support has such an effect.

## WHAT IS PEER SUPPORT?

Peer support interventions harness children's and adolescents' potential to assume a helpful role in tackling interpersonal problems in the peer group. About 80 to 90% of young people express distaste for bullying behavior and disapprove of bullies, though this proportion decreases during adolescence. However, words are one thing and actions another. Only between 10 and 20% of youth actively intervene to help someone in distress on account of the bullying behavior of a peer (Salmivalli, Lagerspetz, Björkquist, Österman, & Kaukiainen, 1996). Approximately 30% of victims of bullying suffer in silence (Cowie, 2002). Peer support systems offer a more structured method of help and create systems in which a peer's potential to be helpful can be fostered through appropriate training, often with the support of regular debriefing sessions (Cowie & Wallace, 2000). Some examples of these systems are reviewed later in this chapter.

## Does Peer Support Work?

There is evidence that peer support is an effective method for improving the quality of peer relationships among school-age pupils (Cowie, 2000; Cunningham et al., 1998; Naylor & Cowie, 1999; Stacey, 2000). Surveying 2313 secondary school pupils and 234 teachers in 51 schools where there was a well-established system of peer support, Naylor and Cowie (1999) questioned peer supporters, groups of service users or potential users, teachers involved in managing the systems, and a sample of teachers not involved in running the systems. They found that while peer support systems do not always reduce the incidence of bullying, they can be an effective preventive measure. Above all, these systems reduce the negative impact of bullying on victims and make it more acceptable for victims to report incidences. The existence of a peer support system was perceived as beneficial to the school as a whole for the following reasons:

- Peers are able to detect bullying at a much earlier stage than adults can.
- Young people are more likely to confide in contemporaries than adults.
- Victims have someone to turn to and see the school as taking action against the problem.
- Peer supporters gain valuable social skills and self-confidence.
- The school enhances its reputation among parents and the local community.
- Over time, the school is perceived as a community that cares.

Naylor and Cowie (1999) found that 82% of pupils who used peer support schemes reported they found these helpful in giving them the strength to cope with bullying.

A follow-up study of a sample of the same cohort of pupils (Cowie, Naylor, Talamelli, Chauhan, & Smith, 2002) confirmed that many pupils appreciated the provision of a service to protect their safety and viewed its presence as a sign that the school was caring. A large proportion of users perceived peer support systems as helpful. Furthermore, peer supporters appreciated the opportunity of addressing a real problem in their school community and being given the skills and structures to tackle it. Peer supporters commented favorably on the usefulness of the communication skills that they learned in the course of training. All peer helpers reported that there were great personal benefits gained through their involvement with the systems. Another frequently mentioned benefit was a gratifying sense of responsibility. In virtually all of the groups interviewed, the peer supporters spontaneously spoke of their satisfaction in helping to make the school a safer place and commented on their pride in being able to make changes to the systems on the basis of their experience. A frequent comment was that the experience of participating in a peer support system had led them to decide on a caring profession for a career.

## Constraints and Limitations

It is important to note, however, that problems exist in establishing and maintaining systems of peer support. Some adults are reluctant to share power with young people (Naylor & Cowie, 1999), and some school environments can be so aggressive that the work of peer supporters is ineffective (Cowie & Olafsson, 2000). Some peers are hostile and try to sabotage the systems through hoax calls and referrals, adverse comments, jealousy, or doubts about the capacity of the service to offer help. Peer supporters who are boys face some derision from peers on the grounds that this type of activity is not manly or macho. Fear of retaliation from bullies is a theme that emerges most commonly from discussions with victimized pupils, and it is also a strong factor in the reluctance of bystanders to offer help. Where dissatisfaction was expressed, it often referred to a failure on the part of teachers to acknowledge peer supporters' expertise, a lack of effective supervision or training, or a reluctance to allow peer supporters enough responsibility for their task (Cowie *et al.*, 2002).

How do we explain the successes and drawbacks of peer support in addressing the challenging problem of bullying in schools? In the next part of the chapter, I consider three explanatory models, each overlapping the other in certain respects. The first concerns the earliest relationships in the family, the second focuses on the immediate network of participant roles in the peer group itself, and the last situates peer support in a wider cultural context.

## THEORY OF MIND AND CLOSE RELATIONSHIPS

Some psychologists argue that before a person can fully understand the nature and complexity of peer relationships during the primary and secondary school years, he or she must first explore the ways in which preschool children have formed their own internal models of relationships through their attachment relationships in their families. In recent years, there has been a growing interest on the part of social/developmental psychologists in the child's *theory of mind*. Having an understanding of other people's desires, beliefs, and their own interpretations of the world is often referred to as having a "theory of mind." It is called a theory because the mind cannot be seen or touched, so inferences must be made about others' mental states. Theory of mind is a rich, interconnected web of ideas that takes account of emotions, desires, pretence, deception, beliefs, and other perspectives of the world. The theory also forges links between two key domains—the cognitive and the social—with the implication that the two are inextricably inter- twined.

Dunn's (1992) research has shown that the development of the child's understanding of mental states is embedded within his or her social world of the family as an interactive network of complex and emotionally charged relationships. The process of talking about feelings and the reasons for actions is also linked to early achievement of theory of mind. Furthermore, Dunn has shown that the differences in how loved a young person feels influence how socially adjusted he or she is. The growth of social under- standing develops out of the child's experience of balancing preoccupation with self against responsiveness to the feelings and emotions of others. She argues that for a young child whose own goals and interests are often at odds with—and frustrated by—others in the family, it is clearly adaptive for him or her to begin to understand those other family members and the social rules of the shared family world. Securely attached children more likely to engage in activities that involve sharing their mental world will have experiences that teach them about how the mind works. This research suggests that the quality of family relationships has a strong influence on the ways in which young people act toward one another and on the extent to which they will actively demonstrate prosocial or antisocial attitudes and behavior toward more vulnerable members of their peer group.

We can apply these ideas directly to the issue of school bullying and to the impact of peer-led interventions to challenge it. It is well-documented in the literature that children who bully have often experienced difficulties in their close relationships with family members, whether because of authoritarian parenting styles or the domineering behavior of an older sibling. These children's family relationships are often characterized by dominance and by a lack of warmth and intimacy (Cowie, Smith, & Barton, 1994; Smith, Bowers, Binney, & Cowie, 1993). One outcome for at least some children who bully is that they lack empathy for others, possibly since they have had to learn to distance themselves from sensitive feelings of pain and hurt to survive emotionally within their families. A substantial proportion of these children become socially skilled manipulators who know how to gather followers and how to avoid detection by adults. They do not temper their relationships with others by empathy or sensitive concern for their feelings (Sutton, Smith, & Swettenham, 1999).

Peer supporters need to have some understanding of these processes if they are to succeed in changing the behavior of their peer group toward those who are the victims of such antisocial behavior. They need to know that they are not only dealing with the leader bullies but also with the cohort of followers that the skilled manipulators have gathered around them. In fact, the evidence from a most recent study (Cowie *et al.*, 2002) indicates a shift away from one-to-one counseling-based peer support systems toward those that involve the wider peer group, such as patrolling the playground during breaktimes or through actively befriending vulnerable pupils. This idea leads directly to the next section where I explore the range of participant roles adopted by children and adolescents when bullying takes place.

## Participant Role Theory

Although early experiences within the family are extremely influential, so are ways in which the peer group norms are formed in the immediate context of the school. Increasingly, investigators are turning their attention to the social context within which bullying takes place and the social constructions of the phenomenon that are made by young people from a range of perspectives. Salmivalli *et al.* (1996) found that, on the basis of peer nominations, it is possible to assign a participant role to 87% of students present at a bullying episode. In addition to *bullies* and *victims*, these include *assistants*, who physically help the bully; *reinforcers*, who incite and encourage the bully; *outsiders*, who remain neutral and inactive and pretend not to see what is happening; and *defenders*, who provide help for victims and confront the bully. Around 10 to 20% of the bystanders arise spontaneously to become defenders, with fewer taking on the defender role during the secondary school years (Rigby, 1997). With the right training and frameworks, such as those offered in schools with a peer support system in place, this percentage of supportive peers can be increased.

Salmivalli, Kaukiainen, and Lagerspetz (1998) found that children and adolescents in similar or complementary participant roles tended to associate with one another. For example, the level of individuals' aggression may be used as a criterion to judge their eligibility for entry to a gang. Young people are selectively allowed into peer group networks, and the network gradually influences the values and behavior of its members. Defenders of victims and outsiders will often form networks with one another. Victims are more likely to be outside all networks, but when they are in one, they share it with defenders, outsiders, and other victims. In fact, *peer supporters* (more likely to be drawn from the ranks of the *defenders*) often include a substantial number of former victims who have developed empathy for bullied peers and who also, through the practice of peer support, find themselves in a supportive and helpful peer group of similar children or adolescents.

## Social Cultural Theory

The discussion now turns to the wider context in which young people learn about culturally appropriate behavior. The norms of one culture can differ extensively from those of another, and this difference can radically affect the ways in which young people learn to behave toward one another. For example, one culture may place a high value on individual achievement, whereas another may stress the achievements of the group. In one culture, it may be desirable to be aggressive toward others; in another, aggression may be met with disapproval. From the sociocultural perspective, young people are viewed as *novice participants* in their culture, and their induction into the culture is achieved through shared joint activity. As they come to understand objects and relationships, they re-create their culture within themselves (Rogoff, Baker-Sennett, Lacasa, & Goldsmith 1995).

Rogoff and her colleagues take the perspective that individual development is inseparable from interpersonal and community processes and that individuals' changing roles are mutually defined with those of other people and with dynamic cultural processes. This is a two-way process. When individuals participate in shared endeavors, not only does individual development occur, but the process also transforms the practices of the community. To illustrate this sociocultural model, this discussion turns to the activities of peer supporters that might explain some cultural changes that take place in school communities as a result of the introduction of peer support systems in schools.

Cowie *et al.* (2002) noticed that peer supporters changed over time. In their study, peer supporters experienced transformations in confidence and a growing identity. They also noted differences that often related to the extent and degree of help that the peer supporters received from others, including the quality of teacher facilitation, parental approval, the extent and relevance of training and debriefing groups, and feedback from other pupils, whether users or potential users. Some boy peer supporters struggled with the issue of gender identity; others managed to find compatibility between the role of peer supporter and being "manly." Each peer supporter had to coordinate his or her individual efforts with guidance from other peer supporters; at the group level, each was guided through training and practices developed by previous peer supporters. The system also provided links with other systems, such as external training agencies (e.g., ChildLine), pressure groups (e.g., the Peer Support Forum), and higher education (e.g., a university-based research project).

Rogoff calls this a process of *guided participation*. Peer supporters did not simply acquire their skills in a vacuum. Rather, they went through a process of personal transformation. In turn, these individual efforts, along with the similar individual efforts throughout the peer support systems in other schools, could potentially influence the historically changing institution of the peer support movement; for example, their efforts could be described in publications that are read by practitioners, or they could be asked to participate in conferences on peer support.

By looking at development from the sociocultural perspective, it is possible to predict that the individual peer supporter develops through participation in an activity and changes in ways that contribute both to the ongoing event (in this case challenging school bullying) and to the peer supporter's preparation for involvement in other similar events in the future (such as training to work in the caring professions as a career).

## SUCCESSFULLY IMPLEMENTED PROGRAMS IN SCHOOLS

It is highly appropriate to introduce peer support systems during the elementary school years since, by this age, many relationship problems (e.g., rejection, isolation, social exclusion, and bullying) have become identifiable. Furthermore, there is great diversity among elementary school children in the extent to which individuals are accepted and liked by their peers and the extent to which they feel left out. This section describes specific examples of interventions that have been successfully implemented in school settings, including cooperative group work, Circle Time, befriending, Checkpoints, the Method of Shared Concern, the No-Blame Approach, conflict resolution/ mediation, and peer counseling. Table 1 provides some guidelines on the ages at which students may be most appropriately trained to offer support to bullied peers.

### Cooperative Group Work

Cooperative group work (CGW) is one of the most fundamental methods in peer support. For it to succeed, it is important that teachers promote cooperative values in the classroom to encourage pro-social behavior and increase cooperative relationships based on trust; teachers should also know their students as individuals. CGW is one method that can promote pro-social values as part of the learning process. It takes a number of forms: working individually but in a group (e.g., students share or evaluate their

TABLE 1
**The Age-Groups That Can Most Effectively Be Trained in Different Types of Peer Support**

|                               | 7–9 yrs | 9–11 yrs | 11–18+ yrs |
|-------------------------------|---------|----------|------------|
| Cooperative group work        | Yes     | Yes      | Yes        |
| Circle Time                   | Yes     | Yes      | Yes        |
| Befriending                   | Yes     | Yes      | Yes        |
| Checkpoints                   | Yes     | Yes      | Yes        |
| Method of Shared Concern      | No      | Yes      | Yes        |
| No-Blame Approach             | No      | Yes      | Yes        |
| Conflict resolution/mediation | No      | Yes      | Yes        |
| Peer counseling               | No      | No       | Yes        |

individual products in a group); working individually on "jigsaw" elements for a joint outcome (e.g., students research different aspects of a topic, and then they fit them together for a group presentation or a group resource pack); working jointly for a shared outcome (e.g., students collaboratively plan and design a role-playing skit around the theme of school bullying). In essence, teachers who use cooperative methods expect participants to show respect for others, to have empathy for their feelings, and to act cooperatively and democractically in their groups. In the cooperative classroom, children and adolescents are taught the skills of collaboration through structured activities, including those that address the issue of conflict. An essential feature of CGW is the time and space that is given to students for regular debriefing and reflection on the events and interpersonal interactions that take place in the classroom. Teachers who facilitate the cooperative classroom are often amazed at the capacity that students have for acting responsibly and providing support for one another.

Students can also be given opportunities to try out different roles within the classroom, such as being a leader, a recorder of classroom discussions, a person who clarifies the goals of the group, a person who uses humor to lighten the atmosphere in a group, a problem solver, or a person who does maintenance work (e.g., tidying up).

As Cowie *et al.* (1994) argue, there are three essential features of CGW in the classroom:

• Students are prepared to work together outside friendship groups. This type of interaction helps to reduce prejudice and fosters trust across gender and ethnic groups as well as helps integrate neglected or rejected children and adolescents into the peer group.

• Students communicate, share information, and divide tasks to achieve a common goal in groups. In the cooperative classroom, the teacher ensures that there are regular opportunities for children and adolescents to engage in tasks that can only be carried out through a group effort. For example, students can brainstorm about ways to improve the school environment or pool information to produce a booklet or poster on a topic of shared concern.

• In cooperative groups, conflicts are discussed and attempts are made to resolve them. Students learn the skills to deal with conflict and to understand the creative potential of conflict in helping individuals to relate to one another in a more authentic way. Students in cooperative classrooms are given chances to reflect on the procedures (or lack of them) in their own school for ensuring their safety, both physical and psychological. These discussion groups can give group members greater insights into their capacity to take responsibility for managing their own relationships and for supporting peers who are experiencing difficulties at a particular time.

## Circle Time

Circle Time is a method for enhancing effective communication among members of a class group and for creating a safe space in which to explore issues of shared concern and difficulty experienced by members of that group.

Circle Time can be an effective preventive measure against bullying because it reduces negative impact of bullying on victims and makes it more acceptable for them to report the victimization incident. There are a number of reasons for this:

- Young people are able to detect bullying at a much earlier stage than adults can.
- Young people are more likely to confide in peers than in adults.
- Members of Circle Time have a forum for sharing interpersonal difficulties, which can result in the school taking action.
- Members of Circle Time gain confidence and valuable social skills.

The creation of Circle Time was influenced by the CGW approach (Mosley, 1996). Circle Time Time is set aside each week for students and their teacher to sit in a circle and take part in games and activities designed to increase self-awareness, self-esteem, cooperation, and listening skills. It usually lasts for about 20 to 30 minutes and provides a useful forum for the discussion of important issues, including peer relationships. The positive atmosphere generated by Circle Time usually spreads into other areas of class activity. Students in Circle Time have the opportunity to consider matters of personal concern, such as relationships with adults and peers, to develop their sense of being in a community, and to learn firsthand about the advantages of shared reflection in deepening understanding and empathy. Circle Time is a very useful method for addressing issues about friendship problems and bullying.

The Circle encourages children and adolescents to develop their own set of ground rules concerning listening to one another, learning to take turns, giving and receiving affirmation, discussing difficult issues from a problem-solving stance, and learning to negotiate ways of resolving interpersonal difficulties.

In one UK school where the Circle Time program was well-established in each class, members of the Circle had the authority to call on a range of peer-led interventions to help resolve interpersonal difficulties (Highfield Junior School, 1997). For example, they could call for the support of a *guardian angel* (potentially any child in the school), a *house captain* (usually a Year 6 pupil aged 10 to 11 years with wide experience as a guardian angel who had been elected by peers), or a *peer mediator* (a pupil trained in mediation skills). Alternatively, the Circle could refer a difficult issue to the school's council, a whole school Circle that met every two weeks as a decision-making forum.

Guardian angels were peers (usually up to three in number) who could "fly to the rescue" and guard a peer from harm or help that peer deal with a situation that they could not handle. Most children could expect to be chosen as a guardian angel at least once during their school career. The guardian angels could be assigned to a bullied child or to an aggressive child who had expressed the wish, witnessed by the Circle, to change his or her behavior. Guardian angels, house captains, and peer mediators would regularly report back their progress to the Circle. The head teacher explained (Highfield Junior School, 1997, p. 30) how the role of peer mediator evolved as pupils worked on issues in a number of Circles:

> They were doing a grand job as guardian angels, and they were developing ways of doing it. They set up their Circles every lunch time to support all the children who were having problems. They were giving advice and using counselling techniques. We realised that they needed training, so that everyone was doing the same thing. We had to adopt ways of resolving conflict fairly and peacefully without giving ill-informed advice, and without making conflict worse. And the way forward was mediation.

The children in the school understood that the guardian angels' and house captains' roles were to help both bullies and victims and that mediation was a constructive and forward-thinking way to change behavior that was aggressive or antisocial and to resolve disputes and disagreements. An essential component of this intervention was that the students "owned the problem" and were treated as responsible citizens in their school community.

## Befriending

Befriending systems involve the assignment of a pupil or pupils to "buddy" or "befriend" a peer. *Befrienders* are volunteers, either same-age peers or older pupils, who are selected by teachers on the basis of their friendly personal qualities. In some systems, existing befrienders are also involved in the selection and interviewing of volunteers. Usually there is some training in interpersonal skills, such as active listening, assertiveness, and leadership. In one UK secondary school, Hampstead School, befrienders, known as *peer partners*, were trained to offer friendship and comfort to fellow students who had come as refugees to the UK, had seen violence and destruction, and were often far from family and friends. These young people were potentially vulnerable to loneliness, social exclusion, and victimization. The peer partners set up an after-school homework/social club where pupils could study, relax, or talk about issues of concern to them. At the club, they also gave advice and information and offered emotional support to pupils who were upset. In addition, they raised funds for the project and delivered speeches about the scheme within school and to outside audiences. Many of the pupils who were helped were so appreciative of the scheme that they volunteered later to become peer partners to "repay" what they had gained (Demetriades, 1996).

Studies of befriending indicate a number of advantages. For vulnerable pupils, the experience of being befriended can be a critical part of the process of feeling more positive about themselves. Through the process of being helped, these pupils are given an opportunity to express their feelings about upsetting aspects of their lives. Befrienders report that they too benefit from the helping process, that they feel more confident in themselves and that they learn to value other people more. Teachers frequently report that the school environment becomes safer and more caring following the introduction of a befriending scheme and that peer relationships in general improve (Cowie & Sharp, 1996).

## Checkpoints

Checkpoints (Varnava, 2000; 2002) is a self-help tool with three main functions: to raise awareness, to facilitate institutional self-audit, and to offer guidance. The use of Checkpoints leads to the formulation of assessment criteria by which the school's progress in behavior management can be measured. This is achieved through the use of a framework representing the main aspects of school life: *home/school/community, values, organization, environment, curriculum, training.* The guide includes a web diagram that, when completed, illustrates a school's strengths in preventing violence and highlights areas where further action may be taken. Varnava's *Checkpoints for Young People* was written for students transitioning from primary to secondary school and offers a second dimension to the process of intervention in that it helps to create a dialogue between young people and adults and provides a framework from which the voices of young people can be heard. In one school, the issues of bullying and violent behavior were explored in the course of a student council conference called "Taking Practical Steps to Make the School a Safer, Happier Place with Improved Facilities." The conference included an introduction to *Checkpoints for Schools,* followed by group discussions, comprising a mix of young people across all year groups, focusing on Checkpoints. Young people from years 12 and 13 (aged 16 to 18) facilitated each group. Each discussion group was invited to make three recommendations for a presentation on the practical steps to make the school a happier, safer place. These were debated, and key recommendations were given to the head teacher for further consideration and action. Key recommendations included:

• Improvement in communication channels among young people, staff, parents, and local community
   • Provision of staff training to deal with bullying and violent behaviors
   • Regular profiling of the school's Antibullying Policy and Code of Conduct to all members of the school community, including parents, and the application of sanctions when necessary

- Provision of alternative areas on the school site for recreation to reduce tension and aggression
- Installation of CCTV systems in "hot spots," such as locker areas and the library
- Refurbishment of school buildings

The conference provided an ideal opportunity to engage young people in the first stages of the school's strategy to address bullying and violent behavior. Student involvement and commitment greatly increase the chances of success.

## Method of Shared Concern

The Method of Shared Concern was devised by Anatol Pikas (1989) in Sweden. It focuses on the students doing the bullying as well as those being bullied and is designed for situations in which a group of pupils have been bullying one or more pupils on a regular basis for some time. The method uses a combination of a simple script and specific nonverbal cues. Training is needed to ensure a thorough grasp of the technique. (A detailed account is given in Sharp and Smith, 1996.) The overall goal of the Method of Shared Concern is to establish ground rules that will enable the pupils to coexist within the same school. It does not aim to create friendships among the pupils or to uncover the details of the bullying situation.

The method starts with a series of brief individual "chats" between the teacher and each pupil involved in a room that is quiet and where there will be no interruptions. The teacher first talks with the pupils doing the bullying. The talks are not confrontational; the premise is that there is a problem because others have witnessed that the bullied pupil is unhappy and has experienced bullying. The teacher follows a structured script with each pupil leading to mutual agreement that the bullied pupil is unhappy and concludes when each pupil agrees to help improve the situation. Common outcomes are that participants leave the bullied pupil alone or become friendly toward him or her.

This is an effective method against bullying. Teachers recommend following-up with the pupils involved to make sure the bullying has stopped and monitoring them to see whether the bullying starts again with even another pupil; if a pupil is persistently involved in bullying, combining the method with some other intervention, such as parental involvement or a change of class, is also recommended. When the follow-up talks are particularly successful, teachers can be tempted to miss out on the final group meeting involving bullies and victims. But it is this final meeting that leads to an agreement about the long-term maintenance of the change in bullying behavior.

The Method of Shared Concern can be effective as part of the graded disciplinary procedure set out by the school's antibullying policy. It is most useful as an interim measure against group bullying. The end result usually involves an improvement in the bullying situation that can be maintained if additional action is taken to change the ringleader's behavior.

## The No-Blame Approach

The No-Blame Approach (Robinson & Maines, 1997) has been used in primary, secondary, and college environments since 1990 (Young, 1998). This method adopts a problem-solving approach by forming a support group for the bullied pupil consisting of those directly involved in the bullying episode and the bystanders. The group is given responsibility for solving the problem and for reporting the progress.

The No-Blame Approach is similar to the Method of Shared Concern, particularly in its identification of shared concern and its nonpunitive stance. The method differs in (1) the order in which the adult facilitator sees the participants, (2) the timing of the individual meetings with bullies (Pikas sees them first individually, while Maines and Robinson see them as a group), (3) the emphasis placed on the victim's feelings (the No-Blame Approach focuses on the feelings of the victim), (4) the importance of an adult facilitator and bully partnership versus a group dynamic (Pikas emphasizes the partnership between adults and bullies while Robinson and Maines focus on group dynamics), and (5) whether the label of "bully" is used (Robinson and Maines do not attach the tabel to any participant).

The first aim of the No-Blame Approach is to arouse in children who bully a sense of empathic concern for those they have bullied. The second aim is to elicit responsible action that will assist in the resolution of the problem. The method is based on the assumption that empathic concern can only be achieved in a nonpunitive context. It assumes that bullying is often a group phenomenon that can be resolved by working with the responsible group. It is also important to monitor the development of new patterns of behavior. There are seven steps in the No-Blame Approach: *talk with the victim, convene a group meeting, communicate to the group how the victim feels, share responsibility, elicit helpful suggestions, hand over responsibility to the group,* and *schedule individual meetings with participants.*

A key aspect of this approach is that it places responsibility for change on the pupils who have participated in the bullying. The group's cooperation involved in the process can have a powerful influence on individual members. Robinson & Maines (1997) have found that in the majority of cases, the bullying stopped completely or the victim no longer required support.

## Conflict Resolution/Mediation

Conflict resolution/mediation is a structured process in which a neutral third party assists voluntary participants to resolve their dispute. The goals of conflict resolution/mediation are to enable victim and perpetrator to identify offender liabilities and obligations and to find a means of restitution; to empower children and adolescents to defuse interpersonal disagreements among peers, including bullying, racist name-calling, fighting, and quarreling; and to ensure that each disputant comes away from the mediation with a positive "win-win" experience and the sense that the outcome is fair to both sides (Cunningham *et al.*, 1998).

These methods are reported to result in a substantial decrease in the incidence of aggressive behavior. In addition, research studies report that both the school climate and the quality of pupils' relationships improve. More than 85% of disputes mediated by peers result in lasting agreements. The frequency of disputes that involve the intervention of a teacher drops by up to 80% after training. Stacey (2000) evaluated the effectiveness of a peer mediation program in primary school and found a reduction in the incidence of bullying.

## Peer Counselling

Active listening methods extend the befriending and mediation approaches into interventions that are based more overtly on a counseling model (for a detailed guide, see Cowie and Wallace, 2000). Pupil helpers are trained (usually by a qualified counselor or psychologist) to use active listening skills to support peers in distress. The goals are to give helpers skills to deal with peers' interpersonal issues, help the victims of bullying, and to challenge pupils who bully. Regular supervision (whether by a qualified counselor or by the teacher who manages the peer support scheme) is an essential feature. Research findings are positive. In one secondary school, 60% of peer supporters reported benefits arising directly from the interpersonal skills and teamwork acquired in the course of training. The majority (63%) believed that the service was having an impact on the school as a whole, with school becoming a place where it was more acceptable to talk about emotional and relationship issues. The adults in charge of the schemes were unanimous in confirming that the work of the peer support service went beyond the help offered to individuals in need—valuable as that was—and that it affected the whole school (Naylor & Cowie, 1999). As a note of caution, however, it was found that when regular supervision is not provided for the peer helpers, the system is likely to be ineffective as a measure against bullying (Cowie & Olafsson, 2000).

# CONCLUSION

Peer support systems are now accepted and valued for their contribution to the quality of life in a growing number of schools. In these schools, the pupils overwhelmingly state that they like the presence of a peer support system, they would use the system if they needed to, and would recommend it to a friend in need. Teachers in charge of systems report that their colleagues are for the most part extremely supportive. There are also external signs of acknowledgment from parent groups. There is a strong sense in these schools of confidence in peer support systems and belief in their usefulness.

The research so far indicates that the key to a peer group system's success lies in a process of flexible monitoring and clear observation of the potential users' needs. Teachers running the schemes also need to take account of the social context in which they operate and make appropriate use of the situated knowledge that the young peer supporters bring to their task. There is a growing appreciation of the role that children and adolescents might play in learning new skills and in reflectively adapting these skills to their particular context.

The phenomenon of peer support offers a rich source of information about the nature of peer group relationships and about the processes involved in change. In this chapter, I have attempted to present some explanatory models that may increase understanding on how and why change can be effected. I also hope that the models offer some integration at different levels of analysis to include the individual, the family, the school community, and the wider social context.

## References

Adcock, M., & White, R. (Eds.) (1985). *Good-enough parenting: A framework for assessment.* British Agency for Fostering and Adoption.

Cowie, H. (2000). Bystanding or standing by: Gender issues in coping with bullying in English schools. *Aggressive Behavior,* 26, 85–97.

Coleman, J., & Warren-Adamson, C. (1992). *Youth policy in the 1980s.* London: Routledge.

Cowie, H. (2002). Youth and violence: A report for the UNESCO Conference Violence in Schools. Brasilia, www.peersupport.co.uk

Cowie, H., Naylor, P., Talamelli, L., Chauhan, P., & Smith, P. K. (2002). Knowledge, use of and attitudes towards peer support. *Journal of Adolescence,* 25(5), 453–467.

Cowie, H., & Olafsson, R. (2000). The role of peer support in helping the victims of bullying in a school with high levels of aggression. *School Psychology International,* 21(1), 79–95.

Cowie, H., & Sharp, S. (1996) (Eds.). *Peer counselling in schools.* London: David Fulton.

Cowie, H., Smith, P. K., & Boulton, M. (1994). *Cooperation in the multi-ethnic classroom.* London: David Fulton.

Cowie, H., & Wallace, P. (2000). *Peer support in action.* London: Sage.

Cunningham, C., Cunningham, L., Martorelli, V., Tran, A., Young, J., & Zacharias, R. (1998). The effects of primary division, student-mediated conflict resolution programs on playground aggression. *Journal of Child Psychology and Psychiatry,* 39(5), 653–662.

Demetriades, A. (1996). Children of the storm: Peer partnership. In H. Cowie & S. Sharp (Eds.), *Peer counselling in schools.* London: David Fulton, pp. 64–72.

Dalrymple, J., & Hough, J. (1995). *Having a voice: An exploration of children's rights and advocacy.* Birmingham, AL: Venture Press.

DES (1989). *Discipline in schools: Report of the committee chaired by Lord Elton.* London: HMSO.

DfES (1992). *Government white paper, choice and diversity: A new framework for schools.* London: HMSO.

Dunn, J. (1992). Siblings and development. *Current Directions in Psychological Science,* 1, 6–9.

Dunne, E., & Bennett, N. (1990). *Talking and learning in groups.* London: MacMillan.

Hazler, R. (1996) Bystanders: An overlooked factor in peer abuse. *The Journal for the Professional Counselor,* 11(2), 11–21.

High field Junior School (1997). *Changing our school.* London: Institute of Education, University of London.

Mosley, J. (1996). *Quality circle time in the primary school.* Wisbech: Learning Development Aids.

Naylor, P., & Cowie, H. (1999). The effectiveness of peer support systems in challenging school bullying: The perspectives and experiences of teachers and pupils. *Journal of Adolescence,* 22(4), 467–479.

Pepler, D. (2003) Kobe/Oxford Seminar.

Pepler, D., & Craig, W. (1995). A peek behind the fence: Naturalistic observations of aggressive children with remote audiovisual recording. *Developmental Psychology,* 31, 548–553.

Pikas, A. (1989). A pure concept of mobbing gives the best results for treatment. *School Psychology International,* 10, 95–104.

Rigby, K. (1997). Attitudes and beliefs about bullying among Australian school children. *Irish Journal of Psychology,* 18(2), 202–20.

Rigby, K., & Slee, P. (1991). Bullying among Australian school children: Reported behaviour and attitudes to victims. *Journal of Social Psychology,* 131, 615–627.

Robinson, G., & Maines, B. (1997). *Crying for help: The No Blame Approach to bullying.* Bristol, UK: Lucky Duck Publishing.

Rogoff, B., Baker-Sennett, J., Lacasa, P., & Goldsmith, D. (1995). Development through participation in sociocultural activity. In J. J. Goodnow, P. J. Miller, & F. Kessel (Eds.), Cultural practices as contexts for development, New directions for child development, vol. 67, Spring (pp. 45–65). San Francisco: Jossey-Bass Publishers.

Salmivalli, C., Kaukiainen, A., & Lagerspetz, K. (1998). Aggression in the social relations of school-aged girls and boys. In P. Slee & K. Rigby (Eds.), *Children's peer relations* (pp. 60–75). London: Routledge.

Salmivalli, C., Lagerspetz, K., Björkqvist, K., Österman, K., & Kaukiainen, A. (1996). Bullying as a group process: Participant roles and their relations to social status within the group. *Aggressive Behavior,* 22, 1–5.

Sharp, S., & Smith P. K. (1996). *Tackling bullying in your school.* London: Routledge.

Smith, P. K., Bowers, L., Binney, V., & Cowie, H. (1993). Relationships of children involved in bully-victim problems at school. In S. Duck (Ed.), *Learning about relationships: Understanding relationship processes,* vol. 2 (pp. 186–212). Newbury Park, CA: Sage.

Stacey, H. (2000). Mediation and peer mediation. In H. Cowie & P. Wallace, *Peer support in action.* London: Sage.

Sutton, J., Smith, P. K., & Swettenham, J. (1999). Social cognition and bullying: Social inadequacy or skilled manipulation? *British Journal of Developmental Psychology,* 17, 435–50.

Talamelli, L., & Cowie, H. (2001). *How pupils cope with bullying: Successful and unsuccessful strategies.* London: HSBC.

United Nations (1991). United Nations Convention on the Rights of the Child. *Innocenti Studies.* Florence: UNICEF.

Varnava, G. (2000). *Towards a non-violent society: Checkpoints for schools.* London: National Children's Bureau/Forum on Children and Violence.

Varnava, G. (2002). *Towards a non-violent Society: Checkpoints for young people.* London: National Children's Bureau/Forum on Children and Violence.

Young, S. (1998). The support group approach to bullying in schools. *Educational Psychology in Practice,* 14, 1, 32–39.

CHAPTER

7

# Schools and Bullying: School Factors Related to Bullying and School-Based Bullying Interventions

ALLISON ANN PAYNE
*The College of New Jersey*

DENISE C. GOTTFREDSON
*University of Maryland*

## INTRODUCTION

On April 20th, 1999, shortly after 11 a.m., Eric Harris and Dylan Klebold entered Columbine High School and began an hour-long attack on students and teachers, using semiautomatic weapons and pipe bombs. When it was over, shortly after 12 p.m., the shooters had killed 13 people and wounded 21 others, before killing themselves. As the public reeled from the deadliest school shooting in history, investigations into the reasons behind the event began. Many focused on Harris's and Klebold's membership in a group known as the "Trent Coat Mafia," a group of students who were known for wearing long black trench coats and were considered "outsiders" by the mainstream student population. After other members of this subculture were questioned, it became clear that these students were frequently harassed and bullied, both individually and as a group, by other students in the school, particularly the school athletes or "jocks."

As the public grew more concerned about these rare yet extreme school shootings, one of the many hypotheses proposed to explain these events drew upon the bullying experienced by the Columbine shooters: Perhaps many shooters had been victims of bullying, and their shootings were retaliation for previous victimizations. To investigate this and other hypotheses, the National Research Council conducted a case study examining seven post-Columbine school shootings (National Research Council and Institute of Medicine, 2003). When investigating the bullying experiences of the offenders, it became clear that although bullying was a problem in many of the schools, the hypothesis that most shooters were victims of bullying seeking revenge did not hold. Four of the eight shooters had been victims; interestingly, however, it was also true that four of the eight shooters had also been bullies (National Research Council and Institute of Medicine, 2003). Therefore, while there does seem to be a connection between bullying and more extreme violence, it is not necessarily due to the proposed victimization hypothesis. In fact, if one takes a more general problem behavior syndrome viewpoint (i.e., Gottfredson & Hirschi, 1990), the more likely connection is between being a bully and engaging in more violent offending.

This more intuitive connection is supported by recent research. Using a nationally representative sample of sixth through tenth graders in the United States, Nansel and her colleagues investigated whether bullying is a risk factor for more serious violence (Nansel et al., 2003). Results indicate that both bullying and being bullied are strongly related to more serious behavior, such as fighting and weapon carrying. These relationships, however, were stronger for the bullies than the victims. Students who bullied others, either at school or away from school, were more likely to be involved in frequent fighting and to carry weapons (Nansel et al., 2003).

Even if bullying was not a predictor for more serious violent behavior, the prevalence of bullying in schools alone is cause for concern. According to Farrington (1993), more than 50% of students have been victims of bullying, and more than 50% have been bullies themselves. Charach, Pepler, and Ziegler (1995) found similar numbers: 49% of students reported being bullied. Findings from others studies, although reporting lower percentages due to differences in definitions of bullying, still support the existence of bullying as a problem. Nansel et al. (2001) found that 30% of students in grades six through ten have been involved in bullying incidents, and the 1999 School Crime Supplement of the National Crime Victimization Survey reported that up to 12% of students have been victims of bullying (U.S. Department of Education, 2002).

This frequency of bullying in schools contributes to a fearful school environment, a climate of intimidation where some students feel unhappy and unwelcome (Batsche & Knoff, 1994). According to the 1999 School Crime Supplement, victims of bullying are far more fearful of being attacked at school and while traveling to and from school than those who are not victims (28% and 12% versus 4% and 4%, respectively) (U.S. Department of Education, 2002). As the public has become more concerned about school violence, prevention efforts have worked to reduce "any condition or act that creates a climate in which individual students and teachers feel fear or intimidation in addition to being victims of assault, theft, or vandalism" (Batsche & Knoff, 1994, p. 165). Clearly bullying is a part of this scenario.

To reduce and prevent bullying in school, one must first examine the correlates and predictors of these incidents. Much of the research investigating factors related to bullying has focused on individual-level correlates of bullies and victims. More general research on delinquency and school disorder, however, has highlighted some school-level predictors, such as school location and size, school social organization, and school norms and values (Gottfredson, 2001). The following section reviews the research examining these school-level factors related to bullying. This is followed by a discussion on a specific perspective of school social organization, communal school organization, that appears to have significant implications for the prevention of bullying. Finally, the chapter presents research on various bullying interventions.

## PREVIOUS RESEARCH ON SCHOOL FACTORS RELATED TO BULLYING

### School Context

School context refers to predetermined characteristics of a school, such as grade level, size of student enrollment, class size, racial and ethnic composition, and school location. Literature examining the relationship between bullying and these factors is discussed in this section. Also reviewed in this section is literature examining the location and timing of bullying; that is, where in the school does bullying most often occur, and does it occur more during school or before and after school?

Although little research has explicitly examined the relationship between grade level and bullying, a few studies consistently show greater amounts of bullying in middle and elementary schools compared to high schools. Olweus (1991) found that the greatest amounts of bullying in Norway occurred in elementary schools. This study determined that the percentage of victims decreased severely as the grade level increased, with second through sixth grade having twice the percentage of victims than seventh through ninth grade. Similarly, Whitney and Smith (1993) reported twice as many bullying incidents in English middle schools than English high schools.

In contrast, the relationship between school size and/or class size and bullying is far from clear. Whereas some studies have not found a relationship between the percentage of victims or bullies and school or class size (Olweus, 1991; Mellor, 1999; Whitney & Smith, 1993), others have found that there is a greater percentage of bullying problems in larger schools and classes (Stephenson & Smith, 1989; Winters, 1997). Even more surprisingly, although Wolke *et al.* (2001) found that school and class size did not affect bullying in German schools, they did find that bullying was a greater problem in *smaller* schools and classes in England.

The racial and ethnic composition of a school appears to have little effect on the amount of bullying. The majority of studies have found no effect (Boulton, 1995; Junger, 1990; Moran *et al.*, 1993; Siann *et al.*, 1994; Whitney & Smith, 1993). Only Wolke *et al.* (2001) found a significant relationship between bullying and a school's racial/ethnic mix, but even this relationship was weak.

As with school/class size, the findings on school location and bullying are mixed. A number of studies have not found a relationship between urban location or socioeconomic status and bullying (Mellor, 1999; Olweus, 1991; Winters, 1997), whereas others have found greater amounts of bullying in schools located in inner-city, low socioeconomic status, disadvantaged areas (Stephenson & Smith, 1989; Whitney & Smith, 1993; Wolke *et al.*, 2001).

Finally, researchers have investigated the timing and location of bullying incidents. That is, is bullying more prevalent during school hours or when students are on the way to and from school or away from school? In addition, when students are in school, where is bullying more likely to occur? Studies have consistently found that students are far more likely to bully and to be bullied while they are at school compared with away from school or to and from school. For example, Olweus (1991) found that students are twice as likely to be bullied at school as on the way to or from school. Other studies have found similar results (Berthold & Hoover, 2000; Boulton & Underwood, 1993; Harris, Petrie, & Willoughby, 2002; Nansel *et al.*, 2003). Not surprisingly, bullying at school is more likely to occur in areas with minimal adult supervision (National Research Council and Institute of Medicine, 2003). The most frequent location for bullying is the playground (Frost, 1991; Mellor, 1990; Smith & Shu, 2000; Whitney & Smith, 1993; Wolke *et al.*, 2001). Interestingly, the second most common location for bullying is the classroom, even when compared with areas such as hallways and bathrooms (Frost, 1991; Mellor, 1990; Smith & Shu, 2000; Whitney & Smith, 1993; Wolke *et al.*, 2001).

## School Climate

School climate refers to the "inner workings of the school" (Ma, Stewin, & Mah, 2001, p. 256), such as the social organization of the school, the system of social relations between and among teachers and students, and the cultural system of norms and values in the school. Research has clearly demonstrated the relationship between school climate and general school disorder (Gottfredson *et al.*, 2003). Although most studies have not explicitly examined the effect of school climate on bullying, suggestions of its importance can be found in studies that report on the bullying-related attitudes and behaviors of both teachers and students (Whitney & Smith, 1993).

The bullying-related attitudes of teachers, whether self-reported or student-reported, hold clear implications for the overall school climate's influence on bullying. Schools in which teachers are more likely to discuss bullying with students, recognize bullying behavior, are interested in stopping bullying, and actually intervene in bullying incidents are less likely to have a bullying problem. For instance, Stephenson and Smith (1991) compared six schools that had a serious bullying problem with six schools that had a less significant problem. Teachers in the schools with less bullying were more likely to clearly articulate bullying problems found in the school and were more concerned with control and prevention. Students, however, do not always perceive teachers as being interested in controlling bullying. Rigby (1996) reported that 30% of students questioned felt that teachers were not interested or only sometimes interested in stopping bullying. Similarly, Harris, et al. (2002) reported that a large portion of students perceived administrators and teachers as not interested in stopping bullying (28% and 21%), with 46% and 44% of students, respectively, saying they "didn't know" if the adults were interested.

This lack of teacher interest in bullying translates into a lack of teacher action. Olweus (1991) found that teachers "do relatively little to stop bullying at school" (Olweus, 1991, p. 420). Between 62 and 76% of students reported that teachers did not talk with them about bullying (Boulton & Underwood, 1993; Smith & Shu, 2000). When considering actual intervenions, only 34 to 54% of students reported that teachers almost always tried to stop bullying (Boulton & Underwood, 1993; Whitney & Smith, 1993), and 34% of students reported that teachers only sometimes or almost never tried to stop the incident (Boulton & Underwood, 1993).

Student attitudes and behavior toward bullying are also an integral part of school climate. Most studies find that the majority of students have anti-bullying attitudes (Boulton, Bucci, & Hawker, 1999; Stevens, Van Oost, & Bourdeaudhuij, 2000). Between 40 and 49% of students do not understand why other children bully (Boulton & Underwood, 1993; Whitney & Smith, 1993; Stevens et al., 2000), and another 23 to 40% of students feel neutral toward bullying (Boulton & Underwood, 1993; Stevens et al., 2000). Rigby and Slee (1991) found that the majority of students were opposed to bullying but that support for victims decreased as students aged. Charach, Pepler, and Ziegler (1995) reported that 90% of students felt that bullying is very or somewhat unpleasant, with 10% feeling indifferent.

These attitudes toward bullying have been linked to the amount of bullying in a school, with more negative attitudes associated with less bullying. Boulton and Flemington (2002) found a negative correlation between attitudes toward bullying and engagement in bullying behavior in a sample of English secondary school students; similar results were found in a sample of Greek students (Boulton, Lanitis, Manoussou, & Lemoni, 1997). Using a sample of Swedish and English students, Boulton, Bucci, and Hawker (1999) also found a negative correlation between antibullying attitudes and bully-ing behavior; in addition, they found that attitudes significantly predicted behavior, such that those students with the most antibullying attitudes engaged in the least amount of bullying.

Antibullying attitudes, however, do not translate into intervening behav-ior, either in terms of telling an adult or actually trying to stop the bullying. Self-report studies find that between 30 and 50% of students try to help when a person is being bullied (Boulton & Underwood, 1993; Charach et al., 1995; Smith & Shu, 2000; Stevens et al., 2000; Whitney & Smith, 1993). Observa-tional studies, however, suggest that these numbers are too high: Pepler, Craig, and Roberts (1989) find that only 11% of students actually helped when another student was being bullied. The link between student antibully-ing attitudes and intervention behaviors appears to be missing.

Whereas these studies support the association between school climate and bullying, they only marginally address the complexity of this relation-ship. The examination of teacher and student attitudes, while important, only focuses on one dimension of climate: school norms. Presumably, other aspects of school climate also predict bullying problems, but more research is needed to investigate this further.

## Communal School Organization and Bullying

One aspect of school climate that would seem to greatly influence the level of bullying in a school is the social organization of the school. Research has illustrated the importance of school social organization in general and specifically the importance of communal school organization (Bryk & Dris-coll, 1988; Gottfredson, 2001). Communal school organization, as illustrated in Figure 1, refers to the organization of a school as a community and

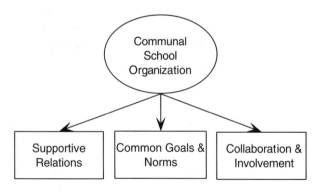

**FIGURE I.**
Communal School Organization and Its Components.

includes supportive relationships between and among teachers, administrators, and students; a common set of goals and norms; and a sense of collaboration and involvement. As defined by Solomon *et al.* (1997), a school that has a good sense of community, is one in which "members know, care about, and support one another, have common goals and sense of shared purpose, and to which they actively contribute and feel personally committed" (Solomon *et al.*, 1997, p. 236). A communally organized school emphasizes informal social relations, common norms and experiences, and collaboration and participation; by contrast, more bureaucratic schools emphasize formal organization, technical knowledge, and regulation and standardization (Lee, Bryk, & Smith, 1992; Rowan, 1990).

Previous research has demonstrated the positive outcomes of communal school organization. Bryk and Driscoll (1988) found that levels of teacher efficacy, work enjoyment, and morale were higher, and teacher absenteeism was lower in schools that were communally organized. These schools also had lower levels of student misbehavior and dropouts and had higher levels of academic interest and math achievement. Similarly, Battistich and his colleagues found that student sense of community was significantly correlated with the students' liking for school, empathy, prosocial motivation, academic motivation, self-esteem, conflict resolution, prosocial motivation, and altruistic behavior (Battistich Solomon, Kim, Watson, & Schaps, 1995; Solomon, Watson, Battistich, Schaps, & Delucchi, 1992). Finally, Battistich and Solomon (1997) found that sense of community was highly correlated with teacher efficacy, teacher work enjoyment, teacher satisfaction, teacher perceptions of principal effectiveness, parental supportiveness, and positive relations between teachers and students. Battistich and his colleagues specifically examined the relationship between communal school organization and deviant behavior and found that higher levels of student sense of school community were associated with lower levels of drug use and delinquency (Battistich & Hom, 1997).

Although much research has demonstrated the positive effects of communally organized schools, the process leading from communal school organization to these beneficial outcomes had not been examined until recently. That is, studies had not examined *why* students in communally organized schools exhibit higher levels of academic achievement or lower levels of problem behavior. Although some researchers propose that communal school organization leads to greater student sense of belonging that, in turn, leads to less delinquency, the first study to specifically test the hypothesized mediating mechanism of student bonding was one by Payne, Gottfredson, and Gottfredson (2003).

Discussions about communal school organization naturally lead to discussions about student bonding. Students in communally organized schools appear to be more bonded to the school: They have a greater attachment to the teachers, have more commitment to the school, and have internalized the norms of the school to a greater degree. They feel as though they belong to the school, as though they are valued and accepted. These ideas provide a link between communal school organization and disorder via Hirschi's social control theory (Hirschi, 1969). As discussed by Hirschi (1969), one domain in which an individual's social bond is formed is the school. Attachment to school is shown by the extent to which students care about the school, the teachers, and the teachers' opinions. Commitment to education is shown by the time and energy students invest in school as they pursue the goal of academic achievement. Involvement is simply the time spent on conventional school activities. Finally, belief is the extent to which students give legitimacy to the norms and rules of the school. In general, students who are well integrated in school are less likely to be deviant. Those who have more positive attachments, who have invested greater effort into school, who are involved in more school activities, and who believe in the rules of the school are less likely to engage in deviant activities (Welsh, Greene, & Jenkins, 1999).

Hirschi (1969) provided support for his theory in the school domain. Students who cared little about what the teachers think and who did not like school were much more likely to report delinquent acts. In addition, those with low belief and low commitment were more likely to be delinquent (Hirschi, 1969). Other researchers have also supported the negative relationship between school bonding and delinquency (Krohn & Massey, 1980; Liska & Reed, 1985; Cernkovich & Giordano, 1992; Jenkins, 1997; Welsh, Greene, and Jenkins, 1999; D. Gottfredson et al., 2002).

Research has demonstrated that students in communally organized schools have a greater sense of belonging, greater commitment to school, and greater internalization of school norms (Solomon et al., 1992; Battistich et al., 1995). As the adults in the school create a school community, the climate of the school becomes warmer and more inclusive and participatory. The students' feelings of belonging or attachment then increase, as do their levels of commitment to school and their levels of belief in or acceptance of school norms and values. Thus, the link between communal school organization and student bonding is clear: Students in schools that are communally organized will be more bonded to the school.

It is important to note the difference between communal school organization and student bonding, as they could be seen as the same concept on the surface. The major difference is where each theoretical concept lies in relation to the individual. Communal school organization refers to the existence of a specific social organization that is external to the individual, such as the existence of supportive relations, collaboration and participation, and a set of shared norms and goals. Student bonding, however, refers to the internal processes that result from the existence of this communal organization in the school: the personal attachment to the school, the commitment to education, and the belief in school rules. Therefore, communal school organization is external to the individual, whereas student bonding is internal.

Based on these ideas, Payne *et al.* (2003) examined the process by which the communal organization of a school influences the level of disorder in that school. Specifically, they tested the hypotheses that (1) schools that are more communally organized will have lower levels of school disorder and (2) the relationship between communal school organization and school disorder will be mediated by student bonding.

Data from a nationally representative sample of 254 public, nonalternative secondary schools were used to examine structural equation models (SEM) representing hypothesized relationships among communal school organization, student bonding, and school disorder. *Communal school organization* was operationalized by two scales measuring the supportive and collaborative relations and the common goals and norms in the school. *Student bonding* was operationalized by three scales measuring students' attachment to, belief in, and commitment to the school and school norms. *School disorder* was operationalized by three scales measuring the level of teacher victimization, student victimization, and student delinquency in the school. Finally, several exogenous variables were added to the models, including *percentage students African American, percentage teachers African American, poverty and disorganization, residential crowding, student enrollment, number of different students taught, urbanicity, percentage students male,* and *grade level.* The EQS Structural Equations Program (version 5.7B for Windows; Bentler, 1995) was used to estimate the SEM of the direct and indirect effects of the exogenous factors and communal school organization and the direct effects of student bonding on school disorder, based on the variance-covariance matrix.

Both hypotheses tested by Payne *et al.* (2003) were supported, but this support did not hold for all three measures of disorder. Schools that were more communally organized did experience less disorder, but the effects were small for the student-reported measures of disorder and statistically significant only for the measure of student delinquency. In addition, levels of student bonding mediated the relationship between communal school organization and student delinquency but not the relationship between communal school organization and teacher victimization.

The results found in this study are valuable, despite these mixed findings. The findings confirm that the social organization of a particular school influences the level of disorder in that school. As predicted by the study's first hypothesis, schools that were more communally organized had lower levels of teacher victimization and student delinquency. In addition, the effect of communal school organization on student victimization was in the expected direction, although nonsignificant. These negative relationships accord with previous research. They suggest that schools in which teachers agree that the relationships among school members are supportive and collaborative and that there are common organizational goals and norms will experience less disorder.

The second hypothesis of this study explored this relationship further. It was predicted that the negative relationship between communal school organization and school disorder would be mediated by student bonding. That is, schools that are more communally organized would have students who are more bonded to the school, which would then lead to less disorder. The first part of this hypothesis was confirmed: Schools that were more communally organized did indeed have students who were more bonded to the school. The second part of the hypothesis was confirmed for student delinquency: The effect of communal school organization on student delinquency became nonsignificant once student bonding was included in the model. This implies that the supportive and collaborative relationships and common norms and goals reported by the teachers were internalized by the students, resulting in higher levels of student bonding. These higher bonding levels, in turn, led to less delinquency.

However, this indirect effect of communal school organization through student bonding was not seen for teacher victimization. The effect of communal school organization on teacher victimization did not change when student bonding was included in the model. This is curious because, presumably, the students' delinquent acts result at least partially in victimization of teachers; one would therefore expect the two disorder measures to act similarly. However, the stronger relationship between the social organization measures and teacher victimization is consistent with previous results reporting similar findings with regard to school climate (Gottfredson & Gottfredson, 1985; Gottfredson et al., 2003). This may indicate that teachers are being victimized by non-students as well as students. Another possible explanation is that the unmediated relationship between communal school organization and teacher victimization is a methodological artifact due to this study's lack of student measures of communal school organization.

Although research has not specifically examined the effects of communal school organization on bullying, recent research has examined concepts that are similar to communal school organization elements or to the concept of communal school organization as a whole. For example, Boulton et al. (1999) found that students who have reciprocated friendships at school are less likely to be involved in bullying incidents, illustrating the importance of the supportive relations element of communal school organization. Similarly, Natvig, Albreksten, and Qvarnstrom (2001) found that students who felt strong support from school members, either teachers or other students, were less likely to be involved in bullying. Natvig et al. (2001) also found that students who are more alienated from school, are less involved, and participate less are more likely to be involved in bullying, demonstrating a relationship between bullying and the participation and involvement element of communal school organization.

Other research illustrates a relationship between bullying and concepts that are similar to communal school organization as a whole. For example, Rigby, Cox, and Black (1997) examined the relation between bullying and student cooperativeness, broadly defined as "acting together in a coordinated way, at work, leisure or in social relationships, in pursuit of shared goals, the enjoyment of joint activity, or simply furthering the relationship" (Rigby et al., 1997, p. 158). This concept of cooperativeness embodies the same elements as communal school organization: common goals and norms, participation and involvement, and cooperative relationships. Rigby et al. (1997) found that cooperativeness was negatively correlated with bullying and victimization. Similarly, in the regression analyses, greater cooperativeness significantly predicted less bullying.

Another concept similar to communal school organization that has been examined in the bullying literature is social support (Rigby, 2000). As defined by Rigby (2000), social support includes elements such as participation in furthering common goals and accepting emotional relationships; again, these elements are clearly related to the elements of communal school organization. Rigby (2000) found that perceived social support at school was negatively correlated with victimization; that is, students who experience support in common goals and are accepted in relationships with other school members are less likely to be victims of bullying.

## SCHOOL-BASED INTERVENTIONS TO PREVENT BULLYING

Whereas most of the research on predictors and correlates of bullying focus on the individual, most bullying interventions focus on the entire school, taking a "whole school approach" (Farrington, 1993). Elements of these types of prevention programs include increasing the awareness of bullying, making antibullying policies clear, and including bullying as part of the school curriculum (Farrington, 1993). Essentially, these interventions attempt to improve the climate of the school by working with all school members, adults and students, to establish antibullying norms and communicate these norms to the entire school community. These interventions are based on the importance of communal school organization and student bonding, initially through the establishment of antibullying norms as part of the system of common values shared by the school community. As school members embrace these norms and work toward improving the bullying problem, participation and involvement increases, relationships become more supportive and collaborative, and school members become more bonded to the school. All of these changes increase the communal organization of a school and decrease all types of disorder in the school, including bullying. Research on these types of interventions has found significant reductions in bullying, ranging from 20 to 50% over the course of two years (Arora, 1994; Clarke & Kiselica, 1997; Olweus, 1991, 1993, 1994).

One example of this type of intervention, Bully Proofing Your School, is detailed by Garrity and his colleagues (Garrity et al., 1994; Garrity & Jens, 1997). This comprehensive program focuses on improving the climate of elementary schools by creating a culture that does not tolerate any kind of aggression, whether physical or verbal. The creation of a more caring and communal school environment decreases both bullying and fear of bullying, which in turn continues to improve the climate of school (Garrity & Jens, 1997).

Several studies have focused specifically on the student piece of the whole-school approach and have presented positive results. Peer support systems, for example, appear to be important and effective elements in the improvement of the social organization of a school and the reduction of bullying incidence (Naylor & Cowie, 1999). Peterson and Rigby (1999) examined the effectiveness of various student programs that were part of a whole-school intervention, such as the Students' Welcomers Program and Students' Antibullying Committee. While an overall reduction in bullying was not seen, there was a significant reduction in bullying reported by first-year high school students (Peterson et al., 1999). This finding is even more significant when considering that these students were most often the victims of bullying in this study (Rigby, 1996), and that the intervention most likely raised awareness and reporting of bullying incidents. The actual reduction in bullying, therefore, was most likely even greater than reported (Peterson et al., 1999). These studies clearly illustrate the importance of student involvement in bullying interventions, which is consistent with the communal school organization view; however, it is important to remember that student involvement is only one element of the whole-school approach and must be accompanied by adult involvement.

Undoubtedly, the most tested and implemented bullying intervention is the Bullying Prevention Program developed by Olweus (1991, 1994, 1997). Like the previous program, this intervention also seeks to improve the climate of a school. The program works toward creating a school "environment characterized by warm, positive interest, and involvement from adults, . . . firms limits to unacceptable behavior, . . . [and], in cases of violations of limits and rules, nonhostile nonphysical sanctions" (Olweus, 1994, p. 1185). This combination of positive adult involvement, clear limits on behavior, and consistent consequences to inappropriate actions is achieved by increased monitoring and surveillance of students by adults in the school as they become more involved in both the academic and social aspects of students' lives. The program has four general objectives: to increase awareness of and education about bullying; to increase adult involvement, both at school and at home; to develop clear rules and consistent sanctions about bullying; and to support and protect victims (Olweus, 1997).

These objectives are achieved through a variety of program core components. The first is an introduction to the program for the adults, making them aware of the bullying problem and their necessary involvement. Next, a questionnaire is administered to the school members to establish the nature of the problem in that particular school. Once program implementation actually begins, school-wide elements include the establishment of a steering committee to oversee implementation, a School Conference Day, increased monitoring in the cafeteria and on the playground, the development of antibullying class rules, frequent class meetings on the subject of bullying, and frequent PTA meetings. In addition, conferences are held with individual students who are involved in bullying incidents, either as the aggressor or victim, and their parents (Olweus, 1997).

Olweus (1997) reported the findings of a two-year study examining the implementation of the Bullying Prevention Program in 42 schools in Norway. Reductions in bullying incidents as high as 50% were found both 8 months and 20 months after the intervention. These reductions applied to both indirect and direct bullying behaviors, to both male and female students, and to students in all grades. Although the program is explicitly aimed at bullying, reductions were also seen in other types of antisocial behavior, such as vandalism, fighting, stealing, drinking, and truancy. Supporting the importance of communal school organization for reducing bullying, Olweus (1997) also found great improvements in the climate of schools. Classroom order, social relationships, and student attitudes toward school and schoolwork all improved as a result of the program. It can be assumed, based on the theory of Olweus's Program, that these improvements in school climate led to the reductions in bullying incidents.

## CONCLUSION

Bullying in schools is clearly a problem. Research has determined that as many as 50% of students have been involved in bullying incidents (Farrington, 1993) and has supported the link between bullying others and engaging in more violent behavior (Nansel et al., 2003). Bullying contributes to a fearful and intimidating school climate that causes many students to feel unwelcome and unsupported (Batsche & Knoff, 1994).

Either as an isolated problem or as a precursor to more violent behavior, schools should focus on the reduction and prevention of bullying. A step in this direction has been the identification of factors related to bullying. Although most research has examined individual-level predictors, some school-level predictors have been investigated. Research has determined that bullying is far more likely to occur in middle schools as opposed to high schools (Olweus, 1991; Whitney & Smith, 1993), to occur at school as opposed to away from school (Berthold & Hoover, 2000; Boulton & Underwood, 1993; Harris et *al.*, 2002; Nansel *et al.*, 2003; Olweus, 1991), and to occur on the playground or in classrooms as opposed to hallways and bathrooms (Frost, 1991; Mellor, 1990; Smith & Shu, 2000; Whitney & Smith, 1993; Wolke *et al.*, 2001). The majority of studies have found no effect of the racial and ethnic composition of a school on the amount of bullying (Boulton, 1995; Junger, 1990; Moran *et al.*, 1993; Siann *et al.*, 1994; Whitney & Smith, 1993). Finally, there is mixed evidence for the effects of school and/or class size on bullying and of school location on bullying. Some studies have found no relationship between school or class size and bullying (Mellor, 1999; Olweus, 1991; Whitney & Smith, 1993; Wolke *et al.*, 2001), while some have found that large schools and classes have more bullying (Stephenson & Smith, 1989; Winters, 1997) and still others have found that small schools and classes have more bullying (Wolke *et al.*, 2001). In addition, while some studies have found no relationship between school location and bullying (Mellor, 1999; Olweus, 1991; Winters, 1997), others have found that schools located in inner-city, low socioeconomic status, disadvantaged areas have more bullying (Stephenson & Smith, 1989; Whitney & Smith, 1993; Wolke *et al.*, 2001). Further research is needed to sort out the effects of these school context factors.

Although previous research has demonstrated the relationship between school climate and general school disorder, most studies have not examined the effect of school climate on bullying specifically. Several studies have indicated that antibullying norms held by teachers and students are related to lower levels of bullying in a school (Boulton *et al.*, 1997; Boulton *et al.*, 1999; Boulton & Flemington, 2002; Stephenson & Smith, 1991), although these antibullying attitudes tend not to translate into antibullying behavior (Boulton & Underwood, 1993; Olweus, 1991; Pepler *et al.*, 1989; Smith & Shu, 2000; Whitney & Smith, 1993). Future research should investigate the intervening mechanisms between these attitudes and behavior. In addition, these studies only address one element of school climate, the norms and beliefs held by school members. Other aspects of school climate, such as teacher and student morale and the relations among school members, should also be examined.

One of these aspects of school climate, the social organization of a school, has been shown to influence general school disorder (Gottfredson, 2001). A specific perspective on social organization, communal school organization, has also been shown to affect disorder (Payne *et al.*, 2003). Communal school organization refers to the organization of a school as a community and includes supportive relationships between and among teachers, administrators, and students; a common set of goals and norms; and a sense of collaboration and involvement. Although the effect of communal school organization on bullying has not specifically been examined, recent research has examined concepts that are similar to communal school organization elements or to the concept of communal school organization as a whole. Research has shown that supportive relationships are related to lower levels of bullying (Boulton *et al.*, 1999; Natvig *et al.*, 2001), as is greater student participation and involvement (Natvig *et al.*, 2001). Rigby *et al.* (1997) found that greater cooperativeness, a concept that embodies many of the same elements as communal school organization, is related to lower levels of bullying. Similarly, greater social support is related to less bullying (Rigby, 2000); this concept, which includes supportive emotional relationships and participation in common goals, is also clearly related to communal school organization.

Further support for the importance of school climate can be seen in the research on school-based bullying interventions. Whereas most of the research on predictors and correlates of bullying focus on the individual, most bullying interventions, by contrast, focus on the entire school, taking a "whole-school approach" (Farrington, 1993). These interventions are based on the importance of communal school organization, initially through the establishment of antibullying norms as part of the system of common values and norms shared by the school community. As school members embrace these norms and work toward improving the bullying problem, participation and involvement increases, and relationships become more supportive and collaborative. Research on these types of interventions has found significant reductions in bullying, ranging from 20 to 50% over the course of two years (Arora, 1994; Clarke & Kiselica, 1997; Olweus, 1991, 1993, 1994).

Research on school-level predictors and school-based interventions clearly indicates the importance of both school context and school climate factors. More research is needed, however, before firm conclusions can be made. The effects of several school context factors, such as size and location, are still unclear. Studies showing evidence on the importance of school climate factors are in the beginning stages; clearer, more explicit tests of the effects of school norms, relations among school members, and other aspects of school climate are necessary. The research on bullying interventions provides the strongest support for school climate influences on bullying, but even this research leaves some questions: What exactly is the process that leads to less bullying? Do the common norms lead to greater participation and more supportive relations, or do the relations lead to the norms? Is the participation by all school members or only specific groups necessary?

Nevertheless, the evidence is clear: School climate matters. This has great implications for school-based prevention of bullying, as several interventions have indicated. Schools that work toward improving the social organization, toward becoming more communal, could experience less bullying. By improving the relationships and bonding among school members, the collaboration and participation of these members, and the agreement on common goals and norms, schools could experience a reduction in bullying. This reduction would, in turn, strengthen the community of the school and allow all members to feel supported and welcome.

# References

Arora, C. M. J. (1994). Is there any point in trying to reduce bullying in secondary schools? *Educational Psychology in Practice*, 10, 155–162.

Batsche, G. M., & Knoff, H. M. (1994). Bullies and their victims: Understanding a pervasive problem in schools. *School Psychology Review*, 23(2), 165–175.

Battistich, V., Solomon, D., Kim, D., Watson, M., & Schaps, E. (1995). Schools as communities, poverty levels of student populations, and students' attitudes, motives, and performance: A multilevel analysis. *American Educational Research Journal*, 32, 627–658.

Battistich, V., & Hom, A. (1997). The relationship between students' sense of their school as a community and their involvement in problem behavior. *American Journal of Public Health*, 87(12), 1997–2001.

Battistich, V., & Solomon, D. (1997). Caring school communities. *Educational Psychologist*, 32(3), 137–151.

Berthold, K. A., & Hoover, J. H. (2000). Correlates of bullying and victimizations among intermediate students in the Midwestern USA. *School Psychology International*, 21(1), 65–78.

Boulton, M. J. (1995). Patterns of bully/victim problems in mixed race groups of children. *Social Development*, 4(3), 277–293.

Boulton, M. J., Bucci, E. & Hawker, D. S. (1999). Swedish and English secondary school pupils' attitudes towards, and conceptions of, bullying: Concurrent links with bully-victim involvement. *Scandinavian Journal of Psychology*, 40, 277–284.

Boulton, M. J., & Flemington, I. (2002). Associations between secondary school pupils' definitions of bullying, attitudes towards bullying, and tendencies to engage in bullying: Age and sex differences. *Educational Studies*, 28(4), 353–371.

Boutlon, M. J., Lanitis, I., Manoussou, V., & Lemoni, O. (1997). Bullying and victimization in Greek primary school pupils: Linkages between attitudes and self-reported involvement. Unpublished manuscript.

Boulton, M. J., & Underwood, K. (1993). Bully/victim problems among middle school children. *European Education*, 25(3), 18–38.

Bryk, A. S., & Driscoll, M. E. (1988). *The school as community: Shaping forces and consequences for students and teachers*. Madison, WI: University of Wisconsin, National Center on Effective Secondary Schools.

Clarke, E. A., & Kiselica, M. S. (1997). A systemic counseling approach to the problems of bullying. *Elementary School Guidance, and Counseling*, 31, 310–315.

Charach, A., Pepler, D., & Ziegler, S. (1995). Bullying at school: A Canadian perspective. *Education Canada*, 35, 12–19, Spring.

Farrington, D. P. (1993). Understanding and preventing Bullying. In M. Tonry, (Ed.), *Crime and justice*, Vol. 17. Chicago: The University of Chicago.

Frost, L. (1991). A primary school approach: What can be done about the bully? In M. Elliot (Ed.), *Bullying: A practical guide to coping for schools*. Harlow, UK: Longman.

Garrity, C., & Jens, K. (1997). Bully proofing your school: Creating a positive climate. *Intervention in School and Clinic*, 32(4), 235–244.

Garrity, C., Jens, K., Porter, W., Sager, N., & Short-Camilli, C. (1994). *Bully proofing your school*. Longmont, CO: Sopris West.

Gottfredson, D. C. (2001). *Delinquency and schools*. New York: Cambridge University.

Gottfredson, D. C. Wilson, D. Najaka, S. (2002). School-Based Crime Prevention. In L. Sherman, D. Farrington, B. Welsh, & D. Mackenzie (Eds.), *Evidence-Based Crime Prevention*. London, UK: Routledge.

Gottfredson, G., Gottfredson, D., Payne, A. A., & Gottfredson, N. (2003). *School climate predictors of school disorder: Results from the National Study of Delinquency Prevention in Schools*. (manuscript under review)

Gottfredson, M. R., & Hirschi, T. (1990). *A general theory of crime*. Stanford, CA: Stanford University.

Harris, S., Petrie, G., & Willoughby, W. (2002). Bullying among 9th graders: An exploratory study. *NASSP Bulletin*, 86(630), 3–14.

Junger, M. (1990). Intergroup bullying and racial harassment in the Netherlands. *Sociology and Social Research*, 74(2), 65–72.

Lee, V. E., Bryk, A. S., & Smith, J. B. (1992). The organization of effective secondary schools. *Review of Research in Education*, 19, 171–267.

Ma, X., Stewin, L. L., & Mah, D. L. (2001). Bullying in School: Nature, effects, and remedies. *Research Papers in Education*, 16(3), 247–270.

Mellor, A. (1990). *Bullying in Swedish secondary schools*. Edinburgh: Scottish Council for Research in Education.

Mellor, A. (1999). Scotland. In P.K. Smith, Y. Morita, J. Junger-Tas, D. Olweus, R. Catalano, & P. Slee (Eds.), *The nature of school bullying: A cross-national perspective*. London: Routledge.

Moran, S., Smith, P., Thompson, D., & Whitney, I. (1993). Ethnic differences in experiences in bullying: Asian and White children. *British Journal of Educational Psychology*, 63, 431–440.

Nansel, T. R., Overpeck, M., Pilla, R. S., Ruan, W. I., & Simons-Morton, B. G. (2001). Bullying behaviors among the US youth: Prevalence and association with psychosocial adjustment. *JAMA*, *285*, 2094–2100.

Nansel, T. R., Overpeck, M. D., Haynie, D. L., Ruan, J., & Scheidt, P. C. (2003). Relationships between bullying and violence among U.S. youth. *Archives of Pediatrics and Adolescent Medicine*, 157, 348–353.

National Research Council and Institute of Medicine (2003). *Deadly lessons: Understanding lethal school violence*. In *Case studies of school violence*. Moore, M. H., Petrie, C. V., Braga, A. A., & McZaughlin, B. L. (Eds.). Division of Behavioral and Social Sciences and Education. Washington, DC: The National Academies Press.

Natvig, G. K., Albreksten, G., & Qvarnstrom, U. (2001). School-related stress experiences as a risk factor for bullying. *Journal of Youth and Adolescence*, 30(5), 561–575.

Naylor, P., & Cowie, H. (1999). The effectiveness of peer support systems in challenging school bullying: The perspectives and experiences of teachers and pupils. *Journal of Adolescence*, 22, 467–479.

Olweus, D. (1991). Bully/victim problems among schoolchildren: Basic facts and effects of a school-based intervention program. In D. Pepler & K. Rubin (Eds), *The development and treatment of childhood aggression*. Hillsdale, NJ: Erlbaum.

Olweus, D. (1993a). *Bullying at school: What we know and what we can do*. Oxford: Blackwell.

Olweus, D. (1994). Bullying at school: Long-term outcomes for the victims and an effective school-based intervention program. In L.R. Huesmann (Ed.), *Aggressive behavior: Current perspectives*. New York: Wiley.

Olweus, D. (1997). Bully/victim problems in school: Facts and intervention. *European Journal of Psychology of Education*, 12(4), 495–510.

Payne, A. A., Gottfredson, D. C. & Gottfredson, G. D. (2003). Schools as communities: The relationships among communal school organization, student bonding, and school disorder. *Criminology*, 41(3), 1301–1327.

Pepler, D. J., Craig, W. M., Ziegler, S., & Charach, A. (1994). An evaluation of an antibullying intervention in Toronto schools. *Canadian Journal of Community Mental Health*, 13, 95–110.

Peterson, L., & Rigby, K. (1999). Countering bullying at an Australian secondary school with students as helpers. *Journal of Adolescence*, 22, 481–492.

Rigby, K. (1996). *Bullying in schools—And what to do about it*. London: Jessica Kingsley.

Rigby, K. (2000). Effects of peer victimization in schools and perceived social support on adolescent well-being. *Journal of Adolescence*, 23, 57–68.

Rigby, K., Cox, I. & Black, G. (1997). Cooperativeness and bully/victim problems among Australian schoolchildren. *The Journal of School Psychology*, 137(3), 357–368.

Rigby, K., & Slee, P. T. (1991). Bullying among Australian schoolchildren: Reported behavior and attitudes toward victims. *The Journal of Social Psychology*, 131(5), 615–627.

Rowan, B. (1990). Commitment and control: Alternative strategies for the organizational design of schools. *Review of Research in Education, 16,* 353–392.

Siann, G., Callaghan, M., Glissov, R. L., & Rawson, L. (1994). Who gets bullied? The effect of school, gender, and ethnic group. *Educational Research, 36*(2), 123–134.

Smith, P. K., & Shu, S. (2000). What good schools can do about bullying: Findings from a survey in English schools after a decade of research and action. *Childhood, 7*(2), 193–212.

Solomon, D., Battistich, D. K., & Watson, M. (1997). Teacher practices associated with students' sense of the classroom as a community. *Social Psychology of Education, 1,* 235–267.

Solomon, D., Watson, M., Battistich, V., Schaps, E., & Deiucchi, K. (1992). Creating a caring community: Educational practices that promote children's prosocial development. In F. K., Oser, A. Dick, and J. L. Patry (Eds.), *Effective and responsible teaching: The new synthesis* (pp. 383–396). San Francisco: Jossey-Bass.

Stephenson, P., & Smith, D. (1989). Bullying in the junior school. In D. Tattum & D. Lane (Eds.), *Bullying in schools.* Stoke-on-Trent, UK: Trentham.

Stephenson, P., & Smith, D. (1991). Why some schools don't have bullies. In M. Elliot (Ed.), *Bullying: A practical guide to coping for schools.* Harlow, UK: Longman.

Stevens, V., Van Oost, P. & Bourdeaudhuij, I. de (2000). The effects of an anti-bullying intervention programme on peers' attitudes and behaviors. *Journal of Adolescence, 23,* 21–34.

U.S. Department of Education, National Center for Education Statistics (2002). Are America's schools safe? Students speak out: 1999 school crime supplement. (NCES 2002-331). Addington, L. A., Rudder, S. A., Miller, A. K., & Devoe, J. F., (Eds.). Washington, DC: Author.

Welsh, W. N., Greene, J. R. & Jenkins, P. (1999). School disorder: The influence of individual, institutional, and community factors. *Criminology, 37*(1), 73–117.

Whitney, I., & Smith, P. K. (1993). A survey of the nature and extent of bullying in junior/middle and secondary schools. *Education Research, 35*(1), 3–25.

Winters, D.L. (1997). Levels of violence in Pennsylvania public schools and efforts to control and prevent violence. *Dissertation Abstracts International,* 58(2020A) (University Microfilms No ?)

Wolke, D., Woods, S., Stanford, K., & Schultz, H. (2001). Bullying and victimization of primary school children in England and Germany: Prevalence and school factors. *British Journal of Psychology, 92,* 673–696.

CHAPTER

8

# Bullying During the Middle School Years

A. D. PELLEGRINI

*Department of Educational Psychology*

*University of Minnesota/Twin Cities Campus*

## INTRODUCTION

Aggression and antisocial behavior in American schools are persistent and very visible problems, particularly as youngsters make the transition from childhood and primary school to adolescence and secondary school (National Center for Educational Statistics, 1995). Much of the aggression in schools during this period involves individuals bullying their peers (Coie & Dodge, 1998; Bosworth, Espalage, & Simon, 1999; Espalage, Bosworth, & Simon, 2000; Perry, Willard, & Perry, 1990). Bullying is characterized by youngsters purposefully "victimizing" their peers by repeatedly using negative actions, such as physical, verbal, or indirect aggression (e.g., Espalage *et al.*, 2000; Smith & Sharp, 1994). Bullying also involves a power differential where aggressors are more dominant than the targets (Olweus, 1993a, b).

Sex differences are also important in this discussion of bullying as they are in more general discussions of aggression. Research has consistently found that boys, more than girls, are bullies at all levels of schooling (Olweus, 1993; Pellegrini & Long, 2001). This difference is part of a more general sex difference in aggression. A recent meta-analysis of sex differences in aggression has shown that males exhibit higher levels of both physical (e.g., hitting) and verbal (e.g., insulting) aggression from childhood through adulthood (Archer, 2001). Females, on the other hand, exhibit higher

*Implications for the Classroom*

levels of indirect, or relational (i.e., aggression to damage social relations), aggression than males. These differences are observed in cases of intrasexual aggression (i.e., male-male and female-female aggression) not intersexual aggression. That males use physical aggression for bullying more than females and females use indirect forms of aggression more than males is consistent with this chapter's more general theoretical orientation that suggests these differences result from sexual dimorphism, or males being physically larger than females. This argument will be explained in more detail later in the discussion.

In this chapter, I will first discuss bullying as a form of instrumental, or proactive, aggression. In the second and third sections I will embed the problem of bullying during adolescence in terms of social dominance theory. This theory integrates the ways in which boys use aggression to accomplish goals during adolescence in a larger theoretical picture of sexual dimorphism, sex segregation, and sex differences in aggression.

Next, I will address the issue of bullying during the period of adolescence. Both social and biological events conspire to increase bullying behavior during this period. In the final section, I will compare different methods used to compile data on bullying and victimization. Traditionally, bullying and victimization have been measured with self-report and, more recently, with peer nomination procedures. As is well known, different procedures used to assess aggression and other social and personality variables (Cairns & Cairns, 1986; Caspi, 1998) yield very different results. This is also true for the field of aggression (Archer, 2002) and for bullying, more specifically (Pellegrini & Bartini, 2000).

## BULLYING AS A DELIBERATE FORM OF AGGRESSION

I argue that bullying is a specific form of aggression and one that is used deliberately to secure resources (Pellegrini, 2002; Pellegrini *et al.*, 2002). In this regard, it is a dimension of *proactive aggression* and distinct from aggression that is used reactively or that is used in response to social provocation (Dodge & Coie, 1987). More specifically, most bullies use aggression in a calculating way. They target someone specific, such as someone who has few allies, and they use this vulnerability to achieve some end; for example, bullies may want to show how strong they are or will get ahead of a peer in the lunch queue. Indeed, these youngsters are often successful at getting their way by using aggressive tactics. It may be the case that this success results in these youngsters being held in relatively high regard by their peers. Both of these outcomes (getting a desired resource and increasing peer status) make bullying a rather attractive, and difficult to change, social strategy with peers.

*Reactive aggression*, on the other hand, is typically a nondeliberate and emotional response to a provocation. For instance, in response to having milk accidentally spilled on him at lunch, Johnny lashes out and punches the child who spilled the milk. This type of child attributes aggressive intent to socially ambiguous provocations. In short, these youngsters see the world as a hostile place. Their default rule in cases of ambiguous provocation is to assume such behaviors are aggressive.

As a result of their "short fuses" peers may provoke these reactive children on purpose to get a response or a "raise." In either case, these reactive youngsters are not effective in their uses of aggression. Indeed, their behavior has the opposite effect. They are disliked by their peers and often victimized. Appropriately, Olweus has labeled these youngsters as *provocative victims*.

The period of early adolescence is important for the study of bullying and victimization because during this period, peers become more important in youngsters' lives and are negatively and positively implicated in bullying and victimization. Specifically, boys use bullying as a way to gain and maintain dominance or leadership status with peers. There is also concern that during this period of increased interest in heterosexual relationships, aggressive boys will victimize girls. The next section introduces the construct of social dominance as a way to explain the role of bullying in adolescence.

## A SOCIAL DOMINANCE VIEW OF BULLYING AND VICTIMIZATION IN EARLY ADOLESCENCE

Following the idea that bullying is a form of proactive aggression is the assumption that in early adolescence, boys use bullying as a strategy to establish and maintain social dominance. Dominance is a relationship variable determining individuals' leadership status within a group that results from a series of agonistic and cooperative exchanges. The most dominant individuals in the group are those who are not only the toughest (often indexed by the ratio of wins:losses in dyadic exchanges or by the attention they receive from peers) but also who are able to reconcile with their former foes. Male groups are often organized in terms of dominance hierarchies with the most dominant being the alpha male. Less dominant individuals are ordered below the leader. Often, but not always (Archer, 1992), these dominance hierarchies are transitive; that is, A is greater than B and B is greater than C; therefore A is greater than C.

Dominance is not an end in itself. That is, individuals do not engage in a dominance-related encounter just to be dominant. Instead, dominance is a means to the end where the most dominant in a group gets prioritized access to resources that are valued for that group. For example, in preschoolers, access to toys is a valued resource. During early adolescence, as will be discussed below, access to heterosexual relationships is a valued resource (Pellegrini & Bartini, 2001).

The function of dominance hierarchies seems to be one of *minimizing* aggression and can best be understood in terms of the costs and benefits associated with using aggression. Specifically, when individuals first come together in a group, they interact with each other to sort out each other's status. Reflecting this sorting out process, the beginning phases of group formation typically witness relatively high rates of aggression. The costs of aggression are high in most cases. Some examples of the costliness of aggression include danger of injury, defeat and public humiliation, and sanction by the school. The benefit of aggression, at least at the beginning of group formation, are high (relative to the costs) and individuals are willing to take the risks. The benefit is access to heterosexual relations, usually in the form of having dates. Thus, aggression at the early stages of group formation can best be understood in terms of aggression used to establish dominance and reap the rewards.

After dominance is established, rates of aggression should decrease because individuals know who are the toughest kids, and to challenge a tougher individual would result in defeat. In cost-benefit terms, the costs of a challenge clearly outweigh the possible benefits. Similarly, a dominant individual should not aggress against individuals of lower status because the bully has little to gain; these minimal benefits are outweighed by the relatively high costs. This logic explains bullying as a form of proactive aggression and also assumes that individuals use aggression rationally. This is clearly not the case for provocative victims because they use aggression reactively.

## Bullying as Social Dominance

This section advances the view that bullying, and physical aggression in general, among boys in early adolescence is part of a quest for social dominance. The model, illustrated in Figure 1, also recognizes the importance of group dynamics in bullying and victimization (Pellegrini & Bartini, 2000b, 2001; Prinstein & Cohen, 2001).

By way of previewing the model presented in Figure 1, this discussion proposes that bullying increases as youngsters make the transition to middle school. They bully in response to their declining or uncertain dominance status during the transition. Bullying is used as an initial strategy to increase dominance status. Bullying decreases after the transition to a new school and as dominance status increases.

This argument is consistent with social dominance theory, which considers the individual, not the group, as the unit of analysis. From this view, groups are organized vertically, and individuals compete with each other for available resources, using both aggressive and cooperative means. This

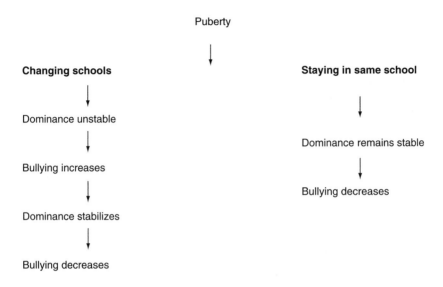

**FIGURE 1.**
Changes in Dominance and Bullying During Adolescence
as a Function of School Change.

process results in a dominance hierarchy. The most dominant individual has first priority to available resources.

This is not to say that individuals are not concerned with reaching and maintaining group goals. Indeed, once dominance hierarchies are established, group level aggression decreases and all members of the group benefit. Further, as long as group membership remains stable, cooperation, not aggression, should characterize group behavior. Cooperation, in turn, maximizes the likelihood that group members will reach their goals (Axelrod & Hamiltion, 1981).

More specifically, leadership status, especially for adolescent boys, is often established by using physically aversive (e.g., hitting peers), verbally aversive (e.g., name-calling), and affiliative (reconciliation) strategies (Pellegrini & Bartini, 2001b; Vaughn, 1999; Vaughn & Waters, 1981). The evidence for this claim, based on data from boys in the first year of middle school, is as follows. At the beginning of the first year of middle school, Pellegrini and Bartini (2001b) observed positive and significant correlations between two measures of aggression and dominance but noted that relations between dominance and affiliation were not significant. Toward the end of the year, the correlation pattern was reversed. Aggression was not related to dominance, but both measures of affiliation were related to dominance. Boys used aggression to establish dominance at the beginning of the year, and once dominance was established, they used affiliative strategies, possibly to consolidate power. For example, leaders often used an aversive strategy in an initial confrontation to establish status. After they "won" that encounter, they often attempted to reconcile "defeated" individuals and gain their support. As a result of a series of aversive and affiliative exchanges, as well as other factors, different role relationships between individuals were formed. From this view, it is not surprising that some bullies are held in relatively high regard by their peers.

Once leadership and status are established, aggression between individuals is minimized as all parties recognize their status in relation to each other. Consequently, lower status individuals do not usually challenge higher status individuals (except in cases of provocative victims) because of the high likelihood of defeat and humiliation, relative to possible benefits. If a subordinate challenges an individual of higher status, the subordinate usually loses (Boulton & Smith, 1990). As noted earlier, the stability of relationships between individuals also supports subsequent cooperation, inhibits aggression, and maximizes the likelihood of goal attainment.

Other aspects of this model have also been supported empirically. Specifically, the assumption that bullying is used in the service of dominance as adolescent males make the transition from primary to middle schools has also been supported. Bullying mediated dominance status from the transition between primary school to middle school (Pellegrini et al., 2002). Bullying during the first year of middle school was a way to achieve dominance status. This process may be the reason that bullying also increased from primary school to the first half of the first year of middle school. After dominance was established, rates of bullying decreased.

Also consistent with the idea that bullying is used to establish peer status was the finding that youngsters who were popular with their peers tended not to be victimized (Pellegrini et al., 2002). Popularity (measured by the number of "like most" nominations received by a person) seems to be a buffer against victimization because bullies would probably damage their reputation and status with their larger peer group if they were to bully a peer who was popular with that same group.

## SEX DIFFERENCES IN BULLYING AND AGGRESSION AND THE EMERGENCE OF HETEROSEXUAL RELATIONSHIPS

As noted above, there are reliable sex differences in bullying and aggression, with males exhibiting more of each relative to females. The vast majority of bullying, and indeed aggression, is intrasexual. That is, boys bully boys and girls bully girls (Archer, 2002). During childhood, this is especially understandable given the existence of sexually segregated peer groups. Sexual segregation among juveniles is a basic component in the social

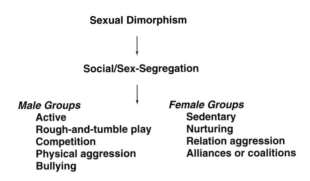

**FIGURE 2.**

A Model for Sex Differences in Aggression.

organization of many human societies as well as in a number of mammalian species (Archer & Lloyd, 2002; Maccoby, 1998).

This section argues that sexual differences in bullying and physical aggression generally are rooted in the differences in size between males and females, with males being the larger of the two sexes. This model is presented in Figure 2.

## Sexual Dimorphism in Size and Physical Activity

Sexual dimorphism, or males being physically bigger than females, among humans has been described as "moderate" (Archer & Lloyd, 2002). Males are typically 18% larger than females and it is the larger size, this text argues, that biases them to be more physically aggressive (Pellegrini & Archer, In press). Briefly, larger physical size results in males being more physically active. This activity is necessary for physical conditioning and skeletal and muscle development (Pellegrini & Smith, 1998). High levels of activity are the ultimate cause for sexually segregated peer groups in childhood (Pellegrini, In press). Males are more physically vigorous than females and join in groups to display their physical traits. Females avoid these groups. Males' behavior in these groups is physically vigorous and, correspondingly, males take on competitive and aggressive roles. Specifically, boys, more than girls, tend to engage in competitive games (Pellegrini et al., 2002), and these games tend to be physically vigorous, such as chase games or ball games. Boys also tend to use physically aggressive strategies with their male peers, whereas girls are not as likely to do so. The combination of physical conditioning, being a leader in competitive games, and the strategic use of aggression result in boys' leadership or dominance status with peers. In short, the competitive and aggressive nature of male groups results in their using physically aggressive strategies with their peers to establish and maintain dominance.

Smaller and more sedentary females try to avoid these physically active behaviors and interact with each other. While males are physically aggressive, active, and competitive, females are more concerned with social relationships in the form of alliance and coalition building. Interestingly, Terman's (1946) chapter on sex differences in the first *Manual of Child Psychology* suggests that differences in physical size and "energetics" may be the basic differences between sexes in addition to dominance and aggression.

It is very important to note that this chapter's argument is not presenting a biological deterministic model. Instead, it incorporates some basic biological tenants (that females and males have different reproductive roles) and that these roles relate to sexual dimorphism, sexual segregation, and differential uses of aggression. The nature of the environment in which individuals develop (from conception to adulthood) moderates the degree of dimorphism. In severe ecological niches (e.g., where there is nutritional stress), there is less sexual dimorphism (Alexander *et al.*, 1976).

This chapter's model predicts that because males are the physically larger (Pellegrini, In press; Plavcan & van Schaik, 1997) and the more competitive sex, they segregate into same-sex groups because of high energetic demands: They can exercise and engage in vigorous and rough behaviors. Relatedly, the social roles that males take in these segregated groups are associated with their being the more competitive sex. Males use physical aggression and dominance-related strategies to sort their status in same-sex peer groups. Segregated groups are the contexts in which males learn and develop the skills necessary for status. They also gain and maintain the physical conditioning associated with successful enactment of these roles in male groups. In adolescence, access to heterosexual relationships is the resource under contention. Higher status individuals have prioritized access to resources.

On the other hand, females segregate into more sedentary, less competitive, and less physically aggressive groups (Maccoby, 1998). When they use aggression to acquire resources, they use indirect or relational aggression because it is less physically vigorous and it aids in coalition building. That is, using indirect aggression does not involve direct confrontation between peers (Bjorkqvist, 1994; Crick & Grotepeter, 1995). Rather, the damage is done indirectly, for example, by spreading rumors and by forming alliances and thus protecting the perpetrator.

Socialization pressures reinforce these differences. Differences are apparent at a very early age when fathers engage in rough and vigorous play with their sons much more frequently than with their daughters (MacDonald & Parke, 1986; Parke & Suomi, 1981). Parents also differentially furnish boys' and girls' bedrooms with toys and props that further reinforce these differences (Rheingold & Cook, 1975). For example, boys' rooms contain more paramilitary toys than girls' rooms (e.g., G.I. Joe), and girls' rooms have more dolls, tea sets, and dollhouses.

These differences continue in segregated peer groups as children them-selves are very reluctant to interact with opposite sex peers (Serbin, Conner, Burchardt, & Citron, 1979). Segregation occurs most commonly in children choosing to interact with same-sex peers during their free time periods with little adult supervision (Blatchford, 1988; Thorne, 1986, 1993). Specifically, segregation is most pronounced in settings where children are institution-ally sorted into the same age groups, such as in schools (Maccoby, 1998). This phenomenon is readily observable in primary school contexts where children are given free choice of social partners, such as during recess or at lunch time. Observations of primary school children on the elementary school playground clearly attest to this segregation, especially in the context of competitive games (Pellegrini, Kato, Blatchford, & Baines, 2002; Thorne, 1986; 1993).

## HETEROSEXUAL RELATIONSHIPS

Just as biology and socialization maintain sexual segregation in childhood, these two forces conspire to bring the two sexes together with the onset of puberty and adolescence (Maccoby, 1998). Hormonal changes during ado-lescence as well societal stress on heterosexual relationships (Collins & Sroufe, 1999) result in boys and girls showing increased interest in one another. This interest is realized by an increase in opposite sex contact and on increased interest in dating (Pellegrini, 2001; Pellegrini & Long, 2003). Interestingly, junior high and middle schools, which house early adoles-cents, afford prime opportunities for youngsters to interact with peers of the opposite sex (Blatchford, 1998). Indeed, Maccoby (1998, p. 73) suggests that school is the "major setting" where children encounter peers of the other sex. Further, the peer culture of middle school often stresses hetero-sexual interaction (Collins & Sroufe, 1999; Furman, 1999). Consequently, middle school is a very interesting and ecologically valid venue to study early adolescents' emerging heterosexual relationships. By extension, to understand the beginnings of heterosexual relationships, it is sensible to study youngsters as they first make the transition into middle school and follow them longitudinally. In this way, the natural history of relationships with opposite sex peers can be studied from the point when youngsters first encounter each other in an institution designed for young adolescents. As Maccoby (1998) noted, schools are very important socialization institutions, but they have not, generally, been studied from this perspective. Thus, research in this area is needed as part of an effort to understand adolescents' heterosexual relationships.

Heterosexual activity for youngsters of this age typically involves group "dating." Dating for young adolescents is an extension of larger social groupings, rather than the intimate dyadic relationships characteristic of adulthood. Dating usually consists of groups of youngsters going out to-gether (Connolly & Goldberg, 1999; Furman, 1999). These groups are often the amalgam of male and female cliques (Furman, 1999). From this view, girls may want to "go out" with a dominant boy because the boys are viewed by peers as leaders (Pellegrini & Long, 2003). Thus, girls may gain status by affiliating with these boys. That dates are relatively large group activities also works to mitigate against possibilities of abuse of girls by boys. Pellegrini and Long's research found that girls tended to choose dominant boys as dates to a hypothetical party (Pellegrini & Long, 2003).

Girls' choosing to affiliate with aggressive boys during adolescence is also consistent with the Moffitt and colleagues extensive longitudinal study (Moffitt et al., 2001). In this study, she found that girls were less aggressive than boys across their lifespans. However, during adolescence, girls' rates of antisocial activity increased, and they tended to affiliate with antisocial boys. According to Moffitt et al., this behavior is due to girls feeling as though they are in a "role trap" in early adolescence. Because girls mature faster than boys, they are often treated as children at a time when they feel like adults. Consequently, they may affiliate with aggressive boys as a way to challenge those roles defined for them by their parents and society at large.

With maturity, most girls revert to form and are no longer attracted to these boys. The exception to this rule is girls who come from aggressive homes. They have both genetic (having inherited aggressive genes from parents) and socialization biases (having been reared in an aggressive home) toward antisocial behavior. These girls, who are antisocial, are attracted to antisocial men not only in early adolescence but also in adulthood.

Girls, as a group, are not as reliant on dominance-related strategies as boys (Pellegrini & Long, 2003). Rather, girls are more concerned with using indirect means to gain access to resources and in choosing males. Girls, more than boys, typically use indirect or relational aggression as a way to manipulate their female peers (Bjorkqvist, 1994; Campbell, 1999; Crick & Grotpeter, 1995). Relational or indirect aggression refers to individuals harming each other and enhancing themselves by damaging reputations and social relations through the use of gossip, rumor, and threats. For example, a girl may damage another girl's reputation by spreading rumors about her morals. This sort of behavior is more commonly observed in females than in males. Girls who use relational aggression against other girls tend to be nominated by boys for dates to a hypothetical party (Pelle-grini & Long, 2003).

To conclude this section, it is important to suggest that adolescent boys are biased (both by biology and socialization) toward using physical aggres-sion against other boys as part of their quest for status. This status makes them attractive to females. Females find these boys attractive for a number of different reasons, thus reinforcing males' intrasexual aggression. Research by Moffitt and colleagues certainly suggests that antisocial girls are especially attracted to aggressive boys (Moffitt *et al.*, 2001). These are the girls who tend to maintain an antisocial profile across their life span.

Girls are also biased by biology and socialization pressures to use less direct forms of aggression. Girls who do this tend to be invited by boys to a hypothetical party. It may be the case that girls use relational aggression as a bullying strategy against girls they see as rivals for dates.

In the cases of both boys and girls, school and society certainly need to make the use of antisocial strategies less rewarding. As a first step, however, teachers need a battery of reliable, valid, and useable measures by which to assess bullying and victimization.

## BULLYING AND THE ROLE OF CHANGING SCHOOLS DURING EARLY ADOLESCENCE

The argument above stressed that adolescent males often use bullying tactics as a way to gain and maintain social status. Aggression increases in circumstances where individuals change schools and thus their social status also changes. This proposition is consistent with data showing that rates and stability of bullying during early adolescence vary systematically according to school organizational factors. Specifically, declines in aggression continue across the school years, *except* in those cases during early adolescence when youngsters make the transition from primary to middle school. When youngsters change schools at this point, there is an increase in bullying; following the transition, the decline resumes. When youngsters of the same age do not change schools, the decline continues without a brief increase in bullying spike. That this trend is more robust for boys than girls (Smith *et al.*, 1999) is consistent with the view that aggression is more important for boys' status with their peers (Maccoby, 1998).

This section presents data from a number of large scale studies to document these claims. The data, for the most part, are based on large and often nationally representative samples. The questionnaires used with children are typically self-reports, asking them questions such as the following: How often have you taken part in bullying other students in school? Do you think it's fun to make fun of other students? How often have you been bullied in school this term?

In Olweus's (1993) pioneering large-scale studies in Norway and Sweden, he reported that the decline in bullying is most marked for primary school children, and for junior high school students, the slope of the decline is less steep. Olweus's data on boys' self-reported victimization shows an increase in bullying from primary school (10.7%) to junior high school (11.3%).

Other data also support the trend whereby the decrement in bullying is reversed with the initial transition to middle school. In two Australian studies (Rigby, 1996, 1997), bullying decreased during the primary school years, increased with the transition to secondary school, and then declined after the transition.

In two American studies, similar trends were reported. In the National Household Education Survey (National Center for Educational Statistics, 1995a), a national sample of students in the sixth through twelfth grades was surveyed, and rates of bullying increased from primary to middle/junior high school and then declined in high school. In another study with American youngsters, using a longitudinal design, Pellegrini and Bartini (2000a) found that boys' bullying scores increased significantly from the end of primary school to the start of middle school and then decreased significantly at the end of the first year of middle school. As illustrated in Figure 3, boys' self-reported bullying (on Olweus' measure) increased significantly from the end of primary school in fifth grade to the start of middle school in the sixth grade. From this point on, however, rates of bullying decreased significantly. Therefore, consistent with theory, boys' bullying increased with the transition to middle school; after status was established, bullying rates declined.

This pattern changes, however, if students stay in the same schools during this same age period because there is less need to establish status in the same school. Specifically, during the period of early adolescence (12- to 13-years of age) for youngsters who stay in the same school (in English and Irish schools) during this time, self-reported bullying continues to decrease. These data are displayed in Figure 4.

The trends reported appear to be robust. The data have been replicated in different countries with different research teams. In most cases, the sample sizes were large and nationally representative. One possible limitation to the national survey data is that the extent to which response bias may have

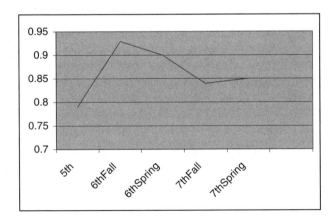

**FIGURE 3.**
Boys' Self-Reported Bullying from Fifth to Seventh Grades.

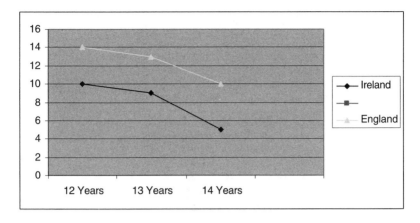

**FIGURE 4.**
Percentage of Students Reporting Being Bullied When
They Do Not Change Schools.

affected the results is not known. This likelihood, however, seems low given the large sample sizes and the replication of results across sites. In the upcoming section, the discussion focuses on what may be causing the increase in bullying when adolescents move from primary to middle/junior high school. The discussion centers around issues associated with puberty and dimensions of school context.

## SPECIFIC ASPECTS OF MIDDLE SCHOOL ASSOCIATED WITH BULLYING

There are many specific features of middle/junior high schools that may be responsible for the documented increases in bullying. It has been suggested that large and impersonal classes (Simmons & Blyth, 1987; USDE, 1998), stress on competition and social comparisons between peers (Eccles, Wigfield, & Schiefele, 1998, p. 1070; USDE, 1998), and teachers' attitudes toward bullying (e.g., "It's part of life, and kids have to learn to deal with it"; Eslea & Smith, 1998) are characteristic of most middle/junior high schools relative to primary schools and are partially responsible for these increases in bullying. In addition, a lack of school community, characteristic of secondary schools relative to primary schools, can encourage subtle forms of bullying by peers (e.g., denigrating peers' efforts or honesty) because students do not support each other (Eccles *et al.*, 1998; USDE, 1998).

The effects of increased competition and school size on bullying were studied directly in Norway and Sweden by Olweus (1993), and he reported no relation between these factors and bullying. Correspondingly, Rutter (1983) found no relations between school size and aggression among high school students. How can the disparate results be reconciled?

It may be that these effects vary with the type of school and age group under study. The results presented by Olweus are for aggregates across primary and secondary schools. The Rutter results are for high schools. It may be that competitive school ethos and school size effects vary in relation to whether adolescents change schools or stay in the same school. Perhaps in the future, researchers could use archival data, such as those in the National Center for Educational Statistics, to examine relations between school size and aggression in different types of schools during early adolescence. That school organization affects aggression during early adolescence is evidenced by the documented increases in bullying when students make the transition to secondary schools but not when similar age students do not change schools.

What might there be about small and cooperative schools that minimizes bullying? Youngsters may be less likely to be aggressive when they are with peers with whom they are familiar and close. Familiarity and subsequently closeness are facilitated by keeping youngsters in physical proximity (Hartup, 1983). Repeated contact between youngsters, in turn, leads to their becoming friends (Hartup, 1996). Organizationally, this can be accomplished by keeping youngsters in intact cohorts during a school year and, in some cases, for multiple years. Many secondary schools currently have students change classrooms numerous times during the day.

That familiarity and closeness of peers should maximize cooperation and minimize aggression is consistent with the *theory of reciprocal altruism*. The theory posits that cooperation and aggression between individuals is determined by the costs and benefits to each participant associated with using each strategy. In a group that is stable (membership does not change rapidly or repeatedly), an aggressive or a cooperative act elicits a similar act from a peer—*quid pro quo*: Aggression elicits aggression and cooperation elicits cooperation. The former strategy is costly to both parties (e.g., injury, sanction) and has fewer benefits (only one or neither may attain their goal) relative to the costs. Cooperation has fewer costs (no injury or sanction) and greater benefits (greater likelihood that both parties will attain their goals; cooperative acts are reciprocated). Consequently, cooperative acts are generally used more than aggressive acts in stable groups.

This *quid pro quo* logic only works if individuals meet repeatedly across time. In cases where individuals do not meet repeatedly, there is a correspondingly low likelihood that the costs associated with aggression will be reciprocated; therefore, it "pays" to be aggressive and it "costs" to be cooperative in transient but not in stable groups.

Support for the *theory of reciprocal altruism* exists. Computer simulations, based on the Prisoners' Dilemma, provide support (Axelrod & Hamilton, 1981) for the ways in which cooperation develops in the context of anticipated, repeated interactions. On the other hand, antisocial behavior occurs and is supported in single encounter scenarios. Specifically, when individuals know that they will meet repeatedly, they are more likely to cooperate with each other than if they know they will only meet once. Any costs incurred with cooperation, such as being exploited, will be minimized as they reap the benefits of partners' cooperative acts. By the same logic, they will not be aggressive in this context because they know aggression will be reciprocated with repeated meeting. The assumption here is that cooperative acts are reciprocated, and each actor benefits accordingly. With reciprocated aggression, costs are greater than benefits for actors. Aggression is more likely to "pay off" when actors only meet once so that initial aggressive acts are not reciprocated.

Relatedly, keeping youngsters together in a cohort with the same team of teachers during the middle school years might also attenuate bullying and aggression. Specifically, keeping youngsters and teachers together for the whole middle school experience would probably increase trust between students and teachers. There are very important implications of this trust for bullying. First, as is discussed in the following paragraphs, most students who are bullied are reluctant to tell their teachers, possibly because of a lack of trust. This results in continued victimization. When students tell teachers, bullying decreases.

Clearly, more schools need to experiment with different staffing and cohort arrangements in middle school. From a personal point of view, my son attended a middle school in the Minneapolis Public Schools system where he stayed with the same cohort of kids for all 3 years of middle school and with the same teachers for the first 2 years. His experience was very positive. Teachers and kids seemed to care about each other.

Lastly, smaller instead of larger schools may inhibit bullying because of the amount of direct supervision afforded in smaller schools (USDE, 1998). Data from a number of sources document effects of supervision on bullying. Olweus (1993), Pellegrini and Bartini (2000a), and Smith and Sharp (1994) all found the inhibiting effect of adult supervision of students on rates of bullying. Olweus (1993b) found a negative and significant relation between the number of adults supervising students' free time and occurrence of bullying in both primary and secondary schools. Similarly, Boulton (1994) reported the inhibiting effects on bullying of adult supervision on the school playground. Specifically, training playground supervisors reduced rates of various bullying behaviors by an order of 40 to 50% (the decreases were noted as statistically significant).

More focus is needed on teachers' and other school personnel's roles in bullying. Teacher self-reports of the problem may bias results. Social desirability and workplace pressures to conform to local norms probably underrepresent the problem. Use of student questionnaires as well as long-term direct observations of teacher-student interactions by neutral third parties are necessary to obtain objective data. Objective data show, as with Boulton's (1994) work in Sheffield, UK, reductions in child-reported bullying after lunchtime supervisors attended awareness training sessions. It may be, as noted above, that an initial step in the process of reducing bullying involves changing teachers' attitudes toward bullying.

## COMPARING METHODS FOR COLLECTING
## BULLYING AND VICTIMIZATION DATA IN SCHOOLS

Collecting information on the perpetrators and targets of aggression in schools is notoriously difficult. Aggressive acts are usually committed in places where and at times when there are few adult witnesses. In addition, aggressive acts, relative to all other behaviors observed during the school day, occur at low frequencies (Humphreys & Smith, 1987; Pellegrini, 1988); therefore, they are very difficult to observe directly. For these reasons researchers typically use some form of informant rating of students (Caspi, 1998), which includes: students' self reports, peer rating/nominations, and teacher questionnaires. The degree to which informants have experience with the target students relates to the accuracy of the measure (Dodge & Coie, 1998). Experience with students for a long period of time and across contexts is ideal. For example, experience with a child can vary from being together for the whole school day (rather than just one or two periods) to spending time with that child for a whole year or more (rather than a semester). Relatedly, experience across contexts can vary from knowing a child only in a math class to knowing him or her in a number of classes, as a member of a sports team, and on the bus.

Various data sources can offer different and complementary sources of information. Thus, it is important to recognize distinctions among data sources and the sort of information each generates. From this view, there is probably no one "correct" indicator. Different measures provide different perspectives on a behavior. Specifically, self-reports are very common in the field, and they tell us about an individual's perception of his or her experiences, which is typically derived from the self-report. A commonly used self-report measure to identify bullies and victims has been developed by Olweus (1993) for use with children and adolescents.

Normative information, or information relative to one's peer group, on aggression and victimization can be derived from peers and teachers (Cairns & Cairns, 1986). Schwartz et al. (1997) and Perry, Kusel, and Perry (1988) have developed different peer nomination procedures which have been widely used with children. Both procedures reliably identify perpetrators (i.e., bullies) and victims of aggression. A teacher rating scale, developed by Dodge and Coie (1987), has been used to identify aggressive middle school youngsters (Pellegrini, Bartini, & Brooks, 1999).

Information from peers and information from teachers generally correlate well with each other and predict long-term outcomes, possibly because they reflect extensive and varied experiences among the raters and nominators (Caspi, 1998). Further, self-ratings and peer nominations should converge when they are both rating "public" phenomena, such as public displays of aggression (Cairns & Cairns, 1986). Aggression is public when youngsters use it as a dominance display for peers. This sort of public display is especially evident during early adolescence, a time when social status is in the state of flux. As the text has presented previously, adolescent boys often use physically coercive strategies to establish or maintain status when they are entering new peer groups, such as in new schools. Girls use other less visible and direct forms of aggression, such as relational aggression (Crick & Grotpeter, 1995), in similar situations but not often in public.

Limitations of these measures are often related to bias. Specifically, self-reports of aggression usually underestimate the problem because aggressors may be reluctant to identify themselves (Smith & Sharp, 1994) due to factors associated with social desirability. Further, some youngsters over-report being victimized, and others underreport being the target of aggression (Juvonen & Graham, 2001).

Relatedly, teacher questionnaires also reflect biases. For example, teachers make different attributions to boys' compared to girls' use of physically aversive social strategies (Pellegrini & Smith, 1998). In addition, they often incorrectly attribute aggressive intent to boys' rough-and-tumble play (Smith, Smees, & Pellegrini, In press). In addition, teachers' ratings reflect and are limited by their experiences with students in specific settings. Consequently, sampling bias (i.e., bias of sampling behavior in different contexts) may also be a problem if teachers spend time with youngsters in a limited number of settings, such as only in the classroom. Problems of bias may, however may be minimized when adults spend months observing focal youngsters in a variety of settings and when their objectivity is maintained by reliability checks and retraining.

Direct observational methods, unlike informant sources, can provide unbiased accounts of focal subjects' actions in specific circumstances regardless of comparisons with others (Cairns & Cairns, 1986). However, observational measures tend not to correlate well across time (Caspi, 1998) possibly because of situational specificity and limited samples of observations (Wachs & Gruen, 1982). These problems can be minimized, however, by sampling behavior in a variety of settings for long periods of time.

It is important to note that, observational methods are "objective" (Caspi, 1998; Kagan, 1998). That is, in well-designed studies, measures of behavior are clearly articulated, reliably sampled, and recorded by unbiased observers. Direct observations cannot, however, be conducted in all settings where bullying and victimization occur (Pepler & Craig, 1995), such as in locker rooms or lavatories. A class of methods, which has been labeled as

**TABLE I**
**Intercorrelations for Measures of Bullying and Victimization**

| Bullying | 2 | 3 | 4 | 5 | 6 |
|---|---|---|---|---|---|
| Peer Noms1 | .47** | .23* | .34** | .28** | .41** |
| Self2 | | .03 | .20* | .24** | .35** |
| Observ3 | | | .01 | .18* | .21* |
| Diary4 | | | | .08 | .09 |
| TeachRat5 | | | | | .50** |
| ObsevRat6 | | | | | |
| **Victimization** | 2 | 3 | 4 | | |
| Peer Noms1 | .32** | .22* | .21* | | |
| Self2 | | .07 | .34** | | |
| Observ3 | | | .08 | | |
| Diary4 | | | | | |

*indirect observational* or *diary methods* (Pellegrini, 2004; Pellegrini & Bartini, 2001a), can be used in settings where participants record their behaviors at predetermined intervals (i.e., interval contingent responses) on standardized forms. Similar methods have been used in the child and educational psychology literature. For example, diaries were used by primary school children to record behaviors and participants during home literacy events (Pellegrini, Galda, Shockley, & Stahl, 1995). The reliability and validity of diaries are maximized when participants are given specific sampling intervals in which to record behavior and a specific vocabulary or categories for recording behavior (Pellegrini, In press).

The following section presents comparative data on these different types of measures and compares the different methods' ability to identify aggressive and victimized youngsters during the school day. Table 1 displays the intercorrelations among different measures of bullying and victimization in a sample of sixth-grade boys and girls (their first year in middle school).

## RATINGS OF AGGRESSION COMPLETED BY TEACHERS AND RESEARCH ASSOCIATES

The Teacher Checklist (Dodge & Coie, 1986) was used to compare the ratings given by teachers and research associates. This measure has been used extensively to identify aggressive children (Dodge & Coie, 1986) and adolescents (Pellegrini et al., 1999). Both teachers and research associates had thorough knowledge of the youngsters they were rating. The research associates' responses should have minimally reflected biases, such as gender and sampling biases, and social desirability. Research associates, however, were trained in objective observational methods and were checked for reliably recording these behaviors. They also had opportunities to observe youngsters in more varied situations (e.g., in the cafeteria, in the halls, and during breaks) and during time periods (from before the start of school throughout the whole school day), relative to teachers (who typically had students in one class and homeroom.

The ratings were intercorrelated, but the magnitude of the correlation coefficient was only modest at .50. Modest correspondence between teachers' ratings and those of other raters is consistent with extant literature (Achenbach, 1985); this result was probably due to three factors. First, the teachers or the research associates may have been differentially deliberate in their completion of the checklists. This conclusion is not, however, supported by the similarly high reliability coefficients for each.

Second, teachers may have been more biased than the research associates and may have more readily rated youngsters in negative ways, such as rating them as aggressive. This explanation does fit our data; the teacher mean was higher (though not at a significant level) than the research associate mean.

Third, each spent time with students in different settings. Teachers observed youngsters in a limited number of settings—usually in homerooms and in one class. The research associates, on the other hand, observed students in many different contexts during the school year (e.g., in the halls, the cafeteria, and at free time). The cafeteria was particularly important for the research associates' ratings of aggression, possibly because of the relatively high social density and the relatively low levels of teacher supervision, both which support peer aggression (Smith & Connolly, 1980).

Relatedly, the contexts in which each rater spent time with children may have elicited behaviors unique to those settings. Differences between raters of youngsters' problem behaviors are often attributed to the different demands of the situations in which each rather spends time with youngsters (Achenbach, 1985). Future research should address this issue by comparing teachers' and external raters' scores in classrooms and in different school settings.

These results have important implications for school policy. If teacher rating scales are to be used in "high stakes" assessments, raters should spend substantial periods of time observing youngsters in a variety of settings. In addition, places where large groups of youngsters congregate with minimal supervision, like the cafeteria, support aggression. Vigilant supervision of such places by adults and peers does lower incidents of aggression (Olweus, 1993).

## DIRECT AND DIARY OBSERVATIONS OF BULLYING/ AGGRESSION AND VICTIMIZATION

Next, this study examined the extent to which direct observations and diaries were interrelated and the extent to which each related to information from peers and adults. The assumption was made that the diaries, being completed by the focal subjects, would indicate a "private" perspective on victimization and bullying. Direct observations, on the other hand, were objectively conducted in public view and would consequently represent a "public" or normative perspective. Despite this difference in orientation, the study expected some overlap between the measures.

Each form of observation, despite lack of direct correspondence with one another, related to specific and predicted sources of information. The diary measures related significantly to the other "private" measure of bullying and victimization, the self-report measure. Moreover, diaries related significantly to peer measures of bullying and victimization but not to the more public teachers' or research associates' ratings of aggression. The direct observation measures of victimization and bullying related to three out of four peer measures of victimization and bullying and to ratings of aggression by teachers and research associates.

That the diaries were systematic correlates of self-report and peer but not adult measures suggests that peer aggression and victimization are phenomena more readily accessible to insiders (i.e., students) than to outsiders (i.e., adults). Much of the aggression and victimization takes place when adults, be they observers or teachers, are not present. Students, however, witness these acts. Indeed, bullies may deliberately victimize peers in the presence of other students as a way to display their physical prowess and, consequently, boost their status with certain peers (Pellegrini et al., 1999). The use of aggression in general to get things done and specifically to establish and maintain peer status is characteristic of the early adolescent period (Pellegrini & Smith, 1998; Pellegrini; 2003).

Further, the diaries, but not the direct observations, were significantly correlated with self-report measures of bullying and victimization. Some instances of victimization are brief and done in a very clandestine and deliberate manner (Pepler & Craig, 1997). Peers were also privy to this information, as indicated by the correlation between diaries and peer nominations. The sampling rules followed in our direct observations seemed to have missed these infrequently occurring behaviors. Future research should address this problem by using event/behavior sampling, which is more sensitive to rare events (Pellegrini, 2004).

There are important implications of these results. Diaries are valid indicators of aggression and victimization as seen through the eyes of students and especially as seen through the eyes of bullies and victims. Students' perspectives should be added to those of external raters, observers, and teachers. Indeed, the diary data accounted for variance in the identification of bullies and victims not available through direct observation. Further, using an approach that enabled sampling rules (i.e., a specific day and a specific event) and recording rules (i.e., using a specific vocabulary list) to be specified may have been especially important (Pellegrini, 2004). A less structured approach may have sampled diverse behaviors and recorded them in a more idiosyncratic fashion, thus attenuating correlations with other measures of aggression and victimization.

## INSTRUMENT UTILITY IN IDENTIFYING BULLIES AND VICTIMIZED STUDENTS

The sensitivity of different instruments in identifying bullies and victims at relatively low levels of severity is a particularly important test of its utility in school settings. It is probably more difficult to identify less severe than more severe problems of aggression and victimization simply because the former are less visible and less persistent. Instruments that can be used with relative ease to identify problems at a lower level of severity could be used to identify and remediate problems before they become more extreme. All three forms of peer and self-report measures were associated in their identification of aggressive youngsters or bullies and victims. Thus, educators could employ any of the three formats in their classrooms as a first step in more thorough assessment. Table 2 presents analyses at two levels of sensitivity: above or below the mean and one standard deviation above or below the mean. The latter case is obviously more extreme and thus should be easier to identify. The case of just being above the mean is obviously more difficult and a more stringent test of instrument utility.

Table 2 shows that both peer nominations and self-reports are equally effective in identifying bullies and victims at different levels of sensitivity. Thus, these measures can be used reliably in school settings to identify instances of bullying and victimization. Both peer nomination and self-report procedures are "practical" for use in school as they are relatively quick and easy to administer and score.

To conclude this section, I have shown the ways in which different data collection procedures complement each other in identifying aggressive and victimized youngsters in middle school. I also pointed out the ways

**TABLE 2**
**Chi-Square Analyses for Self-Reported and Peer Nominated Bullying and Victimization**

| Measure | Severity | N | $\chi^2$ |
|---|---|---|---|
| **Bullying** | | | |
| Peer Nomination/Self-report | Above/Below Mean | 134 | 22.45* |
| | 1SD Above/Below | 273 | 33.49** |
| **Victimization** | | | |
| Peer Nomination/Self-report | Above/Below Mean | 134 | 7.63** |
| | 1SD Above/Below | 134 | 4.35* |

in which different data sources complemented each other. Important distinctions between "public" and "private" uses of aggression were made. Educators and policymakers should be aware of these uses of aggression and know that different measures differentially report aggression. As in most cases of making "high stakes" decisions about children, teachers, or schools, data from a variety of measures should be used as this practice maximizes the validity of the construct under study (Cronbach, 1971).

These results have important implications for educators. I demonstrated that different measures provide different perspectives on the problem of antisocial behavior in school. I showed that "objective" observations of youngsters' behavior were consistently correlated with youngsters' and adults' perceptions of aggression/bullying and victimization. Direct observational methods, however, are probably too expensive for most schools to use. Ratings and nominations completed by youngsters and teachers provide a useful alternative. We should, however, guard against using a limited battery of assessment procedures when conducting "high stakes" assessments. In such cases, a multimethod and multiagent approach should be used. Further, when observations and outside raters are used as part of such a battery, they should observe students in a wide variety of settings across a number of months.

## CONCLUSION

In this chapter, I have suggested that bullying is a deliberate tactic used, by adolescent boys especially, to gain some resource. This view contrasts with other views of aggression suggesting that it is always associated with social information processing deficits. Bullies are calculating and use a combination of aggressive and prosocial strategies to get their way. From this view, bullies may be similar to those youngsters labeled by Coie and colleagues (1982) as "controversial." These youngsters received as many "like least" as "like most" peer nominations, perhaps reflecting their use of antisocial and prosocial strategies. Provocative victims, on the other hand, fit the "rejected" profile of being predominantly disliked by peers.

Some of the more interesting and more troubling findings presented in this chapter relate to the way in which bullies are rewarded for their aggression. Both their peers and their schools seem to reinforce antisocial strategies. Much more research is needed on school policies and environments relating to antisocial behavior. Models from both Scandinavia (Olweus, 1993) and the United Kingdom (Smith & Brain, 200) might be used as bases for the reform of American schools.

# References

Achenbach, T. M., McConaughy, S. H., & Howell, C. T. (1987). Child/adolescent behavioral and emotional problems: Implications of cross-informant correlations for situational specificity. *Psychological Bulletin*, 101, 213–232.

Archer, J. (1992). *Ethology and human development*. Hemel Hemstead, UK: Harvester Wheatsheaf.

Archer, J. A. (2001, October). *Are women or men more aggressive?* Paper presented at the G. Stanley Hall Lecture on Gender and Aggression: Williamstown, MA.

Archer, J., & Lloyd, B. (2002). *Sex and gender*. (2d ed.) London: Cambridge University Press.

Axelrod, R., & Hamilton, W. (1981). The evolution of cooperation. *Science*, 211, 1390–1396.

Bjorkqvist, K., Lagerspetz, K. M. J., & Kaukiainen, A (1992). Do girls manipulate and boys fight? Developmental trends in regard to direct and indirect aggression. *Aggressive Behavior*, 18, 117–127.

Blatchford, P. (1998). *Social life in school*. London: Falmer.

Bosworth, K., Espelage, D. L., & Simon, T. R. (1999). Factors associated with bullying behaviors in middle school students. *Journal of Early Adolescence*, 19, 341–362.

Boulton, M. J. (1994). Understanding and preventing bullying in the junior school playground. In P. K. Smith & S. Sharp (Eds.), *School bullying* (pp. 132–159). London: Routledge.

Boulton, M. J., & Smith, P. K. (1990). Affective biases in children's perceptions of dominance relationships. *Child Development*, 61, 221–229.

Bukowski, W. M., Sipploa, L. K., & Newcomb, A. F. (2000). Variations in patterns of attraction to same-and other-sex peers during early adolescence. *Developmental Psychology*, 36, 147–154.

Cairns, R. B., & Cairns, B. D. (1986). The developmental-interactional view of social behavior: Four issues of adolescent aggression. In D. Olweus, J. Block, & M. Radke-Yarrow (Eds.), *Development of antisocial and prosocial behavior*. New York: Academic.

Campbell, A. (1999). Staying alive: Evolution, culture, and women's intrasexual aggression. *Behavioral and Brain Sciences*, 22, 203–252.

Caspi, A. (1998). Personality development across the life course. In N. Eisenberg (Ed.), *Handbook of child psychology, Vol 3: Social, emotional, and personality development*. 5th ed. (pp. 311–388). New York: Wiley.

Coie, J. D., & Dodge, K. A. (1998). Aggression and antisocial behavior. In W. Damon (Series Ed.) & N. Eisenberg, *Handbook of child psychology, Vol. 3: Social, emotional, and personality development* (5th ed.). New York: Wiley.

Coie, J., Dodge, K., & Coppotelli, H. (1982). Dimensions and types of social status: A cross-age perspective. *Developmental Psychology*, 18, 557–570.

Collins, W. A., & Sroufe, L. A. (1999). Capacity for intimate relationships: A developmental perspective. In W. Furman, B. B. Brown, & C. Feiring (Eds.), *The development of romantic relationships in adolescence* (pp. 125–147). New York: Cambridge University Press.

Connolly, J., & Goldberg, A. (1999). Romantic relationships in adolescence: The role of friends and peers in their emergence and development. In W. Furman, B. B. Brown, & C. Feiring (Eds.), *The development of romantic relationships in adolescence* (pp. 266–290). New York: Cambridge University Press.

Crick, N. R., & Grotpeter, J. K. (1995). Relational aggression, gender, and social-psychological adjustment. *Child Development*, 66, 710–722.

Cronbach, L. J. (1971). Validity. In R. L. Thorndike (Ed.), *Educational measurement* (pp. 443–507). Washington, DC: American Council on Education.

Dodge, K. A., & Coie, J. D. (1987). Social information processing factors in reactive and proactive aggression in children's peer groups. *Journal of Personality and Social Psychology*, 53, 1146–1158.

Eccles, J. S., Midgley, C. (1989). Stage/environment fit: Developmentally appropriate classrooms for early adolescents. In R. Ames & C. Ames (Eds.), *Research on motivation in education* (Vol. 3, pp. 139–181). New York: Academic Press.

Eccles, J. S., Wigfield, A., & Schiefele, U. (1998). Motivation to succeed. In N. Eisenberg (Ed.), *Handbook of child psychology, Vol. 3*: Social, emotional and personality development. (pp. 1017–1096). New York, Wiley.

Eslea, M., & Smith, P. K. (1998). The long-term effectiveness of anti-bullying work in primary schools. *Educational Research*, 40, 203–218.

Espelage, D. L., Bosworth, K., & Simon, T. R. (2000). Examining the social context of bullying behaviors in early adolescence. *Journal of Counseling & Development*, 78, 326–333.

Espelage, D. L., & Holt, M. K. (2001). Bullying and victimization during early adolescence: Peer influences and psychosocial correlates. *Journal of Emotional Abuse*, 2, 123–142.

Furman, W. (1999). Friends and lovers: The role of peer relationships in adolescent romantic relationships. In W. A. Collins & B. Laursen, (Eds.), *Relationships as developmental contexts. The Minnesota symposia on child psychology* (Vol. 30, pp. 133–154). Mahwah, NJ: Erlbaum.

Graham, S., & Juvonen, J. (1998). A social cognitive perspective on peer aggression and victimization. In R. Vasta (Ed.), *Annals of child development*. London: Jessica Kingsley.

Hartup, W. W. (1983). Peer relations. In E. M. Hetherington (Ed.), *Handbook of child psychology* Vol. IV (pp. 103–196). New York: Wiley.

Hartup, W. W. (1996). The company they keep: Friendships and their developmental significance. *Child Development*, 67, 1–13.

Humphreys, A., & Smith, P. K. (1987). Rough-and-tumble play, friendship and dominance in school children: Evidence for continuity and change with age. *Child Development*, 58, 201–212.

Juvonen, J., Nishina, A., & Graham, S. (2001). Self-views versus peer perceptions of victim status among early adolescents. In J. Juvonen & S. Graham (Eds.), *Peer harassment in school: The plight of the vulnerable and victimized* (pp. 105–124). New York: Guilford.

Maccoby, E. E. (1998). *The two sexes: Growing up apart, coming together.* Cambridge, MA: Harvard University Press.

McDonald, K., & Parke, R. (1986). Parent-child physical play. *Sex Roles*, 15, 367–378.

Moffitt, T. E., Caspi, A., Rutter, M., & Solva, P. (2001). *Sex differences in anti-social behaviour.* Cambridge: Cambridge University Press.

National Center for Educational Statistics. (1995a, October). *Student victimization at school.* Washington, DC: U. S. Department of Education, Office of Educational Research and Improvement.

National Center for Educational Statistics. (1995b October). *Strategies to avoid harm at school.* Washington, DC: U. S. Department of Education, Office of Educational Research and Improvement.

Olweus, D. (1993). *Bullying at school.* Cambridge, MA: Blackwell.

Pellegrini, A. D. (1988). Rough-and-tumble play and social competence. *Developmental Psychology*, 24, 802–806.

Pellegrini, A. D. (2001) A longitudinal study of heterosexual relationships, aggression, and sexual harassment during the transition from primary school through middle school. *Journal of Applied Developmental Psychology*, 22, 1–15.

Pellegrini, A. D. (2003). Perceptions and functions of play and real fighting in early adolescence. *Child Development*, 74, 1459–1470.

Pellegrini, A. D. (2004). *Observing children in the natural worlds: A methodological primer* (2nd Edition). Mahwah, NJ: Erlbaum.

Pellegrini, A. D. (In press). Sexual segregation in human juveniles. In K. Ruckstuhl & P. Neuhaus (Eds.), *Sexual segregation in vertebrates.* Cambridge: Cambridge University Press.

Pellegrini, A. D., Bartini, M., & Brooks, F. (1999). School bullies, victims, and aggressive victims: Factors relating top group affiliation and victimization in early adolescence. *Journal of Educational Psychology*, 91, 216–224.

Pellegrini, A. D., & Bartini, M. (2000a). An empirical comparison of methods of sampling aggression and victimization in school settings. *Journal of Educational Psychology*, 92, 360–366.

Pellegrini, A. D., & Bartini, M. (2000b). A longitudinal study of bullying, victimization, and peer affiliation during the transition from primary to middle school. *American Educational Research Journal*, 37, 699–726.

Pellegrini, A. D., & Bartini, M. (2001). Dominance in early adolescent boys: Affiliative and aggressive dimensions and possible functions. *Merrill-Palmer Quarterly*, 47, 142–163.

Pellegrini, A. D., Galda, L., Stahl, S., & Shockley, B. (1995). The nexus of social and literacy experiences at home and school: Implications for primary school oral language and literacy. *British Journal of Educational Psychology*, 65, 273–285.

Pellegrini, A. D., Kato, K., Blatchford, P., & Baines, E. (2002). A short-term longitudinal study of children's playground games across the first year of school: Implications for social competence and adjustment to school. *American Educational Research Journal*, 39, 991–1015.

Pellegrini, A. D., & Long, J. D. (2002). A longitudinal study of bullying, dominance, and victimization during the transition from primary to secondary school. *British Journal of Developmental Psychology*, 20, 259–280.

Pellegrini, A. D. & Long, J. D. (2003). A sexual selection theory analysis of sexual segregation and integration in early adolescence. *Journal of Experimental Child Psychology*, 85, 257–278.

Pellegrini, A., & Smith, P. (1998). Physical activity play: The development and function of a neglected aspect of play. *Child Development*, 69, 577–598.

Pepler, D. J., & Craig, W. M. (1995). A peek behind the fence: Naturalistic observations of aggressive behavior with remote audio-visual recording. *Developmental Psychology*, 31, 548–553.

Perry, D. G., Hodges, E. V. E., & Egan, S. K. (2001). Risk and protective factors in peer victimization: A review and a new model of family influence. In J. Juvonen & S. Graham (Eds), *Peer harassment in school: The plight of the vulnerable and the victimized* (pp. 73–104). New York: Guilford.

Perry, D. G., Kusel, S. J., & Perry, L. (1988). Victims of peer aggression. *Developmental Psychology*, 24, 807–814.

Perry, D., Willard, J., & Perry, L. (1990). Peers' perceptions of the consequences that victimized children provide aggressors. *Child Development*, 61, 1289–1309.

Prinstein, M. J., & Cohen, G. L. (2001, April). *Adolescent peer crowd affiliation and overt, relational, and social aggression: Using aggression to protect one's peer status.* Paper presented at the biennial meetings of the Society for Research in Child Development: Minneapolis, MN.

Rheingold, H., & Cook, K. (1975). The contents of boys' and girls' rooms as an index of parents' behavior *Child Development*, 46, 459–463.

Rutter, M. (1983). School effects on student progress: Research findings and policy implications. *Child Development*, 54, 1–19.

Schwartz, D., Pettit, G. S., Dodge, K. A., & Bates. J. E. (1997). The early socialization and adjustment of aggressive victims of bully. *Child Development*, 68, 665–675.

Simmons, R. G., & Blyth, D. A. (1987). *Moving into adolescence: The impact of pubertal change and school context.* Hawthorn, New York: Aldine de Gruyter.

Smith, P. K., & Brain, P. (2000). Bullying in schools: Lessons from two decades of research. *Aggressive Behavior*, 26, 1–9.

Smith, P. K., & Connolly, K. (1980). *The ecology of preschool behaviour.* London: Cambridge University Press.

Smith, P. K., Madsen, K. C., & Moody, J. C. (1999). What causes the age decline in reports of school being bullied at school? Toward a developmental analysis of risks of being bullied. *Educational Research*, 41, 267–285.

Smith, P. K., & Sharp, S. (Eds.), (1994). *Bullying at school.* London: Routledge.

Smith, P. K., Smees, R., & Pellegrini, A. D. (In press). Play fighting and real fighting: Using video playback methodology with young children. *Aggressive Behavior.*

Terman, L. M. (1946). Psychological sex differences. In L. Carmichael (Ed.), *Manual of child psychology* (pp. 954–1000). New York: Wiley.

Thorne, B. (1986). Girls and boys together. . . . But mostly apart: Gender arrangements in elementary school. In W. W. Hartup & Z Rubin (Eds.), *Relationships and development* (pp167–184). Hillsdale, NJ: Erlbaum.

Thorne, B. (1993). *Gender play: Boys and girls in school.* Buckingham: Open University Press.

United States Department of Education. (1998). *Early warning, Timely response* Washington, DC: Author.

Vaughn, B. E. (1999). Power is knowledge (and vice versa): A commentary on "Winning some and losing some": A social relations approach to social dominance in toddlers *Merrill-Palmer Quarterly, 45,* 215–225.

Vaughn, B. E., & Waters, E. (1981). Attention structure, sociometric status, and dominance: Interrelations, behavioral correlates, and relationships to social competence. *Developmental Psychology, 17,* 275–288.

Wachs, T. D., & Gruen, G. (1982). *Early experience and human development.* New York: Plenum.

CHAPTER

9

# Evaluating Curriculum-Based Intervention Programs: An Examination of Preschool, Primary, and Elementary School Intervention Programs

FAITH L. SAMPLES

*Assistant Professor of Sociomedical Sciences*
*Mailman School of Public Health*
*Columbia University*

## INTRODUCTION

Schools have become the predominant forum for prevention and intervention programs aimed at reducing or ameliorating aggression and violence among children nationwide and across the globe. A number of such programs have been developed and implemented in schools for use with elementary, middle/junior high, and high school students. Although schools represent a logical choice and provide a natural setting for implementing preventive interventions for children, as they provide the primary context for social development (Bronfenbrenner, 1979), very few school-based violence prevention programs have been rigorously evaluated (Elliott & Tolan, 1999; Farrell *et al.*, 2001; Powell *et al.*, 1996; & Samples & Aber, 1998). Research-based interventions, with proven records of effectiveness, represent the gold standard school officials are to achieve when deciding on and implementing prevention programs in their school. Yet, schools are currently using a number of programs with little evidence of their effectiveness.

Although recent reviews of the peer-aggression or bullying literature have summarized the current state of knowledge regarding preventive interventions, communities still do not have effective school-based programs to address youth violence. The lack of systematically evaluated programs has resulted in limited data on which decision makers can draw information about what programs work best with which populations in what community contexts. It has been suggested that the widespread implementation of programs of unknown effectiveness may have the effect of providing false security—that is, believing the problem is being addressed—when in fact the resources devoted to such efforts may be better spent on the development of more effective programs (Farrell *et al.*, 2001).

While violence prevention efforts have largely focused on adolescent populations due to higher rates of violence among members of this group, increasing numbers of preventive interventions have been developed for use with children as young as preschool age. Some programs offer a separate curriculum promoting social competencies in children in preschool and elementary school (kindergarten through the sixth grades); others believe a "whole-school" approach that improves school climate will promote a prosocial approach to life. As with school-based prevention programs, generally little is known about the effectiveness of school-based programs adopted for use specifically in early childhood. The purpose of this chapter is to compile the existing systematic literature on curriculum-based violence prevention programs used with preschool, primary, and elementary schoolchildren. This review will in no way be exhaustive of all relevant intervention programs but rather will concentrate on programs that address the issue of aggression among the target population broadly and on those designed to address bullying specifically.

## BACKGROUND

Increasing attention on youth violence has led to the development of numerous prevention programs aimed at improving children's social competencies (e.g., attitudes, knowledge, and behavior) in an effort to reduce or prevent their involvement in aggressive or violent behavior. Not only has the development of such programs become a part of the national agenda in the United States (Farrell *et al.*, 2001), the development also represents a phenomenon experienced by other industrialized countries confronting similar issues of aggressive behavior, bullying, and violence among their youth.

There is general consensus among mental health and education professionals that the development of prosocial attitudes and behaviors at an early age is critical. Evidence suggests that aggression in early stages of a child's development tends to result in later acts of delinquency if not remedied (Olweus, 1994a; Oliver, Young, and LaSalle, 1994; Slaby *et al.*, 1995). Equally important is the belief that violence prevention programs should be comprehensive, multidisciplinary approaches to nurturing children at school, at home, and in their communities. In so doing, such programs should address all forms of aggressive behavior in which children engage. The U.S.

Department of Education (1999) contends that the most effective violence prevention efforts include measures that prevent all types of misconduct, including aggression, bullying, and harassment (due to differences in gender, race/ethnicity, religion, or sexual orientation) and that require changes in attitude, willingness to report events, and an understanding of respect for personal space (Glover, Gough, & Johnson, 2000).

## CURRICULUM-BASED INTERVENTION PROGRAMS

This section reviews a number of school-based curriculum programs designed to reduce or ameliorate violence among preschool, primary, and elementary schoolchildren. The importance of reviewing violence prevention programs from this developmental and contextual perspective lies in the fact that children are being exposed to and becoming victims of violence at increasingly earlier ages. Concerns about the effects of violence on the healthy growth and development of children have prompted the ever-increasing number of prevention programs developed and implemented in schools. The prevention programs reviewed here have been or are being evaluated using an appropriate empirical methodology. These programs do not represent an exhaustive list of all such interventions; rather, they are programs for which sufficient literature was available. It should be noted that while developmental and contextual framework is used here, it was not possible to categorize the intervention programs by developmental stage. For purposes of illustration, the following categorizations of developmental age and school/grade underlie this work:

1. Preschool
   (Ages 2 to 4)
2. Primary school (kindergarten through the second grades)
   (Ages 5 to 7)
3. Elementary school (first through the sixth grades)
   (Ages 6 to 12)

### Bullying Prevention Program

The Bullying Prevention Program was developed and refined in Norway in 1983–1985 by psychologist Dan Olweus. It is a systematic school-based bullying intervention program for kindergarten through twelfth-grade students and the first comprehensive preventive intervention representing a whole-school approach to reduce the incidence and prevalence of bullying. The program seeks to establish social norms in the school environment that support prosocial behavior and to punish bullying and other antisocial behavior (Cunningham & Henggeler, 2001). Three basic goals guide the program (increased awareness of bullying, adult opposition to bullying behavior, and protection and support of victims) (Ballard, Argus, & Remley, 1999) and are conveyed through a number of tasks that occur at multiple levels (i.e., community, school, classroom, and individual). At the community or school level, forums are held to educate school personnel, parents, students, and community members about bullying behaviors, intervention strategies, and available resources; changes to the physical environment are instituted and school-wide rules against aggressive or violent behavior are established; incentives are provided to encourage prosocial behavior; and a school-wide survey is administered annually and used to guide in-service training with teachers and administrators as well as to tailor the program to the needs of each school (Cunningham & Henggeler, 2001). At the classroom level, a curriculum promoting prosocial behaviors, empathy, anger management, and conflict-resolution skills is used in conjunction with the establishment of classroom rules, sanctions for rule infractions, weekly discussions with students regarding bullying behavior, and consistent communication with parents. The individual level involves teacher identification of bullies and victims, discussions with members and parents of both groups, and role-playing of assertive (for victims) and nonaggressive (for bullies) behavior among all students. The Bullying Prevention Program has served as a model program and has been adapted for use in educational settings in other countries.

Olweus (1994b) conducted an evaluation of the effects of this program in Bergen, Norway, on a sample of 2500 students in the fourth through seventh grades drawn from 42 schools and 112 classrooms. There were three waves of data collection (4 months before program implementation, 8 months after the intervention (post-test), and at 1 year (follow-up) over a period of 2.5 years (1983–1985). A quasi-experimental (age-cohort) design was used with four grade/age cohorts. Results at post-test and at the one-year follow-up showed significant reductions (by 50% or more) in the levels of bullying and victimization problems among boys and girls across all cohorts compared. Similar reductions were reported for peer ratings of the number of students engaging in bullying behaviors as well as for student-reported general antisocial behaviors. Significant improvements were also found on key measures of students' positive prosocial relationships, attitudes toward school and schoolwork, and school climate and culture. The intervention was not only found to reduce the incidence of bullying but also to reduce the number of new victims (Olweus, 1994b).

A number of other researchers have replicated the Bullying Prevention Program and conducted independent evaluations of its effectiveness. For example, using Olweus' model as a basis, Smith and Sharp (1994) developed and systemically evaluated an antibullying program in the United Kingdom. According to Olweus (1999), the DES Sheffield Antibullying Project used essentially the same structure, intervention levels (school, classroom, and individual), optional interventions, and quasi-experimental design as the Bergen project. Differences between the two projects were related to age-cohort assessments, which were done in 1990 and 1992 in Sheffield, and the emphasis placed on a written "whole-school policy" that required schools to define policies and procedures for preventing and responding to bullying behavior. The Sheffield Project was implemented in 16 primary (N=2212) and 7 secondary (N=4256) schools with students ages 8 to 16 (Olweus, 1999).

Although the results were not as strong as those reported in Bergen, data indicated significant results on several important outcome measures. Results of this evaluation revealed significant rates of decline in bully-victim problems after two years, positive changes in students' attitudes, and a decreased frequency in student-reported bullying at both the primary and secondary school levels. Intervention schools showed significant fewer students being bullied, though results were greater among primary school students than among those at the secondary level. Results, at both levels, also indicated more students reported not being bullied. Secondary students were more likely to report an unwillingness to engage in an active bullying incident. Significant increases were found in the rate at which intervention students reported bullying and in the frequency with which teachers discussed bullying behaviors with students. Data also indicated that schools most committed to the program implementation showed greatest signs of improvement. Student-reported perceptions of teachers intervening in bullying situations were found to be nonsignificant.

The Bullying Prevention Program was again replicated in 1993 in Schleswig-Holstein, Germany (Olweus, 1999). Program development, implementation, and study design were similar to that of the original program and evaluation. Olweus (1999) suggests, however, that questionnaire surveys collected from school personnel indicated considerable variation in implementation and program fidelity across schools. The program was implemented and evaluated between 1994 and 1996 using a total of 37 schools. A total of 28 (N=6400) schools involved primary and secondary schools, representing the corresponding students of ages 8 to 16 for whom the program was designed. Data showed significant reductions in student-reported bullying victimization from baseline to follow-up two years later (roughly 18 to 15%, respectively).

## Bullyproof

Bullyproof was developed in 1996 as a school-based curriculum for use with fourth- and fifth-grade students. It is part of the Project on Teasing and Bullying that explores the link between sexual harassment and bullying, and its primary objective is to reduce bullying behaviors. The program consists of an 11-session curriculum using role-playing, group discussions, exercises, and writing and art to facilitate students' distinctions between appropriate and inappropriate boundaries and playful and hurtful behavior. Bullyproof is best employed in a comprehensive school-wide approach. Teacher training is offered, as are parent and community workshops on bullying awareness, appropriate strategies for intervening, and reinforcing connections with the school.

Sanchez et al., (2001) have conducted the most comprehensive study of this program to date. The authors report program effects from a three-year project adapted from the Bullyproof curriculum called the Expect Respect Program: a whole-school approach to bullying, sexual harassment, and gender violence. Results are based on the first year of program implementation in six public elementary schools in Austin, Texas. Program components included staff training, classroom education, parent education, assistance with policy development, and support services. A racially diverse sample (N=1243) of fifth-grade students in schools randomly assigned to intervention and control conditions in matched pairs was used for this study. Intervention schools received a six-hour start-up training followed by an additional three hours of training each academic year, and all fifth-grade students in intervention schools received 12 weekly sessions of the curriculum. Sanchez et al (2001), using data on 747 students, found significant program effects at two points in time (semester's end and year-end). Improvements in sexual harassment knowledge (though not bullying) among program children compared with controls were found to be significant. Results showed no differences between program and control groups on bullying awareness. Significant increases were also found for program children's intent to intervene in a bullying situation rather than rely on adults when compared with controls. Finally, bullying awareness increased significantly from pre-test to year-end post-test for program students.

Focus groups were also conducted at each of the six intervention schools. Groups consisted of boys, girls, and teachers. All focus groups interviews were taped and ran about one hour each. All but one teacher focus group was conducted after school. Student focus groups were conducted during the school day. Results indicated greater student awareness of concepts and recognition of bullying in their environment. Finally, analyses indicated program students were more likely than controls to intervene in a bullying situation. An unintended finding involved postintervention follow-up data: About 20% of students reported they had bullied someone in the past week. The authors also indicated that student self-reports at follow-up showed 37% of students had been bullied in the past three months.

A qualitative study of the Expect Respect Program was also conducted by Khosropour and Walsh in 2001. The authors used a quasi-experimental design in their examination of 40 fifth-grade students drawn from four elementary schools. Two schools received the intervention; two did not. Interviews were conducted four weeks after program sessions ended at intervention schools. They were conducted in a private room at school and were 30 to 60 minutes in duration. All interviews were taped and transcribed for analysis. Results were mixed, with intervention students more aware of instances of bullying and less stereotypical in their conceptualization of bullies and victims than controls. Both intervention and control schoolchildren characterized bullying using a more diverse set of behaviors than expected. Moreover, intervention students were more likely than controls to hold adults at school rather than parents at home accountable for solutions to bullying. Perhaps the most surprising and counterintuitive result indicated that students in the intervention group were much less likely than controls to believe that nothing could be done about bullying.

## Bully Proofing Your School

The Bully Proofing Your School Program was developed in 1994 using a systems approach to change school culture with a teacher-implemented classroom curriculum (Garrity, Jens, & Porter, 1997). It was modeled after Olweus' Bullying Prevention Program and offered two series: one for students in elementary school (kindergarten through the sixth grades) and one for students in middle school (sixth through the eighth grades). Program objectives include teaching students to recognize bullying behavior, set class rules, respond quickly and effectively to bullying, enhance empathy towards victims, develop effective communication in high emotional investment situations, and develop conflict-resolution skills. Components of the program involve teacher/staff training, student instruction, parent education, classroom intervention, creating a caring environment, and victim support. Implementation occurs in three phases beginning with a definition of bullying, a discussion of its impact, and ways to establish classroom rules regarding bullying. The second phase involves developing skills and techniques for dealing with bullying and increasing resilience to victimization. In the third phase, emphasis is placed on change in school culture through converting children who are neither bullies nor victims of bullying—the "silent majority"—into the "caring majority." Further support is provided through the review and revision of school policies and procedures for addressing the problem of bullying.

The first study reporting results on Bully Proofing Your School was conducted in 2001 by Berkey, Keyes, and Longhurst. Berkey and colleagues conducted a two-year study of the Bully Proofing Your School Program in a relatively poor midwestern school district. The program was implemented in elementary, middle, and high schools throughout the district, and the sample included teachers, administrators, paraprofessionals, and students from each of these levels. An interview sample of 200 individuals exposed to the curriculum was used for the study. Interviews were conducted throughout the district using three formats: classroom administration, focus groups, and one-on-one interviews. Results were most encouraging at the elementary school level. At one school, principal reports indicated a sharp decline in suspension rates, fewer disciplinary referrals, and increased student willingness to employ program language and techniques in the resolution of interpersonal conflicts. During year 2 of the study, teacher reports suggested older students used program strategies more frequently and more spontaneously than in year 1. There was no evidence to support students' ability to transfer program skills to nonclassroom and nonschool settings. Other elementary schools used the Bully Proofing Your School Program as a catalyst for additional program development. For example, one school adopted a mentoring program in which 25 students identified with engaging in frequent bullying behavior were matched with teachers or other school staff. Mentoring occurred daily and ranged from casual hallway conversation to intensive problem-solving sessions. Significant improvements in behavior were reported for 16 of the 25 students represented by a decline in suspension rates for fighting, a reduction in the number of disciplinary referrals and actions, and an increase in school attendance.

Although the program offered a middle school (sixth through the eighth grades) version, school officials appear to have adapted the elementary school version for use with middle school students. Berkey *et al.* (2001) note the program was successfully adapted with sixth and seventh graders after one semester. After two years, principal reports indicated noticeable improvements in student behavior, including reductions in absenteeism, class attendance, and classroom disruptions as well as greater student capacity for conflict resolution. Teacher and staff reports suggested that more students were likely to attempt to resolve conflicts or to enlist adult support to resolve interpersonal conflicts than to fight or intimidate others. There was also a reportedly greater increase in students' awareness of consequences associated with bullying or aggressive behavior. No direct impact of the Bully Proofing Your School Program was found at the high school level. Berkey and colleagues suggest this may have been because the program was developmentally inappropriate for this population, and no one at the high school assumed leadership responsibility for adapting the curriculum.

Although this study provides some insight into potential positive benefits of the Bully Proofing Your School Program, there were a number of problems with the methodology. Berkey *et al.* (2001) failed to outline sample characteristics, sampling procedures, or the manner in which data were analyzed. The elementary school version of the program was implemented at and adapted for the middle school students even though a middle school version of the program had been developed. Furthermore, although the Bully Proofing Your School Program was not designed for use with high school students, it was implemented with (though not adapted for) this population.

More recent studies provide more scientific rigor in their evaluations of this program, and results suggest some support for program effectiveness. Epstein, Plog, and Porter (under review) used a pre-test/post-test design in their study of 350 elementary school students (first through the fifth grades) to assess changes in self-reported bullying behaviors and children's sense of safety in several settings. Students were assessed at baseline (before program implementation) and at four postintervention points (immediately following the program; 1-, 2-, and 3-years after the program). Results indicated significant decreases in self-reported rates of physical and verbal bullying across all postintervention points. Epstein and colleagues found no significant improvement in rates of exclusionary bullying immediately following the program (W2) or at the two-year follow-up (W4). Significant improvements in exclusionary bullying behavior were reported at one-year (W3) and three-year (W5) follow-up points. Pre-test data indicated highly rated safety reports from students in two areas of study (i.e., in the classroom and in the lunchroom). Children's sense of safety in the classroom did not change significantly over time; however, there was a marked increase in their sense of safety on the playground at each of follow-up periods. Variations were found across waves for both children's sense of safety in the lunchroom and going to and from school. Data suggested a significant increase in children's sense of safety in the lunchroom from wave 1 to wave 2 and again from wave 1 to wave 4, though no significant increases were reported at waves 3 or 5. The sense of safety going to and from school did not significantly increase until waves 4 and 5 (i.e., two and three years postintervention).

Beran and Tutty (2002) also employed a quasi-experimental design with their study of 197 elementary school students in the fourth through the sixth grades. Their study explored the effects of an adapted version of the *Bully Proofing Your School Program* using varying lengths of implementation (three months, one year, and two years). The intervention school was compared to a nonintervention school, and findings revealed a significant decrease in self-reported witnessing of bullying among students exposed to the program. Rates of bully-witnessing remained constant for students in the comparison group. Program students also remained constant in their reported attitudes toward victims while a significant decline in attitudes toward victims was reported for controls. Outcome data related to length of program implementation showed significantly higher scores on positive attitudes toward victims for students exposed to the program for longer periods of time (i.e., two years).

## Flemish Antibullying Intervention Project

The Flemish Antibullying Project is a curriculum-based intervention designed to enhance positive attitudes toward victims of bullying and to encourage peer involvement to reduce bully-victim conflicts (Stevens, Van Oost, & Bourdeaudhuij, 2000). The program is composed of three modules focused on the school environment, the peer group, and students involved in bully-victim problems. Module 1 focuses on the whole-school approach to implementing the program in schools. It emphasizes a no-tolerance rule for bullying or aggressive behavior. Module 2 consists of a curriculum-based intervention aimed at creating a more supportive environment for interpersonal relationships. Module 3 seeks to provide support to those directly involved in bullying behavior, either as victim or bully.

The evaluation of this program focused specifically on Module 2 in an attempt to measure aspects of the peer environment, such as attitudes and behaviors of students not directly involved in bullying (as victim or bully). An experimental pre- and post-test design with a control group was used to assess students from 24 primary and secondary schools randomly assigned to experimental or control conditions. A sample of 728 primary school students (ages 10 to 12) drawn from 55 classes in 11 schools and of 1465 secondary school students (ages 13 to 16) from 136 classes in 11 schools was used for this study. Four group sessions, conducted in two 50-minute sessions, were directed at student "bystanders." Baseline data were collect in October 1995 with post-test data collected at two points: (1) the end of the school year (May 1996) and (2) at one-year postintervention. Only results of elementary school students will be reported here.

Results revealed low mean scores on probully attitudes and behavior factors indicating negative attitudes toward bullying, but there was little evidence of student intervention in bully-victim problems. Post-test results showed no time effect for attitudes toward bullies or for self-efficacy to intervene in a bullying encounter. Significant findings were reported for attitudes toward victims, for intent to intervene, and for rates of intervening in bully-victim problems over time. The latter two findings showed a decrease over time in both measures of intervention. After nearly two years in the intervention, results showed a slight tendency toward intervention among students in program schools compared with controls. Also, at the second post-test collection point, results showed a greater increase in rates of supporting victims and seeking teacher help.

Stevens, Van Oost, and Bourdeaudhuij (2001) conducted a pilot study of the antibullying intervention in Flemish primary and secondary schools to examine the relationship between program implementation and program outcomes. Using a sample of 12 schools, the researchers conducted a cross-case analysis based on semistructured interviews with school project leaders and survey research among students and teachers. Project leaders consisted of teachers, principals, and coordinators in a school who were responsible for managing the antibullying working group that organized, developed, and coordinated all activities related to the intervention program in schools over the course of two years. Each project leader was interviewed twice: at the beginning of the first school year and at the end of the second school year. Results indicated no differences between the total amount of implementation in primary and secondary schools. This finding suggests a relationship between moderate implementation in primary schools and positive program outcomes. The same amount of implementation at the secondary level did not yield comparable results (Stevens *et al.* 2001). Several possible explanations were offered for these findings. First, it was suggested that differences in the *nature* of the implementation process may have superceded the amount of implementation process at the primary and secondary levels. Second, the researchers contended that differences in organizational structure between primary and secondary schools may have impacted implementation rates. Finally, the question of whether the antibullying program was developmentally appropriate for students at the secondary school level was raised.

## Lions-Quest

The Lions-Quest Conflict Management Program was developed in Toronto, Canada, with three key objectives: (1) changing attitudes about students' interactions, (2) increasing knowledge of nonviolent techniques for dealing with conflict, and (3) fostering behaviors that help children put conflict resolution into action. It is a classroom curriculum offering school-wide activities to promote change in school culture. The program serves children and adolescents from kindergarten through the twelfth grades and has several different components for different age levels. Exploring the Issues: Promoting Peace and Preventing Violence Program was developed for students in the seventh through the twelfth grades and includes 19 sessions in five modules designed to help students understand attitudes and behaviors that escalate from conflict to anger to violence. The Working Towards Peace: Managing Anger, Resolving Conflict, and Preventing Violence Program was developed for use with students in the sixth through the eighth grades. It consists of a 22-lesson curriculum that provides opportunities to learn and practice conflict-resolution skills. The Working It Out Tools for Everyday Peacemakers Program was designed specifically for use with children from kindergarten through the sixth grades. It builds and reinforces skills in the areas of problem solving, cooperation, and peaceful conflict resolution through topics such as recognizing feelings, predicting consequences, managing anger, bullying, and being culturally sensitive. Teacher training is provided and parent involvement is expected and encouraged.

There is no data available on the effectiveness of this program for preschool and elementary schoolchildren. However, there is evidence to suggest positive outcomes of the program for middle/junior high school students. While Lions-Quests materials suggest the program has been evaluated extensively, only one outcome study was found. The two-year study (Laird & Syropoulos, 1996), conducted on 1900 seventh- and eighth-grade students, showed considerable promise for students in the Lions-Quest Working Towards Peace Program compared with those in another violence prevention programs and a nonintervention control groups. Students in the Working Towards Peace Program showed the greatest gain in knowledge of how to handle anger and resolve conflict. Whereas students in both intervention groups showed increases in their grade point average during the first year, there were no such gains found for controls. After two years, teacher ratings of student behavior revealed a 68% decrease in violence-related referrals among students in the Lions-Quest Program. No significant improvements were found for students in the other two conditions. Finally, prosocial interactions among students in the Working Towards Peace Program were five times greater than those of the controls.

Results from Bryd's (1996) content analysis—comparing Lions-Quest with Second Step—provide some generally positive support for this program. Bryd found that while conflict management concepts were comprehensively covered in both programs, the Lions-Quest Program more extensively covered such areas as bullying, prejudice, and classroom conflicts. In addition, Lions-Quest placed a more explicit emphasis on enhancing school climate and was more cost-effective to implement than Second Step.

## Promoting Alternative Thinking Strategies (PATHS)

PATHS is a school-based curriculum intervention designed to develop emotional competence in children (kindergarten through the fifth grades). It was originally developed to facilitate the social adjustment of deaf and hearing-impaired children in the 1980s. PATHS is a 131-lesson curriculum organized into three parts, addressing five conceptual domains: *self-control, self-esteem, emotional understanding, relationships,* and *interpersonal problem-solving skills.* The first unit, Readiness and Self-Control (or the Turtle Unit), is designed specifically for use with kindergarten and first-grade students, children with developmental or communicative delays, or children with serious behavior problems. It is comprised of 12 lessons focused on the development of self-control. The lessons are taught over a period of five to seven weeks and contain reinforcement strategies to be used, as needed, throughout the year. In the second unit, Feelings and Relationships, the curriculum focuses on the development of emotional and interpersonal understanding. This unit is composed of 56 lessons taught after the Turtle Unit or used as the beginning phase of the program for older students or those not requiring a structured model for basic self-control. Students are taught to analyze and judge behaviors and to recognize and respect feelings as well as taught problem-solving and self-monitoring techniques. A third unit, Interpersonal Cognitive Problem Solving, consists of 33 lessons geared toward third- and fourth-grade students. Building on previous units, students are taught to use 11 steps to effective problem solving. A 30-lesson supplemental unit is also available to address varying issues at different grades and/or developmental levels.

Several clinical trials of PATHS have been conducted to date (Greenberg, Kusche, & Mihalic, 1988; Greenberg & Kusche, 1997, 1998). The studies included comparisons of intervention students to matched controls and involved both children with disabilities and regular education students (though not in the same study). One study of 200 regular education students assessed program effects after one year of intervention with a two-year follow-up to test for long-term effects. There were significant improvements in the postintervention period for program students in the areas of problem solving, emotional understanding, and cognitive ability. When compared to controls, students exposed to the intervention were significantly more likely to use prosocial skills and less likely to use aggressive solutions in their resolution of interpersonal conflicts. Follow-up data after one year showed sustained effects on two measures: problem solving and emotional understanding. Intervention students continued to demonstrate less aggressive and more prosocial behavior over time than did their control group peers. Follow-up data after two years also indicated significant differences between intervention and control group students, with program children showing less externalizing behavior problems and more adaptive functioning than children in the comparison group. Intervention students showed fewer signs of depression and anxiety and had fewer behavioral problems than control group students. Findings from this study were supported by results from a second study of 108 behaviorally at-risk first through third-grade students. The research design of this study was very similar to the first, including the one- and two-year follow-ups. Results suggested significant and sustained improvements in intervention students' social competencies, problem-solving skills, and capacity for emotional understanding. A third study examined the effectiveness of the PATHS curriculum on the social, cognitive, and behavioral development of first-through sixth-grade deaf children. A quasi-experimental wait-list control design was used with a sample of 57 children in 11 self-contained classrooms. Again, results indicated significant and sustained improvement on key measures of intervention students' problem-solving, emotional recognition, and social competency skills.

A recent review of promising violence prevention programs by the American Federation of Teachers (2000) also reports encouraging results from an adapted version of PATHS for use with preschool and after-school children. The intervention, implemented by Fast Track—a North Carolina-based comprehensive intervention program including family, academic, peer group, and community-based social services—involves a randomized trial of 5000 students in 50 elementary schools across four states. While the intervention targets children known to have behavioral problems in kindergarten, an abbreviated 57-lession version of PATHS is taught to all students. Preliminary findings suggest significant program effects on measures of classroom atmosphere, classroom disruption, and aggression toward peers.

## Quit It!

Quit It! was developed as part of the Project on Teasing and Bullying by professionals at Educational Equity Concepts and Wellesley College Center for Research on Women in 1997. It was designed to serve children in kindergarten through the third grades and assumes a comprehensive school-wide approach for the establishment and maintenance of safe school climate. Quit It! uses Olweus's model to form the foundation for a whole-school approach. Three sequential themes are presented to students in a ten-session curriculum taught by teachers. Creating Our Rules allows students to discuss and define rules, to consider the benefits and consequences of rules, and to make rules for their classroom. Talking About Teasing and Bullying deals with how students feel and why they feel that way in various school settings, their verbal and nonverbal communication, and appropriate responses to teasing and bullying. Finally, Exploring Courage helps students examine teasing and bullying in the context of interpersonal relationships. Themes are presented to students using age-appropriate activities, including role-playing, group discussion, physical exercises, art, and writing activities, to help them distinguish between teasing and bullying. Teacher training and parent/community workshops are offered to increase bullying awareness, promote strategies for intervening, and ensure support for the program at home.

Froschl and Sprung (2000, 2001) reported findings that suggest potential positive program effects. In a two-year evaluation of the Quit It! Program, Froschl and Sprung (2000) reported a 35% reduction in teacher-observed bullying and teasing behaviors and a 130% increase in staff involvement in such incidents. Reports of teacher-observed incidents of teasing and bullying showed a 45% decline from pre- to post-test in a second study (Froschl & Sprung, 2001), while adult involvement in observed incidences of teasing and bullying was reduced by 29%. The researchers also found less frequent physical conflict as a result of bullying and teasing behaviors among victims and more frequent use of verbal responses among students exposed to the program. This was found to be particularly true for boys.

Results from these Quit It! studies must be considered in light of two important caveats. First, neither study used control groups. Second, no tests of statistical significance were performed to determine reported differences. According to Carney and Merrell (2001), the quality of an intervention program is not relevant in the absence of evaluation data that provide continuous feedback on program effectiveness.

## Second Step

Second Step remains one of very few programs that offer a school-based curriculum to children as young as three years old (Moore & Beland, 1992). The program serves children from preschool through ninth grades (ages 3 to 14). It was designed to meet two primary objectives: (1) to reduce aggression and (2) to increase prosocial behaviors. It consists of 28 sessions conducted two to three times each week for a period of 2.5 to 6 months. The lessons are age and grade appropriate and build sequentially as grade level increases. The training format for elementary school students involves 11 × 17 photo lesson cards that the teacher shows to the class, using the lesson outline on the reverse side. Lesson techniques include story and discussion, teacher modeling of the skills, and role-playing. Transfer of training is encouraged through alerting students to opportunities for using the prosocial skills at school and home and reinforcing them when used. Teacher and parent training are integral parts of the program, with parents encouraged to model and reinforce skills at home.

Summary results of Second Step's pilot studies (Sylvester & Frey, 1994), as well as others conducted with preschool (Moore & Beland, 1992) and elementary school students (Grossman *et al.*, 1997), suggest strong support for the program (see Samples & Aber, 1998 for a detailed review of aforementioned evaluations of this program). Taub (2002) conducted a study of Second Step comparing third- through fifth-grade students in a rural school to a no program comparison school. Baseline data were collected prior to the start of the program, four months postintervention, and at one-year follow-up. A time-series analysis of teacher ratings on the school social behavior scales indicated a significant increase in prosocial behaviors and a significant decrease in antisocial behaviors among students in the experimental group compared to pre-test. An increase in antisocial behavior among controls was found during the same time period. Behavioral observations revealed no significant improvements in peer relations among the experimental group at four months; however, significant improvements were found in how the experimental group engaged with their peers at the one-year follow-up. Other observed behaviors, such as bothering other children and following adult directions, were found to be nonsignificant at both post-test and at follow-up.

Findings from Bergsgaard's (1997) study of Second Step also suggest support for the program among elementary school students. However, it is important to mention that no tests of statistical significance were conducted on differences found between the groups under study. Employing a two-year staged intervention with first through fourth graders—where during year 1, students from only the second and fourth grades participated, and in year 2, first through fourth graders were involved—students were observed and data were collected based on six sessions that each lasted five days. The overall number of conflicts decreased, with a greater decrease in year 2 than in year 1. The average number of conflicts per student decreased over the two-year period. Moreover, Bergsgaard reported less teacher reliance on direct, punitive discipline and more attempts at mediation. Finally, the use of peer mediation increased from 0 to 19% over one year.

## Seville Antibullying in School (SAVE) Project

SAVE is a work in progress but is mentioned here because of the unique manner in which it was developed. While results on program effectiveness are not yet available, the development process for this program is note-worthy. Yielding the call for research-based preventive interventions to address aggression and violence among children, SAVE was designed in response to findings from a 1992 study of bullying in Seville, Spain, schools (Ortega & Lera, 2000). A sample of 859 students, ages 11 to 16, was recruited to assess the level of bullying among students using a Spanish translation of Olweus' questionnaire. Results indicated rates of bullying in Seville that were much higher than originally thought. As a consequence, Ortega and colleagues set out to achieve three main goals: (1) to test the fit of the conceptual model, (2) to use a new questionnaire designed for the study and adapted to cultural circumstances, and (3) to design and implement an intervention program. The sample was composed of 4914 students in 26 elementary, middle/junior high, and high schools in Seville. All schools were state funded and located in socially depressed areas, where it was believed rates of school bullying were most prevalent. Four aspects of children's social relationships were examined, including *social well-being, attitudes toward violence, peer group relations,* and *aggression among peers.* Thirteen schools were invited to participate in program implementation using three principal com-ponents and accompanying "tool bags" or resources to facilitate implemen-tation. Program components included (1) a program for organizational management within schools, (2) a program for cooperative group work, and (3) a program to develop students' emotions, attitudes, and values. Further support for schools was provided through bimonthly staff meetings with the research team for two years, consultation and advisory sessions with teachers/program coordinators, and annual reunions of all teachers working on the program. Evaluative questionnaires were administered at each re-union and all reunions were videotaped for evaluative purposes. Data ana-lyses are currently underway to determine the effectiveness of this program.

## Teaching Students to Be Peacemakers

This peer mediation program began in the 1960s and is currently in its third edition. It uses a peaceable classroom/peaceable school approach to train each student in the school to constructively manage conflicts. Program objectives are to teach students to negotiate nonviolent resolutions to interpersonal conflict, to help classmates negotiate conflicts through peer mediation, to enhance classroom learning, and to improve the quality of school life. Training includes all students and lasts 10 to 20 hours. Training is spread over several weeks, with students receiving 30 minutes every day for 30 days, followed by 30 minutes twice per week for remainder of school year. Teaching Students to Be Peacemakers is a 12-year spiral program, where students learn increasingly sophisticated negotiation and mediation skills as they move through grade levels. The program has four key components that include teaching (1) students to recognize conflict, (2) students how to negotiate integrative agreements to conflicts of interest, (3) students how to mediate their classmates' conflicts, and (4) teachers how to implement the program. Students mediate conflicts (initially in pairs and then independently) on a rotating basis to ensure every student's experience as a mediator.

Johnson and Johnson (1995, 1996) conducted several studies of this program that provide strong and convincing evidence of its effectiveness. Between 1988 and 1994, seven studies of Teaching Students to Be Peacemakers were conducted to examine two approaches to peer mediation—total student body and school cadre. The sample consisted of first-through ninth-grade students from six different schools in two different counties, representing both suburban and urban settings. Training programs were between 9 and 15 hours in length. Johnson and Johnson (1995, 1996) indicate five studies used control groups, four studies rotated teachers across conditions, three studies used random assignment of classrooms and/or controls, and one study randomly assigned students to conditions. Two primary results were targeted: (1) increased student knowledge of negotiation and mediation procedures and skills and (2) generalization of knowledge and skills in settings other than the classroom. Using self-report questionnaires and interviews, three studies found a statistically significant increase in the use of constructive conflict management among experimental groups at post-test compared with controls. A corresponding significant decrease was found among the experimental groups on several other key concepts: using threats to get others to give in, telling a teacher, withdrawing, and using aggressive strategies. Three studies were also used to test the impact of the program on students' ability to generalize negotiation skills to nonclassroom and nonschool settings. One study examined elementary school students' ability to transfer skills to nonschool settings. Results indicated self-reported use of these skills at home among third- and fifth-grade students. Parent-reports of first- and third-grade students also revealed use of these skills with siblings and friends. A second study, employing observation techniques in classrooms and on the playground, showed mediation use at a rate of 50% during conflicts where the emotional investment was very high. A third study found program youths to be significantly more likely to engage in negotiation and mediation skills to resolve conflicts than controls, both during and after training in Teaching Students to Be Peacemakers. A study comparing pre- and post-test scores and pre-test/three-month follow-up scores of trained students indicated significant increases in knowledge and use of constructive conflict management skills at both time points.

## SUMMARY

The intervention programs in this chapter (as outlined in Table 1) represent only a fraction of those available to address the issues of antisocial behavior, bullying, and violence among elementary schoolchildren. I selected to highlight those programs that show, or have shown, the most promise in their attempt to ameliorate this persistent and seemingly growing problem. Although this program review suggests strong general support for primary schoolchildren exposed to preventive interventions as opposed to their peers in nontreatment control groups, there is need for cautious optimism when interpreting these results. This review covered different types of programs, emphasizing those using a curriculum-based approach. As reflected in this review, the vast majority of these programs focused on bullying prevention specifically rather than on violence prevention more broadly. While all of the bullying prevention programs employed a whole-school approach, not all violence prevention programs do so. As a result, it is difficult to generalize about how and in what ways the whole-school approach facilitates the development of a safe school climate for children. As noted in an earlier work (Samples & Aber, 1998), there are several factors to consider when drawing conclusions from any review of intervention programs. These factors include the universal applicability of intervention programs for culturally diverse populations, the comprehensive integration of program services for true long-term effects, and differences in research design and methodology.

Differences in methodology can have profound implications for evaluation results. For example, data from the Lions-Quest Program show real promise although there were clear issues with the methodological approach used in the evaluations of this program. Similar methodological issues were present in the evaluations of the Quit It! Program. While both offered potential positive evidence of program effectiveness, the absence of methodological rigor suggests it is too early to determine the true impact of this program. Another important note involves the lack of evidence to support these programs among culturally diverse populations. Only one study (Sanchez et al., 2001) indicated having used a racially diverse sample when measuring program outcomes. The data clearly suggests the ability to adapt bullying prevention programs, in particular, to different populations

**TABLE I**
**Summary of School-Based Bullying Prevention Programs**

| Studies and Program Names | Age of Children (Sample Size) | Nature and Intensity of Intervention | Research Design | Outcomes |
|---|---|---|---|---|
| Bullying Prevention Program (Olweus, 1993, 1996) | $4^{th}$–$7^{th}$ grades (N=2500) | 1 to 2 days professional development; 12 to 16 discussion groups for teachers first year; annual booster for all staff | Quasi-experimental design | Bully-victim problems E>C School climate E>C Antisocial behaviors E>C Student satisfaction with school life E>C |
| (Olweus, 1999) | $3^{rd}$–$10^{th}$ grades (N=6400) | Same | Same | Bullying/victimization E<C (W2<W1) |
| (Smith & Sharp, 1994) | $3^{rd}$–$10^{th}$ grades (N=6468) | Same | Same | Bullying problems E<C (W3<W1) Positive attitudes E>C Bullying behavior E<C Reported bullying incidents E>C |
| Expect Respect/Bullyproofing (Khosropour & Walsh, 2001) | $5^{th}$ grade (N=40) | 11 sessions; teacher training; parent/community workshops | Quasi-experimental design | Verbal aggression E<C Physical aggression E=C Isolation E<C |
| Sanchez et al., 2001) | $5^{th}$ grade (N=1243) | 12 weekly sessions; 6-hour start-up staff training + 3 hours/year for 2 years | Randomized trial with control group | Harassment knowledge E>C Bullying awareness E>C |
| | | | | Bullying knowledge E=C Bullying Recognition W3>W1 Intervening W3>W1 E>C Relying on adult E<C Intent to |

(continues)

**TABLE I**
*(continued)*

| Studies and Program Names | Age of Children (Sample Size) | Nature and Intensity of Intervention | Research Design | Outcomes |
|---|---|---|---|---|
| | | | | intervene E=C (W1) E>C (W2) Seeking teacher's help E>C (W2) |
| Bully Proofing (Berkey et al., 2001) | 4th–5th grades (N=200) | 1 to 2 years integrated school-based program; teacher training | Quasi-experimental design | Decline in suspension rates Decline in disciplinary referrals Children's willingness to use language and techniques for problem solving |
| Epstein et al., (Under review) | 1st–5th grades (N=350) | 11-session teacher training; parent/ community workshops | Quasi-experimental design | Physical bullying W2–5<W1 Verbal bullying W2–5<W1 Exclusionary bullying W3<W1 W5<W1 Safe in classroom W1=W2–5 Safe in lunchroom W2>W1 W3<W1 W4>W1 W5<W1 Safe on playground W2–5>W1 Safe to/from school W4>W1–3 W5>W1–3 |
| (Beran & Tutty, 2002) | 4th–6th grades (N=197) | 11-session teacher training; parent/ community workshops | Quasi-experimental design | Witness bullying E<C Attitudes toward victims W2=W1 (E) W2<W1 (C) |

**TABLE I**

| Studies and Program Names | Age of Children (Sample Size) | Nature and Intensity of Intervention | Research Design | Outcomes |
|---|---|---|---|---|
| Flemish Antibullying Project (Stevens et al., 2000, 2001) | 5th–6th grades (N=323) | Four sessions with two 50-minute periods each | Randomized trial with control group | Prosocial behavior E>C Attitudes toward bullies/victims E=C (W1/W2) Self-efficacy E=C (W1/W2) |
| PATHS (Greenberg & Kusche, 1996, 1997; Greenberg, Kusche, & Mihalic, 1988) | K–6th grades (1st–3rd at pretest) | 131 lessons; teacher, staff, and administrator training | Quasi-experimental design | Social problem solving E>C (W1) Emotional understanding E>C (W1) Cognitive ability E>C (W1) Prosocial behavior E>C (W2) Externalizing behaviors E<C (W3) Behavioral problems E<C (W3) |
| Peacemaker Program (Johnson & Johnson, 1995) | 1st–9th grades (6–15 years) | 9–15 hours of negotiation and mediation training for students | Quasi-experimental design and randomized controlled trial | Knowledge of negotiation steps E>C Knowledge of mediation steps E>C Retention of knowledge over time E>C Knowledge transfer skills E>C |
| Second Step (Grossman et al., 1997; Moore & Beland, 1992) | Pre-K–8th grades | 28 lessons to teach social skills | Randomized controlled trial | Aggressive behavior E<C Social problem solving E>C |
| (Taub, 2002) | 3rd–5th grade | Same | Quasi-experimental design | Antisocial behavior E<C (W2>W1) |

(continues)

**TABLE I**

(*continued*)

| Studies and Program Names | Age of Children (Sample Size) | Nature and Intensity of Intervention | Research Design | Outcomes |
|---|---|---|---|---|
| | | | | Prosocial behavior E>C (W2>W1) Positive peer relations among experimental group W3>W2 |
| (Bergsgaard, 1997) | 1st–4th grade | Same | Same | Interpersonal conflict W2>W1 Teacher reliance on punishment W2>W1 Peer mediation W2>W1 |
| SAVE (Ortega & Lera, 2000) | 4th–10th grades (8–16 years) | Staff meetings once monthly for 2 years; bimonthly consultations; annual reunion of teachers | Quasi-experimental design | *In process* |

Note: Summary evaluation results for the Lions-Quest and Quit It! programs have intentionally been omitted from this table.

in different countries; however, little remains known about the extent to which there is diversity in these populations. What this review suggests is that the more effective the implementation and the more comprehensive the intervention, the more likely the program will yield promising outcomes. To this end, the programs with the greatest success appear to be those that made some attempt at changing school policies regarding antisocial behavior, violence, and bullying. In the absence of changes in school policies, the question of whether intervention programs affect change in school climate in ways that effectively translate into children's safety continues to loom large. In essence, although we have come a considerable way in establishing effective intervention programs, there is still a need to better discern for whom (i.e., subgroups), under what conditions (i.e., context effects), and why (i.e., mediating processes) do these programs work? Until the field accomplishes these goals, there remains work to be done to further advance work in the area of violence prevention and intervention with young children.

# References

American Federation of Teachers (2000). *Building on the best, learning from what works: Five promising discipline and violence prevention programs.* Washington, DC: American Federation of Teachers.

Ballard, M.B., Argus, T., & Remley, T.P. (1999). Bullying and school violence: A proposed prevention program. NASSPBulletin, 83(607), 38–47.

Beran, T.N., & Tutty, L. (2002). *An evaluation of the Dare to Care: Bully Proofing Your School Program.* Unpublished. Calgary, Alberta: RESOLVE Alberta.

Bergsgaard, M. (1997). Gender issues in the implementation and evaluation of a violence prevention curriculum. *Canadian Journal of Education,* 22(1), 33–45.

Berkey, L.G., Keyes, B.J., & Longhurst, J.E. (2001). Bully-Proofing: What one district learned about improving school climate. *Reclaiming Children and Youth,* 9(4), 224–228.

Bronfenbrenner, U. (1979). *The ecology of human development: Experiments by nature and design.* Cambridge, CA: Harvard University Press.

Bryd, B. (1996). *A comparison of two school-based conflict management programs—Lions-Quest and Second Step.* Toronto, Ontario: Lions-Quest Canada.

Cunningham, P.B., & Henggeler, S.W. (2001). Implementation of an empirically based drug and violence prevention and intervention program in public school settings. *Journal of Clinical Child Psychology,* 30(1), 221–232.

Elliott, D.S., & Tolan, P.H. (1999). Youth violence prevention, intervention, and social policy: An overview. In D.J. Flannery & C.R. Huff (Eds.), *Youth violence prevention, intervention, and social policy* (pp. 3–46). Washington, DC: American Psychiatric Press.

Epstein, L., Plog, A.E., & Porter, W. (under review). Bully proofing your school: Results of a four-year intervention.

Farrell, A.D., Meyer, A.L., Kung, A.M., & Sullivan, T.N. (2001). Development and evaluation of school-based violence prevention programs. *Journal of Clinical Child Psychology,* 30(1), 207–220.

Froschl, M., & Sprung, B. (2000). *Addressing teasing and bullying: A collaboration between Educational Equity Concepts and P.S. 75.* Summary of evaluation report. Unpublished. Wellesley, MA: Wellesley College Center for Research on Women and Educational Equity Concepts.

Froschl, M., & Sprung, B. (2001). *A collaboration between Educational Equity Concepts and Jefferson School to address teasing and bullying in grade K-3: Evaluation summary.* Unpublished. Wellesley, MA: Wellesley College Center for Research on Women and Educational Equity Concepts.

Garrity, C.B., Jens, K., Porter, W.W., Sager, N., & Short-Camilli, C. (1997). Bully Proofing your school: Creating a positive climate. *Intervention in School and Climate,* 32(4), 235–243.

Glover, D., Gough, G., & Johnson, M. (2000). Bullying in 25 secondary schools: Incidence, impact, and intervention. *Educational Research,* 42(2), 141–156.

Greenberg, M.T., & Kushche, C.A. (1997, April). *Improving children's emotion regulation and social competence: The effects of the PATHS curriculum.* Paper presented at the biennial meeting of the Society for Research in Child Development: Washington, DC.

Greenberg, M.T., & Kushche, C.A. (1998). Preventive intervention for school-aged deaf children: The PATHS curriculum. *Journal of Deaf Studies and Deaf Education,* 3(1), 49–63.

Greenberg, M.T., Kushche, C.A., & Mihalic, S.F. (1998). Promoting Alternative Thinking Strategies (PATHS). *Blueprints for violence prevention.* Book Ten. Boulder, CO: Center for the Study and Prevention of Violence.

Grossman, D.C., Neckerman, H.J., Koepsell, T.D., Liu, P.Y., Asher, K.N., Beland, K., Frey, K., & Rivara, F.P. (1997). Effectiveness of a violence prevention curriculum among children in elementary school: A randomized controlled trial. *The Journal of the American Medical Association,* 277(20), 1605–1611.

Johnson, D.W., & Johnson, R.T. (1995). Teaching students to be peacemakers: Results of five years of research. *Journal of Peace Psychology,* 1(4), 417–438.

Johnson, D.W., & Johnson, R.T. (1996). Conflict resolution and peer mediation programs in elementary and secondary schools: A review of the research. *Review of Educational Research*, 66(4), 459–506.

Khosropour, S.C., & Walsh, J. (2001, April). *The effectiveness of a violence prevention program: Did it influence how children conceptualize bullying?* Paper presented at the Annual Conference of the American Educational Research Association: Seattle, Washington.

Moore, B., & Beland, K. (1992). *Evaluation of Second Step, preschool-kindergarten: Summary report.* Seattle, WA: Committee for Children.

Munthe, E., & Roland, E. (1989). *Bullying: An international perspective.* London: David Fulton Publishers.

Oliver, R.L., Hoover, J.H., & Hazler, R. (1994a). The perceived roles of bullying in small town midwestern schools. *Journal of Counseling and Development*, 72, 416–420.

Oliver, R.L., Young, T.A., & LaSalle, S.M. (1994b). Early lessons in bullying and victimization: The help and hindrance of children's literature. *The School Counselor*, 42, 137–146.

Olweus, D. (1991). Bully/victim problems among schoolchildren: Basic facts and a school based intervention program. In K. Rubin & D.J. Pepler (Eds.), *The development and treatment of childhood aggression* (pp. 411–448). Hillsdale, NJ: Lawrence Erlbaum Associates.

Olweus, D. (1993). *Bullying at school: What we know and what we can do.* Cambridge, MA: Blackwell Publishers.

Olweus, D. (1994a). Annotation: Bullying at school: Basic facts and effects of a school-based intervention program. *Journal of Child Pscyhology and Psychiatry and the Allied Disciplines*, 35(7), 1171–1190.

Olweus, D. (1994b). Bullying at school: Long-term outcomes for the victims and an effective school-based intervention program. In L.R. Huesmann (Ed.), *Aggressive behavior: Current perspectives* (pp 97–130). New York: Plenum Press.

Olweus, D. (1996). Bullying at school: Knowledge base and an effective intervention program. *Annals of the New York Academy of Sciences*, 794, 265–276.

Olweus, D., Limber, S.P., & Mihalic, S.F. (1999). Bullying prevention program. In D.S. Elliott (Ed.), *Blueprints for violence prevention.* Book Nine. Boulder, CO: Center for the Study and Prevention of Violence.

Ortega, R., & Lera, M.J. (2000). The Seville Antibullying in School Project. *Aggressive Behavior.* 26(1), 113–123.

Powell, K.E., Dahlberg, L.L., Friday, J., Mercy, J.A., Thornton, T., & Crawford, S. (1996). Prevention of youth violence: Rationale and characteristics of 15 evaluation projects. *American Journal of Preventive Medicine*, 12(5, Suppl.), 3–12.

Roland, E. (1993). Bullying: A developing tradition of research and management. In D.P. Tattum (Ed.), *Understanding and managing bullying* (pp. 15–30). Oxford: Heinemann.

Roland, E. (1998). *School influences on bullying.* Durham: University of Durham.

Roland, E. (2000). Bullying in school: Three national innovations in Norwegian schools in 15 years. *Aggressive Behavior*, 26(1), 135–143.

Roland, E., & Munthe, E. (1997). The 1996 Norwegian program for preventing and managing bullying in schools. *Irish Journal of Psychology*, 18, 233–247.

Samples, F., & Aber, L. (1998). Evaluations of school-based violence prevention programs. In D.S. Elliott, B.A. Hamburg, & K.R. Williams (Eds.), *Violence in American schools: A new perspective* (pp. 217–252). Cambridge: Cambridge University Press.

Sanchez, E., Robertson,T.R., Lewis, C.M., Rosenbluth, B., Bohman, T., & Casey, D.M. (2001). Preventing bullying and sexual harassment in elementary schools: The Expect Respect model. *Journal of Emotional Abuse*, 2(2/3), 157–180.

Sharp, S., & Smith, P.K. (1991). Bullying in UK schools: The DES Sheffield Bullying Project. *Early Child Development and Care*, 77, 47–55.

Slaby, R.G., Roedell, W.C., Arezzo, D., & Kendrix, K. (1995). *Early violence prevention: Tools for teachers of young children.* Washington, DC: National Association for the Education of Youth Children. (ED 382 384)

Slaby, R.G., Wilson-Brewer, R., & DeVos, E. (1994). *Aggressors, victims, and bystanders: An assessment-based middle school violence prevention curriculum.* Newton, MA: Education Development Center.

Smith, P.K., & Sharp, S. (Eds). (1994). *School bullying: Insights and perspectives.* London: Routledge.

Stevens, V., Van Oost, P., & Bourdeaudhuij, I. de (2000). The effects of an anti-bullying intervention programme on peers' attitudes and behaviour. *Journal of Adolescence,* 23(1), 23–34.

Stevens, V., Van Oost, P., & Bourdeaudhuij, I. de (2001). Implementation process of the Flemish Antibullying Intervention Program and relation with program effectiveness. *Journal of School Psychology,* 39(4), 303–317.

Sylvester, L., & Frey, K. (1994). *Summary of Second Step pilot studies.* Seattle, WA: Committee for Children.

Taub, J. (2002). Evaluation of the Second Step violence prevention program at a rural elementary school. *School Psychology Review,* 31(2), 186–200.

Office of Civil Rights. (1999). *Protecting students from harassment and hate crime: A guide for schools.* Washington, DC: U.S. Department of Education. (ED 422 671)

Whitney, I., & Smith, P.K. (1993). A survey of the nature and extent of bullying in junior/middle and secondary schools. *Educational Research,* 35(1), 3–25.

Whitney, I., Rivers, L., Smith, P.K., & Sharp, S. (1994). The Sheffield project: Methodology and findings. In P. Smith & S. Sharp (Eds.), *School bullying: Insights and perspectives* (pp. 20–56). London: Routledge.

CHAPTER

# 10

# Research-Based Interventions on Bullying

JAANA JUVONEN & SANDRA GRAHAM

*University of California, Los Angeles*

## INTRODUCTION

Name-calling, taunting, and spreading nasty rumors are common among children and youth. It is estimated that 40 to 80% of schoolchildren experience bullying at some point during their school careers (Finkelhor & Dziuba-Leatherman, 1994; Harachi, Catalano, & Hawkins, 1999; Hoover, Oliver, & Hazler, 1992). Furthermore, over 60% of 8- to 15-year-old students rate bullying as a big problem affecting their lives (Kaiser Family Foundation and Children Now, 2001). Key questions, therefore, are how can bullying problems be prevented and what type of options do school staff have for intervening with bullying?

There is a range of options available to schools for dealing with bullying. Decisions by school staff involve considering a host of questions, such as the following: What counts as bullying? What should be the consequences of bullying? Is a written policy adequate or should there be an intervention program? Should an intervention target bullies, victims, or both? which programs are most effective?

The goal of this chapter is to provide some practical advice to school personnel about bullying, its antecedents and consequences, as well as research-based prevention and intervention options. We start this chapter by defining the problem and discussing the many faces of bullying that have implications for intervention. We then briefly address some of the common myths or misconceptions about victims and bullies in light of the latest research evidence. Linking the research findings to interventions, we focus on two complementary approaches: school-wide antibullying prevention and social-cognitive intervention targeted at bullies. We end the chapter with some general conclusions about programmatic issues.

Our review and analysis are guided by two particular conceptual frameworks. Based on systemic models of behavior, the discussion examines bullying as a social phenomenon that involves more than the bully-victim dyad. To complement this broader social-contextual approach that highlights the role of bystanders, the chapter also examines bullying from a social-cognitive perspective. That is, we show how certain interpretations of events (or biased perceptions) by victims and bullies can shed light on their emotional reactions and behavior. These two conceptual frameworks also form the theoretical basis for the school-wide antibullying prevention approach and the social-cognitive intervention targeting bullies.

## Defining the Problem

Most researchers rely on a definition of bullying provided by Olweus (1991): "A person is being bullied when she or he is exposed, repeatedly and over time, to negative actions on the part of one or more persons" (p. 413). Olweus emphasizes three specific features in this definition: (1) negative actions are intentionally inflicted, (2) hostile actions target the victim repeatedly, and (3) there is an imbalance of power (physical or psychological strength) between the perpetrator and the victim. Although these components help researchers define the construct of bullying, they are not all necessarily applicable or feasible for schools to use when defining bullying.

It is typically difficult to prove that the intentions of the perpetrator were negative. In most cases, children claim that "they didn't mean to hurt" the target or that the intimidating action was carried out "just for fun" (Garofalo, Siegel, & Laub, 1987; Hoover, Oliver & Hazler, 1992). Instead of negative intent, it is more applicable to consider the reaction of the target. For example, definitions of workplace harassment (e.g., sexual) state that if the targeted person finds the unwanted actions offending, and if the perpetrator will not stop the behavior in the face of complaints, the behavior constitutes harassment. We contend that a school's similar position helps define the problem of bullying in a manner that protects the "rights of victims"—or phrased in a more positive manner, the rights of students to safe schooling (Olweus, 1993).

Another component of Olweus's definition (1991) pertains to the repeated nature of bullying behavior. If the definition states that hostile actions are repeated over time, it is difficult to judge what constitutes adequate repetition of action. Furthermore, by defining bullying as repeated, the effects of single incidents are discounted.

For the purposes of a practical definition, the "imbalance of power" is the most critical aspect of the bullying. This third component of the definition conveys that the bully has the power and is misusing it to put down the less powerful (i.e., the victim). The key here is to contrast bullying with conflict situations in which the children involved have more or less equal power (e.g., two friends having an argument). The definition in and of itself provides an ideal educational opportunity to discuss the meaning and nature of bullying.

## The Many Faces of Bullying

Although it is critical to help define bullying in terms of misuse or abuse of power, this abstract definition is not sufficient for students. Children need concrete examples. Therefore, the many faces or forms of bullying need to be recognized and incorporated in school policies and for prevention and intervention purposes.

Hitting, kicking, shoving, name-calling, spreading of rumors, exclusion, and intimidating gestures (e.g., eye rolling) are all examples of behaviors that constitute abuse of power. It is paramount that school staff rely on a broad definition of bullying. In fact, it may be counterproductive to condemn one type of hostile behavior (e.g., physical aggression or sexual harassment) but not other forms of bullying. Narrow definitions may legitimize forms of peer-directed hostilities that are not included in the school policy.

Name-calling is the most common type of bullying tactic used by children of all ages (Olweus, 1993; Rigby, 1999). Physical attacks (e.g., kicking, shoving, hitting) are common among younger children and boys in general (Olweus, 1994), although girls resort to physical means as well (Cadigan, 2003). But there are other tactics that are more covert and indirect, such as spreading of rumors. These indirect forms of bullying that often involve manipulation of social relationships are used earlier by girls than boys (Crick *et al.*, 2001; Olweus, 1994).

The various forms or types of bullying have implications for intervention. In contrast to some of the overt forms, such as physical aggression and direct verbal harassment, the covert types of intimidation (e.g., exclusion and spreading rumors) are difficult for school staff to detect and intervene. We will return to the issues that pertain specifically to the challenges posed by the most covert forms of bullying when we discuss school-wide prevention programs.

From the perspective of intervention, it is also relevant to distinguish between *proactive* ("troubling to others") and *reactive* ("troubled by others") aggression or bullying. The proactive (also called instrumental) form of bullying is unprovoked, whereas reactive bullying represents a response to a provocation. Provocation—just like the negative intent of the bully—is difficult to observe by others because such judgments rely on the subjective perception of the target. Although it is difficult for anyone else to judge whether bullying is provoked, it is important for school staff to probe the reasons for hostile behavior. Some children tend to interpret unintended, ambiguous actions of others as intentional and react to this perceived provocation or threat. Hence, interventions need to consider and address social perceptual biases of those involved in bullying. We will return to this issue as we discuss some of the social-cognitive biases that are typical of aggressive youth.

## Myths and Facts About Bullies

There are many beliefs about bullies in the professional and lay public discourse that have not been supported by contemporary research. One prevalent myth is that most bullies are rejected by their peers. However, a close look at the developmental literature reveals two patterns of data contradicting that belief. First, at the elementary school level, youth who bully others are a very heterogeneous group. Among those heterogeneous youth, researchers have identified subgroups of aggressive children who are not rejected by their peers as well as subgroups of rejected children who are not aggressive (Bierman, Smoot, & Aumuller, 1993; Cillessen et al., 1992). These findings tell us that there are at least as many nonrejected bullies in elementary school as there are rejected ones.

The second pattern of data concerns the changing relationship between aggression and peer rejection during the adolescent years. By early adolescence, there are almost no studies reporting a positive correlation between aggression and rejection. Many adolescent studies, in fact, report the opposite—a positive association between aggression and peer *acceptance* (Luthar & McMahon, 1996; Rodkin et al., 2000). In our own research, we have found that young adolescents with reputations as aggressive are perceived by their peers as especially "cool," where perceived "coolness" implies both popularity and possession of traits that are admired by others (Graham & Juvonen, 2002; Juvonen, Graham, & Schuster, 2003). As early adolescents exercise their need for autonomy and independence, it seems that deviant and antisocial youth enjoy a newfound but short-lived popularity as more adjusted peers attempt to imitate their antisocial tendencies (Moffitt, 1993).

Another misconception about bullies is that they do not have close friends. Not only are aggressive youth often judged as popular by their peers, but they have well-established social networks (Cairns & Cairns, 1994). They are just as likely as nonaggressive youth to be nuclear (rather than peripheral) members of their peer group and to have reciprocated best friends. What appears to be unique about these friendship groups is that they often are comprised of other aggressive youth who may reinforce bullying behavior (Cairns et al., 1988; Poulin & Boivin, 2000).

Just as it has been incorrectly assumed that bullies are rejected by peers and have no friends, there has been a complementary assumption that aggressive youth are low in self-esteem. That myth has its roots in the known relationship between rejection and low self-regard (rejected youth do tend to have negative self-views) (Parker & Asher, 1987) and in the widely and uncritically accepted view that people who aggress against others must act that way because they think poorly of themselves (Baumeister, Smart, & Boden, 1996; Cairns & Cairns, 1994). Some readers of this chapter may recall the self-esteem movement of the 1980s whose advocates proposed that raising self-esteem was the key to improving the outcomes of children with academic and social problems (Baumeister, 1996). But there is not much evidence in the peer aggression literature that aggressive children suffer from low self-esteem (see Dryfoos, 1990, for a similar conclusion in the risk literature). To the contrary, many studies report that bullies perceive themselves in a positive light, perhaps sometimes displaying overly positive self-views. For example, Zariski and Coie (1996) reported that bullies over-estimated how much their peers liked them and underestimated how much these same classmates disliked them. Thus, not only do aggressive youth appear to have reasonably intact self-concepts, they may believe that they are liked more than they really are.

## Myths and Facts About Victims

One old misconception about experiences of bullying is that they build character. That is, victims of bullying were thought to benefit from experiences of peer intimidation. In contrast to this view, research findings quite clearly show that bullying experiences increase the vulnerabilities of children. For example, we know that children who are passive and socially withdrawn are at heightened risk for getting bullied and that these children become even more withdrawn after incidents of bullying (Schwartz, Dodge, & Coie, 1993). Similarly, Egan, and Perry (1998) have shown that youth who have unfavorable perceptions of their social standing are at risk of getting bullied, but their findings also indicated that bullying has a negative impact on self-views. Thus, certain characteristics or behaviors may mark a child as an "easy target," but bullying experiences also exacerbate these very same attributes.

Another more recent myth about victims of bullying is that the targets of repeated peer maltreatment become violent. This portrayal of victims lashing out at their tormentors was reinforced by the recent media portrayals of school shooting incidents. The truth, however, is that most victims of bullying are more likely to suffer in silence than retaliate. Victims are most likely to display psychological problems, such as depression, social anxiety, and negative self-views, as well as social withdrawal (Hawker & Boulton, 2000; Juvonen & Graham, 2001). These victims are labeled as *submissive victims* (Olweus, 1993, 1994). One of the reasons why submissive victims tend to experience emotional problems is because they often blame themselves for their plight. When children think that they get bullied because of the way they are (e.g., because of their looks, family background, race), they are particularly likely to experience depression, anxiety, and have negative self-views (Graham & Juvonen, 1998).

In contrast to submissive victims, a smaller subset of victims—*aggressive victims*—are indeed likely to retaliate and/or provoke others (Olweus, 1993, 1993; Perry, Kusel, & Perry, 1988). However, this particular group of bully-victims shows a distinct profile of social-emotional and school-related difficulties (Juvonen, *et al.*, 2003) that may indicate other underlying problems, such as emotion regulation problems typical of children who have attention deficit disorders (Schwartz, Proctor, & Chien, 2001).

Another misperception is that there is a victim personality type. Although certain personality characteristics (e.g., propensity to social withdrawal or aggression) indeed place children at higher risk for being bullied (Hodges *et al.*, 1997; Kochenderfer-Ladd, 2003), there are also a host of situational factors (e.g., being a new student in school) and social risk factors (e.g., not having a friend) that increase the likelihood of a child being or continuing to get bullied. We presume that these more dynamic factors explain why there are more temporary than chronic victims of bullying. For example, Kochenderfer and Ladd (1996) found that there was considerable turnover in kindergartners who reported being victimized during their first school year ($r = .24$ between fall and spring). By relying on peer reports rather than self-reports, Juvonen, Nishina, and Graham (2000), in turn, found that only about one third of students who had reputations as a victim in the fall of sixth grade maintained that reputation until the end of the school year. Identification of both personal and social risk factors is critical when considering how to prevent or intervene with bullying.

## Bullying: More than Bully and Victim Involvement

In addition to the myths about bullies and victims, there is another misconception about bullying: Many parents, teachers, and children view bullying as a problem of bullies and victims. Yet, there is ample research evidence demonstrating that bullying involves much more than the bully-victim dyad. For example, bullying incidents are typically public (rather than private) events that have witnesses. Based on playground observations, Craig and Pepler (1997) found that in 85% of bullying incidents, an average of four peers were present. Furthermore, witnesses are not necessarily innocent bystanders but often play a critical part in bullying (O'Connel, Pepler & Graig, 1999; Olweus, 1993, 1994; Salmivalli, 2001). Scandinavian researchers (Olweus, 1978, 1993; Salmivalli *et al.*, 1996) have identified various participant roles, such as *assistants to bullies*, *reinforcers*, *defenders of victims*, and others (Salmivalli, 2001).

*Assistants to bullies* (followers or henchmen) take part in ridiculing or intimidating a schoolmate. They do not initiate the hostile overture but rather join in and facilitate the process. *Reinforcers or supporters*, in turn, encourage the bully by showing signs of approval (e.g., smiling when someone is bullied). It appears that encouragement does not have to be active but can also be passive responding (i.e., lack of interference or help seeking), which is adequate to signal approval (Juvonen & Cadigan, 2002). In comparison to the pro-bully participants, those who defend the victim are rare (O'Connel *et al.*, 1999). In their analysis of bullying in Canadian elementary schools, O'Connel *et al.* (1999) found that 54% of the time, peers reinforced bullies by passively watching; 21% of the time; students were modeling bullies (e.g., following or assisting); and 25% of the time, they were supporting the victim by either directly intervening or distracting or discouraging the bully. Estimates of defending are even lower among groups of students who have just transferred to middle schools (Nishina & Juvonen, 2003).

The apparent support received by the instigator of bullying extends beyond the specific incidents. As reviewed earlier, research shows that bullies are often considered popular, whereas victims have low social status (Juvonen *et al.*, 2003). These findings reflect the differential power status of bullies and victims. Because the power dynamics get played out not only in dyadic terms but on a larger social scale involving group status, some intervention approaches (school-wide bullying prevention programs) focus on changing the entire social system that supports the power imbalance. The idea is to change the behavioral norms or values in ways that no longer support bullying (or the high social standing of bullies) but rather capitalizes on the power that peers have to disapprove of bullying. Before we describe such prevention efforts, we want to briefly lay out the different options that are available for school staff when making choices about how to deal with bullying.

## WHAT CAN BE DONE ABOUT BULLYING AND ITS NEGATIVE EFFECTS?

There are a myriad of intervention strategies to combat and deal with bullying in schools. Some of the programs involve the whole school, while others target at-risk individuals (typically bullies). Certain programs focus on skill building (e.g., fostering prosocial skills, conflict mediation strategies), whereas others rely on the punishment of undesirable behavior (e.g., zero-tolerance policies).

Data on program effectiveness are limited at this time. Especially limited are evaluation studies that would compare different approaches. Hence, we do not know whether instructional programs are better than punitive methods. In the absence of such comparative data, we review two promising research-based approaches: *a school-wide bullying prevention* and a *social-cognitive intervention* targeted at aggressive students. Both approaches are instructional programs, inasmuch that children are explicitly taught norms of conduct and/or behavioral skills that help them react in constructive ways to perceived and actual provocation by peers.

The school-wide bullying prevention approach and the social-cognitive intervention targeting aggressive children represent our own program development and evaluation work, respectively. More importantly, however, the description of the goals and methods of these two approaches provides a meaningful comparison for school staff who are trying to assess the need and capacity of the school to implement a prevention program involving the entire school or to adopt an intervention targeted at children who repeatedly bully others. We suggest that whereas the former is well-suited to change the social context of bullying as well as to address the problems facing the victims of bullying, the latter—by definition—addresses the problems underlying aggression. Hence, the two approaches are not mutually exclusive but complementary.

Our reviews of the two types of approaches are not parallel but reflect some of the fundamental differences between the two. The *whole-school* bullying prevention programs often entail different components (e.g., parent education, staff training, classroom-based lessons, and whole-school assemblies) that are not necessarily prescribed or detailed. In contrast, many of the successful *targeted* interventions are both prescribed and detailed inasmuch as they are curriculum-based. Hence, our description of the whole-school bullying prevention is more global (although we try to highlight some differences between the different variants of the basic model), and our depiction of the targeted intervention approach includes examples of specific lessons of one particular curriculum-based program (Best Foot Forward).

## School-Wide Bullying Prevention

One category or class of antibullying programs consists of school-wide prevention approaches. They are called school-wide or systemic programs because they include all students and staff (even parents to a degree). Bullying is not considered as an individual problem of some students but as a social problem of the collective body of students. Accordingly, the key assumption of school-wide bullying preventions is that to prevent (or decrease) bullying, the social norms toward bullying must be altered. Changing the culture of the school is presumed to require increased awareness of the nature of the problem, heightened monitoring, and systematic and consistent response to incidents of bullying on the part of the school staff.

Most of the school-wide programs are based on a particular model: the (Bergen) Bullying Prevention Program, designed originally by Dan Olweus in Norway (e.g., Olweus, 1993, 1994). This program was selected as the only model program for school-based prevention at the secondary level in the Blueprint Programs by the Center of Prevention of Violence at the University of Colorado at Boulder, along with the Centers of Disease Control and Prevention in 1996.

The school-wide bully prevention program aims to restructure the social environment so that there are fewer opportunities and rewards for bullying (Olweus, 2001). Accordingly, one of the first goals of the Bullying Prevention Program is to increase the awareness of bullying and its negative effects among school staff, students, and parents. To accomplish this goal, one of the first steps is to create clear school rules about bullying.

When the program is first implemented at a school, school staff receive a booklet of basic facts about bullying and a summary of strategies that the school can use to counteract and prevent problems associated with bullying. The school also holds a separate conference or training day on bully-victim problems for staff. In addition, parents receive information about the program. All parents receive a short booklet of basic facts, and parent meetings (e.g., as part of general PTA meetings) are held in which parents receive further information about the school's approach to bullying. Students, in turn, are engaged in class discussions of bullying and strategies to deal with it.

Olweus (1993) recommends classroom-based discussions of bullying based on a 25-minute instructional video consisting of typical episodes of bullying facing students in school. To increase the awareness of the social nature of the problem, the incidents displayed in the video demonstrate the ways in which classmates encourage and reinforce hostile actions of the bully (e.g., smiling, siding with the bully, covering the bully from teachers). By portraying the emotional effects of bullying on the target of the maltreatment, empathy for the victim is evoked. Based on the discussion of the vignettes depicted in the video, children are then asked to provide strategies that help the victim to deal with the bully(ies). Furthermore, students are also asked to consider what bystanders can do to discourage bullying.

In addition to the general school rules about bullying, each class or classroom is expected to create a few rules of its own. Olweus, as well as Rigby (1999), who has designed another whole-school approach to bullying in Australia, emphasize the importance of involving students in constructing such rules. By engaging in the process, students come to better understand the function of the rules. This will alleviate the view that rules are imposed on students. It is presumed that students are more likely to appreciate the rules if they come to see them as protecting their own rights. Such a distinction between behavioral control and protection of rights is rarely emphasized by school personnel in the United States, yet from the perspective of especially older students (e.g., young teens) this distinction may be crucial (Juvonen & Cadigan, 2002). Even if the emphasis on the protection of rights is not likely to deter a child from bullying, it can empower the victim of bullying to seek help or a bystander to intervene.

In addition to providing information that is presumed to increase the awareness of the bullying problem and enlighten students' perspectives of their actions and rights, schools are expected to increase monitoring of student behavior during lunch and recess. The instruction and in-class discussion are not expected to change the social behavior of students unless school staff reinforces the antibullying norms in the school yard and hallways. Incidents of bullying are viewed as instructional opportunities that help students apply the knowledge and insights gained through the classroom-based instruction. Follow-up concerning incidents must therefore be consistent and systematic. Staff discuss bullying incidents with all parties involved. Depending on the seriousness of the transgressions, such discussions can also include parents.

Teachers are encouraged to meet in groups to further develop means to promote school climate. Olweus (1993) recommends groups of five to ten teachers meeting on a weekly or biweekly basis to discuss specific issues with bullying and whether there are barriers to implementing the program effectively.

## Evidence of Effectiveness

Olweus conducted one large-scale evaluation study of the Bullying Prevention Program in Norway in 1983–1985. This evaluation consisted of a pre-assessment approximately four months prior to the implementation of the program and two post-assessments one year and two years after the implementation of the program in grades four to seven (primary and junior high schools). The sample consisted of approximately 2500 students from 112 classrooms.

A quasi-experimental design was used by relying on time-lagged contrasts between age-equivalent groups. By using multiple cohorts, comparisons could be made between age-equivalent groups pre- and post-program implementation. For example, the group of fifth graders who had been exposed to the program for one school year were compared to another group of fifth graders who had not yet been exposed to the program. Various self-report measures were used in addition to student estimates of the "number of students being bullied in class" and the "number of students bullying others."

The comparisons across cohorts over time indicated decreases in self-reported bullying and victimization and decreased estimates of the number of students bullying and being bullied. For example, there was an approximate 50% decrease in the number of students who reported being bullied or bullying others "now and then" or more frequently (Olweus, 1994). Also, decreases in self-reported antisocial behavior and increased satisfaction with school climate were reported. Overall, the effect sizes were substantial (statistically in the range of medium or large). The effects of the program were generally stronger after two years than after one year of the program's implementation (Olweus, 1994). This finding is consistent with other program evaluations, some of which indicate initial negative effects (Alsaker & Valkanover, 2001). It is presumed that increased awareness of bullying problems sensitizes students initially to report more incidents.

Olweus (1994) reports finding dosage–response linkages at the level of classrooms. The reductions in bullying were larger in classrooms in which classroom rules about bullying were established and regular class meetings were held to discuss incidents and strategies to deal with bullying problems. Teachers' perception of the feasibility and effectiveness of the program were among the best predictors of program success. This finding demonstrates how important it is to have the school staff support the program. We suspect that this is one of the key challenges posed by the school-wide approach: Rather than viewing endorsement of rules, facilitation of classroom discussion, and mediation of incidents as an added burden, teachers need to see these efforts as feasible and worth their while. It seems that this can be accomplished more easily at the elementary than at the secondary level and in small rather than in large schools.

## Limitations and Further Program Development

In spite of its general appeal, the original Bullying Prevention Program has been criticized for not providing an adequate level of detail about how staff members are expected to mediate bullying incidents, how they should deal with repeated "offenders" or chronic victims, and how they can engage parents in staff-directed mediation. Stevens *et al.* (2001) also call for clarification of the specific skills needed to implement the program adequately as well as elucidation of linkages between the program goals and methods. Our discussion in this chapter further adds a need to include other measures of both the fidelity of implementation (i.e., how thoroughly and consistently the program is carried out) and program effectiveness besides the ones used by Olweus. For example, indicators of the reliability and consistency of staff mediation of bullying incidents might be critical for adequate level of implementation. Such assessments might include student ratings of fairness of the way school staff deal with bullying (assuming that judgments of fairness depend in part on student perceptions of whether staff responds in a consistent manner to all incidents regardless of who is involved). To better assess program effectiveness in terms of changing the social system that supports bullying, indicators of the social standing of bullies and victims should also be assessed. If this objective is reached, bullies should lose their high social status, whereas victims should gain positive sentiments from classmates. Accordingly, defending victims should become more frequent and widespread.

## An Example of One Particular U.S.-Based Adaptation

As mentioned above, there are several variants of the basic school-wide bullying prevention program in different countries (Pepler *et al.*, 1994; Rigby, 1999; Smith, & Sharp, 1994) as well as in schools and classrooms in the degree to which they follow various program objectives and methods (Stevens *et al.*, 2001). Here we provide a brief overview of one particular U.S.-based model that was developed on the same principles as the original Bullying Prevention Program. This model was adapted in the laboratory elementary school of UCLA (Nishina, Juvonen, & de la Sota, 2000) and is currently called *Cool Tools*. This particular adaptation of a systemic bullying approach emphasizes the explicit instruction of specific strategies that help children respond to perceived or actual provocation.

Like most school-wide bullying prevention programs, *Cool Tools* includes components implemented at the level of the school (e.g., antibullying school policy, two to three special assemblies or events during the school year), classrooms (e.g., integrated curricula materials and activities adapted for different grade levels), and individual students (e.g., staff mediation of bullying incidents). The school policy states that "put downs" of all sorts are not allowed, and specific examples of the various types of incidents are provided. These rules are explicitly taught to the children who are new to the school, while others receive "refresher" or reminder lessons about the policy.

The program name, *Cool Tools*, refers to strategies that can be used in situations when someone is attempting to bully or "put down" another student. Many of the "tools" consist of either preventive behaviors (e.g., "Exit before the situation escalates.") or communication strategies that are relevant either during or right after the bullying episode (e.g., seek help). Other strategies consist of coping responses (e.g., how to re-frame incidents, how to problem solve). These "life skills" are taught to all students—the assumption is that it is not sufficient for students to know what not to do; they also need to be taught what to do. Students are encouraged to explore different strategies (represented as concrete "tools" in a classroom toolbox) when experiencing or witnessing bullying.

Instruction on the strategies involves role-playing and other highly inter-active methods, including discussion of relevant stories and literature. By relying on these multiple methods of instruction, children are presumed to gain further perspective-taking skills and developing insight to understand-ing the consequences of their own actions on others. Most importantly, school staff probe and remind students of the strategies when they mediate bullying incidents in the school yard. Consistent follow-up of incidents is viewed as essential to the generalization of skills, and incidents are regarded as "teachable moments" during which the acquired knowledge can be ap-plied. It is presumed that while young children in the lower grades need adult guidance and reminders, older students in the upper grades should have internalized the values and strategies in such a way that adult mediation is needed only occasionally.

In addition to the on-the-spot mediation of incidents, serious or repeated episodes require additional mediation. In these situations, the Safe School Coordinator goes over the incident with all parties involved. A specific goal of the mediation is to facilitate recognition of alternative or "replacement" behaviors that would result in constructive resolution. In cases of more serious episodes, parents of the involved students also are called in.

In the beginning of each school year, parents receive a copy of the school policy and materials regarding the terminology and procedures used. Additional parent education classes are also provided once a year. By engaging the parents in the process, the goal is to have parents reinforce the behaviors taught in school.

In sum, the primary goal of *Cool Tools* is not to abolish bullying but to help children minimize the negative consequences of bullying. By teaching the same strategies to all students, the goal is that the students will subsequently learn to deal with and mediate bullying incidents more independently.

## Summary of General Guidelines for School-Wide Approaches

Rigby (2001) has identified key elements of school-wide prevention program features necessary for an effective antibullying policy:

1. A strong, positive statement of the school's desire to promote positive peer relations and especially to oppose bullying and harassment of any form it may take by all members of the school community
2. A succinct definition of bullying or peer victimization, with illustrations[1]
3. A declaration of the right of individuals and groups in the school—students, teachers, other workers, and parents—to be free of victimization by others
4. A statement of the responsibility of those who witness peer victimization to seek to stop it
5. Encouragement of students and parents with concerns about victimization to speak with school personnel
6. A general description of how the school proposes to deal with the bully-victim problem
7. A plan to evaluate the policy in the near future (p. 325)

In addition to these general guidelines, Owens, Slee, and Shute (2001) identify specific ways in which schools can respond to covert forms of bullying, such as relational or indirect forms of harassment typical among teenage girls. These guidelines are similar to the general elements identified above. Given their focus on teenage girls, however, Owens *et al.* emphasize the need to develop an understanding among the school staff about the nature of girls' socialization, including their desire to develop close friend-

---

[1] To define bullying, Rigby encourages students to draw what bullying looks like.

ships. Furthermore, teachers need to be educated to recognize that indirect forms of harassment (e.g., spreading of rumors) are not benign but can have devastating emotional consequences. Owens *et al.* also underscore the importance of encouraging victims of indirect harassment to speak out as well as help individual students to find ways to "escape" from old patterns or ways of behaving.

## Targeted Intervention Programs for Aggressive Youth

Unlike school-wide approaches that address the needs of potential (and ultimate) victims and bystanders, most interventions that focus on bullies are programs designed to address the known dysfunctional thoughts and behaviors of the children who aggress against others. Many of these programs focus on some aspect of social skills training because aggressive youth have well-documented deficits in the way they process social information (Coie & Dodge, 1998). One very robust finding in the literature is that bullies have a tendency (bias) to overattribute hostile intent to peers, particularly in ambiguous situations (see Castro *et al.*, 2002, for a recent meta-analysis). Imagine, for example, that you are standing in line and unexpectedly receive a push from the person behind you, but it is unclear whether the person intended the push. Aggressive youth are more likely to infer that the push was instigated "on purpose" (i.e., the person is responsible) and to respond with anger and aggression. Having a low threshold for assigning blame in peer contexts can elicit anger and retaliation from others, including teachers, which can then lead to escalating cycles of hostility and mistrust. In our own research, we have found that aggressive young adolescents, more so than victims or socially adjusted youth, were likely to perceive the school as an unfair place (Graham & Mize, 2003) and that perception, in turn, was related to school suspension (Markoe, 2003).

Hostile attributional bias may be only one part of a larger syndrome of deficits that interferes with the adaptive social information processing. For example, Crick and Dodge (1994) proposed a five-step social cognitive model that has become very influential in the aggression intervention literature. In that model, the information-processing difficulties of aggressive children begin when they inaccurately encode social cues associated with interpersonal dilemmas (e.g., the hypothetical push while waiting in line) and continue as they formulate goals, access from memory a repertoire of possible behavioral responses (e.g., "Should I retaliate or just ignore it?"), and finally enact a response.

One of the best known aggression interventions that includes these kinds of social information processing skills is Fast Track (Conduct Problems Prevention Research Group, 2002a). Implemented at four sites (Durham, NC, Nashville, TN, Seattle, WA, and a rural community in central Pennsylvania), Fast Track identified a sample of 890 high-risk kindergarten children based on parent and teacher report of conduct problems at home and at school. These children were then randomly assigned to either an intervention group or to a no-treatment control group. Those in the intervention group participated in a year-long curriculum with weekly meetings that included training in social information processing, social problem solving, emotional understanding, communication, and self-control. The social cognitive component was accompanied by individualized academic tutoring as needed, and there were parent training components as well. Intervention activities continued to grade ten but there was heavier concentration in the first two years of elementary school and during the transition to middle school. Outcome data for the first three years reported that by the end of third grade, significantly fewer children in the intervention group were displaying serious conduct problems than in the control group (CPPRG, 2002b).

Fast Track is a unique intervention because of its size, breadth, and ten-year time span. It is more of a demonstration project showing the potential of good intervention science rather than a program that could easily be implemented by individual schools or teachers. In the next section, we describe a small scale and more focused social cognitive intervention for aggressive youth developed by Graham, Taylor, and Hudley (2003). This intervention provides a context for concluding the chapter with a discussion of guidelines for implementing school-based interventions.

## Best Foot Forward: A Promising Targeted Intervention

*Best Foot Forward* takes as a starting point two well-known risk factors associated with aggression: Aggressive youth have social information-processing deficits as described previously, and they often do poorly in school. A reasonable way to think about an intervention for aggressive youth is therefore to focus on *decreasing* the motivation to aggress and *increasing* the motivation to achieve a pathway to improving social and academic outcomes. The organizing theme for the intervention is the *social cognitive construct of perceived responsibility* in both other people and the self. The program is designed to consider whether aggressive children perceive that their peers are responsible for negative events, which has implications for reducing the motivation to aggress against those peers. The program also examines the degree to which individuals perceive themselves as responsible for their academic outcomes, which has implications for increasing their own motivation to achieve.

*Best Foot Forward* consists of two separate but interrelated components. The *social skills* component focuses on teaching participants how to make accurate judgments about the causes of other people's behavior, particularly the degree to which others are perceived as responsible for negative outcomes. Accurate beliefs about others' responsibility should then lead to better anger management and aggression control. The *academic motivation* component focuses on training participants to assume self-responsibility for school learning. Strategies are taught that encourage participants to choose tasks of intermediate difficulty, be realistic goal setters, be task focused, and attribute academic failure to lack of effort rather than to factors that are not within their control. All of these strategies derive from principles of motivation that are known to "work"—that is, to increase academic motivation (Graham & Weiner, 1996). The curriculum consists of 32 lessons. We provide here specific examples of some of the lessons.

### Social Skills Training

The social skills component of the curriculum is divided into two sections. The first social component addresses attributional bias or inferring hostile intent in others. Being quick to assign blame following a negative outcome is often an impulsive reaction that can be modified with training. Training involves how to more accurately infer another's intentions and recognize the difference between intended and accidental behavior. In an earlier intervention, it was documented that training aggressive boys to infer nonhostile intent in ambiguous situations resulted in reductions in antisocial behavior as rated by classroom teachers (Hudley & Graham, 1993). This component of *Best Foot Forward* elaborates on those findings. Hypothetical stories demonstrate different intentions, after which students look for examples of such situations in their own lives. Students practice discerning another person's intention by reading nonverbal cues (e.g., tone of voice, facial expression, body language) through matching faces to appropriate feeling labels, pantomiming in small groups, and role-play exercises (e.g., Think Before You Swing, Lesson 11).

The second section addresses account giving. Accounts are explanations or reasons for social transgressions, and they include apologies (confession), excuses, justifications, and denials (Scott & Lyman, 1968). Effective account giving is an important social skill because accounts help students manage the impressions that others have of them—they influence a receiver's judgments about responsibility as well as their emotional reactions to the account giver, such as anger versus forgiveness (Weiner, 1995). We know that aggressive boys show less understanding of the consequences of some accounts (i.e., excuses), and we have hypothesized that they may be less willing to extend forgiveness to peers who offer other accounts (Graham, Weiner, & Benesh-Weiner, 1995). This phase of the intervention teaches participants to understand the characteristics of different kinds of accounts and what they imply about personal responsibility. The goal is for participants to learn to display greater forgiveness when others apologize for their misdeeds, a strategy that should promote better peer relations. Another goal is for aggressive boys to learn the adaptiveness of accepting responsibility for their own misdeeds, such as when they apologize (e.g., The 4 As: Admit, Apologize, Amend, Assure, Lesson 8).

### Academic Motivation Training

The academic motivation component of the curriculum is divided into four sections that focus on risk taking, goal setting, task focus, and attribution retraining. The section on risk taking teaches students how to determine what makes a problem easy, moderately difficult, or hard and to recognize the motivational benefits of intermediate difficulty (Atkinson, 1964). For example, students participate in a weekly spelling game where they choose words that are easy, moderately difficult, or hard. Although more points (exchangeable for prizes) can be earned by correctly spelling more difficult words, participants learn that the best strategy (more points) over the long run is to concentrate on moderately difficult words. Those principles also are incorporated into a number of engaging nonacademic tasks. For example, while playing a competitive game of ring toss, intervention students are taught to adjust their goals (risk taking) upward after success and downward after failure (e.g., Take Smart Risks, Lesson 4). In that way, students are taught about the motivational advantages of continuously revising their goals and level of aspiration in the direction of moderately difficult tasks.

The section on goal setting teaches participants about the importance of setting proximal or short-term goals rather than (or in addition to) distal or long-term goals. Short-term goals help the individual to monitor how much effort is needed to accomplish particular tasks (Bandura, 1997). Using concrete everyday examples where goal setting is likely to be instrumental to success, intervention boys are taught how to set their sights on more immediate attainments that lead to longer-term successes. Over the course of the intervention, they keep a weekly log where they enter daily, weekly, and monthly goals, both academic and nonacademic. They are also given strategies for monitoring their behavior directed toward achieving those goals and for revising their goals in response to success or failure (e.g., The Best Way from Here to There, Lesson 24).

Finally, the attribution retraining section is designed to promote adaptive explanations for achievement failure. Participants read hypothetical failure scenarios and generate possible causes for the outcome, which are used as a context for discussing the characteristics of different causes and why some explanations might be more adaptive than others. Students then work on several achievement tasks that require persistence (e.g, origami puzzles). Here they are taught about the utility of identifying factors within their control, such as lack of effort, and to avoid the endorsement of factors outside of their control, such as low ability and bad luck when faced with academic difficulty (e.g., To Blame or Not to Blame, Lesson 30).

## Implementing the Intervention

Because of the breadth of the curriculum and number of lessons (32 lessons, plus pre-testing and post-testing), the intervention has been implemented as an after-school program. For this evaluation study, participants attended the intervention three days a week for 12 weeks in sessions that lasted approximately one hour. One strength of an after-school intervention is that it provides a structured activity for at-risk youngsters during a particularly risky time of the day. A considerable amount of recent research has documented that the hours between 3 p.m. and 7 p.m. are critical because those are the times when most delinquent activity is likely to take place (i.e., the prime hours when adult supervision is minimal) (Flannery, Williams, & Vazsonyi, 1999).

### Selecting Participants

Participants were selected from a K–5 predominantly ethnic minority elementary school located in an economically depressed community in Los Angeles, California. Using well-established methods in the peer aggression literature, we relied on a combination of both teacher ratings and peer nominations to select eligible participants. We selected African American boys in third through the fifth grades who were identified by their peers and teachers as most aggressive and by their teachers as having serious motivational problems. A total of 31 boys were randomly assigned to the intervention, and 35 were assigned to a no-treatment control group (a few parents only agreed to allow their children participate if they were control subjects).

As one might well imagine, subject attrition can be a problem in studies such as this. Participation was voluntary and required sustained after-school attendance, which meant that there was no "captive" audience that would have been available had the intervention been run during regular school hours. Over the course of the intervention, 9 of 31 boys were lost in the intervention condition. Thus, the final sample consisted of 47 third- through fifth-grade African American boys: There were 22 youth in the intervention and 25 in the control group.

### Outcome Measures

A variety of outcome measures that relied on multiple informants (e.g., self-report, behavioral observations, teacher report, and school records) and included both attitudinal and behavioral assessments were utilized to assess the program effectiveness. The outcome measures assessed improvements from pre- to post-test in both social skills and academic motivation. For social outcomes, changes in children's reactions to ambiguous peer provocation and their understanding of accounts were assessed. Teacher ratings of children's social behavior before and after the intervention also were examined. Among the academic outcomes, changes in students' goal setting and attributions for achievement failure were examined. In addition, students' cumulative records for their semester grade equivalents and teacher comments about academic progress were utilized. Finally, both intervention and control groups participated in a laboratory maze task that simulated ambiguous peer provocation and measured intermediate risk taking.

### Intervention Results

Although our sample sizes were small and the effects therefore modest, the intervention yielded encouraging results, which are briefly summarized here (see Graham *et al.*, 2003, for a complete description of the findings). First, boys in the intervention learned the social skills of giving strategic accounts, honoring the accounts of others, and assuming nonhostile peer intent in ambiguous situations. Second, they learned the academic motivation skills of intermediate risk taking, realistic goal setting, task focus, and attributions for failure to factors within their control. Third, intervention boys used these social and academic motivation skills in the laboratory maze task that simulated ambiguous provocation and provided opportunities for intermediate risk taking and realistic goal setting. Last, boys in the intervention were rated by their teachers as showing more cooperation and persistence than control group boys. They were also judged as having improved more in the social and academic domain based on end-of-the-semester written comments by teachers.

As currently designed and implemented, *Best Foot Forward* was a pilot intervention, and we recognize there are many things that need to be improved. The intervention was generally more successful with *increasing competencies* (e.g., prosocial skills, motivation) than with *decreasing problem behavior* (e.g., teacher-rated negative social behavior). In the language of risk research, that means that we were more successful at enhancing protective factors that buffer against future negative events than we were at reducing current risk. If the target is present risk, then we should consider strategies for increasing the immediate impact of the intervention on antisocial behavior. For example, there could be more lessons on behavior management and anger control in the social skills component. We also need to measure a range of antisocial and problem behavior outcomes, such as school truancy and disciplinary actions, to better test for treatment effects. In addition, procedures need to be developed for studying intervention effects in naturally occurring school contexts (e.g., playground, cafeteria, classroom academic time).

It will be important to design more effective and creative strategies for reducing participant attrition in an after-school program. The incentives used for regular attendance were successful, but there was competition from other after-school activities, including free time for play. It may be that program staff need to work more closely with parents to help researchers sustain their child's commitment to the intervention.

Inclusion of a follow-up component also is a task for the future. We do not know whether the intervention had any lasting effects beyond the end of the school semester following implementation. That is particularly important given our interests in the effect of the intervention on more general outcomes such as academic performance and attitudes about school. We suspect that these outcomes are part of more cumulative intervention effects that unfold gradually over time.

Finally, strategies for monitoring intervention fidelity need to be developed. Some lessons worked better than others, just as some outcomes proved more amenable to change. A system for documenting both the extent to which teacher/trainers remained faithful to the intervention and the variations in implementation (e.g., number of activities and lessons taught) should be obtained in future studies.

## Comparison of the Two Approaches

The school-wide bullying prevention approach and the social-cognitive intervention program targeting bullies—although complementary—also represent different schools of thought, each associated with their unique pros and cons. For example, whereas the former aims to build resiliency of all children, it can be faulted for not addressing the problems underlying aggressive behavior. In contrast, one of the cons of targeted interventions has to do with inaccurate or unreliable identification of students that may result in false labeling.

*Fidelity* and *sustainability*, two important components of good interventions, are also likely to be differentially achieved in the whole-school versus targeted approaches. Fidelity, or the consistency with which all of the components of the intervention are implemented, is probably easier to both monitor and achieve in targeted approaches because there are fewer personnel, both adults (trainers) and children, to keep track of. With multiple activities at multiple levels involving multiple stakeholders, it is more difficult to monitor treatment integrity in the school-wide programs. On the other hand, sustainability may be easier to achieve in the school programs. Systemic changes in peer, classroom, school, and community are needed to build the foundation for long-term prevention of bullying. Targeted interventions, typically imported from outside and implemented by researchers or school staff working with those researchers, usually are too short-lived to achieve that kind of support base (Fast Track is a notable exception).

Also, it should be noted that whereas the school-wide bullying preventions address the needs of victims by fostering resiliency to buffer the effects of *proactive* or instrumental aggression, the targeted interventions aim to correct the biased information processing of *reactive* aggressors (i.e., those who bully in response to perceived provocation). Hence, the two approaches have not only different aims, strengths, and weaknesses but also address different types of problems.

## GENERAL RECOMMENDATIONS FOR
## SCHOOL-BASED INTERVENTIONS

School-based programs are a natural context for prevention of bullying because schools are one of the primary stages for social behavior. Not surprisingly, school-based bullying, aggression, and violence prevention programs have proliferated in the past two decades at an enormous rate and astronomical cost. Some of the demonstration projects conducted by teams of researchers have produced promising results, with effect sizes in the moderate range (see Wilson, Lipsey, and Derzon, 2003, for a meta-analysis). However, the vast number of programs found in schools remain largely unevaluated, and they are often created by professional curriculum developers rather than experts in the science of prevention/intervention research. Furthermore, the large-scale evaluations of those programs that do exist have yielded disappointing results (Gottfredsson, 2001). Based on the two intervention approaches reviewed in this chapter, we conclude with some general guidelines for school staff to consider when choosing a program to deal with bullying.

### Theory Guided Interventions

Unless an interventionist has a clear theory about what causes bullying, it is difficult to avoid what has come to be called a "laundry list" approach—in other words, the curriculum includes a little bit of everything and not much of anything specific to the targeted behavior. The two approaches reviewed in this chapter were each guided by a particular theoretical perspective that identified different causes of bullying. According to systemic theories of behaviors, bullying has social causes; hence, the school-wide prevention aims to boost not only the resiliency of the individual but also the resiliency of the collective against bullying. The targeted intervention approach, in turn, is informed by a theoretical perspective that delineates how inferences about others' and an individual's own behavior affect emotional reactions, reactivity to perceived provocation, and achievement strivings. The conceptual frameworks not only guide the choice of both the program components and activities but also the outcome measures for program evaluation. Thus, the goal is to map specific behaviors targeted for change onto particular outcome measures that allow us to know *why* the programs "work."

### Backfiring of Interventions

In a review of interventions for adolescent problem behavior, Lipsey (1992) reported that 29% of the studies examined were judged as harmful because intervention participants displayed escalated problem behavior in comparison to their control group counterparts. Harmful outcomes of interventions are called *iatrogenic effects*. In targeted interventions, one factor known to produce those effects is aggregating high-risk boys together in treatment groups. The social reinforcement that group members receive from one another for acting out and "talking trash" in discussions of aggressive behavior sometimes functions as a kind of deviancy training that results in increased problem behavior (Dishion, McCord, & Poulin, 1999). At times in *Best Foot Forward*, the interveners were struck with how quickly boys' behavior could deteriorate when such deviancy training escalated. One solution is to have mixed intervention groups that include a balance of high- and low-risk boys and smaller adult: child ratios.

Although less common, school-wide approaches can also backfire if there is not careful thought given to the scope of the problem, where change is targeted, who will be affected by those changes, and what kinds of messages are communicated to students. For example, Zero Tolerance policies in U.S. schools have been criticized because the targets of harsh disciplinary actions are disproportionately African American males (Skiba, 2001). Rather than reducing school violence, those policies sometimes heighten both racial tension and foster the alienation and disengagement that all too often are observed in African American youth. Even the best-intentioned school-wide programs will have negative effects if they are interpreted by stakeholders in unanticipated ways.

## Needed "Boosters"

Many successful interventions adhere to a public health model characterized by problem behaviors that are conceptualized much like diseases that must be both controlled and prevented. Part of prevention involves immunization, as in the prevention of small pox or polio, and booster shots at critical periods. Accordingly, no one should expect bullying to be "fixed" by a one-shot approach. As part of school-wide prevention, policies and practices must be continually assessed and revised. As part of any targeted intervention, brief "doses" of the program (e.g., key lessons with new activities) should in turn be implemented at regular intervals to maintain and maximize program effects.

## Developmentally and Culturally
## Sensitive Interventions

Just like there is a need for boosters, there is a need for school-based interventions at each grade level. There is no magical age or developmental period when interventions stop working. However, because children undergo major cognitive, emotional, social, and biological changes from preschool through high school, interventions must be sensitive to different needs of the various age groups. For example, *Cool Tools* presumes that preschool and sixth-grade students need different levels of adult mediation of bullying incidents. Also, the instructional methods vary for the different age groups from explicit teaching of strategies that are represented by concrete tools (e.g., inflatable foot to remind students to "exit") to the discussion of relevant literature.

In addition, cultural adaptations are needed for programs to be effective. For example, for the *Best Foot Forward* program that was presented earlier, special efforts were made to develop stories and role-play activities that reflected the life experience and cultural heritage of ethnic minority boys. There is evidence that African American youth prefer learning styles associated with physical activity, communalism, and expressiveness (Boykin, 2000). Hence, the role-play activities designed for the program allow for freedom of movement, group work, and an opportunity to express feelings. We also know that the world of sports is a topic that generates a great deal of enthusiasm among inner city boys. Therefore, the activities of this particular program focused on sports as well as academics in the motivation training because the athletic arena is an achievement domain where intermediate risk taking, realistic goal setting, and persistence in the face of challenge are key determinants of success. The success of any intervention designed specifically for minority youth depends in part on the degree to which it is culturally sensitive.

## Interventions: Sensitive to School Transitions

Throughout their school years, children experience many significant and sometimes stressful transitions—the transition to elementary school, then to middle school, and then three years later to high school. Because such changes can produce additional vulnerabilities for youth, it is useful to think about the timing of interventions to determine whether they might serve any protective or buffering function. The underlying assumption is that transitions can result in negative outcomes if they are not successfully negotiated or mastered by those about to experience them. With more intense programming preceding the move to middle school, Fast Track has adopted a transition or milestone approach (Conduct Problems Research Group, 2002a). An intervention like *Best Foot Forward* aimed at aggression reduction and motivation enhancement for fourth and fifth grade at-risk youth is also useful for testing that kind of approach. There is no reason to think that school-wide programs cannot also be timed so that cumulative effects across critical transition periods can be examined.

## About Cost-Effectiveness

It is sometimes difficult to reconcile the costs of intervention research in relation to perceived benefits. However, if effective low-cost interventions can reduce the likelihood of students suffering from emotional distress or of becoming delinquent adolescents, then savings are substantial. Add to this the savings in terms of *human capital*—increased opportunity among *all* youth for education, personal growth, and responsible citizenship—then the potential benefits to society of effective school-based interventions are enormous.

# References

Alsaker, F. D., & Valkanover, S. (2001). Early diagnosis and prevention of victimization in kindergarten. In J. Juvonen & S. Graham (Eds.), *Peer Harassment in School: The Plight of the Vulnerable and Victimized* (pp.175–195). New York: Guilford Press.

Atkinson, J. (1964). *An introduction to motivation*. Princeton, NJ: Van Nostrand.

Bandura, A. (1997). *Self-efficacy: The exercise of control*. New York: W. H. Freeman.

Baumeister, R. (1996). Should schools try to boost self-esteem? Beware the dark side. *American Educator, 20*, 14–19.

Baumeister, R., Smart, L., & Boden, J. (1996). Relations of threatened egotism to violence and aggression: The dark side of high self-esteem. *Psychological Review, 103*, 5–33.

Bierman, K., Smoot, D., & Aumiller, K. (1993). Characteristics of aggressive-rejected, aggressive (non-rejected), and rejected (nonaggressive) boys. *Child Development, 64*, 139–151.

Boykin, W. (2000). The talent development model of schooling: Placing student at promise for academic success. *Journal of Education for Students Placed At Risk, 5*, 3–25.

Cadigan, R. J. (2003). *Scrubs: An ethnographic study of peer culture and harassment among sixth graders in an urban middle school*. Doctoral dissertation, University of California, 2002. *Dissertation Abstracts International, 63*, 2597.

Cairns, R., Cairns, B., Neckerman, H., Gest, S., & Gariepy, J. (1988). Social networks and aggressive behavior: Peer support or peer rejection. *Developmental Psychology, 24*, 815–823.

Cairns, R., & Cairns, B. (1994). *Lifelines and risk: Pathways of youth in our time*. New York: Cambridge University Press.

Castro, B., Veerman, J., Koops, W., Bosch, J., & Monshouwer, H. (2002). Hostile attribution of intent and aggressive behavior: A meta-analysis. *Child Development, 73*, 916–934.

Cillessen, A., van Ijzendoorn, H., van Lieshout, C., & Hartup, W. (1992). Heterogeneity among peer-rejected boys: Subtypes and stabilities. *Child Development, 63*, 893–905.

Coie, J., & Dodge, K. (1998). Aggression and antisocial behavior. In N. Eisenberg (Ed.), *Handbook of child psychology. Vol. 3: Social, emotional, and personality development* (pp. 779–862). New York: John Wiley.

Conduct Problems Prevention Research Group (2002a). The implementation of the Fast Track Program: An example of a large scale prevention science efficacy trial. *Journal of Abnormal Child Psychology, 30*, 1–17.

Conduct Problems Prevention Research Group. (2002b). Evaluation of the first three years of the Fast Track Prevention trial with children at high risk for adolescent conduct problems. *Journal of Abnormal Child Psychology, 30*, 19–35.

Crick, N., & Dodge, K. (1994). A review and reformulation of social information mechanisms in children's social adjustment. *Psychological Bulletin, 115*, 74–101.

Craig, W., & Pepler, D. (1997). Observations of bullying and victimization in the schoolyard. *Canadian Journal of School Psychology, 2*, 41–60.

Crick, N. R., Nelson, D. A., Morales, J. R., Cullerton-Sen, C., Casas, J. F., & Hickman, S. E. (2001). Relational victimization in childhood and adolescence: I hurt you through the grapevine. In J. Juvonen & S. Graham (Eds.), *Peer Harassment in School: The Plight of the Vulnerable and Victimized* (pp. 196–214). New York: Guilford Press.

Dishion, T. J., McCord, J., & Poulin, F. (1999). When interventions harm: Peer groups and problem behavior. *American Psychologist, 54*, 755–764.

Dryfoos, J. (1990). *Adolescents at risk: Prevalence and prevention.* New York: Oxford University Press.

Egan, S. K., & Perry, D. G. (1998). Does low self-regard invite victimization? *Developmental Psychology, 34,* 299–309.

Finkelhor, D. & Dziuba-Leatherman, J. (1994). Victimization of children. *American Psychologist,* 49(3), 173–183.

Flannery, D., Williams, L., & Vazonyi, A. (1999). Who are they with and what are they doing? Delinquent behavior, substance use, and early adolescents' after-school time. *American Journal of Orthopsychiarty, 69,* 247–253.

Garafola, J., Seigal, L., & Laub, J. (1987) School-related victimization among adolescents: an analysis of National Crime Survey (NCS) narratives. *Journal of Quantitative Criminology, 3,* 321–339.

Gottfredson, D. (2001). *Schools and delinquency.* New York: Cambridge University Press.

Graham, S., & Juvonen, J. (1998). Self-blame and peer victimization in middle school: An attributional analysis. *Developmental Psychology, 34,* 587–599.

Graham, S., & Juvonen, J., (2002). Ethnicity, peer harassment, and adjustment in middle school: An exploratory study. *Journal of Early Adolescence, 22,* 173–199.

Graham, S., & Mize, J. (2003). *Aggression, victimization, and their co-occurrence in middle school.* Manuscript submitted for publication.

Graham, S., Taylor, A., & Hudley, C. (2003). *Best Foot Forward: A motivational intervention for at-risk youth.* Manuscript submitted for publication.

Graham, S., & Weiner, B. (1996). Theories and principles of motivation. In D. Berliner & R. Calfee (Eds.), *Handbook of Educational Psychology* (pp. 63–84). New York: MacMillan.

Graham, S., Weiner, B., & Benesh-Weiner, M. (1995). An attributional analysis of the development of excuse-giving in aggressive and nonaggressive African American boys. *Developmental Psychology, 31,* 274–284.

Harachi, T. W., Catalano, R. F., & Hawkins, J. D. (1999). Bullying in the United States. In P. K. Smith, Y. Morita, J. Junger-Tas, D. Olweus, R. Catalano, & P. Slee (Eds.), *The nature of school bullying: Cross-national perspective* (pp. 279–295). New York: Routledge.

Hawker, D. S. J., & Boulton, M. J. (2000). Twenty years' research on peer victimization and psychosocial maladjustment: A meta-analytic review of cross-sectional studies. *Journal of Child Psychology and Psychiatry, 41,* 441–455.

Hodges, E. V. E., Malone, M. J., & Perry, D. G. (1997). Individual risk and social risk as interacting determinants of victimization in the peer group. *Developmental Psychology, 33,* 1032–1039.

Hoover, J., Oliver, R., & Hazler, R. (1992). Bullying: Perceptions of adolescent victims in the midwestern USA. *School Psychology International, 13*(1), 5–16.

Hudley, C., & Graham, S. (1993). An atrributional intervention to reduce peer-directed aggression among African American boys. *Child Development, 64,* 124–138.

Juvonen, J., & Cadigan, J. (2002). Social determinants of public behavior of middle school youth: Perceived peer norms and need to be accepted. In F. Pajares & T. Urdan (Eds.), *Adolescence and Education: Academic motivation of adolescents* (Vol. 2, pp. 277–297). Greenwich, CT: Information Age Publishing.

Juvonen, J., Graham S., Schuster, M. (2003). Bullying among young adolescents: The strong, weak, and troubled. *Pediatrics, 112,* 1231–1237.

Juvonen, J., Nishina, A., & Graham, S. (2000). Peer harassment, psychological adjustment, and school functioning in early adolescence. *Journal of Educational Psychology, 92,* 349–359.

Juvonen, J., & S. Graham (Eds.). (2001). *Peer harassment in school: The plight of the vulnerable and victimized.* New York: Guilford Press.

Kaiser Family Foundation and Children Now. (2001). *Talking with kids about tough issues: A national survey of parents and kids.* CA: Kaiser Family Foundation.

Kochenderfer-Ladd, B. (2003). Identification of aggressive and asocial victims and the stability of their peer victimization. *Merrill-Palmer Quarterly, 49,* 401–425.

Kochenderfer, B. J., & Ladd, G. W. (1996). Peer victimization: Cause or consequence of school maladjustment? *Child Development, 67,* 1305–1317.

Lipsey, M. W. (1992). The effect of treatment on juvenile delinquents: Results from meta-analysis. In F. Loesel & D. Bender (Eds.), *Psychology and law: International perspectives* (pp. 131–143). Berlin, Germany: Walter De Gruyter.

Luthar, S., & McMahon, T. (1996). Peer reputation among inner city adolescents. *Journal of Research on Adolescence, 6,* 581–603.

Markoe, S. (2003). *Aggression, perceived school climate, and suspension.* Unpublished Master's thesis. University of California: Los Angeles.

Moffitt, T. (1993). Adolescence-limited and life-course persistent antisocial behavior: A developmental taxonomy. *Psychological Review, 100,* 674–101.

Nishina, A., & Juvonen, J. (2003). *Daily reports of witnessing and experiencing peer harassment and negative affect in middle school.* Manuscript submitted for publication.

Nishina, A., Juvonen, J., & de la Sota, A. (2000). Violence prevention in elementary school: A systemic Safe School approach. *Connections, Spring* 2000, 3–8.

O'Connell, P., Pepler, D., & Craig, W. (1999). Peer involvement in bullying: Insights and challenges for intervention. *Journal of Adolescence, 22,* 437–452.

Olweus, D. (1978). *Aggression in the schools: Bullies and whipping boys.* Washington, DC: Hemisphere.

Olweus, D. (1991). Bully/victim problems among school-children: Basic facts and effects of a school based intervention program. In D. J. Pepler & K. H. Rubin (Eds.), *The Development and Treatment of Childhood Aggression* (pp. 411–448). Hillsdale, NY: Lawrence Erlbaum Associates.

Olweus, D. (1993). *Bullying at school.* Malden, MA: Blackwell Publishers.

Olweus, D. (1994). Annotation, bullying at school: Basic facts and effects of a school-based intervention program. *Journal of Child Psychology and Psychiatry and Allied Disciplines, 35,* 1171–1190.

Olweus, D. (2001). Peer harassment: A Critical Analysis and Some Important Issues. In J. Juvonen & S. Graham (Eds.). *Peer harassment in school: The plight of the vulnerable and victimized* (pp. 3–20). New York: Guilford Press.

Owens, L., Slee, P., & Shute, R. (2001). Relational victimization in childhood and adolescence: I hurt you through the grapevine. In J. Juvonen & S. Graham (Eds.), *Peer harassment in school: The plight of the vulnerable and victimized* (pp. 215–241). New York: Guilford Press.

Parker, J., & Asher, S. (1987). Peer relations and later social adjustment: Are low-accepted children at risk? *Psychological Bulletin, 102,* 357–389.

Pepler, D. J., Craig, W. M., Ziegler, S., & Charach, A. (1994). An evaluation of an anti-bullying intervention in Toronto schools. *Canadian Journal of Community Mental Health, 13,* 95–110.

Perry, D. G., Kusel, S. J., & Perry, L. C. (1988). Victims of peer aggression. *Developmental Psychology, 24,* 807–814.

Poulin, F., & Boivin, M. (2000). The role of proactive and reactive aggression in the formation and development of boys' friendships. *Developmental Psychology, 36,* 233–240.

Rigby, K. (1999). *Bullying in schools: And what to do about it.* Melbourne, Australia: ACER.

Rigby, K. (2001). Health consequences of bullying and its prevention in schools. In J. Juvonen & S. Graham (Eds.), *Peer harassment in school: The plight of the vulnerable and victimized* (pp. 310–331). New York: Guilford Press.

Rodkin, P., Farmer, T., Pearl, R., & Van Acker, R. (2000). Heterogeneity of popular boys: Antisocial and prosocial configurations. *Developmental Psychology, 36,* 14–24.

Salmivalli, C. (2001). Group view on victimization: Empirical findings and their implications. In J. Juvonen & S. Graham (Eds.), *Peer harassment in School: The plight of the vulnerable and victimized* (pp. 398–419). New York: Guilford Press.

Salmivalli, C., Lagerspetz, K., Björkqvist, K., Österman, K., & Kaukiainen. (1996). Bullying as a group process: Participant roles and their relations to social status within the group. *Aggressive Behavior, 22,* 1–15.

Schwartz, D., Dodge, K. A., & Coie, J. D. (1993). The emergence of chronic peer vicitimization in boys' play groups. *Child Development, 64,* 1755–1772.

Schwartz, D., Proctor, L. J., & Chien, D. H. (2001). The aggressive victim of bullying: Emotional and behavioral dysregulation as a pathway to victimization by peers. In J. Juvonen & S. Graham

(Eds.), *Peer harassment in school: The plight of the vulnerable and victimized* (pp.147–174). New York: Guilford Press.

Scott, M., & Lyman, S. (1968). Accounts. *American Sociological Review, 23,* 46–62.

Skiba, R. (2001). When is disproportionality discrimination? The over-representation of Black students in school suspension. In W. Ayers, B. Dohrn, & R. Ayers (2001). Zero tolerance. New York: The Free Press.

Smith, P. K., & Sharp, S. (1994). *School Bullying: Insights and Perspectives.* Routledge, London.

Stevens, V., De Bourdeaudhuij, I., & Van Oost, P. (2001). Anti-bullying interventions at school: Aspects of programme adaptation and critical issues for further programme development. *Health Promotion International, 16,* 155–167.

Weiner, B. (1995). *Judgments of responsibility: A foundation for a theory of social conduct.* New York: Guilford Press.

Wilson, S., Lipsey, M., & Derzon, J. (2003). The effects of school-based intervention programs on aggressive behavior: A meta-analysis. *Journal of Consulting and Clinical Psychology, 71,* 136–149.

Zariski, A., & Coie, J. (1996). A comparison of aggressive-rejected and non-aggressive-rejected children's interpretations of self-directed and other-directed rejection. *Child Development, 67,* 1048–1070.

# Index